Egyptian Religion

Egyptian Religion

SIEGFRIED MORENZ

Translated by
ANN E. KEEP

CORNELL UNIVERSITY PRESS
ITHACA, NEW YORK

First published, under the title Aegyptische Religion, *by*
W. Kohlhammer GmbH.
© *1960 W. Kohlhammer GmbH.*, *Stuttgart*

© *Methuen & Co Ltd 1973*

English translation first published 1973 by Cornell University Press.
Fourth printing 1990.
First printing, Cornell Paperbacks, 1992.

International Standard Book Number 0-8014-0782-6 (cloth)
International Standard Book Number 0-8014-8029-9 (paper)
Library of Congress Catalog Card Number 73-8401

⊗ The paper in this book meets the minimum requirements of the American National Standard for Information Sciences—Permanence of Paper for Printed Library Materials, ANSI Z39.48-1984.

*Dedicated to the Hohe
Evangelisch-Theologische
Fakultät
of the
Eberhard-Karls-Universität
Tübingen*

Contents

[ix]

Translator's Note

Where standard English translations of Egyptian sources were available, these have been used; in the notes these works are given in square brackets. For the Pyramid Texts use has been made of *The Ancient Egyptian Pyramid Texts*, translated into English by R. O. Faulkner, Oxford, 1969. In transcribing Egyptian words the translator has not adhered to the form used by the author, but used the form now most generally accepted.

The translator and the publishers would like to thank Dr Rosalie David of the Manchester Museum for her advice and assistance in preparing the text for publication.

Foreword

'Enter, also here are gods'
(*after Heraclitus*)

During the present century Egypt has become a centre of attraction for ever-growing numbers of people. The Nile valley and its monuments are visited by tens of thousands of tourists each year. The political and economic life of the Arab peoples evoke equal interest of a different kind. The country's development is taking place in a rich historical context, which reaches back beyond classical antiquity and ancient Israel to the earliest advanced civilizations of the Orient. This growth of interest in Egypt has long since ceased to be the preserve of a few specialists, but finds expression in school curricula and influences the outlook of ordinary men and women. All this creates a need for books which can enable lovers of ancient Egypt to enter into the spirit of its great civilization.

It is only natural that in discussing this literature one should begin with those works that deal with the country's artistic riches. The connoisseur of today has at his disposal numerous illustrated volumes, and also a superb analysis and interpretation by W. Wolf, entitled *Die Kunst Ägyptens. Gestalt und Geschichte* (1957). One is then led to the history of ancient Egypt. In this field some excellent monographs have been published in recent years. Among those in German we may mention A. Scharff's contribution to Scharff and Moortgat, *Ägypten und Vorderasien im Altertum* (1950) and E. Otto, *Ägypten, Der Weg des Pharaonenreiches* (1953; 3rd ed., 1958). In regard to economic conditions, geography and settlement reference may be made to H. Kees, *Das alte Ägypten. Eine kleine Landeskunde* (1955; 2nd ed., 1958; translated by F. D. Morrow and edited by T. G. H. James as *Ancient Egypt. A Cultural Topography*, London, 1961). For cultural history the German reader must still consult earlier works such as A. Erman and H. Ranke, *Ägypten und ägyptisches Leben im Altertum* (1923) and H. Kees, 'Ägypten' (in *Handbuch der Altertumswissenschaft*, III, 1, 3, 1933).

Yet behind all aspects of life of those who dwelt on the Nile in ancient times – behind their art, political structure and cultural achievements – one may sense forces at work which are religious in origin. To penetrate into this alien but fascinating field of inquiry is the desire of many and a necessity for all who seek a clearer understanding of ancient Egypt. In this field also there is no lack of comprehensive studies in German, not to mention textbooks, illustrated volumes and brief summaries in general surveys. In *Die Religion der Ägypter* (3rd ed., 1934) A. Erman provides a lucid account of the external aspects of the phenomenon, making frequent reference to the texts. In regard to spiritual life it needs to be supplemented by H. Kees, *Der Götterglaube im alten Ägypten* (2nd ed., 1956). For problems of detail one may consult H. Bonnet's excellent *Reallexikon der ägyptischen Religionsgeschichte* (1952). The vast subject of the hereafter is discussed by H. Kees in his *Totenglauben und Jenseitsvorstellungen der alten Ägypter* (2nd ed., 1956). Among recent monographs on Egyptian religion published in other countries are: H. Frankfort, *Ancient Egyptian Religion* (2nd ed., 1949); J. Vandier, *La Religion égyptienne* (2nd ed., 1949); J. Černý, *Ancient Egyptian Religion* (1952); E. Drioton, *La Religion égyptienne* (1955; translated by M. B. Loraine as *Egyptian Religion*, 1959); S. Donadoni, *La religione dell'Egitto antico* (1955).

It may at first sight seem superfluous to offer another book on the same theme. Yet each encounter with an important subject cannot but open up new insights. I feel I owe the reader some brief explanation of how I personally view the subject. Above all I have tried to see Egyptian religion as the faith of the Egyptian people. Political, economic and social events are, so far as I am concerned, only 'the conditions in which phenomena appear', to use Goethe's words. The focal point of these phenomena, in my opinion, is man's relationship to God. For this reason I shall begin with some considerations about the gods and those who venerated them, and then shall examine the ways in which the gods acted and their worshippers behaved. I deliberately use the word 'examine'. For it soon became evident to me that in this field far more needed to be done than I had originally assumed in view of the extensive bibliography on the subject. Creation and death, as two realms beyond the confines of our earthly existence, will be treated after the chapters on the living relationship between God and man. For it seemed to me that the actual experience of God's existence is of primary importance, and that the problems of evolution and decay must be secondary.

These matters form the central section of the work. Before discussing them I shall sketch the important part Egyptian religion played in Egyptian culture generally. This introduction may also help to make plain the significance of God for man in every aspect of his life. The main part of the book will be followed by some considerations concerning the essence of Egyptian religion as a cult religion, for this in my view makes for a better understanding of those features which appear peculiar when judged by the yardstick of Judaism and Christianity, which are both scriptural religions. Finally, a description will be given of the influences exercised upon Egyptian religion from elsewhere and its impact upon other lands. This seems necessary to avoid giving the impression that Egypt was a cultural oasis, while paying due regard to the fact that its ways of life did have an inner compactness. In adopting this scheme I have been obliged to select and to omit. For example, I shall discuss the priesthood only in so far as this is essential for an understanding of the divine service; all the relevant facts about the economic and religious history of the priesthood have had to be left out.

While engaged upon this work 1 realized that one has to have experienced oneself the meaning of religion and of God if one is to interpret from the sources the relationship between God and man in an age remote from our own. But one also realizes that the great, simple concerns of mankind are the same through all eternity, whatever variations are induced by physical circumstances and differences of mental outlook. One further perceives that preoccupation with a particular religious creed may open up avenues for an understanding of religion as such, just as the student of a foreign language or culture will often thereby obtain a profounder insight into his own language and culture. I have come to be convinced that Egyptian religion can fulfil the same purpose for those who immerse themselves in it.

It is said of Walter F. Otto that he believed in the Greek gods. I do not know whether this is true; but it seems to me certain that Otto did know that the Greeks believed in their gods. For this very reason he was able to portray them as real. For my part I do not believe in the Egyptian gods, but never for a moment have

I forgotten that to the Egyptians, as to any believer, their gods were real; and in my view this reality of God is *par excellence* the proper theme for a historian of religion.

Inevitably this book has been written in some degree from the heart. I have tried to compensate for the hazards of subjectivity by making no statements without providing evidence for them. I hope that this will make the book more useful to the reader. Since I have had to collect new material for the central section and have often been obliged to interpret it afresh, specialists, too, may find their interest aroused. But in principle I have tried to write in such a way that this volume may be comprehensible to those who are not Egyptologists. In this connection one has of course to bear in mind that religion cannot be made so readily understandable as history, for example, where events can simply be related, or as art, where the objects discussed can be rendered visually.

Throughout this work readers will sense how much I owe to the studies by earlier scholars, especially Sethe, Junker and Kees, as well as to Bonnet, Breasted and Wilson. I should also like to express my heart-felt thanks to my student and collaborator Dr Dieter Müller for his enthusiastic and knowledgeable co-operation in preparing this volume. He has contributed many ideas and pieces of evidence, not all of which has it been possible to note in detail. I have also gained a great deal by the privilege of consulting the manuscript of his work, *Ägypten und die griechischen Isis-Aretalogien* (*Egypt and the Greek Aretalogies of Isis*). I should also like to thank my student and assistant Dr Christa Müller-Kriesel, who drew up the list of deities and also, in collaboration with her husband, compiled the indexes. Finally, I owe a debt of gratitude to the members of my seminars in 1959–60, with whom I was able to hold most helpful discussions of chapters of this book.

Leipzig   SIEGFRIED MORENZ
June 1960

Introduction

Sources

Even the general reader is entitled to know how his image of the ancient advanced civilizations has come to be formed. What is its basis and how reliable is it? This raises the question of the sources upon which our knowledge is founded. We cannot of course provide here a thorough study of the sources relating to the history of Egyptian religion, which alone would fill a fair-sized volume. We shall have to be content with a brief survey to bring out a few salient points.

In the first place we may distinguish between direct and indirect sources. The former are of a textual and archaeological nature and constitute a reservoir so vast that it is hard for anyone today to obtain a comprehensive picture of it. After one hundred and fifty years of philological studies the old Egyptian texts are by and large accessible. They no longer have to be 'deciphered' but merely translated. This does not mean that every passage can be translated with equal ease or reliability. A thorough account would therefore have to indicate which statements are based on words and sentences whose meaning is absolutely certain and which are not. The difficulties encountered in translation are as a rule not of a graphical or grammatical nature but stem from the fact that the Egyptians had a mode of thinking very different from our own.[1]

Chronologically the texts begin in the period when the Two Lands were united, i.e. at the beginning of the third millennium B.C., and extend beyond the Christianization of Egypt, with off-shoots up to the middle of the first millennium A.D.; in this latter period the Egyptian sources overlap with Greek and Roman ones. So far as their subject-matter is concerned, this is not restricted to certain literary genres or types of documents. Naturally, certain types, such as prayers, hymns or mythological tales, yield a particularly rich amount of information on religious matters, but in principle no text can be excluded as devoid of religious content. On the other hand one cannot expect to find religious phenomena treated in a systematic or even continuous way in

Egyptian texts. On the contrary, in order to reconstitute a sacred myth such as that of Osiris, or a cosmogony such as that which derives the world from a flower or an egg, one has to make an extensive collection of textual fragments and arrange them systematically.

The archaeological material reaches back earlier than the written sources. It comprises the entire early period, from the first traces of human activity to the discovery of writing. From the beginning of the Neolithic period onward, around 5000 B.C., we can already obtain a fairly reliable idea of certain manifestations of Egyptian religion, namely funerary customs. So far as the range of archaeological material is concerned, this again is in principle unlimited. The most important buildings, of course, are temples and tombs, with their rich embellishments of sculpture, reliefs and painting; but one should not exclude private houses or certain types of objects which appear to have served merely profane utilitarian purposes.

By indirect sources one understands in the first place those which provide evidence by their mere existence or absence, or by the function they fulfil. Thus the existence of mythology in pre-historic times indicates that an evolution was taking place in religious thought, leading to the emergence of deities; yet the fact that mythology then became subordinated to other concerns and modes of expression shows that the emphasis was shifting and that a new development was under way.[2] Then one must consider the innumerable and varied sources which provide negative evidence about religious forces. Thus Egyptian sculpture, which had once served religious needs alone, was in the New Kingdom elevated to an independent aesthetic plane: inscriptions by visitors praise the beauty of monuments in tourist fashion.[3] This represents a process which we call profanization or secularization, and which in its way characterizes the course of all history, including that of Egypt (chap. 1).

From these brief remarks it will already be plain that the indirect sources are particularly essential for the history of religion. They provide the answers to the questions: When did something evolve? When was it at its strongest? When did it decline? When did it disappear entirely? The direct sources, on the other hand, provide information about phenomenology: What existed? Or, as the specialist tends to ask: Did this or that phenomenon exist in Egypt? True, in view of the absence of certain pieces of evidence, one has to be twice as wary not to form a rash opinion. We have in mind not only the deduction *e silentio*, which is always risky, i.e. the argument that because the sources are lacking the phenomenon itself did not exist either, but the rather more subtle point that certain pieces of evidence are only forthcoming where the necessary prerequisites exist. For example, the fact that laymen are not represented in a praying attitude in the Old Kingdom, whereas such representations are frequent in the New Kingdom,[4] should not be taken to mean that simple persons did not pray during the Pyramid period. For in Old Kingdom private tombs the deity was not represented, and thus one cannot expect to find persons in prayer to be depicted there either. On the other hand the meaning of Egyptian personal names often expresses clearly the relationship between man and God; this shows that the prerequisites for prayer may very well have existed for all men at that time.[5]

Now that we have, as it were, taken the reader into the workshop of the historian of religion by raising the problem of sources, let us explain the principle underlying our survey. The material is arranged topically, not historically. Naturally, the historical evolution will be indicated within each chapter, in so far as this is possible. This phenomenological arrangement has the decisive advantage that the matter itself determines the manner of selecting, ordering and interpreting it. This method has the corresponding disadvantage that phenomena which are also historical entities – indeed, which are part of history – have to be dealt with in different chapters. Thus the religion of Amarna, which by right deserves to be treated as a single entity, is here mentioned at various points in the text. Cross-references will be given to offset this deficiency, which we regard as being a secondary consideration.

Meaning of religion in Egyptian

Before we begin the survey proper, a few remarks may be made on the obvious question, which nevertheless is hardly ever asked, what 'religion' meant in Egyptian. Let us admit in advance that this question is an embarrassing one, since it shows that there is in Egyptian no concept which would adequately convey the meaning of the Latin term *religio*, which developed out of the syncretism of Roman paganism and Christianity. Also the editors of the *Wörterbuch der ägyptischen Sprache* did not find a single word for 'religion', 'piety' or 'faith'. On the other hand, there are abundant terms to denote 'sacrifice' and objects and acts connected with sacrifice. There are also several words for 'priesthood', as there are for 'worship' as an expression of the relationship between man and God; 'prayer' (authenticated from the New Kingdom onward) is even expressed in several different ways, although it is hardly distinguishable from 'praise', to which it is also related in form.[6]

From this we may conclude that the structure of Egyptian religion differed from what we are familiar with from our experience of Christianity. With its sacrifice and its priesthood it is distinguished by a predominance of cult. It may be classified among the pagan cult religions which stand in contrast to Judaism, Christianity and Islam, since the latter were *par excellence* scriptural creeds in which God speaks and demands.[7] But this does not mean that there was no piety or belief, those phenomena which supplement cult to make up what we nowadays call religion. As they were not understood conceptually, they were less evident or else, as was the case with prayer, were in general closely linked to the prescribed forms which evolved from cult.[8]

It will therefore be our main task to seek out the piety of the Egyptian believer within the dominant phenomena of his religion: first of all in the cult itself, then in his ideas on ethics and theology, in his doctrines of creation and in his attitude toward death. Egyptian cult, as we shall see, does not by any means derive solely from duties toward the deity, carried out by command of the state; on the contrary, the worshipper proclaims God's works in the manner which seems right to him, as a member of Egyptian society. He is led by ethical problems to the divine lord of justice, who may grant or deny grace and understanding, and who also sits in judgement upon him. Last but not least, theology serves the needs of the pious man who seeks to invest his God with the maximum amount of power. Doctrines of creation are by no means restricted to the conjuring up of mythical images; they are a means whereby men are told about the great deeds of God, by reference to the various natural phenomena mentioned in these myths. Finally,

God is also regarded as the lord of time and death. Nevertheless it stands to reason that Egyptian society, and the individuals who comprise it, cannot escape from God, but encounter him everywhere. Thus in spite of the paucity of lexical terms we can speak of an Egyptian religion which, for all its structural differences from the scriptural religions more familiar to us, has one fundamental point in common with Christianity: the reality of a God who is in man and above man.[9]

1 · The religious origin of Egyptian civilization

The best justification for the study of Egyptian religion lies in the fact that it was the basis from which Egyptian civilization derived. The cardinal features of that culture and society were determined by the existence and power of its all-pervading religious beliefs. We shall therefore begin by pointing to some well-known facts which illustrate the religious origin of various cultural phenomena.

Art

To take first the simplest and at the same time most impressive: Egyptian pictorial art came into being to perform a function in magic or cult, and for a long time served religious ends alone. Its subject-matter and its structure were both determined by religious notions.[1] This purpose is evident in architectural monuments (temples, tombs) which, since they surpass elementary minimal requirements in their use of space, deserve to be regarded as works of art, as well as in sculptural representations of God (the king) or the dead, and in the cycles of reliefs or paintings which portrayed the same subjects.

Let us illustrate this choice of subject-matter in the case of sculptural works. These did not have to have any aesthetic appeal, and quite often this would have been impossible since they were immured in a dark chamber, far removed from the gaze of potential viewers. They had rather just to be there, by their very existence providing God (the king) or the dead with a body, which could be given vitality by the performance of rites and which could dispense salvation and receive gifts. What is true of images of the gods and occupants of tombs applies also, *mutatis mutandis*, to figures of animals, servants and cycles of reliefs, so far as their religious origin and significance are concerned.[2] It was only much later, at the time of the Eighteenth Dynasty, that aesthetic values gained ground, thereby testifying to the increasing secularization of art (see p. 2) and heralding the emergence of culture from its religious origins.

Literature and drama

The same is true of literature. Language, which at first suffices for the most elementary purposes of speech, becomes a fully fledged medium of expression when it is used in renderings of myth and in the requirements of ritual, and finally combines both functions (often in the form of a play on words). The large number of mythological and ritual royal funerary inscriptions from the later pyramids (the so-called Pyramid Texts) are the earliest examples of Egyptian literature; their function is wholly religious. Here, too, a process of secularization takes place later, but it is worth noting that it is possible to see how profane literary genres had their origin in the religious sphere. It has been demonstrated that various kinds of Egyptian love poetry (descriptive songs, 'songs of the day', 'lamentation at the gate') are derived from religious genres or at least from religious motifs.[3] One branch of literature, drama, brings us to the subject of 'theatre'. This institution, based upon dramatic texts which contained stage directions and notes about the distribution of roles, developed in Egypt at an early date and on a broad scale; it was firmly rooted in cult and remained so rooted throughout the period until the end.[4] One characteristic detail, the mask, evolved out of the general desire of worshippers to see their deities represented. It is known that in later periods priests would don masks and act the part of gods.[5]

Science

What is so clearly true of art holds good also for science. Religion was the basis of Egyptian medicine. Death was seen as caused by a message from the deity, except in those cases where violence was obviously involved.[6] For this reason medical diagnosis, practices and prescriptions are always closely associated with magical utterances – as is quite understandable when the gods and all kinds of intermediate beings are thought to be responsible for the mystery of disease,[7] and much else besides. In retrospect one may perhaps be struck only by the fetters imposed upon Egyptian physicians in their quest for medical knowledge; certainly science, where unlike art the idea of absolute progress is in order,[8] suffered from the fact that religion was so closely bound up with ancient notions about the cosmos, and adhered to them so tenaciously.

But this does not refute the fact that science, medicine included, had its origin in religion. Institutionally the medical profession was associated with the priesthood. Greek authors testify to this connection, and this is amply confirmed by ancient Egyptian sources.[9] Indeed, ritual requirements may even be responsible for the creation of a branch of science.

Thus astronomy evolved in Egypt out of the need to establish the exact periods of time deemed indispensable for the performance of certain rites: in the Osirian cult, for example, the service was divided up on an hourly basis.[10] In the mortuary service, too, astronomical observations played a significant part, in view of the mythical links deemed to exist between the dead and celestial bodies and the need to compile a simple chronology on behalf of the occupant of the tomb (stellar tablets, so-called lists of decans).[11]

The same is true of all the calculations made in respect of the calendar – an invention of the Egyptians which, as is generally known, forms the basis for our own calendar.[12] For this provides a chronological framework for local variations in the Egyptian ecclesiastical year; the 'calendar of festivals' was a list of religious observances and the sacrifices associated with them.[13] Astronomy not only evolves in this way; it is also kept alive by the continuous observations necessitated to fulfil the requirements of the cult; the 'observers of hours' (ὡροσκόποι) are, like most medical practitioners, members of the priesthood.

Physics represents a special case, in so far as it is concerned with the nature of the world and its origins. For it remained completely in the grip of mythology and theology, thereby illustrating the point that although gradual secularization may be the rule in intellectual history, it does not have the character of a universally binding law. First we have the ancient conception of the cosmos: the earth rests on or in the primeval ocean. Above this is the vault of heaven, supported by four pillars, and below it is the counter-heaven which in the very beginning lay beneath the primeval ocean (see pp. 174 f.). This mythical picture was formulated in many variations but was never abandoned.[14] The origins of the world, too, are mentioned only in myth, in the service of theology. The gods, we are told, were the earth's progenitors: air and moisture, and then the sky and the earth, issued from the One and original One and in this way became distinguished from one another (teaching of Heliopolis). Alternatively, the world was deemed to have had its origin in an egg, or in a lotus (teachings of Hermopolis and Herakleopolis). In these cosmogonies one can differentiate between a physical aspect and a religious one; yet they are all bound up with myth. The classic doctrine of creation is that of the eight primeval gods of Hermopolis (see p. 175).

So far as geography is concerned, this was in the nature of things an empirical science, since it set itself much more modest objectives. A people who succeeded in uniting their extensive territories into a single state and later brought other lands under their sway could not help but become familiar with at least a part of the world. They then had to try to master spiritually what they had conquered by military and administrative means. This task, too, was successfully accomplished.[15] In spite of these pressures toward empirical methods, the science of cartography had a religious origin. The earliest cartographic representations known from the lands of the Nile are concerned with the geography of the world hereafter. They are designed to serve as an aid to the dead on their journey. These so-called 'guides to the beyond' are recorded on the bottom of Middle Kingdom coffins (especially the Book of the Two Ways).[16] Not until more than five hundred years later, in the Ramesside period, were maps compiled for economic or other practical purposes. Among them were the plan of the gold mines in the Wadi Hammamat, on a Turin papyrus, and the ground-plans of the tombs of two Ramesside rulers, one on a Turin papyrus and the other on an ostracon in Cairo.[17]

Philology and philosophy

Moving on now to the humanities, we find the same picture. Let us begin with philology. At an early date the Egyptians began to collect and combine words that were identical or had a similar sound. The Pyramid Texts provide us with an abundance of examples. The motive for this was a purely religious one. In the Egyptian view the word and the object were identical, and therefore the magical powers inherent in the word had either to be utilized or eliminated, according to whether the content was benevolent or malignant. In this way there developed the positive and the negative play on words, in which two words which resembled each other were linked together in one phrase.

With such plays on words the Egyptians established a group of relationships between words. To put it differently, in this way they familiarized themselves with nothing less than the study of etymology. The modern reader may smile contemptuously at this. But one should withhold judgement unless one wishes also to find fault with the similar etymological investigations of the Greeks and Romans. Etymology as a science in the modern sense exists only from about 1800, with the beginning of Indo-European philological studies.[18] As for Egyptian plays on words, the rule of gradual secularization again applies: they finally became just a literary device.[19]

On the other hand, with philosophy we have an area of inquiry which, like physics, is an exception to the rule. Indeed, in Egypt philosophy remains so completely embedded in religious thinking that we generally do not speak of Egyptian philosophy, at least in the matter-of-fact way we speak of Greek or Indian philosophy. Yet the Egyptian mind created a linguistic medium whereby philosophical statements could be formulated. To single out a few points: there are two verbs for 'to be', one of which (*wn* [*n*]) can form participles and therefore express what is and what has been – a faculty which Latin did not possess, as is well known. Moreover, statements are also made in a finite form about existence. Thus the well-known personal name Wen-Amon means 'Amon exists'. The same name-usage is incidentally also present in the case of other deities, and the verbal form is varied so as to produce all kinds of such statements about existence.[20]

Finally, let us note the remarkable link between two relative adjectives: 'That which is [and] that which is not (*intt wtt*)'. This means 'everything' and takes account formally of what does not exist in a way which would do credit to Greek philosophy.[21] But the Egyptians did more than supply the linguistic prerequisites for philosophical thinking; we also encounter genuine philosophical modes of reasoning and posing problems. Particular reference may be made here to the common formulae whereby one being 'dwells' in another, or is equated with another. These formulae allow for the independence of the entities concerned. Thus A may be contained in B or A may equal B but A and B do not cease to exist independently or to enter into other associations with C, D, etc. Later (in chap. 7) we shall deal in detail with this question; here we may merely mention that such modes of thinking spring exclusively from theological concerns and seek to answer problems which they raise. In other words, in Egypt philosophical inquiry is the product of theology and never becomes emancipated from it.

Historiography

The third major field in the humanities, historiography, is entirely dependent upon the nature of the subject. Strictly speaking, the only acceptable subject is the Egyptian sacrosanct ruler, through whom or in relation to whom all essential things happen, no matter whether he is appointed by God, who controls his actions, or is free to decide for himself matters of war and peace.[22] To this extent Egyptian history is written as a dogma of sacrosanct monarchy. But once the king has departed from the path of order, the deity punishes this violation in accordance with an almost Biblical theodicy (see pp. 58 f.).[23]

The subject of historiography provides us with the transition from science to the study of the state and administration. For this reason we shall conclude our survey of science at this point[24] and sum up by stating that the religious origin of art and science is fundamental, as is the case in all other cultures as well. There are plenty of examples of this: let us merely recall the dictum of an authority of the stature of J. Fränkel: 'All poetry is in the first place religious. The gifted prophet who marvels at the wonders of the world and tries to interpret them creates cosmic-religious myths which express symbolically the religious feeling of the people. For religion has no other idiom than myth. That is why, in origin, poetry and religion are one.'[25] Only one exception deserves to be noted. It seems that the origin of the science of cartography was not necessarily religious; the earliest testimonies of this science in Mesopotamia are town plans;[26] this may lead one to categorize Egyptian maps as a local peculiarity or a chance phenomenon, the product of the country's traditions. This view may, however, need to be revised if new material comes to light.

Government

With regard to the religious origins of government, we may begin by considering the institution of sacrosanct monarchy. This was a cardinal feature of Egyptian life, and in theory at least survived to the very end (chap. 2). In Egyptian there was no word for 'state', for what we understand by that term was embodied, especially in the early period, wholly in the person of the king, i.e. in the institution of monarchy.[27] Those who attended upon the divine ruler, who looked after his clothing and his residence, gradually came to form a bureaucracy whose members performed specialized functions. These officials were at first recruited among the princes, who by virtue of their high birth were best qualified for such service. They were considered to possess some of the king's magic aura. Later officials were drawn from the aristocracy and finally from the broad masses of the population.[28] The sacrosanct monarch is thus the representative of the Egyptian state and simultaneously the nucleus of its administration. The governmental structure was also influenced by religious factors in yet another way. The Egyptians' peculiarly intense preoccupation with the service of the dead, which involved donations to secure a proper funeral and provision for the hereafter, had a very considerable impact on property relationships and thus also on economic life, administration and law. This was the case right from the feudal Pyramid period, with its vast donations and its priests employed in the service of the dead, to the very close of Egyptian history, when ordinary folk endeavoured to safeguard themselves in the hereafter by making such gifts.[29]

Justice

The last major aspect of Egyptian culture to be considered here is justice. This too, like art, science and government, is rooted in religion. We need not belabour the point that in the very early period the sacrosanct ruler himself made the laws and ensured that they were kept. Let us rather turn to the concept of *maat*, which forms the core of Egyptian justice, so far as it is evident from the texts, and may also be regarded in the technical legal sense as the most widely held concept of justice (for details see chap. 6). It is defined by religion, bestowed by the creator-god (e.g. Atum), and defended and guaranteed by the sacrosanct king who, as is often said, prescribes it instead of injustice (*isft*).[30] From an institutional point of view this religious basis is evident from the fact that judicial officials, including the viziers who from the Fifth

Dynasty onward were in charge of legal matters, and whose office was derived from and conferred by the sacrosanct king, bear the title of 'priests of maat' (ḥm-nṯr Mȝꜥt).[31] Here we thus have the same combination of apparently secular office-holders with priests that we already encountered in the field of science.[32] This initial incorporation of justice in religion remains in effect throughout Egyptian history. One need only consider oaths, in which the deity or the king is invoked,[33] or oracles, which assumed increasing importance in the administration of justice during the Late period. Of these oracles it has been pertinently remarked: 'the focus is merely shifted from the state-centred, institutional aspect of the administration of justice to the original religious aspect'.[34] This likewise indicates that along with the gradual process of secularization new religious impulses made themselves felt.

Religion as matrix of culture

Thus art and science, government and law are founded in religion, which in a nutshell is the womb of culture. Egypt provides particularly clear proof of this fact since in its early history it developed along autochthonous lines, i.e. without being greatly influenced from abroad. We can therefore look more deeply into the basic structure of things here than we can where a new civilization is to some extent indebted to its older and maturer neighbours. In the latter case a distortion of the basic pattern occurs primarily because cultural phenomena are, as we have noted, subject to gradual secularization; for this reason a more recent civilization will often take over the culture of an older neighbour in already secularized form. Be that as it may, the emergence of culture from religion is one of the basic trends of historical development. It is better to avoid calling it a *law* of historical development, since there are exceptions to the rule. In Egypt these exceptions are to be found in physics and philosophy, which remained throughout bound up with mythology and theology.

One may well ask whether this exception is accidental. It does not appear to be so, for the close tie between religion and man's basic outlook on life, his way of thinking (as well as physics and philosophy) creates that fundamental harmony which is so characteristic of this ancient culture. There is abundant proof that the effect which religion exerted upon other cultural phenomena was maintained also during later periods of Egyptian history. Since we are concerned only with the religious origins of culture, we shall not present this evidence here. But one point is worth noting: the continued existence, indeed the impressive power, of *ars sacra*; it still set the tone in all branches of art when the history of ancient Egypt came to an end, and caused the aesthetic emancipation mentioned above to remain a marginal phenomenon. Even the small bronze figures produced in such large numbers bear the stamp of a hieratic style and were commissioned for religious purposes.[35] Let us also recall the indestructibility, however formal, of sacrosanct monarchy, which until the end was the only 'political theory' which the Egyptians had and actually put into practice. Its idiom was taken up later by Macedonian rulers and Roman emperors.

Finally, we may again draw attention to Egyptian justice, which at all times was bound up with religion by the concept of *maat* and by the oath; later, with the spread of judicial oracles, it received new impulses from the belief in God as judge. This bears comparison with the increased importance that came to be attached, in medicine, to the gods of healing.[36] This much must be said to clarify the basic principle of secularization and to show that in the final result its impact in Egypt was quite modest.

Another point deserves to be emphasized, although it is self-evident: it is not the case that with the emergence of culture the force of religion is expended, that it has fulfilled its mission, so that in the further course of history it dissolved or was consumed. On the contrary, religion always remains a vital force, for it is based upon ever fresh encounters between man and God; this is eloquently demonstrated in Egypt by the continued impact which religion had upon other cultural phenomena in later phases of development.[37]

The religious origin of all major cultural phenomena has been emphasized here for several reasons. First, we have endeavoured to show that a knowledge of Egyptian religion is indispensable for anyone who wishes to understand other aspects of life in ancient Egypt. But secondly, and this is far more important, we have sought to provide a highly necessary corrective to the common, and in its own way justified but dangerously one-sided, view that it was man who created God in his own image. Xenophanes' oft-cited phrase is valid in the broadest sense, and is not confined to the person of the deity (chap. 2); it extends also to the manner in which God is deemed to exist and to operate. Thus in Egypt as elsewhere the concept of God the judge and of the judgement of the dead were doubtless based upon an empirical acquaintance with worldly justice. But after the foregoing analysis we should be able to see matters more objectively. With reference to the last example, it follows that a society which is essentially religious regards the things of this world, including its own social order, as being in the hands of divine forces, who ordain and guarantee justice. From this belief there emerge certain legal forms which take account of concrete earthly phenomena; these earthly legal forms are then reflected in the hereafter, once men have begun to draw a conscious distinction between this world and the next. The whole relationship may be termed dialectical, with reciprocal causes and effects. But one must remember – and here we return to our starting-point in this chapter – that it is the religious orientation of society, i.e. the omnipresence of God in the world of man, which determines the origins of culture. This diagnosis does not fit very well into modern notions of historical causation; but it has the undeniable merit of proceeding from fact and not from theory.

2 · The gods

The educated layman, particularly if he is of a religious cast of mind, will find it quite natural that we should now turn our attention to the gods of ancient Egypt. But to the historian of religion this by no means follows automatically. Even if he is a believer, he is obliged to regard matters historically – that is to say, he has to consider religious phenomena as they evolved. This means that one must take very seriously the possibility that God, who objectively is the primary cause and creator of all things and has been extant since time immemorial, was not envisaged by early man in human form. Jews, Christians and Muslims can cope with this difficulty fairly easily because they believe that in the beginning of things God did indeed exist but that later he assumed a particular form and name and proclaimed a particular doctrine. In other words, when faith in God was still in its initial phase, no one asked the question whether God existed objectively or not; instead men were solely concerned with natural phenomena. We may develop this simple proposition by quoting the startling remark by G. v. d. Leeuw, the eminent historian of religion, to the effect that 'God is a latecomer in the history of religion'.[1] By this he meant that all over the world men first worshipped God in a non-personal form. This is only to be expected, for the notion of a divine being presupposes a mode of thinking that could not have existed at the dawn of human history. Let us recall our earlier statement that man created God according to his own image. This also means that the concept of a personal God, i.e. of a 'Thou relationship', presupposes a degree of consciousness that enabled man to regard himself as 'I' and to see other persons as 'not I'.

This was not the case in the early phase of mental development which is usually referred to as 'magical'. At that time no distinction was as yet drawn between being and cause. Neither society nor the individual had yet learned to detach themselves by an awareness of themselves from the natural cause of their existence. In regard to Egypt this becomes clear if we look at the art, where we have the advantage of being able to perceive the object depicted in visual terms. We then see that the view of existence and cause as an integral whole produces two-dimensional form and two-dimensional ornamentation.[2] We are concerned here rather with the reverse: this characteristic of early (neolithic) Egyptian art indicates that at that time men did not distinguish between being and cause. It is only in the next stage, when historical consciousness breaks through (in Egypt, with the invention of writing),[3] the stage which we have come to call 'mythical', that intellectual development reaches the point where God can be comprehended as a person and the concept of God can exist; this stage comes after the ground has been prepared in the late prehistoric (eneolithic) period. Wherever society – though not yet the individual – sees itself as opposed to nature and distinguishes existence from cause, thereby becoming aware of itself and attaining historical consciousness, such a society will seek an antithesis, and find it, in its environment. It is at this point that gods emerge in personal form, and that myths develop in which they are portrayed as persons with name and form, and are ascribed active roles.

Power

What, then, existed before God? Theologians generally refer to it as 'power' (*mana*).[4] Let us briefly see what evidence there is in Egypt of *mana*. As a rule, written evidence is the most reliable, but this is lacking in the early period before writing was invented. We can therefore only say that power left its traces upon the later phases of Egyptian religion, for which we have texts. These traces are evident in a hieroglyph portraying a sceptre (𓌀), which symbolizes power in such a way as to appeal to the imagination. We have to bear in mind, though, that in the early period we are obliged to make deductions *a posteriori*. The first point to note is that Sekhmet (*Sḫmt*), one of the great deities who later became the consort of Ptah of Memphis, simply means the 'Powerful One'; this may or may not have been a taboo name (see p. 22). By way of comparison, we may mention that among the American Indians Manitu and Wakanda originally meant 'power', and that later they became personal gods. It may also be pointed out that in this period 'powers' (*sḫmw*) are sometimes thought to be embodied in the dead; they are often mentioned along with the gods and occasionally in a parallel relationship to them.[5] At the beginning of the Old Kingdom (Third Dynasty) we have royal names of identical structure and meaning: $N\underline{t}r(y)$-$\underline{h}t$ 'divine in body' and $S\underline{h}m$-$\underline{h}t$ 'powerful in body'. 'Power' is also regarded as part of the nature of the deity.[6] The dubious Egyptian word $s\underline{h}m$ acquires the concrete meaning of 'idol';[7] yet we know that the Egyptians thought of a statue or stele as a part of the being it represented.[8] Probably the powers were originally thought of as independent, and were then incorporated into the divine mythology. When the image is conceived as an embodiment of power, this is no doubt connected with the cult of this image and with the hopes and beliefs associated with this visible element of the deity. Admittedly, the original meaning is very often obscured; like 'beauty' and 'beautiful', 'power' and 'powerful' faded out and became mere attributes of the god (see p. 150). Even where power is not explicitly mentioned, one can sense that it forms the basis of worship. It is to be found embryonically in objects and beings which become the centre of pious cult. This very point readily explains why in Egypt everything can in principle be God, from an inanimate implement or object, a plant or animal, to an individual human being.[9]

The ancient theories about fetishes and totemism do not fit the facts and need not be considered further here.[10] The simple concept of power, for which one may also substitute 'efficacy', may serve as a common denominator for the immense variety of cult objects in Egypt.[11] It is preserved in purest form in objects or inferior creatures, but is present in concealed form where it is elevated to a deity in human guise. Finally, in the dynastic periods of Egyptian history powers and gods coexist and influence each other, and it is only from a typological point of view that one group may be said to embody an earlier stage and the other a more recent one. In the history of religion, and least of all in conservative Egypt, it is seldom that the old is wholly ousted by the new.

Conception of the gods

The gods were conceived after the beginning of the historical era, when mythical thinking had come into its own and men had begun to distinguish between existence and cause in heaven as on earth – once individual personality had taken shape. Henceforward gods were to be the exponents, or rather the lords, of power (see chap. 4). This notion of God embraced both concept and form.

As regards the concept, it is hard to explain the origin of the word *nṯr* which we translate as 'God'; three thousand years later it was to become the *nūte* of the Coptic Christians and the Greek θεός. No one today accepts the ancient hypothesis that the symbol (𓊹) represents an axe and indicates the power embodied in God. This sign is actually a staff around which cloth is wound, i.e. a kind of flag, and taking everything into account is apparently a symbol of the sacred district.[12] But despite all the thought that has been given to this question, nothing can be stated with confidence. It is impossible to substantiate the theory that *nṯr* is derived from the word *nṯr*, 'natron', and that this indicates purity because natron was used as soap in ancient Egypt.[13] For the time being at least we shall have to be content with the possibility that a new word was invented to denote a new substance. A similar obscurity surrounds the etymology of the corresponding words used in the Near Eastern realms, such as *dingir* (Sumerian) and *'el* (Semitic).[14] Nor can it be ruled out that *nṯr* may not originally have been a generic name (appellative) at all, but rather a proper name. In any case it is striking that the most human of gods, Osiris, is called *nṯr* in a particular context: in quite a number of puns this word is used almost as though it were his name.[15] The reader must rest content with these inconclusive considerations.

Form of the gods: personification

Turning to the form taken by the deity, we come upon the phenomenon of its personification. A being whom the believer can approach in an 'I–Thou' relationship must be a person and consequently possess form. This is the case even when, as in Israel, he is not represented. By virtue of their existence the Egyptian gods have form – either statically in imagery or dynamically in action. To understand the image it is best to proceed from the form which everyone coming fresh to the subject takes to be characteristic of the Egyptian pantheon: a human being with an animal head. To obtain a clearer idea, it is best to depart a little from the path of scholarship. In an important work,[16] despite its fundamental errors, K. Sethe has assumed that at the beginning of the historical era a general wave of humanization swept over the non-human (especially animal-shaped) deities, but that at the beginning of the Second Dynasty this had already run its course.

Consequently this wave no longer had any effect, even *ex post facto*, on those beings which (according to Manetho) were then extant, but appeared completely in animal guise, like the bull-god Apis. Then Eberhard Otto, with the aid of a drawing on an early potsherd, proved that this very Apis already existed during the First Dynasty, and thus destroyed the basis of Sethe's hypothesis.[17] To this, admittedly, he added the speculative observation that a pure animal cult could no longer have been introduced after the Egyptians had become familiar with the concept of anthropomorphic deities, during the First Dynasty. In this way, to put it crudely, one author believes that pure animal gods, such as Apis, appear relatively late, since they are only conceivable after the wave of humanization had subsided, whereas the other believes that they appeared at an early date, since they could no longer have been conceived after such humanization had occurred.

In our view both these theories are quite mistaken, since they do not take into consideration the fact that 'power' can be personified in many guises and that the differences between them are not chronological. For at a very late date Thoth was conceived and represented, even on the same monument, as Ibis and as an Ibis-headed man, as well as a baboon.[18] The same is true of Amon, who is human being but also goose, ram etc.[19] To return to the gods represented as men with animal heads, we do not deny progress, if such a term be permitted, in this partial humanization. Like other investigators, we see a very close connection between this development and the spirit of this era, which witnessed the dawn of written history and the emergence of human consciousness. But we proceed from 'power' as primary cause, which can elevate to the rank of deity man and animal, even plant and object, so that neither animal nor plant, still less inorganic matter, ever ceases to be God *in potentia*. Yet there is a tendency to make plants and objects attributes of the deity.[20] To come back to the point where we began, we therefore see in the hybrid idols a rendering of the concept of 'Both...And', a tremendously significant theological concept for the Egyptians: they accepted man yet did not reject the animal kingdom. This is the first great example of an intellectual harmony between apparent incompatibilities. Later in the history of Egyptian religion this was to be brought to a pitch of perfection in another way (see chap. 7).

Egyptian artists solved the task they were set with masterly skill and in their own way did the theologians justice. If today one stands before the figure of such a god in human form with animal head, it requires some time before one becomes aware that such a figure represents something unnatural – so cleverly has the sculptor infused it with a higher truth.[21] One then finds it quite natural that these curious hybrid figures should have appeared at the beginning of the historical period, and that they should have maintained their ascendancy thenceforward, like all the great achievements of this superbly creative early era. Here, at the threshold of myth, they occupy their natural place.

By trying to understand their importance in the history of religion, we in no way wish to minimize their potential divine universality. We pay due heed to the multifarious ways in which the gods were given shape, and drawn from the resources of the world of physical phenomena. It is for the historian of mythology to describe the actions of these deities in human form, who often act in a curious way but nevertheless remain recognizable as individuals. Here it will suffice to point to the static aspect of the 'figure' which is united with a dynamic aspect, a dynamic correlative to their static aspect.

Names of the gods

What we have to consider now is another essential element of the gods' personality: their names, which help to characterize them and distinguish them from one another.[22] These names, by their very existence, testify to the personal character of the deities concerned, and thereby to their innermost nature, but they also pose a problem. For almost all the gods' names can be translated and as a rule denote a characteristic feature of their nature or function: for example, Amon, 'the Hidden One', i.e. the invisible air-god; Khons, 'the one who travels across', i.e. the moon-god who journeys across the sky. This raises the question whether these names may not be taboo names, which in practice take the place of the god's real name because pious persons fear to mention the latter, preferring to use a term which conveys the god's nature and activity.[23] This question is by no means an idle one. There is, for instance, a tradition about the true name of the sun-god Re, which remains secret and only in one exceptional case is divulged to his daughter Isis.[24] There are also phrases which designate the name as 'secret',[25] and which may even make it dangerous for anyone to pronounce it.[26]

Moreover, a taboo of this kind was not an isolated case in Egyptian; it also applied to many terms for parts of the body, which were regarded either as having particular magic powers (the eye, the hand) or as being objectionable (the anus, the genitals).[27] Finally, one finds analogies in the history of other religions. One need only mention the rigorous taboo around the name of Yahveh among the Israelites. Admittedly, this raises doubts about the interpretations given above of the translatable Egyptian gods' names. For in the scriptural tradition (to be more precise, treatment) of the name of Yahveh we have a clear indication of the coexistence of a real name and the taboo usage: as is known, the name is written within a framework of consonants (יהוה), but is vocalized in such a way as though it were the appellative of 'lord' (vowels of Adonai, 'my lord'). This is done to make the reader say '(my) lord' and not 'Yahveh'. Here therefore Adonai is a taboo term denoting the real name Yahveh. It is precisely empirical evidence of this kind which, however, is lacking in the case of the Egyptian deities. Our doubts are increased by another consideration of a more general kind: all over the world it is normal for persons to be given names which denote their nature, characteristics or function.[28] Why should this not be possible, or even common practice, with divine persons? The objection that the name enables one to control the person named applies to gods as much as to men, and from this point of view both would be equally entitled to a taboo name.

For this reason we cannot subscribe to the view about the general application of taboo names. In our opinion the Egyptian gods as a rule received the name which they usually possess in our sources either when they were first thought of or when they were incorporated into the pantheon. This name served to define and differentiate them in the same way as their form did.[29] Nevertheless we do not deny the possibility that taboo names did exist in Egypt. Even if they were not used for the common names of deities, which will be discussed in detail below, they were employed for all the numerous terms which designated a god after the place with which he was associated: for example, 'he from [the town of] Nekhen'.[30]

We may now go on to show that names as a rule serve to identify the nature of the deity designated. In doing so we shall acquaint the reader with a number of Egyptian gods, without going systematically into matters of theology, so sparing him the exertions involved in interpreting the myths associated with them. Horus (*Ḥrw*) is 'the Lofty One'; the name strikes exactly the right note for the falcon-like sky-god. Neith (in our opinion derived from *Nrt*) is 'the Awful One' and denotes a war-goddess with two arrows; Sekhmet (*Sḫmt*), 'the Mighty One', likewise a warlike creature, is represented as a lioness and dispenses ailments; Thoth (*Ḏḥwty*), probably 'the Messenger', has a function equivalent to that of Hermes in the pantheon;[31] we have already referred to Amon, 'the Hidden One' (the invisible air-god) and Khons, 'the one who travels across' (the moon-god journeying across the sky). Isis no doubt obtained her name from the 'throne' which she originally personified.[32] Hathor (*Ḥwt-Ḥr*), 'House of Horus', is a suggestive theological designation for a sky-goddess who offers shelter to the falcon Horus. Theological constructs, whose form however cannot be defined with reliability, probably account for the names of Atum, 'he who is the totality', and Nefertem, 'he who has newly appeared is perfect'.[33] From this it is evident that the theologians who devised these constructs were trying to express the nature of the deity through his or her name.

The etymology of the names of three other important gods – Re, Ptah and Osiris – is not yet certain. In the case of Re an attempt was made in oral tradition to interpret the name as 'companion' (Hebr. *rēaʻ*), an allusion to the sun's role as companion of the moon, which was of greater importance in determining chronology.[34] Ptah might be connected with the verb *ptḥ*, 'to sculpture', and denote the god as a sculptor in accordance with his function, were it not for the fact that the verb concerned is only authenticated in very late texts and may have been a loan-word.[35] Osiris has been interpreted in many ways but none of them is satisfactory – not even the one making it a pet name, 'seat of the eye', in the sense of 'delight of the eye', 'darling'.[36] What is true of most of the great gods also holds good for the lesser ones. Pakhet (*Pḫt*), 'the Rapacious One', accurately denotes a lioness. Two falcon-like gods have the appropriate names Anti (*ʻnty*), 'the one with claws' (10th Upper Egyptian nome) and 'the one with outstretched pinions' (*Dwn-'nwy*) (18th Upper Egyptian nome),[37] and so on.

This should suffice to illustrate our point: the gods' names, in so far as they can be interpreted, coincide with all that is known about their respective form, character and function. We also regard it as highly plausible that names were given to the gods at the moment when they were conceived.[38] In those cases involving gods associated with other deities, such as Hathor (House of Horus) and Thoth (messenger of the gods), or intellectual notions based on other gods, such as Atum and possibly also Nefertem, this fact suggests that both the name and the deity in question developed later.[39]

Creation of the gods

The gods are thus individual persons, defined and characterized by their form and their name. In this respect they are like human beings. But they also bear yet another resemblance to men; the strongest reason for this is based upon their personal character. Like men, the gods are created, and, what is more, are created by a primordial god. The various concepts entertained about this matter will be dealt with later (chap. 8). For the present we shall only concern ourselves with two forms of speech which serve to express this notion.

One of them refers only to the creation of the gods. The Memphite primeval god Ptah, for example, is called '[he] who gave birth to the gods' (*msi*).[40] In the other one a parallel is expressly drawn between gods and men. For example, Amon is referred to as 'the one who begot the gods (and) men' (*msi*).[41] The gods thus belong to the realm of what is created, and for this reason it is only logical that, potentially at any rate, they should also be subject to the fate of death. They, too, like men, have a fixed lifetime. This is apparent from an attribute of the moon-god Thoth, who determines time: 'He who calculates the lifetimes of the gods [and] men (*ḥsb*).'[42] It is also evident in a summary formulation according to which the blessed departed expect from Osiris salvation and in exceptional cases immortality: 'I pray thee, let me not fall into rottenness (*ḥwȝ*), even as thou dost permit every god and every goddess, and every animal and every reptile to see corruption (*sbi.ty.fy*)'.[43] Mortality is by no means peculiar to Osiris, the royal god and god of vegetation, for whom this fate is of course particularly relevant. It also affects, quite consistently, the sun-god Re (and the stars), which the sky-goddess Nut swallows up each day and which she bears again after traversing the realm of the dead.[44] Reference may also be made to Amon and the eight primeval gods of his group, whose death and burial (at Medinet Habu) are mentioned in late texts;[45] also to the Ennead of Heliopolis, whose burial-place was located at Edfu.[46] Finally, we possess a text authenticating the mortality of Min, a god in mummy form, around whose death and resurrection the important festivals revolved.[47] Thus Plutarch was well informed when he wrote of Isis and Osiris: 'The priests...relate that not only the bodies of these [i.e., the gods of the Osirian group] but also of other gods who are said to be neither begotten (ἀγέννητοι) nor immortal (ἄφθαρτοι) after their death will rest with them and will be worshipped by them [i.e. the Egyptians]....'[48]

The question of course inevitably arises as to the position in time and place of the primeval god within (or, to be more accurate, vis-à-vis) the gods whom he created and from whom he became separated by this act of creation. The answer can best be given by pointing out that the primeval god is by nature a power of the chaotic shapeless world, and that he resembles the forces of chaos, for in the Egyptian view the orderly sphere of creation is forever surrounded by chaos, in the same way as the primeval ocean surrounds the earth. But as a power of this kind the primeval god is timeless, like the negative forces of chaos, which are immortal despite the fact that they are constantly being combated and destroyed (in the same way as Apophis, the enemy of the gods).[49]

The association we have established between the primeval god and chaos is not just conjured up out of the air. Two texts exist to prove it. In one of them the primeval god (Re) himself states that he 'came into being' before the creation and refers to his original state in a stereotyped way by the expression 'not yet', which characterizes what is chaotic and shapeless all over the earth: 'Heaven had not come into being, the earth had not come into being, the creatures of the earth [and] the reptiles had not been made in that place.'[50] In the other text mention is made of the end of the world, heralded by the primeval god (Atum), when he, as the creator, will, in the form of a serpent, recede again into the chaos whence he had once sprung. 'Earth will appear as a primeval ocean, as a flood, just as it did at the beginning. I am that what remains...after I have turned again into a serpent which no man knows and no god sees.'[51]

Yet another factor suggests a link between the primeval god and chaos. These creatures are either male (e.g. Atum) or female (e.g. Neith), since they are persons; but there is no lack of testimony to the fact that in reality no distinction was drawn between the sexes, for the primordial gods procreated gods and men parthenogenetically, i.e. without a partner. Consider the title of 'father and mother', which was given to Sokaris, for example, or the Greek term ἀρσενόθηλυς ('male-female') for Neith and Ptah.[52] Consider, too, the consecutive equations made in Memphite theology between Ptah and the male god Nun (the primeval ocean) and his female partner Naunet; logically enough, in this context Ptah is first called father, and then mother.[53] We may interpret the lack of distinguishing features between the sexes of the primeval gods as a lack of form, and thus as an element of chaos, since it is precisely the difference between the sexes that represents an otherwise impassable limitation for the Egyptian theologian. The latter may identify one god with another, or one goddess with another, but normally never identifies a god with a goddess.

Negative relationship between gods and man

If the gods, except for the primeval god emerging from chaos, are related to man by the act of creation, they also share with man a personal destiny. They are by no means considered purely benevolent but in certain circumstances may be dangerous; they may then be threatened, attacked, and even killed. We do not allude here to the factions which exist among the denizens of the mythical world, which provide it with its dynamism, as is the case in all pantheons and will be familiar to the reader from Greek religion. We are not thinking of the contendings of Horus and Seth or the rivalry between Osiris and Seth, which had unfortunate consequences for the latter, who was sometimes ostracized (see chap. 8). We are concerned rather with one aspect which affects the relationship between all the gods and man. This is the aspect of hostility, which involves man in defensive and even offensive action. In this, man may seek the aid of benevolent and more powerful gods. Atum, for example, 'protect[s] this pyramid of the king; he protect[s] this construction of his from all the gods, from all the dead'.[54] Such hostilities also involve magic practices, whose meaning and purpose it is to avert undesirable decisions by the gods. The way in which the Egyptians understood their elaborate magical system is evident in the passage from the Instruction for King Merikare (Tenth Dynasty):[55] '[God] made for them [men] magic as weapons to ward off what might happen.' By 'God' the instructions in wisdom mean the effective being who *mutatis mutandis* conforms to the primeval god (see chap. 6). By giving man the weapon of magic he thereby also equipped him to act against malevolent gods. Indeed, in the so-called mortuary texts (see chap. 10) there are abundant threats by man against rebellious or hostile gods.[56] We also have testimonies that such menaces were carried out: for example, the cessation of cult practices, which was popular from ancient times onwards.[57]

It is natural that man will confront God in belligerent self-defence particularly when he is faced with illness. Since, as we have seen (chap. 1), illnesses are dispensed by the gods, medical texts are directed mainly against the divine authors of suffering. There are, for instance, prescriptions for ointments which are said to effect 'the removal of a god and the shadow of the [male] dead and [female] dead'.[58] A particularly radical form of assault upon the gods is encountered in the so-called 'ostracizing texts'. In these, enemies of all kinds are rendered harmless by inscribing their names on vessels, among other objects, which are then smashed. That this magic death rite was also applied to the gods has now been realized.[59] We have deliberately emphasized this negative aspect of the gods, in which they appeared as enemies of man and acted in a hostile manner. For this aspect will be unfamiliar to the casual reader, but serves to bring out fully the personal existence of divine beings, in other words to show that the gods had their darker side. The fact that the gods were also guides, protectors and assistants of man, and were treated with appropriate humility and gratitude, is a familiar point which will be discussed later, in the context of cult and piety, the normal attitude of believers toward their deities (chap. 5).

Local deities

The conception of the gods as persons also helps to explain a development which, although familiar, tends to be seen from a one-sided
point of view. At first the deity appeared to his worshippers in all his
vital power, but later he was regarded by a larger circle of believers
reduced to a lesser form, so to speak, with his functions restricted. In
other words, to begin with God means everything to a small group,
but later comes to mean part of a greater whole to a larger number
of faithful. From the all-encompassing ruler of a very limited
society he becomes the local or particular god of an enlarged one.

In Egypt the all-encompassing god of the small unit has justly
been identified above all in the 'town-god' (*nṯr nwt.j*), who is
bound up with and confined to a particular locality but unrestricted
in his function and expert in everything.[60] It is of course clear
that probably no god in the full sense of the term – i.e. a person
and not merely a personification (e.g. of a concept) – ever ceases
to be everything to his worshippers in the act of worship. The
Egyptian makes sacrificial offerings to Ptah or prays to him
because Ptah exerts a general influence, although in particular he
also acquired the special aspect of a god of craftsmen.[61] It has long
since been justly observed that the political development which
led to far-reaching unity between the 'Two Lands' (Egypt) brought
the ancient local gods together in wide-ranging systems, in which
they were restricted to certain functions. One should not, however,
overstress the political background to this theological development, for one thereby pays too little heed to the nature of the gods
themselves. It should therefore be made clear that in their existence
as persons the gods were as a matter of course active on a comprehensive scale, but that they then at least to some extent suffered
the inevitable destiny of all persons, in that they became subject
to the process of specialization: most of their functions were
restricted and curtailed.[62] Moreover, as is likewise comprehensible
from their personal character, the particular type of specialization
was determined by the specific features of the deity concerned.
In human terms, it was predestined by his aptitudes and talents.
Thus the lioness Sekhmet and Neith, who was characterized by two
arrows, became war-goddesses, since this predisposition was
already inherent in their basic conception.

The personal character of the gods also explains why there was an apparent contradiction between their comprehensive efficacy and their restriction to a particular locality or function. These two basic characteristics appear consecutively in history but are nevertheless present at the same time in living reality. What we have here is nothing other than the survival of personality as a result of specialization, the continuity of the whole despite the accentuation of the individual parts. Just as human beings continue to exist despite their specialized activities, God retains his plenitude of power despite his compartmentalized functions. Moreover, it is only in this way that belief in the gods remains alive beneath what are primarily intellectual constructs. In our view this throws some light on the question of God and the gods, of unity and plurality in the pantheon. In the act of worship, in sacrifice, in hymns and prayers, in the erection of sacred monuments and in moral conduct man normally finds himself facing a single God,[63] and a single God is at first also the counterpart to the community of believers. Then the groups of worshippers coalesce and with them their gods. They come to form a system, are juxtaposed in a group, yet as a rule are still considered as individuals. Thus in the substratum of belief which lies beneath all the great religions of history, there is one God and yet many gods. This is the existential substance of truth in Egyptian theology, which sought to effect an intellectual compromise between unity and plurality and to reconcile them to one another (chap. 7).

Cosmic deities

We have been speaking here of local gods. They may be contrasted, at least typologically, with cosmic deities. Did these also have a personal existence? This question brings us up against the special problem of personification: whether heaven and earth, sun and moon, air and water (Nile) were personified by real gods or whether these were merely deified substances – in the same way as there were deified concepts. Unfortunately we cannot do much more than raise this difficult problem, for the various particular details that one can mention do not take us very far: for instance, heaven and earth were called Nut and Geb as deities but *pet* (*pt*) and *ta* (*tꜣ*) as substances. In the first place, however, this is a rule to which there are exceptions, since these concepts are also cross-linked.[64] Secondly, this juxtaposition could be explained linguistically, in so far as *pet* and *ta* were the sequel to Nut and Geb, who for their part were previously terms denoting substances.[65] In other instances it is possible to explain why different names were given to the substance and the god by the fact that the god originated from a different plane and was associated with the substance only in a secondary way. This may well have been the case with the moon, which as a substance is called *yah* but as a deity is represented mainly by Thoth, who is called the 'messenger' by virtue of an entirely different function he possesses. Thus the evidence does not go far enough to solve our problem.

One could make the existence of a cult the criterion in deciding whether we are dealing with a person or with a personification. But on closer inspection this, too, proves to be misleading: for on one hand what were definitely personifications were occasionally the object of cult,[66] and on the other hand it was not unusual for cults of local gods to be transposed to cosmic deities. In the case of the sun-god Re this occurred in a very early period[67] and with important consequences (solar sanctuaries); it is therefore undeniable that cosmic deities were apt to become the objects of cult, despite their inevitably slight association with the locality. In view of this we can but resort to some general remarks. Why did the 'power' which existed originally not also take on the shape of full-bodied deities, and especially so in the case of the great cosmic powers, which were so impressive in their effect? We are inclined to think that heaven and earth, sun and moon, air and water (Nile) did have the rank of real gods with a personal existence.

This by no means concludes the problems connected with the cosmic deities. Another question of importance to Egyptologists is whether the typological difference between cosmic and local gods incorporated a difference of origin. In concrete terms, did the latter originate as the primeval ancestral deities of nomadic groups, and the former as those of peasant groups? Were the latter in the south and the former in the north (with a link to the Near East)?[68] It is impossible to say. No doubt the peasant way of life invites belief in cosmic forces, which enable the crops to flourish. But can the nomad do without them or escape their impact? The difference does not seem all that important. For the conception of gods as persons arose at the beginning of the historical era,[69] when the belief in myth gained ground, i.e. after the differentiation between southerners and northerners, nomads and peasants, had already taken effect.[70]

One point needs to be emphasized in conclusion: the cosmic deities are as a rule wholly in human form.[71] As we are now familiar with the variety of forms in which the divine made itself manifest, and have gained some idea of the reasons for this variety, it may be suggested that there was a single reason why the cosmic deities assumed wholly human form. They did not have a cultic tradition, or a bond with the ancient local manifestations of power; consequently these did not influence their form.

Revelation

Above we have spoken with some hesitation of the 'conception' of the gods, meaning by this that the time and circumstances of their origin cannot be established. All we can say is that such a beginning took place and that it forms part of the great process whereby man became conscious of history, and human history itself was born. We are obliged to use negative phrases of this kind because an entirely different concept is prevalent about the beginning of historical existence and of the way in which a god manifests himself: we are accustomed to the idea that the deity is not conceived but reveals himself. The God of Israel in particular revealed himself in this way. Thus Yahveh revealed to Moses his name and will (Exodus iii), as well as his commandments (Exodus xx), and later manifested himself as the Lord that created all things to his instrument Cyrus, the king of Persia (Isaiah xlv). The Lord makes himself known on such occasions with the words 'I am'. Also the Jesus of St John says: 'I am the good shepherd' (John x. 11; x. 14 etc.). This raises the obvious question how the God of the Egyptians manifested himself. So much is certain: a revelation as in the Bible was *not* essential. There is no evidence to suggest that such a revelation was ever regarded as forming the inception of a god's life. For this very reason we use the term conception, not revelation.

This negative statement does not, however, mean that there were no phenomena in Egyptian religion which could be called revelations. They are scarce and are expressed in a literary idiom, but have a material power which is evidently strong enough to make itself felt. A revelation is barely hinted at when Min miraculously dispenses rain in the desert and makes himself visible: one 'sees his form' (*mꜣꜣ ḫprw*)', evidently in the falling of the rain (Eleventh Dynasty).[72] In the Story of the Shipwrecked Sailor (from the Middle Kingdom) the hero who is cast ashore on an island encounters a serpent-god, the lord of the place. The elemental force of the apparition and the numinous awe which this encounter evokes on the part of the shipwrecked mariner is described impressively: with a roaring noise and an earthquake the hitherto unknown god appears and the sailor prostrates himself on his belly before him.[73] Finally the serpent instructs the sailor on his home-coming to 'give [me] a good name in thy city'. Thus the revelation ends with an instruction which recalls the revelations we find in the Bible. True, the instruction is by no means the main point, which is that the man makes a speech to the god, in which he describes his mode of life, in response to the latter's question: 'Who has brought thee [hither]?' After the man's detailed story comes an analogous and apparently consoling tale by the serpent, in which one can sense the motive spirit behind this literary work. It is – at least in the form in which it has been handed down – a tale, not a religious document.[74] The revelation must therefore be considered a literary motif rather than an expression of faith.

Similar problems confront us with the so-called 'Sphinx Stele' of Thutmosis IV.[75] Here the god who is personified in the Great Sphinx of Giza appears in a dream to the prince (later the king), as he lies sleeping in the shadow of the Sphinx, and says to him: 'I am thy father Harmakhis-Khepri-Re-Atum, who will give to thee my kingdom on earth at the head of the living', etc. Then the prince learns of the drifting sands which threaten the mighty image of the god. In this testimony we even encounter the formula: 'I am NN.' Yet the revelation in the dream, which has the very limited purpose of freeing the Sphinx from the sand, is very evidently a much-used literary artifice for relating royal deeds.[76] Thus in this case, too, the phenomenon of revelation is scarcely evident and plays no creative part in the structure of religious beliefs.

The same formula 'I am' is to be found in the late inscription on a rock on the island of Sehel, in the area of the First Cataract, which became famous under the name of 'Famine Stele'. We are told in this text, allegedly an ancient document, about something old King Zoser (Third Dynasty) dreamed of. He saw in a vision and heard the god Khnum, who introduced himself with the following words (l. 18): 'I am Khnum, who has fashioned thee', etc. Then the deity tells, among other things, of the power he enjoys over the Nile; this promises the king high floods and thus years of prosperity. In this case, too, admittedly, the revelation is concerned with a single act: on the basis of it the king makes a donation to the god and his temple.[77] On this evidence, quite apart from its late date, no one would claim that Khnum became an Egyptian god through revelation. On the contrary, his emergence, and previous manifestation in the dream, clearly presuppose the reverse, namely that the god already existed and exercised authority. This is nothing other than a special case of the 'appearance' of a god, abundantly authenticated in Egypt. The verbs which we in this context translate by 'appear' (*pri*, *ḥꜥi* and *wbn*) are naturally related to the appearance of the stars in the evening. They therefore refer to the continuous recurrence of what has long existed and is well known. More concretely, they mean, in the metaphysical sense, the (e.g. festive) appearance of ancient and familiar gods.

In conclusion we must once again briefly mention the phrases whereby God introduces himself in the first person singular, the classical form used for revelation.[78] These phrases occur extremely rarely in Egyptian texts except in the cases mentioned above.[79] One example of this is the following: 'I am Thoth, the eldest son of Re, whom Atum has fashioned (*msi*), created from Khepri...I descended to earth with the secrets of "what belongs to the horizon"', etc.[80] This rare example seems noteworthy since phrases of this kind frequently appear in Greek hymns in honour of the Egyptian goddess Isis ('I am Isis', etc.). This leads to the suspicion that they are derived from outside Egypt.[81]

Sacrosanct monarchy

The foregoing remarks on the subject of revelation are offered to the reader with an interest in the phenomenology of religion. We also hope that they will have clarified the way in which the Egyptian gods were conceived, at least by ruling out such erroneous views as the notion that revelation played a creative role. We may now pass on logically to the last section of this chapter, which deals with sacrosanct monarchy. For if for once we interpret the concept of revelation broadly, seeing in it nothing more than the manifestation of the deity in the form of a living person, perceptible to the senses, then we may risk the statement that God was made manifest in the king.[82] From the very beginning of Egyptian history the king was identified in the written sources with Horus – 'the Lofty One', the falcon-like sky-god. He is called 'Horus NN'; the stelae of the earliest kings link the term Horus with the individual name of the ruler, as in the case of the 'serpent Horus', a monument famous for the masterly skill of its sculptor. In performing this task, among others, artists came to the assistance of theologians by expressing religious ideas in an effective way.

To illustrate this, let us call to mind King Chephren, who fuses with the falcon Horus in a singular unity. In this sculpture the 'Horus aspect' of the king is more convincingly rendered than is possible in words.[83] It cannot be ascertained with certainty whether we are confronted here with identity or only incarnation, or whether identity came first and was later reduced to incarnation. In our view the latter is probable, since it would conform to the trend of intellectual development. In the first stage, that of magic power, the chieftain is as much an exponent of power as is the falcon, and they are thus mutually identifiable. But in the second stage, that of mythical deities, when the notion of personality has developed and barriers have been erected between men and gods, chieftain and falcon are differentiated from each other: the person of the ruler can only be the earthly habitation of the falcon-god. In the last resort he is 'he who appears on the throne of Horus ($ḥ^ci$)'.[84] This quality naturally suffices to raise the king far above the human plane and to place him in an intermediate position between God and man. A further step is taken in the same direction when the king is dogmatically categorized as 'the son of Re (s^3 R^c)'. This becomes plain in the titulary of Egyptian rulers during the Fourth Dynasty, when it was rounded off into its classical quinquepartite form.[85] Previously the king had already come to bear three other titles, two of which took account of the morphological and political duality of the country (valley and Delta, Upper and Lower Egypt), as well as the Egyptians' dualistic mode of thinking:[86] 'the Two Ladies' (equivalent to the goddesses of the crown Uto and Nekhbet) and 'member of the rushes and the bee' (a reference to early symbols of Upper and Lower Egypt).[87]

Anyone making his first acquaintance with Egyptian religion will take the epithet 'son of the sun-god' as a special mark of dignity and clear evidence of the Egyptian ruler's divine nature. This is incontestably true, but the matter looks rather different when it is regarded from the standpoint of Egyptian religious history. We then discover that 'son of Re' also conveys the notion of 'only just'. For the king is no longer regarded simply as identical with the god of heaven and earth; nor is he any longer seen as his incarnation; he is simply the son of a divine father. But according to a generally held principle which was especially strong in the ancient Orient, a son is *responsible* to a more powerful father. Nothing confirms this better than the fact that when the king acts he merely carries out his father's commands. Thus Sesostris I says, in an account of the foundation of a temple, that God had 'formed him in order to do for him what should be done for him'.[88] The pharaohs of the New Kingdom, beginning with Thutmosis III, undertake their campaigns at the command of their divine father (Amon-Re), etc. [89] This idea became so common that it is hardly possible, and also unnecessary, to provide exhaustive evidence of it. Instead, we may make use of an entirely different sort of evidence: architecture. Buildings which serve the purposes of cult, and not infrequently of theology, provide striking testimony of the way the king lost his earlier paramountcy. When sun worship became dominant during the Fifth Dynasty, great solar sanctuaries were built near Abu Sir to discharge in an architectural form the ruler's debt to his divine father. In size they vie with the pyramids, which were royal tombs and places of worship. Behind the change of dogma whereby the king ceased to be Horus and became the son of Re there was probably a struggle between south and north; the cosmic god now in the ascendant had his spiritual centre in the north,[90] and the way in which nature is depicted on reliefs in his sanctuaries is in accord with the northerners' inclination towards the sensual representation of life in all its abundance.[91]

We shall not pursue this point any further but, changing the method of discussion, shall try to clarify the dialectic inherent in this situation. We spoke earlier of the king ceasing to be Horus and becoming the son of Re. This might suggest that some breach of continuity took place, which would be quite misleading. Egyptians would not have been Egyptians if they had not preserved the old along with the new, juxtaposing them if not actually reconciling them. In this case, at least, the ancient title of Horus continued to exist in juxtaposition with the new rank of 'son of Re'. This of course accorded with the general trend whereby sacrosanct kingship was subject to progressive diminution, passing from identity to incarnation, and thence to a father–son relationship. In each case what was new was no doubt what seemed at the time to have the greatest merit and significance, even if it did not wholly oust what had gone before.

The doctrine of 'son of the sun' was later embroidered in myths which turned out to have momentous consequences. A story from the Westcar Papyrus (late Middle Kingdom) has it that the Fifth-Dynasty kings were born from a union between the sun-god and a mortal, the wife of a priest.[92] Above all this doctrine is documented in dogmatic form in the cycles on two of the most famous buildings at Thebes (Eighteenth Dynasty), on the north wall of the central colonnade in Queen Hatshepsut's mortuary temple at Deir el-Bahari, and in one of the halls built by Amenophis III in the temple of Luxor.[93] In both cases the procreation and birth of the king concerned are depicted as proceeding from a union between the national god (Amon-Re) and the consort of the ruling pharaoh: God, in the guise of the pharaoh, is shown approaching the woman thus blessed. The images and the text depict the scene with a fine delicacy, yet dwell frankly upon the act of sexual union. There is nothing here of that ascetic spiritual treatment so characteristic of the late Hellenistic age, which led to the Christian idea of the miraculous birth of Jesus. The traditional mode of representation remained alive right down to the threshold of Christianity, to the birth of Caesarion, Caesar's son by Cleopatra VII.[94]

The king's two bodies

We mentioned above that once the king became just an incarnation of the deity he ceased to be God in the full sense of the word. This diminution of his stature did not spring merely from the differentiation that came with the emergence of personality and the development of myth. It was also rooted in the fact that men became increasingly aware, through their powers of ratiocination, that the pharaoh was indeed a human being. Today we know that the original godliness associated with the chieftain during the Old Kingdom (evident from the Fourth Dynasty) was superseded by a fully fledged doctrine of the king's two bodies. In other words, his stature was diminished. It can be shown that an astonishingly consistent distinction was drawn terminologically between the divine character of the royal office and the human nature of the person holding it. The documents of this period, especially inscriptions on tombs of eminent persons and royal decrees, use a different expression for the person of the individual ruler and for the bearer of the impersonal office. In one case (leaving out the finer nuances) they employ the term *ḥm*, which rather unfortunately has to be translated as 'majesty', although it really means 'the body';[95] if the bearer of office is meant, the term *nłswt* is employed, which is also a component of the titulary that proclaims the king's divine nature.[96]

We are concerned less with the political and legal aspects of the matter, important as they are, than with the theological, and in the last resort psychological, implications. According to the Old Kingdom conception, as we learn from royal mortuary texts, the living king is both man and God, and, as we shall see presently, only when he is dead does he become God.[97]

It is admittedly rather misleading to speak of a *doctrine* of the king's two bodies, as if this were laid down didactically. The existence of this idea has to be deduced from the terminology in each case; yet precisely the fact that these phrases occur regularly shows that the idea existed and was clearly perceived.

How did man become king and thereby the bearer of divine office? To this question the Egyptian sources afford no systematic answer. But we do know of something which testifies to this transition from man to king, this acquisition by a select individual

of a dual nature: the ceremonial act of coronation. This act, together with the fixing of the titulary and the royal name, indicated
that a new kind of being had been born. Crowns are particularly
efficacious visible symbols of power. The king acquires this power
in the most drastic manner, by swallowing them. In the Cannibal
Hymn of the Pyramid Texts, which bears the imprint of primitive
vitality, the ruler devours the crown of Lower Egypt and thereby
gains dominion over its territory.[98] In the same text, as well as in
other collections, hymns are addressed to the crowns, which are
praised as conferring dignity and power upon the man who wears
them.[99] In the royal mortuary cult these crowns play an enormous
role, in real life as in myth; for example, crowns have their own
separate sanctuaries, etc.[100] The reign of the new ruler, and thus
his existence as king, commences with his coronation, the climax
of which, as the name suggests, is the receiving of the crown.[101]
Ideally, coronation took place on New Year's day, as was certainly
the case with Hatshepsut; if these two dates did not coincide, the
years were calculated from the day of the ruler's coronation, beginning on that very day.[102] This shows what epoch-making
significance was attached to the act of coronation. Later, it is true,
ideologies developed which asserted that the king was predestined
to rule, at or even before his birth. The Instruction for King
Merikare states that God created for man 'rulers from the
womb';[103] Sinuhe praises the ruling king (Sesostris I), saying
that 'he [already] conquered while yet in the womb; on that was
he set ever since he was born'.[104] The former formulation may have
had a bearing on the dynastic principle, and may have sought to
emphasize continuity of lineage; the latter may be regarded as
a retrospective and hyperbolic glorification of the present king's
manly vigour. Both formulations (and many others besides) go
back far beyond the empirical phenomenon of coronation, and
seek to elevate the royal and superhuman ruler to the plane of
what is essential and permanent, from the plane of becoming
(*werden*) to that of existence (*sein*). The coronation raised the
divinity of the king into the state of 'becoming'. One *was* not king;
one *became* one. As man, one became the bearer of a divine office.

Then came the other decisive event in the ruler's life: his death.
According to Old Kingdom teaching, just as coronation enabled
a man to enter the world of the divine, so upon his death he ceased

to belong to the human world. Proof of this may be found in the innumerable utterances in the royal mortuary texts recorded in the pyramids, among which there is not one that mentions *ḥm*, the terrestrial, bodily nature of the king. This has ended with his death.[105] Another proof of this belief is to be found in the denial of the king's physical mortality, and the assertion that he has entered upon a new life: 'You have not departed dead, you have departed alive'[106] – or again, 'Grasp the king by his hand, and take the king to the sky, that he may not die on earth among men.'[107] It is in this way that the Egyptian rulers pass into the beyond. Later we shall become acquainted with impressive testimonies of the king's existence in the celestial hereafter (see pp. 204 f.). Finally, evidence of this belief is afforded by the 'becoming of Osiris', whereby the king entered into the eternal nature of this god and, instead of just acting analogously, as at first, acquired an identity of existence with him (see pp. 54 f.).

So far so good. But death must have presented a psychological problem both for the ruler and for his subjects. For the monumental royal tombs were visible to all, especially during the Old Kingdom, and these complexes had a twofold function, in accordance with the twofold nature of the ruler. They comprised a temple, erected for the worship of the sacrosanct ruler, whose power was still effective even though he had passed into eternity, but were also a place whence the deceased ruler obtained the supplies he needed in the afterlife.[108] The sceptical literature that appeared after the collapse of the Old Kingdom bears witness to the radical decline of royal power by speaking frankly of the king's death. Reference is even made to the deplorable spoliation of royal tombs: 'Behold, he that was buried as a hawk [i.e. the king] lieth on a bier. What the pyramid hid [i.e. the sepulchral chamber in the interior or even the sarcophagus itself] will become empty.'[109] The same directness is to be found in one version of the so-called Songs of the Harpers, where we hear of 'gods [i.e. kings] that were aforetime [and] rest in their pyramids; this realization of the transitoriness of life prompts the conclusion "carpe diem"'.[110] It is therefore hardly a coincidence that the king, when faced with death, appears in his most human form. When Neferikare sees how his faithful vizier Weshptah is suddenly overtaken by death, 'he prayed to Re', i.e. he turned to God, the helper in distress, like

any other mortal.[111] The human element in the notion of the
king's two bodies could not be brought out more impressively.
When a new kingdom took shape after the collapse of the Old
Kingdom and the troubles of the Intermediate period, a political
pamphlet ascribed to the murdered King Amenemhet I, as though
they came from the beyond, the following words: 'Hold thyself
apart from those subordinate to [thee]...approach them not alone.
Fill not thy heart with a brother, nor know a friend and do not
provide for thyself any confidants. This is of no use.'[112] This
moving document testifies to the loneliness and anguish of a ruler
who has experienced the limits of human existence in the most
palpable form.

The king as intermediary with the gods

Thus the Egyptian king is simultaneously God and man. His role
as an intermediary becomes especially evident in the fact that he
alone is entitled to communicate with the gods. In principle he
alone was entitled to carry out the daily ritual of the cult, although
in practice he obviously had to entrust this function to a whole
class of priests, as we shall see later (chap. 5). The king's sacerdotal
function was not just a privilege which set him apart from other
men, but also a service to the gods. This is clear, for example,
from the regulations governing the ritual of daily service, where
the priest-king has to say 'I kiss the earth, I embrace [the earth-
god] Geb', and there are chapter headings which run as follows:
'utterance: to prostrate oneself', 'utterance: to kiss the earth face
downward'.[113] There are sculptures in which the king is portrayed
prostrate (before the deity); recently some of these have been
found which date from as early as the Middle Kingdom and the
Eighteenth Dynasty and not just from the Ramesside period. It is
therefore impossible to attribute them to foreign (for example,
Syrian) influences during the late New Kingdom; they must rather
be seen as appropriate to the institution of sacrosanct monarchy
itself.[114]

The paradox inherent in the king's position as an intermediary
between God and man comes out especially clearly when, during
the New Kingdom, the king is portrayed, sometimes in his
priestly capacity, confronting his own divine image.[115] A tension
was latent in the very conception of kingship as entertained during

the Old Kingdom, which placed the king between two rival poles of attraction, the human and the divine; it was responsible for the double aspect of his sacerdotal function, whereby he was numbered among the gods yet was forced to kneel before them.

The above remarks will have made it plain that sacrosanct monarchy, which at the very beginning was still a simple affair, became ever more complex and intricate as it developed. It is tempting to assume that the attribution to the living ruler of two natures, one human and the other divine, runs roughly parallel to the differentiation between this world and the beyond, i.e. with the idea that a terrestrial existence, prolonged beyond the grave, was to be followed by a completely different world; with this notion we shall deal later, in connection with the judgement of the dead (see pp. 126 ff.). Nor shall we consider here the secondary deification (by comparison with the original one in the early period) of the living ruler, which reached its climax in the Amarna kingdom. Let us rather conclude by returning to our point of departure: that the king *reveals* the deity by being a visible incarnation of it. This capacity and function of the divine ruler is expressed by Ramses II, who lived in a late period when the tendency was to deify the living king. He adopts a propagandist manner, making use of apostrophes, for his audience, who in an earlier age would have intuitively grasped his meaning. He uses the formula 'I am', which as we know introduces a revelation: 'Hear ye! I speak to you, all ye men (*rmt*), ye mighty ones of the earth [and] all my soldiers (*mnfꜣt*): I am Re, Lord of Heaven, who is upon earth. For you I do fine deeds, as would a father...'[116] All this accords with the quality of 'fame' (*hmhmt*), often ascribed to the king during the New Kingdom; this was a value which evidently sprang from the hearts of the common people.[117] In this case we should be grateful to the propagandist style, for it expresses neatly how the king now saw his theological position and how he wanted others to see it.

3 · The worshippers

The national religion of the Egyptians

The student of Egyptian religion who approaches the subject from the Christian vantage-point will, as we have seen, reach a negative conclusion: that the Egyptians did not have a revealed religion, at least in the strict sense of the word. If we now turn to that group of people for whom the worship of Egyptian deities was a firm reality, and still retain the same outlook, we shall once more come to a negative conclusion: namely that the Egyptians did not create one of the world's great religions. Let us, however, put the matter differently and say that they did establish a national religion.[1]

First, of course, we must prove that this statement is true. It will be as well to proceed from the remarks made at the end of the last chapter, where it was pointed out that in the sacrosanct monarchy, God is incarnate in the king, who represents him in the eyes of the people. This alone suggests that the worship of Egyptian gods was confined to subjects of the Egyptian ruler. This assumption may be substantiated on two levels: by the Egyptians' conviction that their country was the centre of the earth, beyond whose borders other lands stretched outward indefinitely, and by their conviction that they were superior to all other peoples. These views were modified in the course of time, but they fixed once and for all the lineaments of Egyptian religion as a national religion.

The Egyptocentric outlook: the country

In the earliest stages of its development each nation regards its territory and especially its principal sanctuary as the centre of the earth; they do not know where the limits of this territory run or deem such a question to be in any way significant. This attitude found its classical expression in the Greek notion of the 'navel of the earth' (ὀμφαλὸς τῆς γῆς), which they identified with Delphi. The same expression is encountered among the Israelites (*ṭabbūr hā-āreṣ*);[2] the idea that their own country was the focal point and nucleus of the earth was retained tenaciously even in later stages of Jewish history, although the term navel is not always to be found.[3] This general and familiar notion[4] is also present to a marked degree in Egypt. It takes a form which seems particularly appropriate to the character of a country which each year is flooded and re-emerges from the water. We have in mind the conception of the primordial mound which at the beginning of time arose out of the floods and from which a procreator-god fashioned the world. The efficacy of this topographically most convincing concept is shown by the fact that for a long time to come every Egyptian sanctuary was regarded as an image of this primeval mound and thus as the centre and nucleus of the earth.[5] Originally the idea of the primeval mound was linked with Heliopolis. In one play on words the primeval god of that place, Atum, is addressed simply as 'mound': 'May you be high (kʒi) in this your name of "Height" [kʒ, i.e. mound].'[6] It was then appropriated by many other centres of political and intellectual life, among them of course the royal capitals of Memphis and Thebes;[7] at Memphis it could scarcely avoid being associated with the local god, Ta-tenen ('the land rising from the primordial water').[8] It seems as though in the course of time Hermopolis, the town in central Egypt, obtained a reputation as the oldest place; certainly it had such honour at the close of Egyptian history. In any case all manner of cosmogonic concepts became localized here, among them that of the primordial mound, the Isle of Flames, and of God seated upon a lotus-flower. If we add to this that the notion of the cosmic egg and the teaching of the eight primeval gods evidently sprang from Hermopolis as well (chap. 8), then this place was the centre of all the Egyptians' ideas about the origin of the world.[9] We cannot do more than state the following fact here: it may have been connected with the intellectual rank of Hermopolis during the Late period, and/or with its central geographical location in Egypt, but neither of these hypotheses can be proved.

A different and unique image was coined for the role of Thebes, the southern capital, as the country's original nucleus. It was taken from the sphere of geology and mining, and ran as follows: 'Thou art the maternal rock (bʒt nɩ̯wt) of cities.'[10] If we can again offer a hypothesis, perhaps the metaphor was in this case prompted by the city's most impressive mountainous surroundings. But there is another statement about Thebes which provides a very clear picture of the way it stimulated development in its environs: 'Thebes testifies to every city...Mankind (*ḥrw*) then came into existence, in order to establish (*grg*) every city'...[11] Here the country is said to have been colonized by settlers from the oldest place on earth. In other cases it is simply said that a place had been 'the nome of Re at the beginning', etc.[12] Admittedly, all the pieces of evidence we have cited have one common characteristic. They do indeed prove our point, by showing how the world was deemed to have developed from certain places in Egypt. But they are primarily related to the rank which these cities enjoyed within Egypt itself: Heliopolis, Memphis, Thebes, Hermopolis and several other places were claimants for the honour of being the original centre of the creation of the world.

What can be said about the relationship between Egypt and neighbouring countries? In the first place the very fact that different Egyptian places claimed various cosmogonies, and were thus rivals (although probably not hostile ones) suggests that it was regarded as a matter of course that an *Egyptian* place was seen as the ὀμφαλὸς τῆς γῆς. But we also have testimony that, like Egyptian towns on a small scale, so also on a broader scale Egypt itself was seen as the centre of the earth. For the earlier period we of course have to be content with indirect allusions. In the first place there is the well-known classical list of the chief neighbours of the Egyptians: the Libyans, Nubians (later also Negroes) and Asiatics, who together make up the known world. These peoples inhabit contiguous territories to the west, south and east of Egypt, which consequently occupies the central place.[13] Only the name of 'Middle Kingdom' is lacking to complete the parallel with China, likewise surrounded by barbarians to the north, south, east and west.

From this central position the pharaoh's power extended outwards in all directions to the very ends of the earth. 'The south', says the deity to the king, 'is given to thee as far as the wind bloweth (*rᶜ ṯꜣw*), the north to the end of the ocean, the west as far as the sun goes, [the east up to the point where] it rises as Shu.'[14] Two rites performed during the ceremony of coronation are relevant here. The new king lets arrows fly toward all four cardinal points of the compass and releases birds to announce his accession to the throne.[15] These two ceremonies make it impressively clear that the Egyptians regarded their country as the centre of the earth. If in comparison with these indirect indications it is objected that direct and concrete statements are of late date, this stems from the fact that the intellectual prerequisites for such formulations *expressis verbis* were not present until the Egyptians had grown into a single family of peoples (see pp. 50 ff.). These sources comprise both written texts and works of art. A sarcophagus in New York from the Late period (fourth–third century B.C.) bears a representation of the earth as a circle, with the nomes of Egypt forming a ring in the centre, as though this were a matter of course. Another example, slightly earlier, was found in a Cairo antique shop and has been published.[16] As for the written evidence Horapollo says distinctly that the Egyptian land forms 'the centre of the [inhabited] earth',[17] and Stobaeus likewise mentions Egypt as 'the very holy land' (ἱερωτάτη χώρα), located in the centre of the earth (γῆ).[18] Finally, one author of the so-called hermetic literature, known to scholars as Pseudo-Apuleius, modifies the theme by praising Egypt (*terra nostra*) as 'the temple of the entire world' and 'the likeness of the sky';[19] the country's privileged position is thus given a metaphysical foundation.

We could leave the matter here were it not for Greek quotations that raise an interesting question that merits a brief digression. Egypt is said to be the centre of the γῆ or οἰκουμένη. What did the Egyptians understand by these Greek terms for earth? Did they also have a word for κόσμος, 'world'? The second question may definitely be answered in the negative. The Egyptians, like their neighbours the Israelites (Genesis i. 1), spoke of the 'heaven and the earth' and often added 'the nether world' or 'the water'. The terms for 'world' given in the Egyptian dictionary[20] are very late and – just as we also use the terms world and earth indiscriminately – either refer to the earth or are of a poetic or paraphrastic nature: 'What the sun traverses (*nmt ȝḫt*)', 'what the wind blows through (*nmt n ṯȝw*)'. It may be stated quite confidently that the Egyptians could not have conceived the term 'world' in the sense of κόσμος, i.e. an ordered universe, because in their view the ordered areas (heaven and earth) were always surrounded by the powers of chaos (the nether world and the waters, which continued to exist).[21]

Let us now inquire a little closer into their terms for earth and what they understood by them. The principal word (*tȝ*, in hieroglyphics ▭) has a very wide range of meaning. On the one hand it denotes the earth as part of the world (together with heaven, etc.: see above); on the other hand it can also mean the earth as material (soil, even dirt); finally, it can signify the ground upon which one stands. Furthermore, it is used to denote the land (to be more accurate: the low country in contrast to mountainous country), and even foreign lands as well as Egypt. Thus the plural form 'the lands' may have the sense of 'the entire earth'. These meanings are used idiomatically, which brings us back to the point about Egypt's special position among her neighbours. There is, for instance, the following enumeration: low-lying lands (*tȝw*), mountainous country (*ḫȝswt*), Egypt (*Kmt*, also *tȝ-mrỉ*);[22] in this case Egypt has its own name and is contrasted with other flat or mountainous tracts of territory as something apart. Above all there is the term 'the Two Lands' (*tȝwy*, in hieroglyphics ▭), based upon the political and topographical duality of Upper and Lower Egypt, the Nile valley and the Delta. It contains the general word *tȝ*, 'land', but elevates it and accords it a special usage as a term applicable to Egypt alone. The dual term 'the Two Lands' was thus quite consistently rendered into Greek by the proper name 'Egypt' (Αἴγυπτος).[23] Thus the use of special terms for earth and land shows that the Egyptians claimed an exceptional position for their country.

Other evidence indicates how the Egyptians related the geographical or climatic conditions of other regions to those with which they were familiar in their own territory. When they learned of the Euphrates, which unlike the Nile flows from north to south, they called it 'that inverted water which goes downstream in going up-stream'.[24] Their terminology, oriented to the Nile, combined the terms for 'up-stream' and 'south' and for 'down-stream' and 'north'; all they meant about the Euphrates, therefore, was that it flowed in a southerly direction. The water systems of other countries, too, were envisaged in relation to the Nile. In the Hymn to Akhnaton of Amarna we read: 'Thou art a Nile in heaven (*ḥʿpy m pt*), for the strange nations (*ḫȝstyw*)..., [but] a Nile which issues from the underworld for Egypt (*tȝ-mrỉ*).'[25] Certainly we already have here a notion of a highly universalistic kind (which we shall come to presently): that God manifests a concern for foreign poeples. But the image remains Egyptocentric and the distinction made between the north-eastern areas, almost arid but fed by the young Nile, and Egypt itself enhances the latter's privileged position.

The Egyptocentric outlook: the inhabitants

What holds good for the country is also true of its inhabitants. If Egypt was the nucleus and centre of the earth, the Egyptians were naturally its only legitimate inhabitants. This is clear from the way in which concepts which were originally limited to a single politico-religious group came to mean 'man' and 'mankind' in general. The Egyptians themselves compiled encyclopaedic lists of these words, and the whole question has been thoroughly investigated.[26] We know, for example, that the concept p^ct, which later merely had the general meaning of 'mankind', originally denoted the primeval inhabitants of Egypt at the time when the earth was separated from the sky and the earth-god Geb ruled upon earth.[27] We may consider here in some detail the most important of these concepts, particularly since they have not as yet been studied adequately.[28] The word in question is *rmṯ*, which definitely came to mean 'human being'. In this sense it is used to distinguish men from God or from animals; it may also mean 'man' as distinct from woman or boy. Now there is reliable information to show that the word *rmṯ* originally also had a restricted meaning. At the beginning of the Old Kingdom the Admonitions of Ipuwer contain a lament that foreigners are pouring into northern Egypt and gaining power there. Near the beginning of the surviving text we read: 'The tribes of the desert [?] (*ḫȝstyw*) have become Egyptians [?] (*rmṯ w*) everywhere.' Here, in view of the antithesis, *rmṯ* cannot on my account mean 'man', but rather means 'Egyptian', whose incontestable ancestral rights had been appropriated by foreigners, wrongfully and contrary to the natural order.[29] Elsewhere, too, *rmṯ w* are mentioned alongside other peoples and are evidently a term denoting 'people'. This meaning even asserts itself at a time when the general tendency is towards universalism and when *rmṯ*, as we shall see directly, had long since acquired the meaning of 'man'. We have in mind the scenes in the so-called Book of Gates, one of the guides through the nether world recorded in one of the royal tombs of the Ramesside era (Seti I, Merenptah, Seti II, Ramses III, Ramses VI), and also in the Osireion at Abydos; in these guides, which represent the creation of human races by Horus, the Egyptians are referred to as *rmṯ w* in contrast to their neighbours. Here the term in question is again used to designate a people, since it is on the same level with the other names referring to the Egyptians' mighty neighbours. Its character as a *nomen proprium* is further enhanced by the fact that *rmṯ w*, like the terms for Asiatics (*ꜥꜣmw*), Negroes (*nḥsyw*) and Libyans (*ṯmḥw*), is made up of plays on words and is given an etymological explanation.[30]

The belief in the privileged position of one's own people necessarily implies an ability to distinguish strictly between other foreign peoples. This the Egyptians did from the Old Kingdom onwards, in effective and artistically outstanding portraits of men of various races. These accurately registered not merely external features, such as the style of hair, beard or clothing, but also facial features.[31] Those who had such an acute eye for differences between peoples will have arrived at a universal concept of man in the historical, and not zoological sense; they will have done so gradually, probably by identifying the basic elements pertinent to each, giving them a name, and so building up a composite picture.

But let us return to the history of the word *rmṯ* and trace further some of the essential landmarks in its development. In the early Middle Kingdom the meaning of *rmṯ* seems to have faded to that of 'man'; it no longer corresponded adequately to 'Egyptian'. In any event Sinuhe, who fled to Syria, speaks of *rmṯw Kmt*, 'Egyptian folk', when he refers to his own people.[32] One could at a pinch qualify this statement by assuming that he wanted to make himself absolutely clear and designate as 'Egyptians' those who journeyed about in Syria and by virtue of their Egyptian origin could produce credible testimony about Sinuhe to one of the local princes. In that case *rmṯw Kmt* would not have the primary meaning of 'Egyptians' but rather people who, unlike the *émigré* Sinuhe, still had their residence in Egypt. But this is only one possible interpretation, and the reader will be aware of the shaky ground upon which systematic expositions often rest.

On the other hand, the picture is completely clear during the Eighteenth Dynasty. For now the once exclusive term *rmṯ* is applied even to prisoners of war, that is to say to foreigners of the lowest social category, whose lives were forfeit and who were therefore also called 'living ones to be slain' *sk̠r ꜥnḫ*); such people were as a rule taken into slavery. The term *rmtw kfꜥw* literally means 'captives' i.e. 'prisoners of war'.[33] It is therefore not surprising that both in Coptic, the vernacular used during the last millennium B.C., which later became a literary language, and also in the juridical and literary demotic language, this line of development was continued. The term now used for 'Egyptian' was *rmt̠. n km.t*, 'man of Egypt' (pronounced rᵉmᵉnkēme).

In conclusion it is worth pointing to one tendency which operated in the reverse direction. Herodotus speaks of 'the *rmt̠*' (with the article *p* and a Greek ending = πίρωμις) and adds the initially surprising statement that in Greek this means 'nobleman' (καλὸς κἀγαθός).[34] He does not reproduce the meaning of 'human being' (ἄνθρωπος), which had become the normal one in the Late period. This, taken together with the strong classicist trends among his contemporary Egyptian informants, may reflect a revival of the old specific sense of the term *rmt̠*, i.e. one particular select human being rather than 'man' as such.[35]

Extent of Egyptian gods' influence

From the above it should be clear that to the ancient Egyptians their country was the centre of the earth and their people its only rightful inhabitants. The history of the word *rmt̠* shows clearly that the latter belief was modified in the course of time. We now have to consider the question of how this Egyptocentric outlook affected the extent of the area within which the Egyptian gods were worshipped and the extent of the latter's impact upon men.

The first question can best be approached by making three general points: Egyptian gods were primarily worshipped in cult (see chaps. 5 and 10); in principle the ruler alone was entitled to communicate with the deity (see p. 40); the king, the representative of the Egyptian land and people, acts on their behalf in the name of the gods, with whose authority he is imbued. The king and Egypt are accordingly the subject of history, the environment merely its object. This idea could not be expressed more plainly than in an inscription of Ramses III, the last great emperor in Egyptian history: 'Mayest thou [king of the gods Amon-Re] let it be known in all the low country (*tȝ*) and all the hilly country (*ḫȝst*) that thou art the power of the pharaoh, thy son, against all the low country and all the hilly country. Thou grantest victory to Egypt (*tȝ n Kmt*), thine only land (*pȝy.k tȝ wˁty*), without the hand of a soldier or any man [being involved], but only thy great strength which ensures salvation...'[36] In other words, the representative of the Egyptian pantheon, Amon-Re, operates through the medium of the king for the benefit of the chosen ('sole') land of Egypt against all its neighbours.[37] Another note-worthy phrase occurs in the Hymn of Victory of Merenptah, which has become famous as the 'Israel Stele': 'As for Egypt', it says, 'since [the time of] the gods, [she has been] the sole daughter of Re, and his son is he who is on the throne of Shu.'[38] Here, too, emphasis is laid on the singular character of Egypt, whose ruler occupies the ancient throne of the gods with all its rights and duties.

Thus there are two aspects to the strong political affiliations of Egyptian religion and its consequent limitation to a single country. Firstly, the king was a priest and lord of ritual as well as a political figure; secondly, the Egyptian gods had a political role, since they led Egypt to victory through the medium of the pharaoh.[39] Of course the gods were more than just political figures. Where their aid was invoked by pious individuals in distress, acting in a private capacity, there is no question of their having a political function (see chap. 5). But this does not mean that this aspect did not exist, for it was part of the very nature of Egyptian deities. Indeed, it can even be shown that the devout cherished the ideal of their Egyptian homeland as a truly divine gift. A single prayer to Amon, elaborated into a hymn, runs: 'Whosoever is in Syria [says]: come, take me to Egypt.'[40] Later we shall see that burial in Egypt, too, was regarded as a privilege (see p. 204) and that during the last centuries of the pagan era the pious were strictly admonished not to leave the country for foreign lands, where there were no ancestral local gods (see p. 139).

The extent or range of the Egyptian gods' impact must have been considerable, if only because they had to bring or keep foreign peoples under Egyptian rule. What is doubtful is whether the relationship between the gods and the foreigners was an exclusively Egyptocentric one or not. In this respect a characteristic development may be observed: during the New Kingdom (especially perhaps during the Amarna period) the Egyptians allowed these peoples, if not actual equality of status, at least comparability with the Egyptians in their relationship to their gods. This is evident from two testimonies which we have already cited: the Hymn to the Aton, according to which God (the sun Aton) created rain, as a celestial Nile flood, for the inhabitants of the upper country;[41] and the Book of the Gates, in which the deity (Horus) is represented as the creator of all the main races of mankind. There are other pieces of evidence to support this, and a few at least are worthy of note. In the passage cited from the Book of the Gates an Egyptian deity is portrayed as the protector as well as the creator of foreign peoples: Horus or Sekhmet 'protect the souls' (*nḏ bȝw*) of Asiatics, Negroes and Libyans. Moreover, in the Hymn to the Aton of Amarna the creation of human races was already praised as a deed of God, and a reference made to the linguistic differences between them: 'Their [men's] tongues are separate (*wpỉ*) in speech, and their nature as well, their skins are distinguished (*sṯny*). So hast thou distinguished (*sṯnỉ*) the peoples (*hȝstyw*).'[42] The theme of the multiplicity of languages was often reverted to, and none other than Thoth, the god of wisdom, was singled out as responsible for creating and separating them.[43] But not only that: in the very structure of the realm of the dead the existence of foreign peoples seems now to have been taken into account. According to the well-known chapter on the last judgement (Book of the Dead, 125), Thoth appears as 'the interpreter of the Two Lands' to act as intermediary between the gate-keeper and the stranger to Egypt. On the other hand the deceased is introduced to the judges of the dead as 'a man who comes from Egypt' (and who *inter alia* is distinguishable by his odour). From these two cases it might be deduced that interpreters and foreigners were expected to be present in the realm of the dead; but unfortunately we have no information about the fate that awaited such foreigners in the beyond.[44]

The above testifies clearly to the fact that the Egyptian horizon was enlarging itself in a universal sense. The gods are seen as having created other peoples as well and as having given them names and features, languages and climatic conditions of their own. What at the beginning of Egyptian history had applied solely to the Egyptians and their gods now also applied to foreign peoples, in the Egyptian view: they had a personal existence, an individual stamp, derived from their divine origin.

We noted that this development towards universality was evident during the New Kingdom and may have been especially strengthened during the Amarna period.[45] One day it will undoubtedly be possible to describe the course of this process more precisely. Here we may merely observe that this development was not confined to the religious sphere but accorded with a general historical tendency which naturally is most obvious in political history. For the New Kingdom was the period when Egypt became a member of the international community, when it came into contact with alien polities which were not far inferior to Egypt in intellect and power but its equal both culturally and politically. Political treaties and economic agreements offer proof of this, as do the marital ties between the rulers' courts.

To sum up, it may be said that only Egyptians worshipped the Egyptian gods and that the Egyptian gods at first worked solely on their behalf, but were later regarded as the creators and protectors of foreign peoples as well, as guardians of their natural and spiritual order. This latter development, which we have ascribed to the general tendency toward universalism in later periods of Egyptian history, does not by any means imply that Egyptian religion became a world religion, that it had any claim to universal validity, or still less that it sought to assert such a claim in practice. This was excluded from the start by its political aspect, to which we have referred; it may be added that this imposed a similar limitation upon foreigners. Even when the idea of universalism was in the ascendant, the poet could put the following words into the mouth of the king, fighting on the battlefield: 'What are these Asiatics (ʿȝmw) to thee, Amon? Wretches that know not God (ḥmw nṯr)?' This passage is followed by one in which the pharaoh points to his achievements on God's behalf in maintaining the national cult.[46]

At this point mention may be made of a special case: in places which came under Egyptian rule we also encounter fairly numerous traces of Egyptian cults. They are to be found south of the First Cataract in Nubia and, to a lesser extent, north-east

of the Delta in Syria.[47] But these very locations show that the
cults merely reflect the fact of Egyptian domination. If Syrians
were enlisted to perform services or pay dues in kind for
Egyptian temples on Syrian soil, this was evidently due to considerations of a political and juridical nature: the pharaohs had
ordered Syrian places to provide for the upkeep of these
sanctuaries to the Egyptian gods (Amon, Ptah).[48] Furthermore,
even the epithets given to Egyptian gods abroad quite often
distinguish them as Egyptian. This may occur topographically,
as when, for example, Satis and Anukis, two goddesses of the
First Cataract, are called 'mistresses of southern Elephantine',
in the Nubian fortified town of Buhen on the Second Cataract,
i.e. the foreign place of worship itself is given an Egyptian
name. Alternatively, their Egyptian character may be expressed
in political terms: Amon-Re, when worshipped at Napata in
the deep south by the Fourth Cataract, is referred to as 'Amon-
Re, the Lord of the thrones of the Two Lands on the Sacred
Mountain at Napata', i.e. the epithet designates him as the king
of the gods of Egypt.[49]

Some further points will emerge from our discussion of the
impact which Egyptian religion had abroad and of its survival
through the missionary work carried out in the Hellenistic and
Imperial Roman periods (chap. 11). But this information
will not lead to any modification of our verdict on the national
character of Egyptian religion in the pre-Hellenistic period. As
final corroboration of this, we may point to two other pieces of
evidence. One of them indicates the strict national exclusiveness
of the spiritual centre of Egyptian religion. This is an instruction
concerning the so-called 'House of Life', which served mainly
as a place where sacred writings were compiled (see chap. 10).
It is categorically placed out of bounds to foreigners. 'An Asiatic
(ˁ3m) may not enter into (ˁḳ) this House of Life, he may not see
it.'[50] The other text shows how exclusive were the festivals
which the Egyptians held in honour of their gods. It prohibits
foreigners from entering the temple of Khnum, with reference to
the evening before the great festival of Opet (19th/20th day):
'Do not permit any Asiatic (ˁ3m nb) to enter the temple (ˁḳ r ḥwt-
nṯr) whether he be old or young.'[51] Such prohibitions lead directly
to the prescriptions governing personal cleanliness and diet which,

according to Greek sources, distinguish Egyptians from foreigners just as they did in the case of the Jews.[52]

Extent of Egyptian gods' influence within the country

We cannot conclude our remarks on this theme without devoting at least a few lines to the question: how large was the proportion of Egyptians within the country who worshipped the gods? The casual observer may easily gain the impression that during the Old Kingdom only a small upper class engaged in such worship, and that it then spread more broadly among the people as time went on. But this impression is only due to the fact that during the Old Kingdom the relationship between simple men and the deity was not represented directly; we do not have any representation from that period depicting laymen in prayer.[53] But let us bear in mind the principle enunciated on p. 3: in Egypt not everything which existed in reality was represented; since the deity was not portrayed in private tombs during the Old Kingdom, men in prayer could not be represented either. What seems to be significant here are the indirect sources: personal names which indicate a relationship between the individual and the deity, which are statements of belief. Such names mention that God was 'gracious' or that he 'came to the mother [in labour]', 'kept [her] alive' or 'let [her] prosper', etc.[54] It maybe true that the names preserved from the Old Kingdom are predominantly those of members of the upper class. But we also have a good many persons buried in poor graves – lesser mortuary priests who occupy an intermediate position between the aristocracy and the common people.[55] Why should those whose names have not survived not have had names with similar statements of belief or prayers? This is not to deny that religious privileges existed which were later gradually curtailed. But here it is not a matter of worshipping the gods but of something entirely different, being equated with them. This equation was based in the dual character of the king, as both divine and human: the living pharaoh was God so long as he fulfilled his office (see pp. 37 f.), and when he was dead he was equal or identical with the great gods. From the abundant statements made to this effect we may single out those indicating that he did the same as Re,[56] that he raised himself up like Osiris,[57] and that he was at one with

Osiris.[58] But the latter inspired first the nobility and later all segments of the populace to claim for themselves what belonged to the king, and so led to the phenomenon which in Egyptology has long since come to be called 'the democratization of mortuary beliefs', i.e. the appropriation by the community of texts which were originally reserved for the king and expressed the eminent role he was to play in the beyond, up to the point of being equated with the deity;[59] it also led to the entire ritual complex of Osirian burial, including mummification itself, which enabled the dead to become Osiris *ex opere operato*.[60]

We should not think of this democratization as a single event, even though its climax came when the Old Kingdom collapsed. Traces of it have been observed even on the threshold of the Roman period, since it is only then that renderings were made of the ablution of deceased private persons by the gods (Horus and Thoth).[61] Indeed, during the late Antonine period it even became an international phenomenon, in that Roman marks of dignity, the so-called *clavi*, were taken over as magic symbols for Greco-Egyptian dead.[62] This development of mortuary beliefs for the benefit of ever broader sections of the population did not, however, deter the living from maintaining a devout attitude, as emerges from memorial stones erected by Ramesside artisans at Thebes (see chap. 5).

We have thus returned to the phenomenon of worship itself. We may conclude by citing evidence in which the Egyptians' equality before their God is formulated in an almost unbelievably modern way. Whilst on one hand it takes for granted the *specifically* Egyptian feature of the Nile flood, it bases on the creator-god the notion that the deities were worshipped by all Egyptians *universally*. This evidence is to be encountered in the Coffin Texts, and as yet only there. It originates from a spirit of contestation between belief and scepticism which came into being with the collapse of the Old Kingdom.

> I made the four winds that every man might breathe
>   thereof like his fellow in his time. That is [the first] of the
>   deeds.
> I made the great flood waters that the poor man might have rights
>   in them like the great man. That is [the second] of the deeds.

I made every man like his fellow. I did not command that they
might do evil, [but] it was their hearts that violated what I
had said. That is [the third] of the deeds.

I made that their hearts should cease from forgetting the west,
in order that divine offerings might be made to the gods of
the provinces. That is [the fourth] of the deeds.[63]

In retrospect we may say: the Egyptian gods were worshipped
by the entire population, and at no time merely by the upper class.
The gradual democratization of mortuary beliefs did not affect
worship of the gods, but only the magical assimilation of the former
to the latter. However, the worshippers were limited to the population of Egypt so long as it remained an independent kingdom and
so long as the gods had a political aspect as creators of Egypt, the
ὀμφαλὸς τῆς γῆς, and as counsellors and protectors of its privileged
inhabitants.

4 · Divine commandments, guidance and inspiration: the functions of the gods

Having dealt with the Egyptian gods and their worshippers, we may proceed to our next field of inquiry: the relationship between them. How did men approach the gods and vice versa? We are not raising the question of the degree of intimacy in the relationship, for which we would need full information about the behaviour of both parties. We are concerned for the present with the way in which the Egyptians visualized their gods as conducting themselves. There is no need here to sketch their functions as creators of the world and preservers of life; this will be discussed later in the context of cosmogonies (chap. 8). We shall rather examine the ways in which men's conduct and destinies were influenced by obedience to divine commandments. We shall show that the gods not only issued commandments but offered spiritual guidance, and that in some cases one can speak of divine inspiration.

The problem of free will

A commandment is addressed to man by God, calling upon him to perform some action. Fulfilment of the divine command necessarily implies action on man's part. Where God fixes man's destiny, his role remains a passive one. In either case we have a problem relating to the link between life on earth and the law of God. This in turn leads inevitably to the problem of freedom: can man resist God's commands? (More will be said on this point on pp. 137 f.)

Egyptians were faced with this difficult question at a time of great crisis, and they gave a clear answer. We came across it at the end of the last chapter. 'I did not command them (*n wd̲.ỉ*)' – says the creator-god as he looks upon man – 'that they might do evil (*ỉsft*) [but] it was their hearts that violated what I had said (*ḥd d̲dt.n.ỉ*).' According to this view man is free to act as he

[57]

pleases. The evil in the world is the consequence of this freedom
to forsake God's will. This is very similar to the Biblical teaching
on the Fall of Man, and also the ancient Greek view formulated
in the *Odyssey*:

> My word, how mortals take the gods to task!
> All their afflictions come from us, we hear.
> And what of their own failings?
> Greed and folly double the suffering in the lot of man.[1]

The general maxim in the Coffin Text cited above recurs in
an account from the Ethiopian period, recorded on the so-called
'Banishment Stele': 'They [priests of Napata] have done something without a command by the god [meaning Amon]: they
made an [evil] plan (*wꜣwꜣ*) in their hearts: to kill a man who was
innocent. God [Amon] did not command this to be done.'[2] Here
an illegal action is attributed to the hearts of men and the culprits
are expressly debarred from pleading that their deed was ordered
by the deity. Myths also tell of men accepting this dubious freedom
of conduct. We hear that one day men rebelled against the sun-god
and at his command were slain by Hathor, although not all were
put to death. An allusion to the myth is encountered in the
Instruction for King Merikare,[3] but as an integral whole it is
known only from the royal tombs of the Ramesside era.[4] In this
case, too, man enjoys freedom, and again it leads to a falling away
from God. The god's vindication of his actions in the Coffin Text
cited above bears the same relationship to the myth about the
annihilation of mankind as, in the Old Testament, the Fall of
Man does to the Flood.

Theodicy

Consequently we have in Egyptian texts the idea of theodicy,
i.e. a justification of God by attributing evil to man, who brought
it about by his sinful conduct. It is worth while pausing here
briefly (see also pp. 96 f.). Merikare's royal father utters the
following admonition and confession: 'Do not hack up graves,
do not hack up, do not hack up. I did the same, and the same
happened as is done to one who transgresses the way of the god.'[5]
Later he tells of the destruction at This (Abydos) which, although
it was not carried out by him, occurred during his lifetime and is

therefore still his responsibility. Incidentally, this is probably the earliest known confession of a political sin, and is certainly older than the plague prayers of the Hittite king Mursilis.[6] Merikare goes on to mention the consequences and sums up as follows: 'A blow is to be repaid with its [own] like. This is the application of all that has been done.'[7] The same causal relationship between crime and punishment is deemed to exist in the lives of individuals. It is to be found almost as a matter of course in inscriptions on Ramesside tombs by artisans at western Thebes (Deir el-Medina),[8] but also with an underlying tone of reproach to God, for a widow says in a lament for her dead husband: 'There is no support for the bereaved, my fault has certainly not been found.'[9] Finally let us recall the superb evaluation given in earlier times to those who died an unnatural death (eaten by a crocodile, bitten by a snake, etc.).[10]

Now one has freedom not only in the negative sense but also to undertake positive action. In obeying God's commandment one can also do the right thing, and a reverse theodicy comes into play: God rewards man for his righteousness. This is likewise apparent in the Instruction for King Merikare, where we read: 'Do right so long as thou abidest on earth.'[11] It is already present in the stereotyped formula of Old Kingdom biographical inscriptions in which the deceased sought to justify himself by describing his good conduct: '[I did good] since I wanted that on account of this I should do well with the [great] God.'[12] Even if by 'great God' the king is meant here, divine rule is surely implied.[13] In fact men were at that time convinced that the word of God gave men just reward for good and evil: 'Justice was given to him who does what is liked, and injustice to him who does what is disliked. Thus life was given to him who has peace and death was given to him who has sin.'[14]

This has been a welcome opportunity to emphasize that the Egyptians had a theodicy, a phenomenon which played an enormous part in neighbouring Israel and later even more so in the rabbinic tradition; here it was developed with a logical consistency which sometimes produced grotesque results;[15] its problems were made manifest in the Book of Job, and it was also censured by Jesus for its obvious simplicity (Luke xiii. 1 ff.). We must now return to our starting-point, which the above digression was designed to illuminate: the relationship between life on earth and the law of God. We may begin with the commandments, which express God's will most emphatically.

Divine commandments

The earliest evidence of a commandment is to be found in myths about the pantheon, such as the one addressed to the threatened Horus child: 'Horus, who came forth from the acacia, to whom it was commanded: 'Be thou aware of the lion''.'[16] The dead king is of course included in this world of the divine and receives analogous directives from the gods: 'Anubis...has commanded that you go down as a star, as the Morning-star.'[17] The amount of testimony is enormous; even where the *nomen ipsum* of commanding or being commanded is lacking, and we have just a simple imperative, these are commandments.[18] Also subject to such divine commands are the living, the survivors, who are ordered by the earth-god Geb to provide food for the dead: 'Barley is threshed for you, emmer is reaped for you, and offering thereof is made at your monthly festivals..., being what was commanded to be done for you by your father Geb.'[19] The command addressed to other deities by a superior or supreme god is also found in later times and evidently forms a constituent element in the divine hierarchy. Thus the potter Khnum fashioned on his potter's wheel the child Hatshepsut and her *ka*, embellishing her with blessings 'according as Amon-Re...has commanded'.[20] Even at the close of Egyptian history the idea is still alive that the deity disposes of beings who are in his service and act 'as he had commanded them to do'.[21]

In spite of this mythological evidence, the concept of divine commandments must have taken shape from men's experience of matters terrestrial. Egyptians were familiar with 'commands of the king' (*wd nsw*) issued to regulate juridical and administrative problems. It was the peculiarity of such royal decrees that – by contrast with the law – they were designed to settle individual cases, even where a number of such cases might be dealt with by a single regulation.[22] Divine commandments were thought of as similar to such decrees. Thus Thoth announces to the gods a command of Amon, by virtue of which Thutmosis III is to occupy the pharaonic throne for ever: 'Hear ye this decree (*mdw pn*) which Amon-Re has commanded (*wd*) the king of Upper and

Lower Egypt *Mn-ḫpr Rᶜ*: "effect a union between the two crowns, accede to the throne, celebrate millions of jubilees..." '[23] It was at Amon's command that this great general, who planned his campaigns so systematically, went into battle: 'His Majesty went to Syria to cast down foreign lands in the north in his first triumphant campaign, as Amon-Re had commanded him.'[24] Amon also ordered him to make donations for festivals and sacrifices at the great temples of the king of the gods at Karnak, and to erect monuments there. The king 'did not forget anything he [Amon] had commanded him to do'. He 'did it for him in conformity with his command'.[25]

This also throws light on the dual nature of the king (see pp. 34 ff.): he is God, but simultaneously the obedient servant ('the son') of the national god, whose commands he carries out as his official duty.[26] He is thought capable of disobeying these instructions, which should not surprise us in view of the Egyptian notion that the individual enjoyed freedom of action. Ramses III assures Amon: 'I have not transgressed (*thi*) what thou hast commanded, what I have been directed to do (*nty m ḥr.i*)'.[27] The danger in which the individual thereby finds himself is recognized by Piankhi, the Ethiopian king, who says in regard to his divine father (Amon): 'There is nothing which I shall do without his knowing it (*m ḫmt.f*); it is he who commands me to do it.'[28] Later still a similar emphasis is laid upon God's knowledge of all men's actions in the so-called 'Stele of the selection of the King', referring to the Ethiopian Aspalta: 'We do nothing without thy knowledge. Thou art our guide (*sšm.n*).'[29]

We have begun with divine decrees that concerned the whole kingdom and were therefore central to Egyptian life. Besides these there are others which refer to temples and the order maintained in them. One example may suffice: the rules governing the famous sanctuary of Abaton, on the tiny island of Bigga near Philae, were laid down in a decree of the sun-god, elaborated by Thoth. Re says to Osiris, the Lord of Abaton: 'In your favour I issue a command (*wḏt*) to all countries to sanctify (*nṯry*) your glorious abode, the Abaton.' Of Thoth it is said: '[he] sanctifies [the place] by the following deed (*sš*)', the text of which then follows.[30]

In this way divine commandments regulate both secular and sacred matters, as the occasion demands. The question now arises how such decrees affected the lives of individuals. Here we may again revert to the important phrase in the Coffin Texts, where we are told: 'I did not command that they do evil, [but] it was their hearts which violated what I had said.'[31] From this it transpires that God has said something to men and that this utterance concerns their mode of life. For the violation consists in their leading a mode of life which causes them to do evil. One might be tempted to draw the bold conclusion that in Egypt, too, there were divine commandments like those of the Old Testament. But none of these have yet been discovered. Indeed, we shall show that although ethical teachings tended increasingly to be associated with the deity and the judgement of the dead (see chap. 6), they are not usually represented as divine commandments; the chief reason for this is that in Egypt ethical teachings never acquired the character of holy writ as they did in Israel (see chap. 10). This must explain the noteworthy fact that only in exceptional cases do biographical statements by private persons, which are present in great abundance, contain references to divine commands as the basis of men's actions and mode of life.[32] One dignitary of the Libyan period, Hornakht, does attribute at least his career as a priest serving the ram of Mendes to a command by this god. He heard 'the command that sprang from thy [the god's] mouth'.[33] Here, admittedly, one might think that the god had commanded the man to enter his service. We can only speak for certain of an exception to the rule where the divine command is given in response to a petition. This is the case with the husband of Taimhotep, who beseeches God (to be precise, the *heros* Imhotep) to grant him a son and is ordered by the god to enlarge his sanctuary, whereupon his wish will be fulfilled.[34] The sparsity of references of this kind is due, as we have just said, to the character of ethical teachings in Egypt. The biographies were written in accordance with the same precepts that we find in the so-called instructions in wisdom; indeed both kinds of document underwent the same modifications in the course of their history.[35]

Divine guidance

Turning now from divine commandments to divine guidance, we see that the latter is much more common where private individuals are concerned, since the former are almost entirely confined to

the public sphere, whether secular or sacred. The idea of divine
guidance is indirectly linked with that of God the shepherd.
Admittedly, there are not many references to this notion in Egypt,[36]
but the Instruction for King Merikare was elaborated by popular
usage in such a way that we find mankind referred to as 'the
small cattle (ʿwt) of God'; compare, for instance, the phrase: 'care
is taken of men, the small cattle of God'.[37] However, much more
frequently divine guidance is mentioned directly. Thus in the
Leyden hymns to Amon there are, for example, statements that
God 'leads the people' (sšm.f ḥrw), or that 'it is he who leads the
people to every way'.[38] In the second passage Amon has been
equated with the sun-god Harakhti, and is mentioned in the same
context; we may assume that his guidance stems from the function
attributed to the sun, at first simply a physical one but then given
a spiritual meaning: God, who makes everything clear and
visible, guides men along the paths they have to tread – that is
to say, he illuminates their way literally and figuratively.[39] To
quote one of many testimonies, Amon of Napata, who likewise
possesses the aspect of the sun-god, 'leads the king on each of his
admirable enterprises'.[40]

But we do not have to be content with instances where God
seems to provide illumination from without. There is ample evidence that the Egyptians felt that they received divine guidance
from within their hearts. Nor need one be surprised at the role
given to the two bodily organs which in the Egyptian view had
a decisive influence upon human actions: the tongue, which makes
known decisions and ideas, and the heart, in which these are
formed. A high priest of Amon says of the god Khnum that 'he
had steered his tongue (ḥm)'.[41] A slight variation occurs in a much-
quoted passage from the Instruction of Amenemope, where man
is warned against steering himself with his tongue because 'the
Universal Lord is the pilot (iry-ḥ3t)' of the ship of human life.[42]
As far as the heart is concerned, in which men's decisions are
brought to maturity, God seems to offer guidance at moments
either of complete confusion or of deepest insight. The former is
the case where Sinuhe describes his flight, which he later regards
as involuntary and devoid of political motives, in the following
words: 'My body quivered, my feet began to scurry, my heart
directed me, the god who ordained this flight drew me away.'[43]

One cannot help seeing here in the heart the organ through which
God guides a man lacking in willpower, or at least unable to make
up his mind. In contrast deepest insight is implied where it is
maintained that the deity has instructed a man (since for the
Egyptians, of course, the heart was the seat of the intellect). Such
a case occurs in the biography of Mentuemhat, governor of the
Thebaïd at the close of the Ethiopian period, who even today is
famous for the masterly standing statues bearing his portrait. The
success and benevolence of this high official are explained by the
concept that he was 'one of those whom God has instructed
(*sbꜣ*)'.⁴⁴ Already long before this, during the Hyksos period, a scribe
had proudly inscribed on his writing implement, a palette, that
he was 'one of those whom Thoth himself has instructed'.⁴⁵ It
may also simply be said that 'the heart of a man [is] his God
himself (*nṯr.f ds.f*)' – from which consequences follow for the
man's conduct.⁴⁶ Behind this lies in the last instance the ancient
popular belief that God is at work within man and determines his
entire nature by way of his heart.⁴⁷

Divine inspiration

Moreover, we encounter in many different forms a concept which
by contrast might be called more sublime, and which we shall
dwell upon briefly since it has remained completely unnoticed:
inspiration of the heart. By this we do not have in mind the phrase
in which it is said that men themselves 'give [something] into
their hearts', the sense of which consequently weakened to that
of 'planning', 'deciding'.⁴⁸ We are concerned rather with inspiration by a deity. This may be confined to single acts, such as
the erection of buildings by royal or private persons,⁴⁹ in which
case it has a function very close to that of a divine command.
We also encounter divine inspiration, for reasons that may
readily be understood, wherever a god has taken a decision which
subsequently needs to be confirmed orally by man, i.e. wherever
the divine and the human decisions correspond to one another.
This is the case (although the idiom is slightly different here)
when the names of Queen Hatshepsut are proclaimed by lector
priests who at that moment appear to be inspired: 'Then they
proclaimed her [Hatshepsut's] royal names of Upper and Lower
Egypt for the God caused that it should be in their hearts (*rdi.n*

nt̠r ḫpr m ỉbw.sn) to make her names according to the form with which he had made them before.'[50]

There are other examples of men receiving divine inspiration in all kinds of situations. Let us first consider an account in which the subject, who admittedly later does become king, is represented in a private capacity. This is the story about Amenophis II's glory as a young man. Mention is made of the boy's unusual readiness to prepare himself for his future office, which is attributed to divine inspiration: 'God puts it into his heart to do [it].'[51] Emphasis is here laid upon divine action, as is clear from the sentence structure, where the subject comes at the beginning. Later the same formula is again encountered in a distinct reference to a private person. On a statue of Hor, a priest of Amon, dating from the Bubastite period (Twenty-third Dynasty), King Petubastis, the owner of the memorial, attributes his success in life to divine inspiration: 'God put [all] this into my heart so as to make my lifetime on earth long [literally: high].'[52] In this case, too, God is given grammatical emphasis. The positive picture drawn of Hor's achievements in life brings out the kindly and wise guidance he received, as was the case with Amenophis. There is no trace of the imperatives one associates with a commandment. There is a hint of a theodicy in the background, in that God, the author of Hor's good thoughts, grants him the reward of longevity. We also come upon the question of man's will: can man co-operate in this inspiration by opening his heart toward it? It is hard to answer this. In Egyptian there is a construction *wbꜣ ỉb* 'of an open heart', which has rather the sense of 'clever'; one can be 'of an open heart' in relation to 'the words of God', meaning the holy scripture in the broadest sense of the term.[53] Could man also lock up his heart just as, according to our passage from the Coffin Texts, he is capable of doing evil from his heart aganist God's command? Here, too, there is little to be said. Ptah-hotep, an Old Kingdom sage, teaches: 'It is the heart which brings up its lord as one who hears [or] as one who does not hear.'[54] Here the heart, which elsewhere is a gate through which God can enter, is regarded primarily as an organ, indeed almost as man's property, as though he had the power of decision and the responsibility.

But there is yet another, and even more difficult question: can

God also inspire men to commit destructive actions? Here we do have a clear answer, which will take us far afield. The answer is yes, for we read: 'God places it [evil thoughts] into the heart of him whomever he hates in order to give his goods to another whom he loves.' This weighty sentence, crushing in its implications, is recorded in the inscriptions of Petosiris, a man who lived at the dawn of the Ptolemaic era and who built an impressive tomb for himself near Hermopolis.[55] What Petosiris says is no different from what the Israelites called impenitence and the Greeks delusion, attributing it to the deity.[56]

This leads us on to the last and longest section of this chapter. For the god who loves and hates, i.e. chooses and condemns, and who acts so arbitrarily in granting inspiration and so influencing human conduct, is neither a god who commands nor one who guides. This negative aspect of inspiration reveals him rather as a lord who works through fate and as fate. How this happens deserves thorough examination.

Fate

We are now concerned with the role of fate – the force which circumscribes the passive aspect of human life.[57] We may conveniently proceed from the Petosiris inscription just mentioned, which is on the borderline between inspiration and determination. The deity appears here as an arbitrary power: loving or hating, accepting or condemning, liking or disliking. This arbitrariness determines the kind of inspiration imparted, which in turn determines the course of a man's life – in this case from wealth to poverty. Now it could be held that this testimony was not only of late date but born out of the spirit of resignation and pessimism that reigned at that time. But this would be a false conclusion. Election to grace and condemnation are encountered already in an Old Kingdom doctrine, that of Ptah-hotep (see chap. 6). Close to the sentence about the heart, making its owner either one who hearkens or one who does not, and which probably advocates human co-operation, we find the aspect of divine determination: 'He whom God loves, hears, [but] he whom God hates hears not.'[58] Thus in this teaching determination does not stand alone. Elsewhere we are told of a son who has proved a failure and is to be driven out: '[It is] he who has acted [in a hostile fashion] against you and whom they [the gods] hate; he is one whom they have condemned in the [very] womb...'⁵⁹ Finally, the covetous type, whom Egyptian officials were prone to identify roundly with evil, is represented in the same doctrine as an incurable invalid, i.e. his fate is considered as sealed by his nature: [covetousness is] a grievous malady in a man who must be given up, for he cannot be treated [medically].'⁶⁰ Thus during the Old Kingdom we have a concert of voices in favour of determination. Nor do these voices sing in unison: what is determined is now the ability to hearken to God's word, now a man's very nature (indeed, this is even predestined), now an irresistible determining power is merely ascribed to an evil character, who has brought the wrong upon himself.

All this obliges or allows one to say that belief in fate already existed at this time, even though the concept of 'fate', as we shall see, only came into being later. Phenomena of this kind not only affect a man's nature and character, but also the career he follows. In a Middle Kingdom teaching, that of Khety, it is said: 'Behold, I have set thee on the way of God. The Renenut of a scribe is on his shoulder on the day of his birth...Meskhenet is [the source of] the scribe's welfare, he being set before the magistrates.'⁶¹ Here two deities, entrusted respectively with birth (Meskhenet) and upbringing (Renenut), determine at a child's birth how successful he is to be in his professional career. Another example of this, on a grand scale, is to be found later (after the close of the New Kingdom) in the Instruction of Amenemope: 'For man is clay and straw, and the god is his builder. He is tearing down and building up every day. He makes a thousand poor (*twȝ*) men as he wishes, he makes a thousand men as overseers (*ḥy*).'⁶² The sage here attributes not only the existence of mankind but also the distinctions between men to the arbitrary power of their creator, and thus strikes a note which, developed by Hebrew divines, is echoed finally in the Apostle Paul's teaching on God's ability to confer honour or dishonour.⁶³ In view of this one could say that this passage contains the sharpest division known to Egyptian literature between an arbitrary creator and those whom he creates, whose characters are by and large determined. There is of course a possibility that this is not an authentic Egyptian statement but a translation from Hebrew or Aramaic collections of proverbs which found no place in the Old Testament canon and have since been lost.[64]

The foregoing dealt only with an indirect determining influence upon men's characters and careers; but by 'fate' we also understand particular events in a man's life, ordained from above, which guide him directly. This belief is also met with in Egypt even before the concept of fate came into being. In the so-called Admonitions of Ipuwer – a document dating from the period after the collapse of the Old Kingdom, which was concerned with this universal catastrophe – a number of most deplorable events are explained as having been determined at a very early stage by the gods: 'this was predestined for you in the time of Horus, in the age of [the Ennead]'.[65] This destiny was thought of as afflicting Egyptian society as a whole, but the fate of each individual in it was also included implicitly, since great political events must necessarily affect the lives of numerous individuals. What distinguishes this ancient Egyptian statement is the firmness with which the author estimates as predestined those events which he considers to be entirely evil.

Foreknowledge; prophecy

Together with predestination goes foreknowledge or prophecy; the relationship is similar to that between a decree and its promulgation. Now we do not of course have any evidence that the Egyptians reflected upon the logical connection between these two entities, as did the philosophers of classical antiquity or Islamic scholars.[66] All we can do is to quote testimony to the effect that they did anticipate future events, and evidently thought that these were predetermined. In the Admonitions of Ipuwer mentioned above we encounter, again related to events judged as being dreadful, the phrase 'which the ancestors had foretold';[67] the technical term for 'prophecy' (*sr*), used here, is encountered in many other passages. At a later date in the First Intermediate period, when princes of Herakleopolis in central Egypt (Tenth Dynasty) held sway over much of the north of the country, Merikare's father tells his son, in the instruction with which we are already familiar: 'Generation will oppress generation, as the ancestors prophesied about it.' And: 'Do not [deal] evilly with the southern region, for thou knowest the prophecy of the Residence

City concerning it.'[68] This prophetic tradition may have been passed on orally or in writing; it may have been no more than a literary fiction, although this is less probable, but in any case we have here a historical plan, deemed to be long established and cognizable. He who knows the plan refers to his knowledge with a touch of pride. A certain Neferti (formerly erroneously called Nefer-rohu) was the presumed author of a prophecy which stems from the beginning of the Twelfth Dynasty, but on account of the form of address may be assigned to the period of the ancient King Snefru (early Fourth Dynasty). This reads: 'I will speak of what is before me and foretell nought that is not also come.'[69] Naturally one must take care not to see each occurrence of the verb *sr* as a sacred announcement of the future of the state or an individual. One should exclude those cases in which a man's natural talents or professional experience enable him to anticipate what is impending, such as the mariners, in the well-known central Egyptian Story of the Shipwrecked Sailor, who are praised twice: 'They foretold (*sr*) a storm or ever [= before] it came, and a tempest when as yet it was not.'[70]

We spoke of a historical scheme, predetermined long before. We may expect that such a plan would cover not only exceptional events, predominantly those of a negative character, but also those which strictly speaking were part of the natural order, and so of positive value. Among the latter a prominent place is of course occupied by the monarchy and its successful representatives. Indeed, we find Hatshepsut, for example, the queen who ruled at the beginning of the Eighteenth Dynasty, saying of herself: 'I was foretold for a [future] period of years as a "born conqueror".'[71] Or again, the belief that a king was destined to assume his office already in childhood was based upon prophecy: 'You have foretold him as a king when he was a child', says Ramses III to Amon, referring to his son Ramses IV.[72]

The concept of fate in general and the belief in the existence of a historical scheme in particular make it necessary to understand clearly how the Egyptians comprehended time. Since this would entail a long digression, we shall simply point to the connection between the concepts of fate, of a historical scheme and of time; on the latter see pp. 75 ff.

Terminology for 'fate'

The next point we may turn to is how and when was there created in Egyptian a fixed terminology to express this belief in fate, time, and particularly for the word 'fate' itself. Such terminology may appear essential, but we should not forget that there was none in Hebrew religious literature. For although the Jews, too, knew the phenomenon, they took refuge in such concepts as '[assigned] share' or '[fixed] time'; since the notion of fate challenged the idea of an omnipotent god, it could only take shape outside the framework of the religion of Yahveh (Isaiah lxv. 11). Egyptian religion, on the other hand, had the capacity to innovate without abandoning what was old. Bold attempts were made to forge concepts for 'fate' which then, as we shall see, were built into ancient religious beliefs. The term is derived from the verb *šꜣ* 'to ordain', 'to fix'.[73] The earliest evidence of this verb known to us is again found in the Instruction of Ptah-hotep. The sage warns against conflict and declares that one day every matter automatically finds its way to the proper persons: 'He cannot escape from him who predetermined him.'[74] Then the Story of Sinuhe provides two unequivocal testimonies. In the first the hero of the tale invokes the deity of providence: 'O God, whosoever thou art that didst ordain this flight, show mercy...'[75] Thereupon he goes on to say (in a context we have already considered: the heart as a gateway for divine guidance, see p. 63): 'The god who ordained this flight drew me away.'[76] In the early Eighteenth Dynasty we encounter the first evidence of the concept of 'determination' or 'fate' derived from the verb *šꜣ*. In the biography of Ahmose of El-Kab we are told about a rebel: 'His fate (*šꜣw*) made his death draw near.'[77] The evidence becomes abundant, almost with explosive force, in the Amarna period. Now Aton, the god of the reformer king, or the pharaoh Akhnaton himself are called 'the Fate that gives life'.[78] The state of the evidence suggests that the concept of 'fate' had come into being earlier but made a decisive breakthrough in literature at this time. In this case its origin may be ascribed to popular belief. There are two reasons for thinking so. In the first place, the substance existed long before the concept; in other words, at the beginning it was not formulated intellectually. In the second place, during the Amarna period the con-

temporary vernacular on the whole came to be regarded as
acceptable for literature. Perhaps we may go a stage further and
surmise that belief in fate derives ultimately from the primordial
belief in certain impersonal 'forces' deemed to exist alongside the
gods as well as in them (see pp. 17 f.). In support of this hypothesis
one may adduce the group of the Seven Hathors, who played
a great part as harbingers of destiny; because they appeared in
such number, or rather because there were more than one of them,
they tended to be associated with these 'forces'.

Once the Egyptians had the concept of fate, how did they
interpret it? What is the basic and chief significance of the terms
used to express the concept?[79] A clear answer is provided by two
passages in the well-known texts from the Ramesside period and
from the close of the New Kingdom, which of course only corroborate what, as we know, occurred in the Amarna period. 'Fate'
(literally, destination) primarily means a fixed life-span. The
Leyden hymns to Amon say, of Amon, 'he makes a lifetime long
or shortens it'; the hymnist then goes on: 'He gives more than
that which is fated (*š3yt*) to him whom he loves.' The context
makes it abundantly clear that 'fate' is considered important, and
is a synonym for 'lifetime'.[80] Later, in an account rendered by the
temple official Wen-Amon (Twenty-first Dynasty) of his unhappy
journey, told in an almost ironic vein, it was suggested to a Syrian
prince that the following words be inscribed on his memorial stone:
'I sent them my [messengers] to reach Egypt in order to beseech
for me fifty years of life from Amon over and above that ordained
for me [by destiny (*š3*)].'[81] The prince was therefore asking for
exactly what Amon was able to give, according to the hymns:
extra years of life over and above those ordained by destiny.

It is only logical that the problematic terms *š3w* or *š3* and *š3yt*
should denote the opposite of lifetime, i.e. the fate of death. Thus the
hymnist extols Amon because 'he saves from fate (*š3yt*) as his heart
directs'. The context here is one of curing disease, so that *š3yt*
clearly means death.[82] Moreover, it is said of the physician Horus
that his words 'preserve that man whose destiny is behind [him]',
and here again the context makes it certain that death is implied.[83]
Hence the euphemism whereby fate takes the place of death. 'The
goodly destiny has come to pass', runs a well-known phrase in one
of the Songs of the Harpers.[84] The fate of death also includes the

manner of dying. One need merely point to the New Egyptian Tale of the Enchanted Prince in which we are told: 'Then the [Seven] Hathors came to decree him his destiny, and they said: "He shall die either by the crocodile, or by the snake, or by the dog".'[85]

Consequently in the Egyptian view fate is primarily the fixing of a man's span of years, but also the hour and the manner of his death. The terms have a secondary meaning of 'good fortune' (or 'misfortune'), in which case destiny refers not to the chronological framework of a man's life but to its content; the events he experiences may bring either good fortune or misfortune. But this is much less frequently the case than was assumed by the editors of the *Wörterbuch der ägyptischen Sprache* and various translators.[86] When God is praised above all else as the dispenser of fertility, and it is said of him that *š3yt* was 'with him for everybody', this refers to the gift of well-being and prosperity, and the term *š3yt* may be rendered as 'fortune'.[87] The same holds good of a scribe of whom it is said that 'he gives no taxes from his writing' (probably meaning that his work brings in so little that he has no cause to pay tax); consequently, '*š3yt* is not with him'.[88] In this case, too, *š3yt* must mean the 'good fortune' which did not befall the scribe, who was unsuccessful and therefore remained poor.

The grammatical aspect of this question is by no means irrelevant for the historian of religion. When the Greeks say εἱμαρμένη and the Romans 'fatum' they employ a passive form. What kind of verbal form is *š3w*? This question unfortunately cannot be decided with certainty by the grammarian, as the word has not been found in sufficient graphic representations. *š3w* may mean 'he who determines', 'determining' or 'what is determined'.[89] The right meaning depends on the context, and thus the historian of religion himself has to make a decision. He asks the question: was there a primal cause? Where the term means 'he who (actively) determines', the answer is no; but where it means 'determining' or 'what is determined', both passive concepts, we must logically postulate a subject, a primal cause or source. What other such subject could there be than God?

God as lord of fate

Usually there is indeed a logical subject, and it is the deity who is seen as the author of fate, here playing a passive role. Thus our grammatical inquiry has led us directly to the central point in the history of Egyptian religion: the relationship between God and fate. From the testimonies we have drawn upon above, and from countless others of which only a few can be mentioned here, it is apparent that in Egypt the gods are thought of, praised and believed in as lords of fate. In resorting to texts cited above and to a number of others, of which we can mention but a few here, it appears that even before the concept of fate had evolved it is the anonymous God of the wisdom literature who predetermines the character of man, by electing him to grace or by rejecting him, by love or by hatred (Ptah-hotep). The decision about a man's career is taken at his birth by the deities Meskhenet and Renenut (Khety). The procreator-god, who is sovereign in his decision-making power, allots men to particular social groups (Amenemope). It is God who takes a vital decision which seems to rule out human volition (Sinuhe). When the concept of fate is formed and is related primarily to man's lifetime and death, the gods appear as lords and creators: Amon may give one more life than one is fated to have, and can be implored to prolong one's life (Leyden hymns, Wen-Amon). We may add: even in cases where the term 'fate' is not used, the gods determine men's destiny: thus it is said of Thoth that he 'calculates' one's lifetime.[90] The span of the king's reign in particular is fixed by the gods.[91] We shall come back to the link between time and God on another occasion.

The situation is most striking during those centuries when the Egyptian gods came into close contact with the Greek and Roman world, when they were worshipped all over the Mediterranean, to the furthest extremities of the Roman empire, and acquired some alien attributes, particularly Greek ones (see chap. 11). Now, as is well known, the Greeks, and also the Romans, saw their gods as dependent upon fate. Already with Homer – the tendency became more pronounced as time went on – the gods cannot regulate fate but have to submit to it. It is *moira* which above all determines the cause of events, especially death; the gods, who belong to the sphere of life, can accomplish nothing if death has been ordained. 'Here is a fixed limit to their power, a basic "so far and no farther!" That is death.'[92]

Let us now see what is said in Greek and Latin sources about the Egyptian gods. The Greco-Egyptian god Sarapis says of himself in an aretalogy of the second century B.C.: 'I change the garb of the moirai!' – i.e., 'I give them a different aspect'.[93] An analogous predication in the first person singular spoken by Isis, who was in many respects hellenized, the aretalogy of Kyme, reaches a final climax with the pretentious words: 'I conquer Heimarmene. Heimarmene is obedient to me.'[94] Instead of listing further Greek testimonies, which are to be found in large numbers in magical papyri and contain variations on the same theme,[95] we shall adduce a statement from Latin literature. It appears in that section of the *Metamorphoses* of Apuleius which tells of the initiation of Egyptian gods into the hellenized mysteries. The goddess promises the sufferer (xi, 6, 6): 'Nay, if by sedulous observance and religious service and persistent chastity thou bear thee worthy of my godhead, thou shalt know that I alone have power to prolong thy life (*vitam tibi prorogare...*) beyond the space ordained by fate (*ultra statuta fato tuo spatia*).'[96] This is at once reminiscent of the faculty ascribed by Egyptians of the New Kingdom to their god Amon; but there is also much later and more relevant Egyptian testimony. This, like the statement in Apuleius, is concerned with Isis, and comes from the Ptolemaic period: 'Isis who disguises life, the Lady of Philae...' – runs a passage in a hymn inscribed on the Great Pylon of the Isis temple in that place – 'who prolongs the years of him who is submissive to her'.[97] These data from Greek and Roman times invite the conclusion that the inherited superiority which the Egyptian gods had over fate was so powerful and so characteristic of them that it prevailed even in a milieu where gods had an entirely different relationship to fate. We shall hardly go wrong in assuming that this consoling power over fate was not the least reason for the Egyptian deities' appeal to the Greeks and Romans. In this respect the gods of the Nile closely resemble those of the Near East. We have already stressed the point that Yahveh in particular is absolute master over fate; indeed, that he was so powerful as to prevent the emergence of a genuine concept of fate among the Israelites (see p. 70). To make this absolutely clear one detail deserves to be noted which invites comparison with Egyptian findings. Like Amon or Isis, Yahveh too could prolong a man's lifetime; Hezekiah, king of Judah, had his supplication granted for fifteen years to be added to his span (2 Kings xx. 6).

Egyptian view of time

Thus we have proved the statement made at the outset of this chapter to the effect that fate was seen by the Egyptians as one of several modes of action through which the gods made their presence felt. [98] In conclusion we have to examine their concept of time, a question posed by their belief in predestination, prophecy, a historical scheme, and divine power to determine men's lives. This is closely linked with the role of fate and its relation to the deity, but it deserves to be treated as a subject in its own right.

Let us recapitulate briefly some basic points, and begin with the evidence that God rules over time. Our discussion of fate has been much concerned with time, because it is the dimension within which the drama of human history and human life is played out. Destination, as we saw, was in part predestination, in so far as decisions were believed to have been irrevocably taken in the distant past or at a man's birth. Foreknowledge and prophecy presuppose some sort of chronological plan, however vague. We have seen how the deity was lord of fate and that in particular he set the limits of men's lives. But we also have statements of a more general nature about the connection between time and a superior being with his own will. Not long ago an important piece of evidence was discovered from the early Ramesside period. It comes from one of the wisdom texts and runs as follows: 'Prepare not thyself on this day for tomorrow ere it be come. Is not [?] yesterday like today upon the hands of God?'[99] The same idea is formulated similarly, only in a simpler form, several generations later in a hymn to Amon-Re: 'The years are in his hand.'[100] It is tempting to trace the adoption of this graphic motif of the Egyptian texts by the Biblical and Christian tradition, right down to the hymns of our own time: in 1938 J. Klepper wrote: 'Thou who hast time in thy hands.'

General statements of this kind are valuable because they bear witness to God's mastery of time. But they are still more helpful to us because it turns out on closer inspection that for the Egyptians time had several aspects and was structured in a different way. Two of these, not the most important for our immediate purpose, have been clarified during the past few years. One is the cyclic line of periodicity, which manifested itself to the Egyptians above all in the regular repetition of the Nile flood-waters and the flourishing of crops. From this was derived the year (*rnpt*) as a unit of time: this term means literally 'the juvenescent', and of itself indicates the cyclic character of time. It had striking political implications, too, since the reign of each pharaoh was considered to be a new beginning. The second aspect of time is expressed by the idea of time stretching lineally to infinity (chronologically speaking: to eternity); it is exemplified by the aspiration to the fulfilment of the *cursus honorum*[101] on the part of Egyptian officials, and by the urge for indestructibility impressively symbolized by the mummy.[102] These ideas of the structure of time are certainly most characteristic, and we shall return to them again when discussing doctrines of creation (see p. 171).

For our present purposes it will suffice to bring out the point that the Egyptians preferred to relate time, whether it was viewed as cyclic or linear, to living creatures or to events. That is to say, they did not envisage it as an absolute quantity, or at least only as this, but related it to something else and thereby gave it quality. To put it in more concrete terms, they attributed to substances and objects a 'right moment', what the Greeks called καιρός. One of the several Egyptian words for time and units of time, *tr*, apparently sometimes has this meaning. Of a child wrested from life at a very early age and now alone in its grave it can be said that it had not yet been 'in its time (*tr*) of solitude', i.e. that the right moment for its death had not yet come.[103] But mainly the relationship is indicated by a personal suffix. Somebody is said to be 'in his time' (the time ordained for him); something occurs 'in its time' (the time provided for it or suited to it). We referred a moment ago to the Greek concept of καιρός, but here we can draw a comparison with passages in the Old Testament where we hear that something is 'in due season' (עִתּוֹ: Psalm civ. 27) or where certain events have their particular 'time' (עֵת לְ: Koh. 3, 1–8).[104] From the vast amount of testimony we may pick out a few items which will indicate the main points of view.

So far as persons are concerned, it can be said of a god or of a man that he is 'in his time'. The best known of all such statements are no doubt the parallels drawn between the deities and Ramses II, the hero of the poem commemorating the battle he fought at Kadesh. On the First Pylon at Luxor we are told that he was 'like Seth in his time (*m ȝt.f*)'. Or the king himself cries out: 'I am as Baal in his time (*m ẓt.f*)', and finally he returns triumphantly 'as my father Month in his time (*m ẓt.f*)'.[105] When in a later epoch history was mythologized, the irresistible god Horus of Edfu was praised with the words: 'Thou destroyest the enemies in thy time (*m ẓt.k*).'[106] One can hardly go wrong in interpreting these or similar passages if one regards the time of the god as the culminating point of his power, as the most propitious moment at which he functions, i.e. exactly what the Greeks understood by καιρός.[107] On the same level, but in exact contrast, are statements about someone's 'time' which mean the most unfavourable moment, when his defences are at their weakest. Such statements naturally relate to hostile persons or creatures. Thus we hear of Apophis, the serpent-like antagonist of the sun-god: 'Thou art crushed and repelled in thy moment (*m ẓt.k*).' Or the assistant of Re says: 'I fell Apophis for thee in his moment (*m ẓt.f*).'[108] It is also Apophis whom the hymnist has in mind when he praises the sun-god with the words: 'Thou repellest the dragon in its time' and: 'he [the god] has felled the rebel in his time (*m ẓt.f*)'.[109] Seth, another antagonist of the gods, meets the same fate as Apophis. There is a ritual book which has the avowed purpose of 'repulsing Seth in his time (*m ẓt.f*)';[110] it cannot of course be established with certainty whether Seth is to be struck at the moment when he is most dangerous or, as we believe, at the moment when he is most exposed. One further testimony may be quoted from the pantheon which has the advantage of providing a kind of exegetic corroboration of our interpretation of 'time' as the culminating point. In the Horus myth of Edfu, Thoth utters magical incantations for the ship 'in order to calm the sea (*ym*) in his time (*m ẓt.f*) when it rages (*m nšnỉ.f*)'.[111] The 'time' of the sea seems to be imagined – as in the so-called Astarte tale – as personified, i.e. in a state of the utmost agitation. Finally, let us point to one item of evidence for καιρός in the human sphere. In the Instruction of Ptah-hotep counsel is given how one should conduct oneself vis-à-vis a *ḏẓỉsw*., probably a partner in conversation or negotiation. The advice is introduced with the words: 'If thou findest a *ḏẓỉsw*. in his time (*m ẓt.f*)...'[112] This may simply mean the time of the action: the man is in the act of speaking. But of course it also might mean what we would call today 'to be in form': the speaker is in full voice. In any case *m ẓt.f* here has to do with καιρός.

Like persons, objects, too, or to be more precise natural phenomena and systems, possess their 'time'. In the first place this is
naturally true of the great annual events in the life of the land on
the Nile. It is hardly possible to count the statements, in their
several variants, to the effect that the flood comes at its time. Of an
official of Hatshepsut we are told: 'Thou hast seen the flooding
of the Nile (*Ḥꜥpy*) come about in its time (*r tr.f*).'[113] The Nile
itself speaks: 'Each year I emerge from the nether world in my
time (*r tr.i*).'[114] Khnum, lord of the Cataract region, promises
the king, in this case Ptolemy IX: 'I give you the Nile, full at its
time (*r tr.i*)',[115] and so on. Just as the Nile, when its moment has
come, floods the land and makes it fertile, so also vegetation has
its due time. Horus can promise the king: 'I give you the lands of
the shore (*idbw*), being green (*wꜣḏ*) in their time (*r tr.sn*).'[116]
Similarly, the peasants' activities have their due time. The inscription to a ploughing scene runs as follows: 'Great ploughing –
its time is good (*nfr tr.f*).'[117] For the connoisseur the particular
charm of this construction lies in the fact that the word *nfr*,
'good', itself hints at the suitable moment. In the same source the
rendering of sowing is accompanied by the sentence: 'Sowing...
that thou mayest find benefit from it in its time (*m tr.s*)'; in this
case the reference is to the harvest which will reward the sower
when it has ripened.[118] Naturally it is also said expressly about the
harvest that it has its 'time': 'It [the crop] will be reaped (*ꜣsḫ*) for
you [Hathor] in its time (*r tr.s*).'[119]

It is likewise natural that fixed times are allotted to the principal
acts of cult, sacrifices and festivals. We read in the Pyramid Texts
the statement: 'Your bread is [in] its due time (*ḏr tr.f*), your
bread of worship [?] is [in] its due time';[120] this may mean that
there was a separate time for the sacrifice. Temple inscriptions
from the Greek period speak distinctly of 'the [sacrificial] bread
in its time (*r tr.f*)', and of 'the cake in its time (*r sw.f*)'.[121] An
Ethiopian prince lets it be known: 'I performed [rites of] lament
at festivals in their time (*r tr.sn*)',[122] and so on. All profane things
have to be ordered chronologically. We hear of boats making their
way up and down the Nile 'at their times (*r tr.sn*)', and a regular
time-table of this kind is regarded as a praiseworthy achievement
of one notable, governor Mentuemhat,[123] whom we have already
mentioned.

In considering the evidence presented here, in which the technical terms have always been given their Egyptian equivalent in transcription, the attentive reader will have realized that when referring to persons (to which may be added the sea, personified as *ym*) the Egyptians used the term *ȝt*, but when referring to natural phenomena they used the term *tr*. Subject to the findings which a detailed examination would show, we may conclude that, in principle at least, a distinction was made between time relating to persons and time relating to natural phenomena and objects. This distinction at any rate holds good for qualitative time, which is related to persons or things by a personal suffix, i.e. for καιρός, whether conceived positively or negatively. If this is the case, one cannot resist the temptation to link these two spheres with the Egyptian structure of time, which we have already analysed. The time for persons (*ȝt*) has its geometric location on the straight line leading to infinity: here, with one sign or another, are the καιροί for gods and men. This does not exclude the possibility that a qualified moment such as this may not be followed by another one somewhere along the same line of direction. But the time for natural phenomena as well as for objects relating to cult etc. (*tr*) is linked to the cyclical line and here the repetitive character of καιρός is logical and necessary. It seems to me that this classification can be corroborated and clarified by looking at what appears to be an exception. In a mythical work which describes the destruction of the cosmic order as a dangerous possibility, we are offered, by way of a date for this unique catastrophe: 'At that time (*ȝt tf*) which should not happen.'[124] One thing that is interesting here is the idea of a malicious καιρός, hovering like a kind of Damocles' sword over the future, but which can be wished or conjured out of existence. Above all, however, we are concerned with the fact that in this context *ȝt*, not *tr*, has been chosen to denote 'time', although the matter in question is chiefly the overthrow of the natural order. The choice of *ȝt* must therefore be explained by the fact that this overthrow of natural order, because of its uniqueness, occupies a place on the straight line, and not on the cyclic one. Be that as it may: we hope to have proved and illustrated sufficiently the existence in Egypt of the καιρός idea, the presence of a notion of time which obtained, by its non-absolute character, quality as well as quantity.

Let us finally look back once more to the part played by fate, which was the starting-point of this digression on the Egyptians' concept of time. 'Fate' was in the first place the fixing of a man's lifetime, and thus of his death. To this extent it is logically in line with καιρός, of which we heard that it also comprises the negative aspect: Apophis is destroyed 'in his moment', etc. For this simply means that within the context of a qualitative and relative time there are fixed nadirs, which so far as human life is concerned are the end, death.

In conclusion, to substantiate this point, let us turn to a text. In an inscription in the temple of Ramses III at Karnak Amon says to the king: 'Thy enemy is smitten in his time (*n* [for *m*] *ȝt.f*).'[125] There could be no clearer way of expressing the idea that there is a time for a man's decline and death, and it seems only logical that the Egyptians should have evolved their concept of fate from this idea of time as thoroughly determined. This led them in the first place to see men as having a fixed term of life, decided upon in advance and occasionally modified by the gods, as the lords of time. Birth and death were the cardinal moments in the life of every man, be he king or commoner. In Egypt as nowhere else in the world a man could be told: *tua res agitur*.

5 · Cult and piety: the conduct of men

The Egyptians perceived God as an active force – commanding, guiding, inspiring and ordaining man's destiny. Active, or passive, man felt its power, and naturally he reacted in accord with it. What forms did this reaction take? This is the question we may now proceed to examine. The cult and piety referred to in the heading of this chapter should not be thought of as two separate entities. Our task is rather to seek out piety in cult. Old Testament studies, if not the Old Testament itself, have almost accustomed us to call in question the religious value of cult. We may therefore begin by pointing out that for some years past historians of religion have come round to a more positive and, as we believe, fairer appreciation of ritual forms in the Old Testament. There is an apt quotation that runs: 'From the days of Amos and Wellhausen onward it has been the custom of theologians to inveigh against ritual in religion',[1] but attempts have even been made to show that Amos, that mighty master of word and spirit, did not reject cult on principle.[2] We should make it clear that in the history of religion, wherever the Hebrew-Christian (especially Protestant) scriptural tradition is lacking (see chap. 10), there has hardly been any other way whereby pious persons could come into contact with the active deity except through ritual. The fact that attempts have been made to lead a devout life based on moral values does not impair the worth of ritual piety. Ethics are certainly part of man's attitude towards God, but they are not identical with religion; here they will be treated as a separate issue (chap. 6).

Relationship between cult and myth

Let us now explore the terrain we have thus roughly marked out. At once we come upon a great stumbling-block: the relationship between cult and myth. This problem is discussed by all historians of religion. Modern writers have called in question the chronological priority of cult,[3] and therefore it is interesting to see how matters stood in Egypt, where religion came into being independently of foreign influences. It is difficult to arrive at a final judgement because we do not have enough facts about the

divine cult, as distinct from the mortuary service. In the period
before the discovery of writing, we have no means of entering
into the thought of the faithful. We do know that in the Neolithic
era the dead were provided with funerary gifts,[4] and we can deduce
from this that offerings were rendered, perhaps with a different
intent, to supernatural forces or gods. From the time of the unification of the Two Lands we have the temple of a falcon-god at
Hierakonpolis, in which were found gifts of the most varied kind,
including the famous archaic cosmetic palettes and mace-heads.[5]
We also know that temples existed, and what shape they had; the
evidence for this comes from hieroglyphic records in the case of
the ancient southern and northern sanctuaries by the name of
Pr-wr and *Pr-nw* (i.e. *Pr-nsr*), and from drawings on contemporary
ivory tablets.[6] This was the time when writing was being invented,
but long texts, including those of a mythical character, were not
yet written down. Thus we do not know, and presumably shall
never know, whether offerings and observances were already
associated with words used in myths.

Consequently we are also debarred from knowing whether the
ancient Egyptians drew a distinction between primordial magic
rites and religious cult in the proper sense of the term. Rites
served primitive man as a practical means of communicating with
magic forces and influencing them in his favour; religious cult was
practised by men who had become aware of God's existence and
had been 'touched' by him.[7] In other words, we cannot show
clearly where the boundary ran between the magic and mythical
modes of thought, between force and God. Yet there is one means
of deciding the question concerning the priority of cult and myth,
although it must be used with caution: it would be wrong to think
that cult began later than it did just because we have no mythical
literary sources during the Archaic period, and because the
earliest archaeological evidence is of sanctuaries and offerings.
There is plausible evidence which suggests that the cult act came
first and the mythical vocabulary later. For the so-called offering-
utterances in the Pyramid Texts refer to rites in which offerings
are made for a dead king, who by virtue of his nature is classed
among the gods. We may therefore speak of offerings to God. Often
there seems to be a connection between the utterance and the gift
offered: the utterance indicates the gift by a play on words, and

the name of the object offered is added, separated by a line from the rest of the inscribed panel, like a stage direction in a play. The utterance itself expresses, albeit briefly, a statement of mythical character, i.e. it refers to a pantheon of gods who have assumed some definite shape. For example: 'Take the Eye of Horus which he has entrapped ($ʿḥ$), [Horus] has given it to thee – two bowls of $wʿḥ$ grains.'[8] Put in readily comprehensible terms, the deified king in his tomb is here requested to take something for himself; this something is in reality two bowls of cereal from which food may be prepared and which we frequently find mentioned in the lists of provisions for the dead. But in the text the substance is referred to as the 'Eye of Horus' and is said to have been entrapped. This is an allusion to one of the most common Egyptian myths: the eye of the sky-god, in its guise as the moon, is injured, but is then restored; to possess it is thought beneficial.[9] What is of particular interest to us here is the way in which the substance offered and the myth are combined with one another. The gift in question is called $wʿḥ$; the word 'to entrap' in the brief mythical text is $ʿḥ$. Both words have a similar sound and this makes possible a kind of pun.[10] The word play we have here is implicit, i.e. a negative one. The related words are not connected with one another in an explicit statement, as is the case in our next example. In this mention is made of a particular form of Osiris (Andjeti): 'Horus has revived thee ($sʿnḫ$) in this thy name of "Andjeti" ($ʿnḏty$).'[11]

This comparison gives us a clue to our question about the priority of cult or myth. For in the second kind of pun the persons or objects are first mentioned in the utterance and it is mentioning them that causes them to be present; they are not present beforehand. Where the pun is implicit, an object must already exist beforehand, to which the utterance can be related. In other words, one starts with actual acts of sacrifice, and then builds up myths around them. In our first example, to begin with there was an offering of $wʿḥ$ grains, and later these were interpreted as 'the entrapped ($ʿḥ$) Eye of Horus'. The play on words gave the literary meaning. It may be noted that mythical tales based on offerings of this kind are limited to small details. Thus although this cannot be proved for certain, it seems likely that in Egypt cult came before myth.[12]

The attentive reader will no doubt have become aware from the above of the deeper relationship between the two. For one cannot but ask oneself the question: what happens if a real sacrificial offering – and one might add, all imaginable accoutrements employed in ritual[13] – are accompanied by mythical statements which do not really have anything to do with them? What happens is that the real objects are reinterpreted symbols, representations of the myth. Egyptian thinkers never ceased to seek new interpretations of objects associated with the cult – sacrificial offerings, ablutions, burning of incense and other observances.[14] This is to say that from a given point in time the Egyptian cult comprised an aggregate of actions which had a special significance over and above their obvious one. Individual rites and myths might be correlated in various ways,[15] but ritual and myth as such were intertwined. At an early date Egyptian cult became a representation of the mythical pantheon.

This is not to deny that eventually myths, too, exerted a decisive influence upon forms of cult – for example, on the tightly knit dramatic plays, in which the action was determined very largely by the mythical content, since drama as such presupposes the existence of myth and a belief in a personified God. But we must return once more to our point of departure. The ritual act, we have argued, came before myth and was the subject of myth. Was the ritual act therefore conducted silently? We shall never be able to answer this intriguing question with certainty. In our view it may originally have been accompanied by some simple descriptive words, complete in themselves, such as 'here is the offering'. This could have been said even if the offering was made, not to a being in a thou-relationship to the donor, but to some magic force that had not yet assumed personal shape (see pp. 17 f.).[16]

Cult in dynastic times

We have a much sounder scholarly foundation to go on when we turn from the origins of cult to its nature in dynastic times. We may speak of the temples and what transpired therein. True, we do not have as much information as we would like for all periods of Egyptian history. Thus there is not a single temple to the gods from the entire Old Kingdom which is in a state of preservation comparable either to that of contemporary complexes of royal mortuary and devotional temples at Giza, Abu Sir and Saqqara (for instance, those of Chephren, Sahure or Unas), or to that of the New Kingdom temples to the gods at Luxor and Karnak, to say nothing of those from the Ptolemaic period in southern Upper Egypt. One has to bear in mind not only that the preservation of monuments depends in part on chance factors, but also that during the Old Kingdom the deified king played a much greater role in relation to the gods than he did during the New Kingdom, which was bound to have an effect upon the size and quality of the monument concerned. The worship of the deified ruler, repeated in regular acts of cult, was thought to do more for the prosperity of society during the Old Kingdom than later. The deified king might have said of God, in the words of John the Baptist: 'He must increase but I must decrease.' As we know, the king was degraded to the rank of son of the sun-god, and later took orders from the national god (see pp. 35 f.).

To keep within the framework we have set ourselves, we cannot go into the history of Egyptian temples, which is the province of the art historian.[17] We shall only single out two facts which are of equal importance for the historian of religion.

One is the conservatism that dominated temple architecture, which allows us, at least as far as the basic concepts are concerned, to take data relating to later buildings as valid also for earlier ones For a book containing traditional schemes of temple construction was in complete conformity with the texts found in a temple library: time and again we encounter the statement that a temple has been built according to the old regulations and plans. A 'book about the plan of the temple' was included in the register of books kept in the temple library at Edfu.[18] Its author is said to be none other than the ancient vizier Imhotep, later heroized, who built the Zoser complex at Saqqara; this is said to have been the model for the Ptolemaic temple at Edfu, probably the best preserved architectural monument of antiquity.[19] The temple at Dendera, likewise dating from the Ptolemaic period, also claims an ancient tradition dating back through Thutmosis III to Cheops.[20] The correctness of its ground-plan is ensured by a phrase normally met with only in connection with holy scripture: 'without taking [anything] away from it or adding to it...'.[21]

The second point we should like to underline is the influence
which ritual could always exercise on temple architecture. New
(that is to say, altered or expanded) requirements of the divine service, most of which were deeply rooted in past beliefs, often
exerted an influence upon the form of a building. Although we
cannot prove it beyond all doubt, the connection between ritual
needs and the form of the building, if nothing more substantial,
must have been worked out when the Old Kingdom royal mortuary temples were erected.[22] The form of the complexes at Giza
in particular has been traced back to the link between the Osiris
myth and royal dogma. The king's death was seen in mythical
terms as an act of fate, which called for dramatic representation
at the burial ceremony. This required a sequence of chambers
which matched the form taken by this rite; Wolf calls it 'a require-
ment which was given a perfect architectonic solution by the processional platform of Fourth-Dynasty mortuary temples'.[23]

Among temples built to honour the gods, those for the sun-god
had open courts, but had no chapel to accommodate a cult image.
The intention was that the sun-god himself should pour in freely;
there was no need for him to be represented in any other form.
We can see this in the Fifth-Dynasty solar sanctuaries near Abu
Sir and in the temples of the Aton at Amarna.[24] In this case it was
the (static) nature of the god which determined the form of the
temple; in other instances this was the result of historical evolution. For example, the transformation of an Eighteenth-Dynasty
peripteral temple into a longitudinal temple at Medinet Habu by
architects of the Late period[25] cannot be explained except as
a response to changes in ritual, which created a need for a space
in which processions could be held. Detailed studies of this would
be welcome, although the subject is not an easy one.

The Egyptian temple

We may therefore take a well-preserved temple from a later period
as a prototype of the normal Egyptian 'house of God' (this is in
fact the name given in Egypt to a temple: *ḥwt nṯr*). Let us choose
the one that is best preserved, the Horus temple at Edfu, whose
layout, as we have just learned, conformed so closely to tradition.
Entering by the pylon and following the central axis, one finds at
the end an oblong chamber. One's eyes and steps are naturally

drawn towards it, for it is the focal-point, the *telos*, of the whole
design: the sanctuary which contained the image of the god.
Reliefs indicate how the priest-king or his official representative
had to attend to the image: we shall speak more of this below.[26]
From the corridor surrounding the sanctuary small chambers lead
off, which are used for various cult purposes and for the storage
of equipment employed in the divine service. In front of the
sanctuary, placed exactly along the axial line, are two small
vestibules and a fairly large columnar hall. In these chambers the
god dwelt; their width is equal to that of the main room in a human
habitation. This completes the main structure of the 'house of
God'. In front of it was a columnar hall which in turn opened on
to a large court enclosed by colonnades. The entire complex was
walled off from the turbulent world outside. On the façade is
a massive pylon, used both as a gateway and also as a watch-tower
and emblem. Anyone can see at once the necessity for and the
purpose of the sanctuary as well as the protective wall. However,
the other architectural elements cannot be explained solely in
terms of a desire to build a dwelling-place worthy of God and of
those who built it: they, too, had ritual functions to fulfil. The court
serves to accommodate the crowds of faithful who attended religious festivals, as well as individual worshippers. For this reason
it is called 'chamber of the multitude (*wsḫt mš*ᶜ)', rendered in
Greek as ἐπιφανέστατος τόπος: 'place of full public'.[27] The term
occasionally encountered, 'offering chamber (*wsḫt wdnt*)',[28] suggests that offerings were also made in the courtyard. But also the
names given to the broad halls, whether columnar or not, show that
they served a cult purpose: 'offering chamber', 'chamber of
appearance (*wsḫt ḫ*ᶜ*ỉ*)'. These chambers were therefore used for
rendering sacrifice or for holding processions around the image of
the deity.[29]

Daily service for the image

As far as the actual divine service is concerned, we may distinguish
two main forms in Egypt: daily care of the image and festival.
Of the former we have representations in the sanctuary referred
to above. But we are also lucky enough to have the actual book of
rites according to which the care of the image was carried out; it
is a New Kingdom papyrus illustrated with pictures of the temple.[30]

This incidentally throws light on the origins of our word 'cult': the image of the god is 'cultivated' (*colere*), i.e. cared for. Each morning the priest opens the shrine containing the image, prostrates himself before it, cleanses and perfumes it with incense, adorns and embellishes it, places crowns upon it, anoints it and beautifies it with cosmetic. Finally he wipes away his footprints. Each motion is carried out with due ceremony. The words spoken by the priest give each event a mythical interpretation: this accords with what we know to be the characteristic combination of cult and myth in Egypt.[31] In the context of religious ideas (chap. 7), we shall later discuss the purpose of this cultivation: it was to furnish the image with vital force and to ensure that the deity – with whom it is not identical – lodges within it. One point, however, may be emphasized here: the service performed about the image takes place in private. In theory at least, it is the privilege of the priest of the highest rank.[32] It takes place at that point in the temple furthest removed from the entrance and the court, in a chamber where there is no room for the general public, in pitch darkness. For the structure of the temple, including the sanctuary, was completely roofed over; light penetrated the ante-room only sparingly through apertures in the ceiling and walls. The Egyptian gods would have shared Yahveh's wish 'that he would dwell in thick darkness' (1 Kings viii. 12). Consequently it is said of the divine image that it is 'less accessible (*ḏsr*)[33] than that which is in heaven, more secret than the affairs of the nether world, more (hidden) than the inhabitants of the primeval ocean'.[34] What transpires in private nevertheless serves the general well-being and is actually done on behalf of the community. We are told, although only briefly: God, the Distant One, is made present in the image by the daily service. Therefore he is really present in the temple, which is also visualized as an image of the world, combining heaven and earth; it is in fact a representation of the world.[35] In particular the shrine of the deity is simply called 'heaven', or with an eye to its doors 'the doors of heaven'.[36]

Festivals

God also makes himself manifest to all people in the other basic form of divine service, the festival. We have already seen that the general public had access to the enclosed court and that sacrifices

were also performed there. It stands to reason that large-scale
public rites did not take place daily, but were restricted to festive
occasions. In every temple there was a large number of these;
they differed in form according to the location and the deity
concerned, possibly also from one period to another.[37] There is
yet another way in which festivals may be classified. There are
those that are linked to the principal seasonal natural phenomena
(e.g. the appearance of vegetation); then there are festivities that
concern the monarchy (coronation days, jubilees etc.); finally
there are the feasts of the gods themselves, the observance of
which is rooted in myth. It is unlikely that the mass of the people
made much of a distinction between the religious content of these
three types of festival, for God was lord of nature – over the Nile
as over the heavenly bodies[38] – and the monarchy was a religious
institution, especially once the pharaoh was seen as God's appointed and the recipient of his commands (see pp. 35 f.).[39] In the
popular view all festivals were occasions for the deity to manifest
himself.[40]

What mattered was the deity's encounter with the people. This
is clear from the philological evidence. At the festival the deity
'appeared', i.e. its image left the sanctuary and, borne by the priests
in a shrine (which may have been kept closed) upon a barque,
went out among the crowd. On certain occasions it was even taken
out of the temple precincts to another place where festivals were
held: for example, Hathor of Dendera went to Horus of Edfu
or – the most famous example – Amon of Karnak went to his
harem at Luxor (Opet).[41] The word for 'appear' is $ḫꜥı̓$, from
which was later derived $ḫꜥ$, 'festival'; in Coptic, the demotic
language of the last millennium B.C., which later became a vehicle
of literature,[42] this term alone held the field (in the Sahidic dialect
ša, in the Bohairic dialect šai). Thus the appearance of the deity
among the believers, indeed in the country-side, was seen as the
key element in the festival, which was accordingly named after it.

If further proof is needed of the public character of Egyptian
festivals, it is provided by the Greek rendering of 'great appearance
($ḫꜥ ꜥꜣ$)': πανήγυρις δημοτελής, 'public festival'.[43] The populace,
although debarred from performing the daily service, can not only
behold the holy shrine but can also participate actively in the
festival. The sage Ani tells us what a cult image needs to receive

at a festival: 'Singing, dancing, and incense are his food, and to receive prostrations is his property [right].'[44] The participation of the public can take the most varied forms, and such all too human traits as drinking to excess and tumultuous behaviour are not ruled out.[45] These traits were the hall-mark of the joyous festival of Bastet, in her native town of Bubastis, where the local people were joined by large numbers of strangers who came to the ceremony in the town expressly for that purpose.[46] The houses were lit up, thus spreading the festive mood from the sanctuary to the whole town; this we know from a ceremony at Saïs.[47] The participation of large masses of the population was necessary at the so-called mysteries, which were celebrated with tournaments and other events in honour of Osiris.[48] Finally, the significance which festivals had in people's lives is reflected in personal names, which from the Middle Kingdom onward often refer to them.[49]

Professions of belief; hymns

Ritual, whether in the form of caring for the image or of festivals, whether private or public, may seem from the above account to have been solely concerned with myth, moreover myth of a fairly superficial kind. Such a view would be quite incorrect. Let us now turn to examine the problem of the worshippers' profession of their belief in God. Here again we find ourselves in difficult terrain. The trouble is that we have to rely for textual evidence on hymns, which in the nature of things are most likely to contain such professions of belief in God. It is true that quite a number of Egyptian hymns have been well edited, translated and interpreted, but so far as we know no one has yet investigated the position they held in ritual. Thus we have to undertake a brief investigation of our own. Some of our hypotheses would no doubt require further research to substantiate them, and others might need modification.[50] But we cannot ignore this material, since it is of the utmost importance for a study of Egyptian piety as manifest in cult.

We shall not attempt to elucidate a question which everyone working on Egyptian hymns for their own sake would naturally embark upon first: their history and quality as works of literature. These hymns seem to be especially strictly bound by traditional canons regarding their form and content, with the result that individual specimens resemble one another closely.[51] But we cannot disregard this aspect completely, for it raises an interesting problem relevant to our concerns. Hitherto writers have noted the literary character of individual hymns,[52] but at the expense of overlooking or denying their use in cult. This obliges us to stress the latter point, and to demonstrate the role they played in the divine service, their religious content and the range of their appeal. Only once this has been done can one gauge what evidence these so-called literary hymns can offer about popular piety.

The first point to note is that hymns formed part of the daily service ritual. According to the ritual books mentioned above, when the image received its daily service it was also addressed with hymns of glorification on two occasions.[53] One involved a litany, which was an awakening call and morning hymn to the deity: 'Awake graciously [or in peace]; thou awakest graciously [in peace], let god NN awaken graciously [in peace].' We know of such 'morning hymns' from other sources: for example, a complete cycle was used in the cult of Sobek at Crocodilopolis in the Faiyum. It has rather engagingly been suggested that they were originally presented to the king, then were transposed to the sungod who arose afresh each morn, and were finally applied to the gods in general.[54] This can as little be proved as one can prove the numerous borrowings made by the worshippers of one god from those of another, which in their way reflect the latter's efforts to magnify the power of their specific god (see chap. 7).[55]

Another question is whether the role that hymns played in cult was limited to their function in the service of the image. On the face of it this seems rather unlikely, and indeed hymns can also be found in use at other moments in the divine service. At festivals, as we know, the image, i.e. the shrine containing it, is brought out into the antechambers of the temple. We have an account by Thutmosis III of his election through the agency of Amon's image at Karnak. The god appears there in procession, lingers before the blessed youth, and in this manner designates him as king. In a tale of this kind one can as a rule take as historically reliable the incidental external circumstances, in this case the fact that 'subjects' (rḥyt) are present in the temple precincts and 'offer praise'.[56] Perhaps what is meant is merely a brief acclamation, to which the term hymn would be inappropriate.

In any case, facts of this kind lead one to other pertinent material:

hymns which by their nature and style belong to the public part of the divine service. Let us consider first the so-called Berlin Hymn to Ptah.[57] According to its heading (II, I) it is a morning greeting to God, and in fact it does contain a morning hymn of the kind mentioned above;[58] on this account it could be assigned to the daily service in the sanctuary. But it also contains two elements of an entirely different character, which owing to their form could not (at least originally) have been used by a solitary priest in the sanctuary.[59] For one line, written vertically, is repeated at regular intervals alongside the rest of the text. At one place (VIII, 1–9) it reads: 'Hurrah, let us praise him (*rdi ḥknw*)'; and at another: 'Come, let us acclaim him (*iri hnw*), let us praise (*rdi iȝw*) his glorious image in all its beauteous names.' The text itself gives the reasons why praise should be bestowed upon God, employing participial sentences or appositions in the vocative. He is referred to as 'He who has created all gods, men and animals, who has created all lands and shores and the ocean in his name as "fashioner of the earth" ' (VIII, 2). Or '[thou] hidden one, whose nature nobody knows' (IX, 10a). In each case we thus have a stereotyped entreaty for glorification, directed to a number of persons, and on these grounds the text must be said to have been used in ritual. Those to whom the entreaties were addressed were probably not members of the community at large, for there are too many such invocations, and some of them may have been too difficult. We should rather think of the choir of singers, especially women, attached to the temple, who partnered a leader or principal singer (or perhaps one part of the choir).[60] In other cases we know exactly that hymns were recited by a choir with instrumental accompaniment, and we even hear that the choir addressed the people as follows: 'Rejoice, men and people... Horus has taken possession of his throne', etc.[61] So much is at least certain: hymns were not recited by a choir in secret; on the contrary, they were designed to be broadcast to the multitude and listened to. In the rite they will have greeted the image as it appeared and accompanied it.

Perhaps we have been over-cautious in estimating the number of those involved in such recitals. For in the following example all the people are called upon to recite a hymn and are literally brought into the dialogue: 'Oh ye men (*tmw*) who exist and live here... [62] grant reverence to Sobek, lord of Ombos' – then follow, as in the passages of the Hymn to Ptah, predications about the nature, position and actions of the god.[63] The structure of the text suggests a dialogue between a choir leader and the choir (literally, the entire community). The words 'grant reverence ($snd\ n$) to the god NN'[64] are repeated at regular intervals and are followed each time by new participial constructions of sentences or appositions, in the manner of responses, which give the reason for this glorification: e.g. 'He who keeps alive the herbs'. There are a number of hymns in just this form, and it is noteworthy that the place where they were written down may be accessible to the broad public. In the temple of Khons at Karnak, for example, they are inscribed on the outside of the propylon.[65] Naturally we cannot be quite certain, and for this reason we have erred on the side of caution, whether one should imagine that these entreaties addressed to all men were complied with in practice. For we also have a hymn to Isis, constructed in the same fashion, in which the whole of creation is called upon to offer praise: not only men but also birds, creatures of the deep, and even worms.[66] Here we are clearly not dealing with a ritual injunction, but with religious lyricism such as we find in the psalms of the Old Testament: 'Let everything that breathes praise the Lord.'

Even though the linguistic evidence does not permit firm conclusions about the number of people who joined in the hymns sung at festivals, we do know for certain that individual believers addressed songs of praise and prayers to the deity during the divine service. Words in praise of Thoth, accompanied by personal entreaties, 'are spoken by a man after he had presented offerings to Thoth'; the man makes it clear that 'it is I alone who worship thee'.[67] This piece of evidence is admittedly ambiguous. We cannot tell for sure whether the act of worship in question took place in the temple. For sacrifice could also be offered on domestic altars, and of all the gods it was Thoth, as we know, whose image was set up in private homes and who was extolled with songs of adulation.[68] We shall come back to this point at the end of this chapter, when discussing forms of personal piety (see pp. 104, 108).

For all this it can be said that hymns played a part both in the private cult of images and in the public divine service (festival). In the former case they were recited by the priest; in the latter case they often seem to have been recited in a dialogue between a speaker and a choir. That the congregation joined in the hymn is possible, but cannot be proved; on the other hand, it is not certain whether the recital of hymns and prayers which accompanied sacrifice by individual believers took place in temples. In spite of these uncertainties we have enough information to answer the second of our two main questions: what does the content of these hymns signify, and to whom did they appeal?

To put it briefly, the hymns tell of the nature and workings of the god they glorify. They mention his name and his ties to the locality, allude to the myths associated with him, and describe his appearance, especially his attributes of divinity. This content has been dismissed as empty rhetoric,[69] but this view is quite unjustified. Since every god had political aspects and was consequently linked with certain sites, these needed to be brought home to believers; since he was the subject of a myth, or several myths, these likewise needed to be pointed out to them; and finally, they needed to have at least a description of the invisible deity, whose image was concealed from ordinary men, perhaps even when it was transported about in the shrine.[70] The significance of these hymns for the faithful is quite obvious where they praise the workings of the deity. These passages contain professions of faith which strike a responsive chord in the hearts even of those of us today who have been brought up in a religious atmosphere devoid of images and myths. The hymns praise God 'who has created all gods, men and beasts, who has created all lands and shores and the ocean'; or God 'who grants life to the herbs'. Yet God remains 'the Hidden One, whose nature nobody knows'. These few examples, which could be multiplied a hundredfold, have puposely been taken from texts whose function in public ritual we have discussed above. By this means God the creator and preserver, in special cases even the *deus absconditus*, is made known to the faithful, who are invited to open their hearts to him. By 'the faithful' we mean any participant in the divine service, other than the daily ritual, in which hymns had their place. Of course it could be limited to those who really listened and kept their hearts open, and no historian can say how numerous they were. Even if they were a minority compared with those whose ear was attuned to more worldly things, this is no objection against the religious possibilities of ritual, any more than it is in any other part of the world.

We may now pass on to the last part of this section, which forms a kind of appendix: the question of the value to the student of religion of the so-called literary hymns. Let us assume that some of these songs of praise were composed as works of literature, i.e., that they had no function in ritual. I share with Gardiner the view that this is so in the case of the Leyden hymns to Amon, although their acrostic arrangement need not be just a literary artifice, but might be a means of sanctifying the textual sequence.[71] If we grant this, two things follow.

First, the authors will not have indulged in fancies, but will have kept to what was said in the cult about the god they were extolling. To this extent these texts may be seen as variations on the religious theme that was officially professed. In this case the Leyden hymns would greatly enrich our knowledge of the deepest levels of this faith, and show that God was thought of as omnipresent and caring for individuals in distress: 'To him belong eyes as well as ears wherever he goes, for the benefit of him whom he loves. Hearing the prayers (*snmḥ*) of him who summons him, coming from afar in the completion of a moment for him who calls to him.'[72] This is followed by the utterance about Amon's power over a man's lifetime, which we discussed in the previous chapter (see p. 71).

Secondly, the songs of praise testify to a phenomenon which is of the utmost value for our purposes: to the poet's personal piety, or to be more precise, the piety of the educated class, which alone was capable of producing works of this kind. We shall come back to this point at the end of this chapter.

Divine service as expression of a juridical relationship between God and man

Although some points of detail remain to be cleared up, we have now demonstrated that profession of faith formed an integral part of the divine service. It both evoked and satisfied a sense of piety. By this we do not wish to minimize the significance of ritual. Even if in Egypt the divine service satisfied men's religious needs to a greater extent than many of us used to think, it still remained quite literally a service for God. God is served when the king builds a temple, donates images or has them restored and cleaned; when priests look after the temples and images; when the people honour and glorify God in festive observances. King and citizen, society as a whole and each individual in society, have their own varied experience of the workings of the deity; each feels that God has a right to such service on his or their part. The relationship between God and worshippers is a juridical one. To be sure, men have a less clear perception of God's nature than they have of his efforts on their behalf; and consequently they seek to repay him by efforts of their own. There thus develops the idea that God and men have mutual claims upon each other, that service is rendered in the expectation of some other service in return.[73] Indeed, Egyptian ritual offers an abundance of testimony to the acceptance of that principle we usually call *do ut des*. This development carries with it two risks or dangers, which merit our attention. One is a stress on the external, material side of ritual; the other is the temptation to *hubris*, whereby the tables are turned on God whom man dares to threaten and punish by denying him performance of the cult.

In this reciprocal service relationship, in Egypt as elsewhere, gratitude and piety go hand in hand with hopeful expectation. One serves God because he has given something and in order that he should give more. Along with *do ut des* we have *do quia dedisti*. Both motifs are apparent in an inscription of Thutmosis III at Karnak, in which the king takes counsel with his elders about erecting buildings for his divine father Amon. In the text, which has in part been destroyed, the king says that it had been his wish 'to do something good to him who created my beauty; for I am he whom he has crowned king instead of himself; I will do good to him who has begotten me', etc. The elders reply by expressing their joy at the work the king has done at the sanctuary and speak of the divine reward which followed, namely that the king possesses energy, is 'alive, new and young like Re every day'.[74] This kind of relationship between king and deity is expressed in pithiest form in a text relating to Amenophis IV, which runs: '[the king] who is "useful" to the [god], who is "useful" to him (*ꜣḫ n ꜣḫ n.f*)'.[75] In some texts we have merely gratitude, and in others merely expectation. Thus the same king says of Amon: 'He has made great the victories of my majesty above [those of] any king who has been before. My majesty commanded that his altar should be supplied with every good thing.'[76] Thus the king is thanking the god with a sacrificial offering for the aid he has given him during the war. In another extract the Ennead praises before Amon the well-known festival hall which Thutmosis III erected for the national god in the eastern part of the vast temple complex at Karnak: 'He has rejuvenated you and restored your temple – reward him with many years, may he be joyous upon the throne of Horus eternally like Re.'[77]

Private individuals, too, can enter into a juridical relationship of this kind. When Petosiris of Hermopolis had work done on his local sanctuaries, he was assured, according to his son, of divine reward: 'The gods [in return] will let your lifetime be high eternally.' A postscript follows which is characteristic of the desire men had in this late period for lasting earthly *gloria* (see chap. 8): 'When you reach this necropolis, you will not be forgotten.'[78] Petosiris himself puts an even higher price on the reward he expects from his building work and the material provision he has made for the cult: '[God] has raised [me] above my equals as a reward for having furnished him (*irì šps*) worthily with all good things, with silver and gold, with offerings...I did all this for the reward of a long lifetime in contentedness', etc.[79]

What was said above in regard to individual cases was generalized in wisdom literature. 'Work unto God', Merikare is advised, 'that he may work for thee the like; with offerings to replenish offering-tables and with a carved inscription.'[80] Or: 'Increase the permanent offering – that is profitable to him that doeth it', etc.[81] This principle was followed by the pharaoh to a point where Ramses III ordered the exaggerated formulae recorded in the Harris Magical Papyrus.[82] Later, Ani was to formulate the idea summarily: 'He is made great who makes great', the object here being the deity to whom correct ritual observance is made.[83]

What we have here is clearly the reverse side of the phenomenon we discussed earlier (see pp. 58 f.) under the name of theodicy. There it was a matter of exempting God from responsibility for human suffering, which was attributed to man's own guilt; here it is a matter of men expecting their actions, in particular their service of the deity, to be rewarded by the latter. A regular *lex talionis* is formulated. But we do not wish to denigrate the divine service on account of this idea that service brought an automatic reward. The chilly criteria of Kantian ethics would do injustice to the vital law inherent in ritually bound piety. For according to this view a man is pious if he comprehends that God is at work in the world, and therefore serves him, in the implicit or explicit hope of reward.[84]

As we have pointed out, this principle carries with it certain risks or dangers, which we have illustrated from the sources. The first, that ritual acts may become superficial and lose their spiritual character, arises out of the material character of so many ritual acts. The Egyptians were aware of this risk. In the same Instruction for King Merikare which commends cult and sacrifice as pleasing to God, indeed in direct proximity to these commendations, we find a sentence which has deservedly become famous: 'Make fair thine house of the West, and stately thy place in the necropolis, even as one that is just ($ck?$), as one that hath done right ($irt\ m?^ct$). That it is, whereon their heart reposeth. More acceptable [to God] is the virtue ($b??t$) of one that is just of heart ($ck?-ib$) than the ox of him that doeth iniquity.'[85] It has long been realized that this great maxim raises a problem known to the prophets of the Old Testament; it is even formulated in a similar way.[86] We shall come back to this passage when we discuss the links between ethics and religion; we shall then explain some of the terms used and analyse the meaning of the critical remarks made about mortuary practices (see chap. 6). For the present we are concerned only with ritual, and so may explain that it is 'the ox of him that doeth iniquity' which is debased; there is no mention of the ox of him that doeth right. Or, to put it in more general terms, reference is made to the risks in cult, but cult itself is not called in question. Thus the wisdom literature, which is concerned with the right attitude to be adopted by man in everything he does, gives express instructions about ritual observances. 'Make offering to thy god', Ani teaches; here and elsewhere he lays down rules for attaining that piety in cult which is pleasing to God.[87]

The other risk is *hubris*: the false reasoning that 'if I do something for God, he is dependent upon me; I can threaten him by ceasing my efforts.' Such a line of thought is alien to modern man; for the Egyptian, who clung tenaciously to the magic practices associated with ritual, and whose words and actions were powerfully influenced by workers of magic, such ideas were always attractive. We may merely recall the spirit behind the magical mortuary texts which utter menaces toward the deity, or the actual suspension of cult practices until God complied with human wishes and hopes.[88] However, we do not want to overstress this point, but just to make it plain that the mortuary texts, although they contain religious material, are not themselves religious but magical in nature and purpose (see pp. 229 f.). One might conclude by saying that in Egypt cult, despite the risks latent in it, was never contested as the dominant form of religious practice, but on the contrary was actually promoted by the wisdom literature, and was considered by the compilers of biographies to be a meritorious achievement.

Sanctity

In conformity with the aim of our investigation, we have sought out the element of piety in cult. We have examined the public parts of the Egyptian divine service and the hymns through which the members of that public expressed their faith in God. Without detracting from what we have said we must now pay some attention to those aspects of ritual which were not public. As we have seen, the daily care of the image was carried out in secret. We may now go on to explain that this reflected an awareness of God's sanctity. What did this actually mean in Egypt?

Let us once again start with the linguistic material. The words for 'sacred' or 'sacred district' often seem to be derived from a term having the meaning of 'to segregate',[89] just as in Greek τέμενος is derived from τέμνειν, 'to cut off'. For the historian of religion the implication is that God (and what is connected with him) is 'the Other', that which is powerful in every respect and therefore also dangerous. Contact with this 'Other' necessitates strict precautions – hence segregation. We have seen this segregation in the concealment of the image in a dark and remote sanctuary, where it may be handled only by a high priest who has undergone special initiation;[90] it may have been kept in a closed shrine even when carried about in procession. But even specialists seem to have devoted little attention to the fact that *dsr*, one of the words used mainly to denote God's sanctity and sacred things, means 'set apart', 'segregate' in its original sense. We cannot here set out the development of this well-authenticated word stem; this, again, is something that would deserve closer analysis. Gardiner noted the point;[91] we may add that a necropolis is called in Egyptian *tꜣ ḏsr*; originally, at least, this did not mean 'glorious land' but 'segregated land', since necropolises were located away from inhabited places, once the custom of interring the dead in settlements had been abandoned. In the Elysian fields which the dead must traverse there is an area called *tꜣ ḏsr*; it is closed off by a door, watched over by a guardian.[92] This may be associated with the fact that, according to a spell in the Book of the Dead, the deceased person, who appears as a falcon, describes his magic freedom of movement in the following words: '[The gods] open up for me the shut-off (*ḏsr*) ways.'[93] Quite consistently, the term *ḏsr* used here later appears alongside *štꜣ*, 'secret', and *imn*, 'hidden'. Finally, a priest may also say that he was 'hidden as regards his innermost self (*imn ḫt*), shut off [= keeping to himself] toward that which he has seen (*ḏsr ḥr mꜣ.n.f*)'.[94] When we read, as we often do, that God, his image or his abode are *ḏsr*, which is rightly translated as 'sacred', this implies the concept of 'segregated'; this, as we know, comes close to meaning 'secret' and 'hidden'. This is confirmed quite explicitly by a Greek rendering of the term for the location of the image, where the Egyptian words *bw ḏsr*, 'segregated place', correspond to the word ἄδυτον, the usual term for the holy of holies in oriental temples, where no man may enter.[95]

Priesthood

This 'segregated' sanctity of God is also the point at which the institution of priesthood originates. A priest had to be initiated into the secret of the service performed for the deity[96] and to know the forms that had been evolved for it; indeed, he actually had to belong to the divine sphere if he wanted to associate with God. For this reason the Egyptian priesthood in theory only represented the deified king. In practice it developed as a result of a delegation by the king of his rights and duties.[97]

The development of the priesthood had a considerable impact upon, and was greatly affected by, the social and economic structure of the country. Its character is in the last resort determined by the fact that it derived its origin from the king. To describe this evolution is an important if laborious task, which we shall not attempt here since it would take us outside the limits of our field.[98]

Here we shall only consider the question whether the priesthood drove a wedge between the deity and the faithful and whether it was a handicap to personal piety. In a nutshell, the answer is a clear no. We have seen that the highest function a priest could perform was to care for the image, but that by this very service he made the deity a living presence for everyone in the temple. Now we must demonstrate that the faithful also definitely had contact with God in the course of private worship. Let the evidence speak for itself in each case. Of the sanctuary it is said: 'No man may ascend to it except he who is the "great priest" (w^cb $^c{\cdot}{\cdot}$), and who is to perform the divine ritual.'[99] And the poet can say piously of the great Amon that he is 'coming from afar in the completion of a moment for him who calls him'.[100]

To understand the institutional aspect of this tension between public and private manifestations of the deity, we would do well to remember that the service in the sanctuary, except for that rendered to the divine image, rested upon the shoulders of lay priests, who took turns to do it while continuing to earn their living as laymen. They formed a broad stratum of intermediaries between the faithful and the sanctuary. In small places especially they will have constituted a most vital element. The lay priesthood flourished during the Old and Middle Kingdom. Later it was displaced by a class of priestly officials.[101] This, however, was primarily a technical and economic process and did not impair the vigour of religious life. This is evident from the mere fact that the most important evidence of personal piety comes from the New Kingdom and the Late period. Nevertheless it is worth inquiring whether the bureaucratization of the lower clergy in the sanctuary promoted the free expression of pious sentiments outside the temple. This process was a limited one and did not lead to a separation, still less to an alienation of believers from the temple, as we shall see.

Personal piety; oracles

We may now briefly consider what is meant by 'personal piety' and, where we are thinking of large bodies of people, 'popular piety'. It will be clear that this is something different from the official divine service. Let us begin by looking at the evidence on the relationship between personal piety and the temple. First, there are some texts which leave no doubt that people went to the temple to bring their private troubles to God. These texts are to be found on statues themselves which important office-bearers erected in the temple precinct, to provide the public with intermediaries in approaching the deity. Two of these statues are of Amenophis, son of Hapu, who was a scribe of recruits during the reign of Amenophis III; his magnificent tomb, equal to that of a king, on the western bank at Thebes later became the starting-point of the heroization he enjoyed. These statues were erected in front of Pylon X at Karnak, and the texts run as follows: 'Ye people from south and north, all ye eyes that see the sun, all ye who come from south and north to Thebes to entreat (*snmḥ*) the lord of gods, come to me! What ye say I shall pass to Amon at Karnak. Say the "offering spell" to me and give me water from that which ye possess. [For] I am the messenger (*wḥmw*) whom the king has appointed to hear your words of petition (*snmḥ*) and to send up [to him] the affairs of the Two Lands.' The other text reads: 'Ye people of Karnak, ye who wish to see Amon, come to me! I shall report your petitions (*sprwt*). [For] I am indeed the messenger of this god. [The king] has appointed me to report the words of the Two Lands. Speak to me the "offering spell" and invoke my name daily, as is done to one who has taken a vow.'[102] There are two other statues of persons who likewise held the rank of 'scribe of recruits', located respectively in the temple of Mut at Karnak and in the forecourt of the sanctuary of Isis at Coptos. One runs: 'I am the messenger of my mistress [i.e. Mut]; I am going so that your entreaties may ascend.' The other text says: 'I am the messenger of the mistress of the sky [i.e. Isis of Coptos], I belong to her outer court. Tell me your petitions so that I can report them to the mistress of the Two Lands, for she hears my supplications.'[103]

These texts are of interest in several respects. They testify to the role the statues played as points of contact in worship; they tell of the private individual's concern with his *gloria*, since the image was intended to keep his memory fresh among his con-temporaries and among later generations, who were expected to mention his name in their prayers as they rendered sacrifice; they throw light on the growing role played by mediators with the deity; finally, they illustrate indirectly the position of the scribe of recruits as a recipient of quite concrete formal petitions. But what seems most important in our context is the testimony they afford to the fact that individual believers journeyed to the house of God for the purpose of submitting personal entreaties to him. Some of the terms characteristic of these inscriptions above (*wḥmw*, 'messenger'; *sꜥr*, 'to let ascend') introduce us to a whole area of personal piety which is very closely linked to the temple, where men bring their personal affairs before God according to a specific procedure. We are referring here to the phenomenon of the oracle.

It has been rightly noted that oracular sources like the bull-god Apis and Mnevis were messengers (*wḥmw*) of Ptah or of Re, and that they 'let ascend the right thing [the truth, *mꜣꜥt*] to the great god whose mediators they were, thus providing the factual basis for the divine judgement delivered by the oracle.[104] Recently the title 'servant of God who carries the message' (*ḥm-nṯr wḥm*) has been interpreted as a member of the highest sacerdotal rank who alone had the right to draw up the written questions submitted to the oracle and also to expound the god's pronouncement.[105] If we could go into detail, we would see that these pronouncements are concerned not only with right and wrong but with every imaginable kind of question relating to human life. They are sought after equally by king and commoner.[106] Oracles were an important medium for linking the personal piety of ordinary folk with the temple and with its high priests.

Let us now return from the oracle, a special and limited medium of communication with the deity, to the general phenomenon of such communication. The well-known memorial stelae from Deir el-Medina, the Theban city of the dead,[107] provide some remarkable evidence about this. It is to be found on the stele which contains what is probably the most important of these inscriptions, and not so much in the text as in the image it bears.[108] This represents, in a triangular panel, a man kneeling in prayer before a massive statue of Amon, seated upon his throne in front of the pylon of his temple. It is a splendid illustration of the contemporary personal name 'I have seen Amon'.[109] Scholars have already pointed to the highly unconventional character of the praise, supplication and thanks expressed by an artisan, the painter Neb-Re, to God for curing his ailing son.[110] The manner in which the god is addressed in itself leaves no doubt that the petitioner regards Amon as the official lord of the great temple at Karnak.

This address reads: 'Amon-Re, Lord of the Thrones of the Two Lands, the Great God Presiding over Karnak.'[111] But the image portrays the pious Neb-Re in the national temple of Amon. We cannot be quite certain how this should be interpreted. Is the petitioner really kneeling before a statue of the god in the forecourt,[112] or is he experiencing in prayer an apparition of the god, emerging from the pylon of his sanctuary and manifesting himself to Neb-Re? But there cannot be any doubt that here a most intimate happening, whether real or spiritual, is linked in an impressive way with the great temple of Amon at Karnak.[113]

In conclusion we may mention an instruction by the sage Ani about the correct manner of praying in the temple. The believer should pray silently, and at the same time make sacrifice: 'The dwelling (*ḥnw*) of God – its abomination is clamor. Pray thou with a loving heart (*ỉb mr*), all the words of which are hidden, and he will do what thou needest (*ḥr.t*), he will hear what thou sayest, and he will accept thy offering...' We can hardly conceive of finer testimony to the link between the individual believer and the temple, or to the attitude he adopted in it.[114]

Amon's role in personal piety

Thus popular piety is by no means divorced from the temple. As we have seen, the faithful also went to the temple when no ritual was in progress there, simply to have contact with God. We have mentioned Amon in this context not for any reason particular to this deity but because he exemplifies the way in which an Egyptian god could be lord over all gods and kings, yet at the same time a refuge for and consolation to ordinary folk in their everyday troubles. Amon was the mightiest and wealthiest god ever to have been worshipped in Egypt; of humble origin, he had 'the most brilliant divine career ever known in all antiquity'.[115] But Amon never ceased to be simultaneously helpmate and saviour.

Of all the gods, therefore, Amon is the linchpin between national ritual and popular piety. Among the people the range of his impact extends from simple artisans to the profoundest religious thinkers. It would be superfluous to list evidence of Amon's role as lord of the gods and the embodiment of the pomp of the national ritual. Suffice it to recall that he played a mighty political role as the initiator of the policy of imperial expansion during the reign of

Thutmosis III; that he became a powerful landowner as a result of the endowments made to him in gratitude, and thus a factor of the utmost importance in domestic affairs; and finally that he became the patron of a regular theocracy. As is well known, at the end of the New Kingdom the high priest of Amon, Heri-Hor, accepted royal office.[116]

The importance of the other side of Amon's nature has become increasingly obvious as a result of recent research. We have quoted some of this evidence already. It seems that he was the patron of mariners, probably in his capacity as lord of the air and winds. At any rate his name is inscribed upon ships' rudders like a charm, in a kind of secret script.[117] This explains the form of address 'pilot who knowest the water, Amon, thou rudder'.[118] We may also quote a statement in the Leyden hymns to Amon: 'A water-charm (ḥsw) is Amon when his name is on the flood (nwn): the crocodile has no power, when his name is pronounced.'[119] In this capacity, for which the evidence could be multiplied,[120] Amon is the predecessor of Isis εὔπλοια or *pelagia*, which gained such importance in Hellenistic times and whose worship bears such distinct personal traits.[121] Amon's helpfulness to the pious was not restricted to mariners. Next to the passage cited from the Leyden hymns he is referred to as accessible to anyone in distress and sovereign over the lifetime of the individual (III, 16 ff.). It is therefore not surprising to find Amon designated boldly as a 'safe stronghold' on unpretentious little monuments of private origin: 'No refuge of the heart (pḥrt ỉb) is to be found except Amon (-Re).'[122] If a comparison with Luther's *Ein' feste Burg* seems too far-fetched, consider the personal name 'My god is a mountain (ḏw) for me'.[123]

It would also be a mistake to imagine that personal veneration of this kind for Amon was limited to ordinary folk. The author of the Leyden hymns to Amon, which by virtue of their literary character we have considered as a private non-ritual work, must have been an important religious thinker, or at least a man who was able to reproduce ideas of great significance. He leaves no stone unturned, running the gamut from his role as water-charm to his beneficial omnipresence, and comes up with a theological formulation whose full import will be made clear in chapter 7: 'All gods are three: Amon, Re and Ptah..."Hidden" is his name as Amon, he is Re in face, and his body is Ptah' (IV, 21 f.).[124]

Not only theologians, who may have also been priests serving Amon in an official capacity, but also the king, whose function it was to maintain the juridical relationship between the national god and the land of Egypt, entered into a relationship of personal piety with this all-encompassing deity. There is plenty of testimony showing that individual rulers 'chose' Amon from among other deities as one who was peculiarly their own. This was connected with the decline of institutionalized religion during the New Kingdom. We find god and king conferring benefits upon one another, because one of them 'loves [the other] more than anybody else'.[125] What emerges from all this is that in Amon the national cult and popular piety were combined in an exemplary fashion. He was both a political factor and the friend of the common man. How could it be otherwise, one might add, if God really is God?[126]

Images

Amon is the god who, more than any other, personifies the profound oneness of religious phenomena. This unity can be seen also in the forms which ritual and piety took – for example, in the images of the gods, to which we may now turn.

As we know, the daily service of the image had the purpose of filling the lifeless idol with the god's vital power. The plentiful sources which substantiate this iconology will be dealt with in chapter 7, where we shall be concerned with the philosophical implications. Simple people had an appreciation of the vitality of these images, although they will not have understood the complex ritual or its philosophical motivation. In their eyes these 'living images of god' had a simple objective quality. Among them were small figures which expressed vital bodily functions. In the Berlin Museum there is a faience figurine of Thoueris, the patroness of women in labour, in the shape of a pregnant hippopotamus. The goddess is depicted in a standing position and suckling her young, her right paw holding her left breast. In lieu of the nipple there is a circular aperture, and the figure is hollow inside. When it was filled with milk, this dripped out of the goddess's breast.[127] This piece, no doubt an offering to Thoueris, may be classified as serving the purposes of analogous magic. It is designed to ensure for the nursing mother a healthy period of breast-feeding, i.e. to confer blessing upon her and her child. But this figurine also shows that

Egyptians saw such images as filled with vital force. It would therefore be wrong to dismiss the intervention of images in human affairs, for example when oracles were consulted at elections, as the product of fraud by the priests. No doubt there was a good deal of stage-management, but the principle on which the veneration of images rested was that there existed a living God, whose word was equally binding in cult and private piety, upon priest and people.[128] Only if we bear this in mind can we appreciate the popular appeal of Egyptian religion.

We could develop our argument along various lines, and only a few avenues can be explored here. The deities portrayed in temple reliefs were regarded by believers as particularly efficacious. A portrait of Ptah in the passage of the High Gate at Medinet Habu was venerated as 'Ptah of the High Gate' and invoked as a mediator.[129] The same may also have been true of a group at Karnak which shows Amon receiving the sacrifice and veneration of Ramses III, with Ahmes Nofret-ere as intermediary. The god's head was embellished with precious inlays, which have not survived, which may well imply that the image was designed for public worship.[130] In such cases the faithful themselves chose which image was to be displayed in the temple; the reasons for their choice are no longer comprehensible to us.[131]

Another point worth making is that priests sometimes combined their performance of the official ritual with a kind of divine service that appealed to ordinary people in need. We know of a fourth prophet of Amon at Karnak, i.e. one of the chief priests in the god's principal temple, who was simultaneously a prophet of 'Amon of Luxor, the helper ($p3\ dr$)' – a sobriquet which suggests that personal piety had priority in this Amon cult.[132]

It also seems worthy of note that a priest should mention his services in looking after and embalming sacred animals, in the same breath with his good moral conduct, as deserving divine reward: 'I gave food to the living ibises, falcons, cats, jackals and I interred them according to ritual [with] balm and linen.'[133] The interpreter of this passage faces a difficulty: is the deceased priest speaking of the correct fulfilment of his official ritual duties or did he undertake these actions from motives of piety, common during the Late period, when they were extended to sacred animals of every species? Without having other evidence on this point we cannot distinguish between official ritual practice and personal piety. Probably such a distinction would be artificial, anyway.

Finally, we may mention the custom of assigning to a place of worship an adjective showing that it was 'great in fame'. The expression used was ꜥꜣ hmhmt, which was of popular origin and previously denoted the 'reputation' which persons or objects enjoyed among the masses.[134] Characteristically enough, this adjective denoting popularity was linked with the sacred place of Osiris at Abydos, which throughout the land was celebrated as rich in grace, because the myth of this god expressed so vividly the common human lot of death, which Osiris overcame by being born again. In this case we have literal confirmation of the popularity of a particular place of worship, the centre of a cult sustained by the hopes of countless individuals for immortality.

We have endeavoured to show the intimate link that existed between temple and ritual on one hand and personal piety on the other. This was a link based upon a single belief in a living God at work everywhere in the world. This does not mean that there was no piety outside the temple. On the contrary, as a vital force in people's lives, it was to be found everywhere. It often made itself felt at the naming of a new-born child, when the person naming it spoke phrases indicating the bond between the deity and himself or the child: that God gives, protects, saves, provides for one, etc.[135]

Images were put up in the home, and these were offered praise and gifts (see p. 93), naturally using the established rituals. There were also regular domestic altars. Unfortunately this tradition is known to us principally from Amarna, because here most dwellings happen to have been fairly well preserved. These altars have folding doors and represent the royal family, upon which the sun-disk (Aton) shines and confers blessings. One may seriously wonder whether these altars should be taken as indisputable evidence of piety. The élite at Amarna consisted mainly of careerists who had made cause with Akhnaton and who subscribed to his doctrine.[136] It is therefore not being malicious to compare these dogmatic images on Amarna altars to the obligatory 'images of rulers' with their standardized beards[137] – all the more so since the idolization of the person of the living ruler, unknown during the Old Kingdom, now reached its zenith (see pp. 41, 148).

Coexistence of official cult and personal piety

Finally, let us sum up the essential points. The official cult co-existed with expressions of personal piety, but there was apparently never any conflict between them. This does not seem quite natural to us, brought up on the history of western Christianity. We think with anguish of the profound contradiction that existed between the Church and lay piety during the Middle Ages, and the struggles that this led to. But these conflicts had a spiritual source that was non-existent in Egyptian religion: an authoritative holy writ which served as the criterion in judging ecclesiastical controversies. Thus the Biblical piety of the laity became suspect to the Church, and laymen grew to hate the gulf between the ultra-Biblical ritual practice of the Church and the anti-Biblical conduct of its servants. It has quite justly been said that in the cataclysmic Waldensian movement 'the laymen were as though overcome by the incomparable force of the great religious monument which the Church possesses in the Bible'.[138] Egyptian religion was a ritual religion in which holy scripture had no place in a normative sense (see chap. 10). It could therefore tolerate all manner of expressions of lay piety, and be certain that they would remain in accordance with the forms of the official divine service; certainly, often enough they even utilized its holy places.[139]

We cannot offer a summary of the multiple forms which this personal piety took. We would have to mention the fact that, apparently during the Eighteenth Dynasty, the ancient idea that every deity provided help in distress gave rise to an independent 'saviour' god,[140] and that there was an increasing tendency to venerate healing deities. This important subject would deserve a monograph of its own, which seems to me to be one of the most urgent tasks facing historians of Egyptian religion; no justice could be done to such a topic by a cursory examination.[141]

6 · Ethics and its relationship to religion

In Egypt, as elsewhere, man responds to God's call by serving him. This service acquires fixed forms, and this leads to ritual in the narrower sense of the term. But piety, openness toward God, is a changing reality, and it too takes changing forms with the passage of time. These forms are akin to those used in ritual and complement them. Their prime function is to express men's needs as individuals, rather than as members of society. God appears as helper in need, as well as ruler. In the nature of things ritual may degenerate into something superficial and become petrified into a material affair. This can happen without fatal damage to religious belief: the law of *ex opere operato* applies. It is likewise in accordance with the nature of things that personal piety should draw upon fresh sources daily; for the unceasing spring of religious faith ensures that God remains a living presence in men's hearts, even if worship in the temples becomes just a formal observance. Piety and ritual are the flesh and blood of Egyptian religion. Yet are they men's sole response to the call of God?

Religious foundations of conduct

This question leads on to the religious foundations of human conduct in ancient Egypt. Since ethical norms influence man's conduct towards God, this chapter is a logical complement to the preceding one. But ethics is not identical with religion: it is something both more and less than religion. It lays down what is 'custom' or 'habit' (ἦθος); the Latin word for morality, *mos*, has the same meaning. Egyptian moral philosophy includes matters which one would not normally ascribe to religion: for instance, table manners or behaviour towards one's superiors.[1] On the other hand, the heart of religion, man's spontaneous turning to God in adversity, involves only a minimum of habit, and no one would include under the heading of ethics pious prayers addressed to God as a helper in distress. Here we shall be concerned with the extent to which, in ancient Egypt, ethical principles governed man's behaviour towards the deity. This means that we must first investigate the nature and basis of Egyptian ethics as well as the relationship between ethics and religion.

Sources

Let us begin with a brief survey of the sources. This might be thought superfluous, in that the sources on religious phenomena in Egypt are limitless (see pp. 1 f.). But so far as ethics is concerned matters are somewhat different, since there are certain categories of texts on which we principally rely: the so-called instructions in wisdom, along with certain biographical mortuary inscriptions (the ideal biographies), and finally confessions of the dead before judgement is passed on them in the hereafter. With regard to the instructions in wisdom, which really ought to be called 'directives for life' or simply 'teachings', some will be familiar from previous chapters where they have been cited: for instance, the Instructions of Ptah-hotep, Khety, Ani, Amenemope, and, last but not least, the Instruction for Merikare, devised for a king. It will be apparent that these texts do not deal exclusively with ethical matters but contain much information about religion as well. Among other instructions which have survived in more or less complete form are those of Hor-dedef, those compiled for Kagemni, dating from the Old Kingdom, and those recorded in the demotic Insinger Papyrus from the Late period (probably Ptolemaic). We also have documents of this kind known simply by the author's name, including one attributed to Imhotep, the statesman and architect of Zoser's reign (Third Dynasty).[2]

Since this is a special genre, one is made particularly aware that the texts which have survived are a haphazard selection, and that at any time new ones may be found, although these are unlikely to contain anything revolutionary. These finds may not even come from new archaeological excavations or from the antique market; a mere search through old museum collections or archives could prove remunerative. Thus some years ago among the treasures in Berlin there was discovered an admittedly unpretentious fragment (ostracon) of an instruction which resembles that of Ani.[3] On another recent occasion fragments of instructions were brought to light from the well-known group of manuscripts unearthed at the site which later became the Ramesseum; among them was the Ramesseum Dramatic Papyrus.[4] A little later came the publication of a British Museum papyrus of quite considerable size and importance containing the (demotic) instructions of one Onchsheshonqy, probably dating from the middle of the first millennium B.C., embedded in a framework of a long-drawn-out narrative;[5] almost simultaneously some rules in demotic were found in a manuscript in the Louvre.[6] Things are thus in a state of flux, and one can do no more than state general principles, since many details are liable to subsequent correction. In particular one has to guard against making deductions *e silentio*, unless they follow plausibly from these basic principles.

The second group of sources we mentioned are the idealized biographies: the stereotyped statements in Egyptian funerary inscriptions about a man's character which supplement the particulars given about his career. These strike an ethical rather than a historical note;[7] since they are usually couched in the first person singular, they look like confessions. Naturally, the content of these brief maxims tallies with that of the wisdom literature and influenced its historical development.[8] In the case of the vizier Kagemni, for whom an instruction was composed and whose biography is known to us, we come close to the ideal case of a direct quotation from didactic literature in the funerary inscription of the person instructed. Sentences such as 'Do maat (*bw mȝꜥt*) for the king, [for] maat is that which the king loves! Speak maat to the king [for] that which the king loves is maat!' read like maxims of an instruction, and it is regrettable that the Instruction for Kagemni has been lost, except for the conclusion, so that we cannot establish the link with absolute precision.[9]

The third type of source material comprises the confessions of the dead before judgement was passed on them in the beyond. How the idea of such justice evolved and what sort of function these statements by the dead fulfil are important and difficult questions in their own right, which we shall have to discuss separately. To classify them we need only state that they are contained in the very popular, i.e. widely disseminated, Chapter 125 of the Book of the Dead.[10] Their ethical teaching covers men's conduct towards their neighbours, the gods, society and even themselves (if the interpretation of certain sexual practices is correct).[11] The foregoing analysis of the sources should of course not be taken as implying that there were no other texts containing information about ethical principles or their relationship to religion. We have simply indicated the central core of the material, and do not wish to suggest that it was demarcated clearly from other kinds of sources.

What is maat?

There are some matters which can only be understood if one tackles them from their most intimate aspect. Among these are Egyptian ethics and its innermost element, *maat*. What is maat? This is like asking Pilate's question – for maat does indeed mean 'truth' among other things[12] – and it cannot be answered by a simple translation of the Egyptian term. At least four sentences must be added by way of explanation. Maat is right order in nature and society, as established by the act of creation, and hence means, according to the context, what is right, what is correct, law, order, justice and truth. This state of righteousness needs to be preserved or established, in great matters as in small. Maat is therefore not only right order but also the object of human activity. Maat is both the task which man sets himself and also, as righteousness, the promise and reward which await him on fulfilling it.

These assertions need of course to be substantiated and illustrated. The first point one should make is that originally maat seems to have been something simple, a concrete geometrical and physical term denoting 'straightness' and 'evenness'.[13] The earliest hieroglyph for it (⊂⊐) probably represents the straightness of the socle of the pharaoh's throne, which in turn may be regarded as a stylized form of the primeval mound (see chap. 3).[14] The transference of meaning from something physical to something ethical is philologically plausible and is not at all startling. There is a parallel in Hebrew, for example, where *iāšār* first means 'straight' and 'even' in the geometrical sense, and later comes to mean 'right' and 'correct' in the ethical sense. One must bear in mind that it was this transference of meaning which gave the concept its significance and made it a fundamental concept in Egyptian thought and behaviour. Its ultimate range of impact can in no way be explained by examining its derivation from such simple origins. This compels us to consider the testimonies themselves, where maat is always mentioned in a metaphorical sense. We shall confine ourselves to looking at some of the factual material relevant to the field of our inquiry, since if we were to deal fully with the term maat, this, as one expert puts it, 'would grow into a history of Egyptian culture'.[15]

The first point to make about maat is that it originates with the creation: it is brought into being by the primordial god and then constantly refreshed or restored by the king. This is plain from the information contained in the following three texts, arranged here in chronological order, without any accompanying commentary: 'The sky is at peace, the earth is in joy, for they have heard that [the deceased king] will set right in the place of disorder (*isft*).'[16] '[Amenemhet II] drove out disorder (*isft*) by appearing as Atum himself.'[17] '[Tutankhamon] drove out disorder (*isft*) from the Two Lands and maat is firmly established in its place; he made lying (*grg*) an abomination and the land is as it was at the first time.'[18] The crucial formulations are these: maat is equated with 'the first time', i.e. the act of creation; the king who drives out disorder, the antithesis to maat, is an incarnation of Atum, the primeval god and god of creation; the end of disorder goes hand in hand with the establishment of maat; finally, heaven and earth, the entire cosmos, are joyful at this. There are other points of interest to Egyptologists in these passages, but we cannot pursue them further here.[19] Instead, we may go on to cite a formula from the Greek period in which the primeval era (of the Ogdoad) is represented as a golden age; in this maat appears as a celestial force. 'Maat descended (*h3i*) to earth in its time [that of the primordial gods] and fraternized (*snsn*) with the gods'; or again: 'maat came from heaven at its time and joined (*hnm*) those who lived upon earth'.[20]

Thus the sources bear out our definition: maat is the order established by the act of creation (we may add: by the primeval god), which has to be preserved or re-instituted (that is to say, as we now know, by the expulsion of its antithesis).

We now have to substantiate the belief that each individual participated in the maat – in other words, that maat had to be preserved, not only by the king for the entire community, but also by each individual in the community, even for his own sake. This is exactly the main theme of the instructions, and it is echoed in the biographies. The sage Ptah-hotep teaches: 'Maat is great, and its effectiveness lasting; it has not been disturbed since the time of Osiris. There is punishment for him who passes over its laws, [but] this is unfamiliar to the 'covetous one'. Fraud gains riches [yet] wrongdoing has never brought its undertaking to port. When the end is nigh, maat lasts.' And later: 'Long-lived is the man whose rule of conduct is in accordance with maat...but the covetous has no tomb.'[21] At the beginning the text reads like a hymn to maat, with whose divine origin we are familiar. In this case emphasis is laid upon its unbroken continuity from the mythical time of Osiris onward and its everlastingness, for it outlasts human life. Man, however, is judged by it, and whoever is in accord with it is himself granted longevity. The nature of maat is thus determined in relation to its antithesis, namely covetousness (^{c}wn-îb), which actually means ruthless personal accumulation, involving every unjust means including deceit and violence;[22] such behaviour is especially to be deplored among the officials to whose milieu the Instruction of Ptah-hotep is addressed. What is couched here as a didactic statement is found elsewhere as an injunction. We have already come across the sentences from the inscription of the vizier Kagemni, which may be taken as a quotation from the instruction he himself received: 'Do maat (bw m3^{c}t) for the king, [for] maat is that which God loves! Speak maat to the king [for] that which the king loves is maat!' It may be that 'God' here was just a synonym for the king.[23] For the sage bases his admonition to do and to speak maat on the fact that its earthly guarantor loves it, and that consequently he finds pleasure in pursuing it. A combination of injunction and praise of maat is found in an utterance by a peasant dwelling in an oasis who had been grievously wronged, and who repeatedly seeks justice from a high official, saying: 'Speak justice, and do justice; for it is mighty (^{c}3), it is great (wr), it endureth long (w3h).'[24] Since the utterance is presented as a quotation – it is said to originate 'from the mouth of Re himself'[25] – one is tempted to link it with the injunctions in the Kagemni text and also with the Ptah-hotep passage, whose hymnic character it almost resembles.[26]

This then is some of the evidence for the existence or desirability of a normative link between the individual and maat in human action as well as in speech. The passage from the biography of

Kagemni already expresses the hope of a reward. The king, we are told, loves maat. But what the king loves he usually rewards. We thus have direct testimony to substantiate the last part of our definition, according to which maat was the compensation for righteous actions. There is a lapidary sentence in the Memphite theology, at least the core of which is ancient, where maat is promised to whoever does right; moreover, right is paraphrased as 'that which is loved', so that the Kagemni passage may be seen almost as a commentary on this. The passage concerned comes after the account of the creation of gods and forces of growth and reads: 'Thus justice was given to him who does what is liked and injustice to him who does what is disliked. Thus life was given to him who has peace and death was given to him who has sin.'[27] The idea of reward in dispensing justice is clearly emphasized by the parallelism: justice means life (at first in the juridical sense). In conclusion we may say that this throws some further light on the basic Egyptian notions of theodicy and talion, which we have examined above (see pp. 58 f.). In sum it may be said that maat was the order established at the creation and the rightful order which the king and every member of society had to maintain, as well as the just reward promised to those who kept it faithfully.

Maat, we have said, was the heart of Egyptian ethics, and we have now seen something of its rich treasury of meaning. Several questions now arise. Is maat made so explicit that a man can know what it actually means in the circumstances of everyday life? What is the basis for injunctions to behave in accordance with maat? What possibilities exist for a man to become conscious of maat? Finally, how is a man's life judged by the criterion of maat, and what consequences follow for the individual concerned?

It will be obvious that these questions are framed with a view to elucidating the interaction between ethics and religion, or to be more precise, its role in man's conduct toward God. These questions take us away from the aspect of maat as order guaranteed by the king, and direct our attention toward that aspect of maat where it implies the right dealing which God sets as the individual's task, and the justice he receives in compensation. Of course we cannot ignore the first aspect entirely. To forestall possible misunderstanding, we may state at the outset that in Egypt the duties of the individual are substantially determined by his relationship to the society and milieu in which he lives; consequently ethics lies within the framework of the general order.

Relative explicitness of maat

Our first question, about the degree to which maat was made explicit in the context of everyday life, may be approached by looking at the situation in ancient Israel, and its later development among the Jews. This is territory which will be very familiar to theologians, and also to ordinary Jews or Christians.[28] Here we have the classic case of detailed juridical maxims which were regarded by the Jews as a law handed down by Yahveh and thus as the quintessence of the scriptures (regardless of whether these laws were formulated with apodictic brevity or in casuistic profusion, whether they were introduced in early nomadic days or were adopted from the Canaanite cities, with their advanced legal culture, after they had been conquered).[29] In the way these laws were interpreted and further developed by the rabbis, they hedged about the life of the faithful with an impenetrable thicket of prohibitions. We need only think of the many rules governing cleanliness and the Sabbath, familiar to every reader of the New Testament as the stuff of many conflicts with Jesus and the first Christians.[30] The final objective of this extreme legalistic piety was to regulate men's entire lives in such a way that they could do nothing wrong, provided that they were knowledgeable and obedient. This throws some light on our questions about the explicitness of maat and the authority of those who interpreted it. For the Jews the law was laid down in detail, and the detail became more complex as time went on; for the Egyptians maat was a basic value, a general norm. In Egypt, if someone gives specific instructions about some line of conduct, he does so only in the spirit of maat, not in conformity with some precise legalistic wording. Ptah-hotep and the peasant in the oasis, for instance, praise maat for its magnitude and continuity, and for its effect on man: 'Great is maat, lasting and effective'; 'a man lives on who conforms to maat'. The teacher of Kagemni makes maat the basis of one's speech and actions: 'Do maat...speak maat.'

We may add: the Egyptians developed an ideal character type, the man who conforms to maat, which they commended to others.

This was 'the silent man (*grw*)', i.e. one who was wise and cautious, and also modest and reticent; they spoke, too, of 'the really silent man (*grw mꜣꜥ*)', whose whole character was infused with maat.[31] The Egyptian never says 'such and such is prescribed by maat,' or 'this is what God has commanded in the spirit of maat for such and such a case'. What he does offer in a particular case is rather his own experience, as that of a man who takes maat as his guide. The teacher of Merikare confesses at the end of his instructions, with almost touching simplicity: 'Behold, I have spoken to thee the profitable matters of my [very] belly (*bw ꜣḫ n ḥt.ì*).'[32] This shows clearly that the instructions are compiled in the spirit of God-given maat but do not claim to be themselves of divine origin. This is all the more important since some writers have claimed that in Egypt certain texts were of divine origin (see chap. 10). These instructions proffer no more than the fruits of an experience that springs from the innermost corners of the soul. They are, so to speak, educational material; thus a well-instructed son can have a proper discussion with his father and teacher about their expediency, and characteristically enough the father does not fall back upon divine commandment but only invokes his authority as a pedagogue, drawing realistic parallels with the training of animals.[33]

In our view, if maat is not an explicit divine law, it follows logically that one cannot interpret it as of divine authorship. It is true that we have some isolated passages in which phrases about maat are attributed to God. One of these is in the Memphite theology, which we have already cited twice: 'Thus justice was given to him who does what is liked, [and] injustice to him who does what is disliked...' With good reason it has been assumed that this sentence is based upon the word of the creator-god (Ptah), and that here, too, one is dealing with the formula we find elsewhere – namely, that the divine order came into being 'through what the heart thought and the tongue commanded'.[34] This may be coupled with the injunction uttered by the oppressed oasis-dweller to the high steward: 'Speak justice, and do justice, for it is mighty, it is great, it endureth long. If its trustworthiness [?] is discovered, it bringeth unto revered old age.' Here, according to the text (whether this is the work of the oasis-dweller himself, a writer, or an editor), we are dealing with 'a fine word which

cometh forth from the mouth of Re himself'.[35] However, even in
these cases, which are offered to us as the word of God, and
undoubtedly were regarded as such by Egyptians, maat is only
referred to as a basic value, as a goal and reward to which the
individual concerned may aspire.

Let us finally add the apology from the Coffin Texts – again
a passage we have quoted earlier (see p. 62) – in which we are
told: 'I did not command [men] that they do evil (*isft*) [but] it
was their hearts which violated my word.'[36] Earlier we raised the
possibility that there might be a hint here of explicit commands
such as one finds in the Old Testament, but we rejected this idea
at once. Now we may go on to argue that what is meant by the
word of God is nothing other than that brief proclamation of
maat which (in one variant or the other) we came across in the
two pieces of evidence just cited. For the word used in the Coffin
Text, *isft* ('evil', 'injustice'), is the common antithesis to maat;
the best way that one could turn this negative text into a positive one would be simply to cite the words 'speak maat, and
do maat', the authoritative 'word of Re' from the Eloquent
Peasant's tale. Now everything is in right order. According to the
spell in the Coffin Texts, therefore, the creator-god simply issued
a brief general command to abide by maat and nothing more.
Maat is established by God, commanded by his word; but it is
a basic value, not an explicit law. Thus the laws of Egypt are not
divine injunctions but edicts which the king issues from time to
time 'in the exercise of his supreme power, but by virtue of his
insight into the nature of maat'.[37]

By calling maat a basic value, we might have created the impression that it was a colourless concept, or at least that it became
one in the course of time, and that it lacked any concrete content
for the individual Egyptian. But this is by no means the case.
Maat could be given an appropriate specific meaning at any time
by drawing upon its wide range of meaning. In the instructions
it acquired a very clearly defined profile according to the circumstances. It was the truth that one ought to speak in a court of law
and also the justice which the court ought to put into practice.[38]

Finally, let us take another look at Judaism, where, as we have
seen, the divine law was made very explicit, with the thousands
of details mentioned in the Talmud. Men must have often felt

themselves hamstrung by these pettifogging regulations. They accordingly tried to reduce them to a single basic value. It is said of one pagan that he offered to become a proselyte on condition that he would be taught the law while standing on one leg, i.e. in the shortest possible time. Thereupon the liberal rabbi Hillel, an older contemporary of Jesus, summed up the Torah in a brief golden rule which has entered our treasury of sayings: 'Do as ye would be done by.'39 This pithy commandment was developed by Jesus into a dual one 'to love God and to love one's neighbour as oneself'.40 Equally terse, and no doubt just as significant to Egyptians believers, was the command 'to speak and to do maat', which often enough meant speaking the truth and doing what was right, although there was more to it than that.

Means of becoming cognizant of maat

It is to be hoped that the above remarks have done historical justice to maat and its succinct norms. This brings us to the burning question: what chances did Egyptians think they had to know maat, if God's word was not made explicit? What *was* truth, what *was* justice, what *was* the right thing to do in each specific situation? How could one know? In answering these queries we must distinguish strictly between the king and the private individual. The belief that the king was divine made itself felt right down to the close of Egyptian history precisely in his relationship to maat, which had been established at the creation and which it was his function to preserve. Like the deity himself, he maintained an intimate link with maat, which to him seemed very real. Hatshepsut says with regard to her divine father Amon: 'I have offered the maat which he loved, since I know that he liveth by it. [Also] it is my bread and I drink from its dew. I am of one body with him.'41 In this passage the ruler offers maat to God as nourishment, i.e. presents him with the quintessence of his righteous conduct of his royal duties; but the divine king is himself an embodiment of maat, and has become food and drink. In principle, at any rate, a union takes place between the pharaoh and maat. Haremhab formulates this in the introduction to the well-known edict designed to restore order in the land: 'Maat has come after it has united itself (*ḥnm*) [with King Haremhab].'42 Here the existence of maat in the land is based upon its having become one

with the king. The wordy inscriptions on temples built in Hellenistic and Roman times record many characteristic nuances of this
idea. Two examples may suffice, which portray the deity as dispensing maat to the king: 'I [Horus] give thee maat into thy heart
so that thou mayest exercise it toward all the gods';[43] and 'I
[Hathor] give thee maat so that thou mayest live from it, so that
thou mayest unite closely (*snsn*) with it and so that thy heart may
rejoice'.[44] In each instance maat is in concrete terms undoubtedly
the divinely-established pattern of government, and the pharaoh,
by virtue of his divine nature, receives it substantially like a
sacrament. It will at once be clear that in this process the king
is not regarded as an individual person but as the bearer of the
royal office. One must assume that the maat at work in the ruler
was thought to be of benefit to each individual Egyptian. If he
lived in a realm governed by maat, he could not but become
imbued with it. This inference can be substantiated. At Abydos
Seti I is extolled as follows: 'Thou hast fixed (*smn*) maat in Egypt;
it has become united with everyone (*ḥnm.n.s bw nb*).'[45]

Nevertheless we cannot be satisfied with these testimonies,
however important they are for the dogma of sacrosanct monarchy
and however impressively they are registered alongside the royal
titulary right down to the close of the pagan era. We are left with
the question how the individual Egyptian in his everyday existence became aware of maat, whose existence he took as his guiding
norm and which he thought, at least ideally, directed the state.
The answer seems simple enough: one could *learn* what maat
was; one could become cognizant of it. But on closer inspection
this only raises a further question: how could this knowledge be
obtained?

It has with justification been said that all wisdom literature
was based on the assumption 'that virtue means knowledge',[46]
i.e. that right conduct in life could be taught and that it was based
upon insight. For this reason a young man is anxious to be like
his teacher: 'Alas, if only I were like thee by being knowing (*rḫ*)
in thy way.'[47] A concluding chapter in the Instruction of Amenemope commends them in the following words: 'They make the
ignorant (*ḥm*) knowledgeable (*rḫ*).'[48] With this we have the characteristic antithesis which already dominated the Instruction of
Ptah-hotep: 'The fool who does not hearken, he cannot do any-

thing. He regards knowledge as ignorance...He does everything blameworthy, so that one finds fault with him every day', etc.[49] In another passage in a later manuscript, rather characteristically, the ignorant man (*ḥm iḥt*) takes the place of the evil stereotype, the covetous man (*ʿwn ib*): 'There is punishment for him who passes over its laws [those of maat], but the ignorant man does not know this.'[50] Relevant here is the postscript to a spell in the Coffin Texts, according to which the man who knows the text shakes off the sinful life he has hitherto led, and acts 'as does a man who was ignorant and who came to know'.[51] Since in this case it is a matter of knowing an occult mortuary text, the knowledge referred to likewise has an occult character, and we shall have something to say about this presently. But simple pious people also attribute to ignorance the failure to do the right thing. Neferabet, a minor official in western Thebes, introduces his confession of sins by saying that he was 'an ignorant and witless man (*s ḥm n iwty ḥȝty.i*)'[52] who 'knew not good or evil (*nfr bin*)'.[53] Quite similar is the confession made by a man who prays to the sun-god for remission of punishment for his many sins: 'I am one that knoweth not himself (*ḥm ḏt.f*), I am a witless man (*rmt iwty ḥȝty.f*).'[54]

It would of course be useful to have direct evidence that private persons could be cognizant of maat. Such evidence is fortunately available. The peasant dwelling in the oasis, to whom we have referred frequently, enjoins the high steward: 'Be patient that thou mayest discover justice.'[55] Our translation of *wȝḥ ib* can do no more than indicate that the man is asked to open his heart. An instruction in Papyrus Beatty IV runs as follows: 'I bring it about that thou mayest know (*rḫ*) in thy heart the matter of maat (*bw-mȝʿ.t*); mayest thou do what is right for thee.'[56] It is not surprising that Egyptians should have seen good conduct on earth as based upon knowledge. In another context we pointed out that private persons in Egypt did not base their actions upon God's command (see pp. 61 f.). Let us now supplement this by saying that they based their conduct on knowledge instead. An official of the Saite period states that he has been just and charitable; characteristically, the reason he gives is: 'for I knew that God is content with the man who acts thus'.[57] One of several contrasting statements that could be quoted is the following: 'I was one who liked maat and hated sin (*iswi*, probably standing for *isft*). For I knew that [sin] is the abomination of God.'[58] Such knowledge comprises the concept of reward implicit in maat, along with its other meanings. This is plain from a New Kingdom funerary stele: 'I was glad (*ḥꜥ i*) to speak the maat, for I knew that it was useful (*ꜣḫ.s*) for him who practises it upon earth.'[59]

Cognizance of maat based on insight and experience

How did Egyptians arrive at a perception of maat? Ordinary insight and experience played their part. Since maat is the criterion by which men lead their lives, it appears reasonable and beneficial. The teachings appeal to men's insight and are based upon their experience; this is the main reason for their pragmatic character, which sometimes embarrasses modern readers.[60] But in our view the Egyptians realized quite well that there are deeper wells of spiritual experience; they knew that correct perception of the truth is in the last resort a sign of God's mercy.

To explain this we may revert to our remarks about guidance, instruction and inspiration (see pp. 62 ff.). We know of a Bubastite priest who confessed that 'Khnum had steered his tongue'. In our considered judgement this means: 'Khnum guided him to preserve maat when speaking.' At the close of the Ethiopian period a high official claimed that his beneficial activities were due to the fact that he was 'one who was instructed by God'. We would say: God provided him with the perception to act in accordance with maat. The same term was used for God's activity as was employed for human teachings: *sbꜣ – sbꜣyt*.[61] Several individuals, starting with the young Amenophis II before he became king, are credited with divine inspiration, in taking decisions or actions which we may now say were carried out in accordance with maat. But if these insights came from God, it was also in his power to grant them or to deny them.[62] This was why already Ptah-hotep formulated a sentence which on the face of it has a pedagogic purpose, but at a deeper level is imbued with a belief in the divine determination of human affairs: 'He whom God loves, hears, [but] he whom God hates, hears not' (see p. 66). Here we may add that the divine gift of hearing is the basis of perception: 'The fool who does not hearken, he cannot do anything. He regards knowledge as ignorance.'

After all this we need items of evidence which combine perception (i.e. the gift of maat) with divine instruction or inspiration.
Two such are known to us. One concerns one of Ramses II's sons,
Prince Ramses-mer-Atum, and is inscribed in the western passage
of the rear chamber in the Mut temple at Karnak. Although the
context of the statement has been destroyed, it is certain that the
prince is referred to here as one 'who knows the truth, whom God
has instructed'.[63] The other comes from a prayer of Nefer-hotep
(Nineteenth Dynasty), addressed to Re: 'Since thou hast ever set
Truth over my heart (*dd.k m3ᶜt ḥnty*), I offer it to thy ka.'[64] It is
therefore not an imaginative reconstruction, but a fully substantiated fact that the perception of maat and divine instruction or
inspiration belong together. More studies in this field would be
needed to take matters further. We must be content with the
knowledge that in their conduct Egyptians felt that they were
guided, instructed and inspired by God. The philological
evidence does not permit us to go beyond this self-evident truth.
But we may also point to the consultation of oracles, which
provided information about many vital questions, since here
instruction was deemed to be imparted by God. Then there are
the innumerable prayers offered up to the Egyptian gods by
persons in distress, which open up a deeper level of experience.
Who dares tell us that, when Egyptians, in torment of soul, could
not find satisfactory answers to their quest for right direction,
they did not pray to God in the same spirit as that of Paul
Gerhardt in his Advent hymn:

> *O Jesu, Jesu,*
> *setze mir selbst die Fackel bei,*
> *damit, was dich ergötze,*
> *mir kund und wissend sei.*

Such pleas for the gift of wisdom must have preceded acknow-
ledgements that correct knowledge came from God, and that one's
ignorance was a cause of sin and suffering. We may therefore say
that in Egyptian ethics there was more than just intellectual perception, attained by insight and experience; there was also
a charismatic element, enlightenment by God.[65] In just the same
way very ancient occult knowledge was used by men later, in
historic times, to overcome their fear of the beyond.[66] Thus we

are suggesting that intellectual, charismatic and magic elements all had parts to play in the act of perception, and that this led to a striving for salvation through knowledge which we call gnosis, and which in later centuries was to find such fertile soil in Egypt.

Maat as measure of judgement upon men

If men were so anxious to attain cognizance of maat, this was because their lives were measured by it. This brings us to our last question about this basic concept. Now there can be no doubt that this criterion was applied also in earthly justice. As justice, maat was the basis of the Egyptian legal system. The vizier, who was responsible for the administration of justice, was from the Fifth Dynasty onward called 'the priest of maat'.[67] In later times judges wore an image of maat on a chain about their neck.[68] Maat also appears personified in human guise, like fate (see p. 74). It has been pointed out that personified maat was also familiar to the Jews who lived in the Upper Egyptian town of Elephantine and that this led, by way of the Aramaic *Words of Ahiqar* (part of which was available there), to the hypostatization of 'wisdom' in the Book of Proverbs (Proverbs viii).[69] But we are concerned here with ethics, not with the administration of justice. We therefore have to consider that aspect of the matter where maat is the standard whereby human conduct as such is judged. Such comprehensive judgements are not delivered in an earthly court. We need not raise the question, beloved of the Romantics, whether, during some past golden age when all aspects of human life were allegedly in harmony, the law instinctively took account of all facets of a man's conduct, so that justice and ethics were integrated and social justice prevailed. It is not the place of the historian to discuss such matters; he can do no more than point out that the later Egyptians did have such a retrospective view, when they could write, for instance, that in the era of the primordial gods 'maat came from heaven and joined those who lived on earth'; at that time, it was believed, there was no injustice, no pain, no hunger – in short, no everyday problems whatever.[70] On the other hand it is a fact that in historical times ethics existed as an independent quantity alongside justice, and that it was based upon a more comprehensive interpretation of maat than had underlain the concept of justice. The basic principle of Memphite theology is as follows: 'Thus justice [maat] was given to him who does what is liked, and injustice to him who does what is disliked. Thus life was given to him who has peace and death was given to him who has sin.' This principle can be applied both to justice and to ethics, which are still seen as closely allied. It can be interpreted either as a judicial verdict or as something broader: a non-judicial principle whereby, in accordance with the concepts of talion and theodicy, men are rewarded for right conduct by the grant of longevity (see pp. 97 f.). This idea of right conduct is the basis of ethics, as we shall see. It comes to be seen as something independent of and superior to the law, although its norms were undoubtedly modelled upon earthly judicial processes. Logically, a man's actions must be assessed according to criteria of right and wrong before he can be rewarded or punished. Another factor was involved here. The early Egyptians regarded life after death simply as a continuation of life on earth; mummification and the lavish furnishing of tombs are eloquent and familiar testimony to this simple idea, which was later supplemented by other notions (see chap. 9). In the beyond, it was believed, men not only combined to live a static existence; they also maintained their dynamic relationships with other members of society. This meant that in the realm of the dead, too, there were courts of law in which one could prosecute and be prosecuted. One could commit an offence even when in the tomb, and also be sued over some injustice one had committed on earth. The deceased Egyptian faced 'a tribunal which was brought into being only when needed, if the deceased person was sued by others, or if he himself sought the court's protection from torts committed against him'.[71]

The judgement of the dead

What is generally called 'the judgement of the dead' in Egypt comprised two elements: a belief that ethical norms had a higher validity than mere judicial ones, and a belief that earthly justice continued in the beyond. The judgement of the dead is met with in its most developed form, as is generally known, in Chapter 125 of the Book of the Dead. Here the vignettes accompanying the text (the details of which vary) show that the dead man's heart, deemed to be the seat of the intellect and will as well as the life-giving centre of the physical body, is weighed against the symbol of maat (usually depicted as a feather), which serves as an ethical standard. Anubis, who has become an attendant of Osiris, lord of the nether world, is master of the balance (*iry mḫȝt*), and is in control of the pointer; the scribe Thoth records the verdict and announces it. If the verdict should be unfavourable, the sinner falls victim to 'the devourer' (*ᶜm*; also *ᶜm mwt*, 'devourer of the dead'), a hybrid monster with the head and jaws of a crocodile.[72] If the verdict should be favourable, the deceased is invested with the attribute of maat and as 'one who has been vindicated (*mȝᶜ ḫrw*)' is brought before Osiris, seated upon his throne. The characteristics of this tribunal, which according to our text had forty-two judges, were the product of a historical evolution which we need not consider here.[73]

We are interested only in the question when and why the judgement of the dead began, in its strict sense of an automatic general judgement upon every mortal. Its origins are difficult to ascertain and have therefore been much debated. In our view there is good reason to think that the doctrine arose from a reinterpretation of the fifth maxim of Ptah-hotep, i.e. a document of the late Fifth Dynasty. This reinterpretation took place in a most characteristic fashion. The text, set forth by the author in an ambiguous way, first speaks of atonement through immanent earthly justice and then of evil being thwarted in the nether world. Lines 90–92 in Papyrus Prisse contain first the statement about immanent earthly justice: 'There is punishment for him who passes over its laws [those of maat], [however] the covetous person [i.e. the evil person] knoweth this not. [It may be that] it is fraud that gains riches but wrongdoing has never brought its undertaking into port.' But in the same text we find a reference to justice being rendered in the beyond: 'He is punished who trespasses against the laws [of maat], [however] to the covetous person this is something distant. Evil [indeed] lasts a lifetime, [but] never has misconduct reached [the world beyond] intact.' This passage seems significant for two reasons. Firstly, it displays a conscious ambivalence between an apparently older, in any case naive and optimistic, belief in automatic atonement, and another belief that atonement is granted only in the beyond; this shows that the new concept was coming to be accepted as a corrective to the earlier one, which was losing validity. Secondly, it affords incontestable evidence of a belief in a general judgement of the dead, such as we find subsequently in the Instruction for Merikare: 'Put not thy trust in length of years; [the judges of the dead] regard a lifetime as an hour. A man remaineth over after death and his deeds are placed beside him in heaps.'[74] The presence of a number of ambiguous keywords suggests very plausibly that the later instruction (Merikare) quoted the earlier one (Ptah-hotep); this evidence is marshalled by Fecht, who discovered the connection.[75]

The foregoing leads to the hypothesis that in the chain of instructions[76] the caesura occurs before that of Ptah-hotep. The little we possess from the Instruction of Hor-dedef, a prince of the Fourth Dynasty, suggests that the future existence of the deceased was still thought to be entirely dependent upon fine funerary furnishings: 'Embellish thy house of the necropolis, [and] enrich thy place of the West. Accept [this principle, for] death is oppressive ($d\underline{h}\dot{s}$) to us; accept [this principle, for] life is held in high regard by us. The house of death serves life.'[77]

Let us now consider the even more important problem of the historical conditions which gave rise to the belief in the judgement of the dead, and its deeper significance. In our view social changes have to be given very serious consideration here. The poor man who could not afford funerary furnishings, but who was quite familiar with maat as a criterion, will have adopted, or at least will have been prepared to adopt, the idea of an ethical judgement once this was made available to him.[78] Such ideas were bound to be in the air at a time when the harmonious and self-sufficient order of life in the Old Kingdom, guaranteed by the king as a personification of the cosmic god, was put out of joint by the sun-god Re, who won supremacy and demoted the king to the rank of his son, responsible to him (see p. 34). It was now that a distinction was drawn between the terrestrial world and the hereafter; previously life in the beyond had been just a continuation of life on earth. Henceforward the king and his subjects had to render account of themselves to God. This is the moment when the idea germinates of a tribunal in the beyond passing ethical judgements.

This reconstruction – and in a problem of this kind we can do no more than offer such a hypothesis – corresponds to the fact that Re apparently held a privileged position as the lord of the judgement of the dead. We are deliberately expressing ourselves cautiously here. For only from the First Intermediate period (Merikare) and the Middle Kingdom is there completely reliable evidence that the sun-god was associated with judging the dead.[79] In the Coffin Texts he is described *expressis verbis* as handling the balance, and the implement is called 'that balance of Re, in which he weighs maat'.[80] Since we are arguing that the conception of judging the dead arose as early as the Fifth Dynasty, we need earlier evidence of a link between Re and maat. Such evidence is to be found in the title 'lord of maat', which is assumed by Re as a falcon (Re-Harakhti) in his sanctuary of Neuserre. This monumental place of worship was built and dedicated to him (at the cost of curtailing work on his own pyramid) exactly at the time when the king became the son of the sun-god, responsible to the latter.[81] Admittedly, there is no mention here of judging the dead. But if it existed according to other evidence, then the 'lord of maat' is its obvious chief. On the other hand, recently scholars have pointed to certain passages – pyramid utterances and formulae of funerary offerings from the late Old Kingdom – which refer to Osiris as 'lord of maat' during this early period, which would qualify him for this office.[82] But in our view this very fact points the way to a solution of the problem: *both* Re and Osiris became 'lord of maat'. The king was originally in charge of justice; subsequently his title was extended to cover maat; it was simultaneously applied both to Osiris, the king of gods, and to Re, who as lord of the cosmos displaced the king as the supreme authority over justice in Egypt.[83] At this point it may be added that the Horus names of Kings Snefru (Fourth Dynasty) and Userkaf (Fifth Dynasty) are respectively 'lord of maat' and 'doer of maat (ir $m\beta^ct$)'.[84] If our hypothesis about Osiris should not prove acceptable, on the grounds that it is more correct to regard his quality as nb $m\beta^ct$ in the sense of 'possessor of maat', and to derive it from the fact that Osiris for his part had obtained justice against his adversary from a divine tribunal,[85] this simplifies matters, and what we have said of Osiris applies to Re alone. We shall not deny that this simpler solution seems more attractive.

However this may be, we may confidently state the following. The concept of maat as the criterion for measuring men's achievements, coupled with the notion of a tribunal in the beyond operating as a continuation of an earthly court, gave rise to the idea of a general judgement of the dead under divine supervision. This came to pass during the Fifth Dynasty, at a time when men began to distinguish between life on earth and life in the hereafter. The Instruction of Ptah-hotep, with its ambivalence over the question of atonement in this world or the next, illustrates the decline in the ancient belief in a homogeneous, harmonious world. The god who passes judgement is probably in the first instance Re, who takes on the additional function of 'lord of maat' (which, as we showed earlier, belonged to him anyway in his capacity of creator-god). We may also note that, as lord of maat, Re was naturally regarded, even in later periods, as lord also of the terrestrial order (see chap. 9). According to the pessimistic Instruction of Onchsheshonqy he was even capable, when in a rage, of expelling maat from his country and thus of imposing collective punishment: 'When the sun-god is enraged against a land ($ḫꜥr$), he expels ($ty lg$) maat from it.'[86]

Consciousness of sin

We have now answered our four questions about maat. Before we can draw conclusions about the relationship between ethics and religion, we must take a brief look at the substance of ethics in Egypt and the consciousness among Egyptians of a sense of sin. For practical reasons we may begin with the latter. We said above that our knowledge of the judgement of the dead in its fully developed form comes from Chapter 125 of the Book of the Dead. The attentive reader will have noted that we did not quote this source textually but drew our evidence from the representation showing the weighing of hearts. There was a good reason for this. For the text does not mention any hearing of the person judged, at which his maat could have been brought before his judge.[87] The text consists mostly of assurances by the deceased that he is innocent of lapses of a general ethical, ritual and criminal kind. These are followed by other statements claiming that he has adhered to certain moral precepts. Where a hearing takes place, it is not concerned with the man's conduct, as given in his statements, but with knowledge of certain occult matters, including a particular personal name, e.g.: 'What is thy name?'; 'where didst thou pass?'; 'what didst thou see there?'; 'what did they give unto thee?'; 'what hast thou done with them?'[88] Finally the deceased on trial must know the components (threshold, etc.) of the gate leading to the hall of the two goddesses of Maat, which leads to a detailed interrogation about the parts concerned.[89] In brief, we are dealing here with that magic knowledge which we identified as so characteristic of Egyptian thinking, along with intellectual and charismatic elements (see p. 125).

The statements by the deceased about his conduct are impregnated with the same spirit: the assurances of innocence and good conduct are intended to have a healing effect through the magic power of the formulae used. The same is true of the representation of the heart and maat being weighed: it is designed to bring about the desired balance of the two elements.[90] It has long been realized that, in what at first seems a strange fashion, magic practices eliminated the significance of the judgement of the dead – precisely where, according to our reasoning, it was fully developed.[91] It has also rightly been pointed out that these statements of one's innocence and virtue, which are derived from earlier ideal biographies and thus also correspond to the instructions, convey what Egyptians understood as an ideal way of life to which all should aspire.[92] But one can hardly accept the hypothesis that the deceased here speaks 'not as an individual but as the representative of what is generally held to be valid...', or that 'before the tribunal of the dead, where he is divorced from the particularities of his earthly life, he speaks as the pure representative of what is generally held to be valid'.[93] It is much more reasonable to assume that the idea of judging the dead, which presupposes an individual judgement on each heart, seemed too vast, too dangerous, and that Egyptians were loath to make their future existence for all eternity dependent upon passing through this terrible trial. For this reason they reverted to the magical equation with Osiris, brought about by funerary ceremonies, and extended it to include everyone in the country. This made the man summoned before the tribunal not an accused but 'one who has been vindicated (m^{3c} $ḥrw$)' in advance, in the same way as Osiris had once been vindicated (see also p. 210). Thus the passing of judgement on individual mortals was not repudiated, but was evaded by resort to magic. Chapter 125 of the Book of the Dead is a worthy contribution to mortuary literature, whose magical character must always be borne in mind (see pp. 98 f.).

All this means – and here we return to our starting-point – that the assurances of innocence in Chapter 125 testify to the Egyptians' deep anxiety to avoid sin. For in truth the Egyptian by no means regarded himself as free from sin. In the postscript to a spell from the Coffin Texts quoted above, we read that its purpose is to help this man, who has spent one hundred years living in 'incrimination (*sḏb*), impurity (*ᶜbw*) and wrongdoing (*ḫbnt*)', to escape this vicious circle for the rest of his days.[94] Consequently the Egyptian normally passes his life in the shadow of sin. The editor of Chapter 125 himself recognized this full well, for he gives the claims of innocence the most characteristic and appropriate title 'So that he may be separated from every sin (*ḥww*) which he hath done'.[95] When the sage Amenemope finally exhorts his readers: 'Say not: "I have no wrongdoing (*btȝ*)"',[96] this reads almost like a warning to living mortals, who are responsible toward God, not to take too literally the statements in the Book of the Dead, which are only designed to serve magical ends.[97] To this we may add, last but not least, the direct evidence of those who confess their sins to God in humble piety in the hope of mercy:

> Though the servant was disposed to do evil (*btȝ*),
> Yet is the Lord disposed to be merciful.

And they ask to be forgiven:

> Punish me not for my many misdeeds (*btȝ*), [for]
> I am one that knows not himself.
> I am a witless man.[98]

Lest anyone should think that such confessions were just ignoble chatter by people of no significance, we may recall the Instruction for Merikare (see pp. 58 f.), which contains the earliest known Egyptian confessions of sin. True, one should not seek in Egypt the idea that man is intrinsically wicked and burdened with original sin.[99] Man's consciousness of sin was adventitious and quantitative, and did not become ontological. But it is worth making it clear that even ancient Israel at its zenith did not attain such depths of insight into the nature of sin. For St Paul's parallel between Adam and Christ (Romans v. 12 ff.), based on the Old Testament tale of the Fall of Man, which later developed into the doctrine of original sin,[100] was a late fruit, and cannot be taken as evidence of Old Testament 'religious anthropology'.[101]

The statements of innocence in Chapter 125 of the Book of the Dead, which at first sight seem to show that Egyptians had no sense of sin, in fact demonstrate the opposite, if one interprets them correctly. There is other evidence attesting to this as well. We are obliged to confine ourselves to a general view of this subject, although we may certainly assume, on the basis of our own historical experience, that individual Egyptians differed in the degree to which they were cognizant of sin; that some of them were men of ethical and religious sensibility; that some of them felt themselves to be responsible toward God while others did not, and yet others were indifferent; and that these variations became more marked among individuals who succeeded in emancipating themselves from their social milieu. Where, in later times, we encounter a member of the élite with a strongly develped moral sense, like Petosiris of Hermopolis, whom we have often mentioned, such a man will have taken very seriously the judgement of the dead, as an inquiry into man's earthly life, and also the possibility of sin. He does not escape into magic or claim the respect due to his rank. 'No one reaches [the salutary west] unless his heart was righteous ($^{c}ḳȝ$) by doing maat. There no distinction is made between the inferior and superior person; [it matters] only that (wpw) one is found faultless when the balances and the two weights stand before the lord of eternity. No one is free from the reckoning. Thoth as a baboon holds [the balances], to count each man according to what he has done upon earth.'[102] This echoes, and even underlines, the message given to Merikare, when righteousness ($^{c}ḳȝ$) and doing maat were proclaimed as the criterion for obtaining a good place in the beyond and proper conduct on earth took the place of funerary furnishings (see p. 98). It is no accident that this was the source of the first confessions of sin. But this does not rule out the fact that, from Merikare to Petosiris and beyond, there were always plenty of people who acquiesced in magical practices, were indifferent to ethical or religious matters, and gave no thought to the morrow.

Substance of Egyptian ethics

A few words still remain to be said about the form and substance of Egyptian ethics.[103] There is little point in enumerating individually those plentiful and varied utterances in instructions, ideal biographies, or statements before the divine tribunal from which one could compile a moral code of Egyptians throughout the ages. It stands to reason that one had to conform to maat in one's speech and actions; statements to this effect are to be found among ancient funerary inscriptions.[104] As regards the endeavours made to make maat more explicit, two facts seem to be of prime importance. In the first place, there were formulae exhorting men to avoid evil deeds as well as those urging them to carry out good ones. The former were later to play a major role in declarations of innocence before the tribunal in the beyond. They are apparently among the earliest funerary inscriptions,[105] and from this we may conclude that they had a defensive character, like ideal biographies, and that they covered both specific actions and underlying principles of conduct. We therefore find many well-known sentences expressing helpfulness and a rather militant sense of righteousness, such as: 'I have given bread to the hungry man, apparel to the naked man'; 'I carried over him that had no boat'; 'I saved the weak from him who was stronger than he';[106] and next to them general confessions such as: 'I have not inflicted pain' (*smr*), or 'I have not made any man weep (*smr*)'.[107] This shows clearly that the Egyptians possessed general maxims of conduct, such as the need to avoid inflicting pain upon one's fellow beings, but did not attempt to describe exhaustively all the possible wicked actions whereby this could be done. They may be said to have had an ethic of an attitude of mind, which obliges men themselves to apply to the concrete circumstances the general moral maxim that one should show consideration for one's fellows. Thus Egyptian ethics are oriented toward commission and omission, but also toward facts and toward mental attitudes. It is precisely this latter tendency which shows us once again in conclusion what importance the Egyptians attached to the grace of insight into right dealing.

The range of human affairs permeated by ethical principles was as broad as it could be. It included man's conduct toward his fellows, toward the gods and toward society.[108] We might assign to justice such precepts as those which forbade fraud in weighing corn or measuring land; and we might classify as ritual regulations other precepts such as those prescribing the right way to celebrate divine festivals. Nevertheless all these testify to the comprehensiveness of maat. It underlay every step one took in Egypt. It imbued justice and ritual with an ethical spirit.[109]

Ethics and religion

Our exposition of the chief features of Egyptian ethics has indicated the religious basis of everyday life. The fundamental criterion of every action, maat, was established by God at the creation. The ability to perceive it everywhere as life demanded, and to comply with it are granted by God through insight and experience. It is to God that man is responsible. He rewards and punishes, in this world as in the next.

We may therefore conclude by asking: who is this 'God' referred to so often in instructions and inscriptions, whose name is not mentioned although the pantheon is teeming with suitable figures? Occasionally one can work out from the text whom the author has in mind in a particular case. Merikare's teacher is clearly alluding to the sun-god,[110] and the biographical inscriptions of the Late period generally refer to the specific local god;[111] in one instance it is apparent that the local embodiment of the sun-god is meant.[112] This is the most powerful argument in favour of the view that, despite their highly articulated pantheon, pious Egyptians only felt a bond to one specific deity, so far as their general conduct was concerned. This deity was of a comprehensive nature. The local god, although limited to a particular area, was comprehensive as regards his nature and efficacy (see pp. 28 f.).[113] It may help to clarify the matter if we recall that it was also the custom in Greece to speak simply of 'god' or 'the gods' whenever one had in mind the deity responsible for a particular effect upon human life.[114]

An investigation of ethics thus has its place in a study of Egyptian religion, but one must continually keep an eye on its religious foundations. Without wishing to repeat here the conclusions we have drawn in regard to particular problems, let us end by emphasizing two points relevant to our general theme. First, the way in which the Egyptian conducted himself depended very largely on the manner in which he behaved toward God. In his daily life he was in profound and permanent contact with God. The experience of personal suffering, regarded as a punishment for sin, could lead to an outpouring of piety; anxiety about his life on earth or in eternity could make him keenly aware of his responsibility toward a god who wanted him to uphold righteousness. Secondly, ethics is embedded in religion (see pp. 12 f.), from which it obtained the idea of a divinely established order; this became a norm which man had to preserve. Upon it depended his fate in this world and in all ages to come.

7 · Egyptian theology

Nature of Egyptian theology

We have dealt in some detail with man's relationship to God, because in our view this is the heart of Egyptian religion, and hitherto seems to have received less attention than it deserves. Nevertheless the three preceding chapters have by no means exhausted our theme. For example, we have only touched upon the question of (moral) free will. We learned that man was given the opportunity of transgressing the word of God and of allowing his heart (thought to be the seat of the will) to lead him into evil. We have also discovered that God himself may deny man the grace of true insight and may inspire him to negative actions. Thus free will and determinism coexist.

This should not come as a surprise to us, for these questions abound in logical ambiguities. Even in modern philosophy (moral) freedom is ranged among 'the antinomies of pure reason' and is regarded solely as 'the postulate of practical reason' (Kant), being thus assigned to a plane beyond that subject to logic and cognition. Perhaps we may attempt to form an opinion by looking first at the concept of fate. As we have seen, the Egyptians regarded fate primarily as responsible for determining one's life-span. From this it may be cautiously inferred that by and large they did not see human actions as predetermined.[1] In any case we have a text in which a sage warns man not to take refuge in the plea that his actions are fatally predetermined. 'Beware lest thou say: "Every man is according to his [own] character (*bỉȝt*); ignorant and learned (*ḥm rḫ*) are all alike; Fate and upbringing (*šȝy rnnt*) are graven (*ḫtỉ*) on the character in the writing of God himself." '[2] To put it differently, man is responsible for his actions. He cannot excuse himself by the plea that human nature causes him to act as he does. A great distinction is made (in judicial proceedings) between knowledge and ignorance which, as is generally known, are equated with hearing and not hearing, obedience and disobedience (see p. 122 and especially Papyrus Prisse 575 ff.). If a man refers to *šȝy* and *rnnt*, which foreordain his lifetime and development (see p. 70), he must not link them with his character and so seek to absolve himself from responsibility.[3]

But it is not these problems of human existence which will preoccupy us in this chapter. By religious thought we understand the intellectual efforts made by Egyptians to put into order and to systematize the large number of deities which developed historically, and likewise to harmonize this multiplicity of deities with the idea of one single God, as the object of worship and the guardian of good conduct. We shall also undertake the spiritually analogous task of determining the relationship between this deity and its various images. It will at once be evident that we are here encroaching upon the domain of theology. But the theologian has to take account at every step of historical data as well as of political factors; indeed, these are often the motive force behind theological developments. This incontestable fact has been conscientiously demonstrated by numerous scholars.[4] But this has led them to neglect the fact that religious thought has to take account of the elementary spiritual needs of ordinary people, who generally visualized the deity as a single figure, invested with the full panoply of power, and who consequently also wanted to see him represented in this way.[5] Yet it is this that constitutes the really religious element in Egyptian theology. This was the mighty force which attracted into the pantheon the thinkers' philosophical speculations. We have seen, at the end of the last chapter, how important 'God' was for men aware of the morality of their actions; earlier we noted that personal piety was closely bound up with the temple and with ritual; it will therefore not be difficult for us to grasp that Egyptian theology was greatly concerned with the intellectual relationship between 'God' and the empirical multiplicity of deities, and also with the iconography of these gods. In this respect our attempt to describe Egyptian religious thought is organically linked to what has been said above. In our view theology has religious as well as historico-political consequences. It grows out of the relationship between man and God: in the mind of the believer, the multiplicity of gods (or some of them at least) become fused with the One God whom he visualizes, as he worships him, as an encompassing totality. One might say that Egyptian theology is the divine service of the thinker – an act of veneration which, for all its intellectual subtleties, redounded to the believer's spiritual benefit. The historico-political factors are, in Goethe's words, only 'the conditions under which phenomena appear'. They no more 'cause' these phenomena than they 'cause' the creation of works of art.[6]

Fortunately, in regard to Egyptian theology we can base our analysis to a considerable extent on some excellent preliminary studies, which can be confidently recommended to the reader. These works cover the source material,[7] the principles underlying religious thought, and the sprititual attitudes that informed them.[8] We shall proceed from our view that in the act of worship, as well as in the general orientation of their lives, Egyptians normally saw themselves as confronting a single God (see p. 29). In many cases, if not in all, this single God was the specific local god; as we have just seen (see p. 135), when 'God' is mentioned in instructions and biographies, without further identification, it is often the local deity who is meant.

Local deities; 'syncretism'

We may therefore legitimately begin by taking a closer look at these local deities. As the smaller units in Egyptian society – clans, localities, nomes – were united to form larger ones, until a single Egyptian state came into existence, so likewise their deities had to be brought into some kind of mutual relationship. In principle, this could take one of two forms. Either the local god could be incorporated into a higher one, and lose his separate identity, or he could assert himself and be allotted a place with other deities in a hierarchically structured pantheon. It was, however, characteristic of Egyptian theology that it avoided the first course but did not adopt the second either. Right down to the close of their history the ancient Egyptians never abandoned their local gods. On the contrary, the latter were very much in evidence during the Late period;[9] this was a logical development, which accorded with the diminishing appeal of the idea of national unity. In the instruction in the Insinger Papyrus there is a whole section warning against emigrating to foreign lands, which reaches its climax in the words: 'The god who is in the town is he upon whom depend the death and life of his people. The ungodly man who goes abroad places himself in the hands of [the enemy].'[10] On the other hand, Egyptians were never satisfied with the idea of a pantheon, even though they invented it by speaking frequently of 'all the gods (*ntrw nbw*)', who were thought to assemble on special festive occasions (in the context of the Sed-festival);[11] similarly, the priests of all the gods, in their capacity as delegates of the king, formed a single body, and the Egyptian people formed a single body of worshippers (see chap. 3). The Egyptians preferred that their local gods should become infused with other deities, for this would augment their qualities and enhance their power.

This led to that characteristic phenomenon which is generally called 'syncretism'. This term means precisely the process we have described: the coalescence of one god with another. This point is worth discussing in detail. We ought to abandon the infelicitous term 'syncretism', which contrary to accepted opinion is not derived from συγκεράννυμι, 'to mix' (which is really συγκερασμός or σύγκρασις (or σύγκρησις)), but from Κρής, 'Cretan', and denotes the union of the Cretans against a common enemy.[12] We frequently find two Egyptian deities coalescing (in a manner that we shall examine presently). Such unions are not confined to local gods and their superiors (national god, a cosmic entity), but extends to the relationships between the national god and cosmic entities as well as to deities with kindred functions. The relationship is evident in the first place simply from the name. We say Sobek-Re, for instance, by this meaning that the two gods are united. Naturally the crocodile-god Sobek and the sun-god Re continue to exist as separate entities, and indeed enter into other relationships: e.g., Re with Amon, Sobek the crocodile with Horus the falcon, etc.[13] This patently suggests that the union is not a static or lasting one, but rather a dynamic inhabitation ('indwelling') by one of the other, which does not limit the independence or mobility of either partner.

To comprehend this, let us recall our description of the way in which, as human consciousness developed, the gods ceased to be factors of power and became personal embodiments of it – although the concept of 'power' continued to exist alongside the concept of 'God' (see p. 18). The way in which deities seem to have come into being in men's minds helps to explain how they were able to merge or coalesce with one another. The concept of magical power comes in here too, in a rather appealing way. The greater of the gods concerned, it is said, takes up his abode in the other (e.g., Re in Sobek), by imbuing his partner with his power. This explains how each can retain his or her personal identity, and why such unions are neither permanent nor exclusive. When Re gives his power to Sobek, he raises him to the quality of Sobek-Re, but does not deprive Sobek or himself of individual personality, or inhibit either of them from concluding other such liaisons.[14]

The results of these unions are most clearly apparent in the hymns of praise offered up to the deities concerned. Let us for the present keep to Sobek, the local god of Kom Ombo, and his liaison with Re. In the hymn the crocodile-god is referred to *expressis verbis* by the name of Sobek-Re, as the sky-god: 'the great god whose eyes emit the two discs of light, whose right eye shines by day and whose left eye shines at night, whose two large eyes light up the darkness'. Here the sun-god Re has grown into the sky-god, and the title 'prince (*sr*) of maat', ascribed to Sobek, has been borrowed from the substance of Re, the paradigmatic 'lord of maat', and so on.[15] Characteristics are transposed on such a scale that, for example, a hymn in which Ptah is mentioned neither by his name nor by his characteristic titles, but where we hear of Re and Amon, is in one manuscript entered under the title of Hymn to Ptah.[16] It was possible, and even common practice, to refer to Ptah, like Re, as 'the child that is born each day' and as 'the old man that is within the bounds of eternity'; alternatively, he was referred to, in the manner of Amon, as the 'Hidden One (*imn*) whose nature no one knows'.

At this point we may add a word about the degree to which the Egyptian gods were personified. We said earlier that the gods were conceived by investing magic power with a personal form. But we must draw a distinction between personality and individuality, the latter implying that the individual concerned has a sharply delineated character peculiar to him alone. The Egyptian gods had personality but not individuality. This is evident from the unstable liaisons they formed (usually confined to the same sex) and the transposing of qualities from one to the other.[17] To make this clear, we may cast a glance at the situation in Greece. During the classical period, at any rate, the individual gods were individuals, each of whom had unmistakable characteristics. The so-called Homeric hymns to Aphrodite, Apollo, Demeter, Hermes, etc. portray them as such with reference to their prosopography, myths and character. The indeterminateness of Egyptian gods corresponds, *mutatis mutandis*, to the relative lack of individuality in Egyptian art and literature;[18] it may thus be called typically Egyptian.

But we would be making a one-sided and subjective judgement if we left matters there. For this formlessness is but the necessary counterpart to an attitude of mind that is of the utmost importance; it explains why the Egyptian gods merged in the way they did, and – again in contrast to Greece – called into being a great system of theology. This theology accentuated the existing tendency to strengthen the local gods by fusing them with higher ones, for it led to earnest theoretical speculations about the problem of how the numerous deities in the pantheon could be reconciled with a single God. In their efforts to this end thinkers took the course we have indicated above: namely, they avoided liquidating individual gods but did not remain content with building up a hierarchical pantheon; they boldly went on to advance the theory that behind the plurality of gods there was a basic unity. The pantheon was classified in two ways: according to families of kindred deities and according to the specialized functions which particular gods performed. We shall not go into the details here; the reader may consult the list given as an appendix to this volume (see pp. 258 ff.). We have already dealt with the gods' specialized functions (see p. 28), and noted that these never became so elaborate as they did in Greece.

Unity in plurality; Egyptian trinities

Let us turn now to the idea of unity in plurality, and see what the sources tell us. We shall choose one particular relationship, that of three to one (the figure three may serve as the quintessence of 'plural'),[19] and examine the various possible ways of formulating the proposition of unity in plurality. First of all there is the kind of association of gods that we have already encountered: first a pair, and then a trinity. The best known example of this is the union of Ptah, Sokaris and Osiris. Sokaris, who was a local god at Memphis, was associated with Ptah, who was powerful there but whose influence was also nationwide; through his function as god of the dead, he was associated with Osiris, who was supreme in such matters. There is ample evidence that this trinity was regarded as a unity. For instance, the association Ptah-Sokaris-Osiris is found in mortuary formulae. Or we read in numerous cases: 'may *he* offer ($d\hat{\imath}.f$) [the gifts, etc.]' – i.e., the trinity is rendered a unity by the singular pronoun.[20] Sometimes the plural is used instead: e.g., 'that *they* may give ($d\hat{\imath}.sn$)'; but this is not so much proof of inconsistency as a reflection of the dialectic inherent in a problem which was, to to speak, open-ended.[21] It seems highly characteristic of the impact made by Egyptian theology that Syrian goddesses, who in their homeland (according to the information that survives) were never associated in this way, were in Egypt combined to form a trinity: Kadesh-Astarte-Anath.[22]

Other unions of gods were more complex than such simple combinations of names, which only yield a modest amount of information through an analysis of grammatical usage. In the theology of Apis, the god of Memphis, incarnate as a (whole) bull, there are two statements which serve to enhance the nature of this relatively humble god by making two great deities take up their abode in him; these statements shows clearly that the three gods are one. The earlier one dates from the Ramesside period. It represents the bull as a mortal who has become Osiris, and runs as follows: 'Osiris = Apis [a single quantity] – Atum – Horus at the same time (n sp), the Great God.'[23] The more recent one is to be found as an invocation of an oracle in the so-called Demotic Chronicle. It runs: 'Apis, Apis, Apis! That is ($\underline{d}d$) Ptah, Pre, Horsiese...Apis is ($p\hat{\jmath}y$; i.e., the copula) Ptah, Apis is Pre, Apis is Horsiese.'[24] The texts speak for themselves; by various linguistic devices they formulate the unity of the three gods in Apis. His power is greatly enhanced by being associated either with the Heliopolitan primordial god Atum and the god-king Horus or with his mighty neighbour Ptah, the sun-god Re and a manifestation of Horus. Thus there are two possibilities: in the first case two gods are combined with Apis; in the second case he incorporates three gods. The purpose of these trinities is, as we saw at the beginning of our analysis, to enhance the nature and increase the power of a low- or medium-ranking deity. This was the first step along a path of spiritual development that was fraught with tremendous consequences.

By contrast, other trinities lead one directly to the problem of unity in plurality by making three stand for plurality as such.

This appears to be the case in that important theological statement in the Leyden hymns to Amon which runs: 'All gods are three: Amon, Re and Ptah, and there is no second to them. "Hidden" (*imn*) is his name as Amon, he is Re in face, and his body is Ptah.'[25] Already at the beginning of this century the editor of this text realized that this was a 'trinity as a unity',[26] and the tension between singular and plural brings out the inherent dialectic: *three* gods, no second to *them*, but hidden is *his* name, *he* is Re, etc. How the three gods mentioned here represent the pantheon will be immediately evident to the Egyptologist. For the hymns, which were written down and probably also composed during the early Ramesside period, have chosen in Amon, Re and Ptah the three gods whose real power (possession of temples, etc.) surpassed that of all other gods, with Amon far in the lead.[27] It is also worth noting that the theology in question by no means occupied a vacuum. For Re and Ptah had daughter sanctuaries in the complex of Karnak, Amon's main temple, so that the three great gods were worshipped next door to one another. Moreover, we have already heard that texts addressed to Amon could be put up in the Ptah temple at Karnak.[28] Finally, the trinity as a unity of Amon, Re and Ptah, like that of Ptah, Re and Horsiese, can be embodied in a fourth god, Apis. In the Ptolemaic Opet temple at Karnak Thoth is praised as 'the twofold Great One, Lord of Hermopolis'; he is called 'the heart of Re, the tongue of the Tatenen [= Ptah], the throat of the one with the hidden name [Amon]'.[29] This shows that this trinity was still important in a very late period; we shall take up this point again in chapter 11, when dealing with the impact of such Egyptian theological doctrines. One other point deserves to be emphasized. In conformity with the principles governing the association of Egyptian gods, the Amon-Re-Ptah trinity did not put an end to the independent existence of the three gods concerned. This is absolutely clear from the continuation of the Leyden hymn, which lists the localities where the gods concerned were first worshipped and brings out what was peculiar to each of them (IV, 22): 'Their [the three gods'] cities are on earth, abiding forever: Thebes, Heliopolis, and Memphis unto eternity.'[30] If one makes use of Christian theological terminology to categorize Egyptian doctrines, the Leyden trinity would have to be called tritheistic, not modalistic.

To indicate the whole range of opportunities open to Egyptian theologians in the matter of trinities alone, we can do no better, by way of contrast to the foregoing, than to draw attention to a unity in trinity which is definitely modalistic. This is to be found in the notion of one sun becoming visible in three aspects (modalities). These modalities are the three phases of the sun in the morning, at noon and in the evening. Already in the Pyramid Texts these were identified, by characteristic plays on words, as Khepri (one who rises), Re and Atum (one who sets).[31] During the Ramesside period, however, they are expressly referred to as the unity which they in fact are: three manifestations of one sun. The sun-god is made to say: 'I am Khepri in the morning, Re at noon, Atum in the evening.'[32] This modalistic trinity, in which the one 'I' appears three times, is in our opinion reflected in a spell in the Book of the Dead, where the sun is addressed as 'the aspect of the three (*bꜣ n ḫmt*)'.[33] This is in accord with the common notion that Re was 'a child in the morning, a youth at noon and Atum [as an old man] in the evening',[34] which once again shows clearly that this is in fact the extreme borderline case of primary and intrinsic unity.

These extremes of tritheism and modalism do not exhaust the wealth of Egyptian trinities. In the Leyden hymns we saw the problem of plurality and unity represented by three gods and one. A trinity can also come about by suspending, as it were, the process whereby the gods were created out of the primordial god at the decisive initial moment, and so formulating a 'trinity of becoming', comprising the primordial One and the first pair of gods to be begotten. In one theological text this reasoning is applied to the god Shu, who according to Heliopolitan teaching was begotten parthenogenetically, together with his partner Tefnut, by the primordial god Atum (see pp. 162 f.). This text survived in the spells of the Coffin Texts, where it is transposed to the dead man who equates himself with Shu. It runs as follows: 'I am "life", the lord of years, alive until infinity, a lord of eternity, [I am he] whom Atum, the eldest, has brought forth through his might (*ꜣḫw*) [at the time] when be brought forth Shu and Tefnut at Heliopolis, when he was One [and] when he became Three (*m wn.f wꜥi m ḫpr.f m ḫmt*).'[35] This formulation, with its contrapuntal rhythm of being and becoming, one and three, makes it clear to anyone familiar with such ways of thinking that the original unity is thought of as continuing to exist after the act of creation. He, the one Atum, performed the act of creation; he is still deemed to be singular after he became three, i.e. after he had begotten Shu and Tefnut; thereafter further evolution could take place by natural procreation. It could be held that in the Leyden text we have a static and simultaneous type of plurality, whereas the one in the Coffin Texts is dynamic, called into being by the triad.

The development of many out of one can of course also be expressed differently. Thus in a coffin inscription from the Bubastite period one mortal, again magically identifying himself with the gods, says: 'I am one [Atum] who became two. I am two [Shu and Tefnut] who became four. I am four who became eight.'[36] The eight referred to here, which together with the primordial One form the Heliopolitan Ennead (see pp. 163 f.), may be regarded as a concept of totality, i.e. a symbol of plurality.[37] But what is lacking is the characteristic link between unity and plurality; we can indeed see plurality developing, but the basic harmony that characterizes unity, which makes the trinities what they are, is not sustained. This is not so true of that extreme borderline case in which Amon, the primordial god, is said to be 'the only One who made himself into millions (ḥḥ)'.[38] For in this case the unity of the primordial god is nevertheless preserved by the fact that the hymnist praises the one God even though he has developed to the point of infinite multiplicity.

Doctrine of Amenophis IV

However, in the history of Egyptian religion there seems to have been a moment when the problem of the tension between unity and plurality was solved in a way that appears plausible to our Christian way of thinking: in the sense of a *tabula rasa* favourable to monotheism. In any case, this is the customary interpretation of Amenophis IV's profession of faith, which was not only in opposition to the paramount national "church" of Amon at Thebes but left no place for the countless deities in the Egyptian pantheon; the person of the sun-god alone was deemed a worthy object of religious belief. Let us for the moment assume that this is the right way to look at Amenophis IV's reform. Since it was undeniably a failure, we may conclude that Egyptians regarded it as strange and disagreeable to have to abandon their familiar deities, the number of which had continually increased, in favour of the simple idea of a single god. For one could not explain the king's demonstrative abandonment of his dogmatic ideas simply by such political factors as the conflict with the national church and his catastrophic failure in Syria, although these factors are clearly important in arriving at a general assessment of his achievements. Matters are more complex than that. It is quite clear that, even in his early radical phase, Amenophis IV was in no sense an advocate of simple monotheism. On the contrary, what he proposed was precisely a trinitarian formula such as we have described above. The quintessence of his dogma lay in the so-called instructive name which he coined for the god whose cause he propagated. This name is traditionally (no doubt erroneously) rendered as 'Aton' (*itn*); at the time it probably had the form Jāti (i.e., the '*n*' was dropped), in accordance with contemporary pronunciation.[39] The name (surrounded by cartouches) has two parts and runs as follows: 'Re-Harakhti who rejoices in the horizon – in his name: as (*m*) Shu, who is Jāti ['Aton'].' Whether Shu here is simply, as most scholars have assumed,[40] a term for the sun or whether, as seems more probable, it is an allusion (or *also* is an allusion) to Shu as son (Shu as the son of the primordial god Re = Atum of Heliopolis), thereby raising the god-king Akhanjāti ('Akhnaton') to unity with his father[41] – in either case this is a trinitarian formulation.

One can almost hear the theologians hammering out these sophistries, and gain a useful insight ino the way their minds worked. What was it all about? Either (*a*): the ancient sun-god Re = Harakhti, who had long since become a unitary figure, was simply fused with two more recent manifestations of the sun-god, Shu and Jāti, to form a trinity; this one could call a modalistic trinity, comparable *mutatis mutandis* with the modalism we have just examined – which concerned precisely such a solar trinity. Or (*b*), which seems more likely, Re = Harakhti is on the one hand equated with the new aspect of the sun-god, Jāti, who incidentally comprises and represents the sun both as a natural phenomenon and as the father of the king,[42] but on the other hand is equated with the son of 'Shu', i.e. with the king himself; he was worshipped as a deity above all in Amarna, as we know from the domestic altars with the image of the radiant sun and the royal family (see p. 108). If this latter view is correct, we have in this example a trinity comprising successive generations (father and son). This was of course already implied in the 'trinity of becoming' referred to in a spell in the Coffin Texts (Atum-Shu/Tefnut). Perhaps we may regard this as the embryo – and certainly as an example – of the idea that the creator continues to exist in what he has created, and that the father continues to exist in the son he has begotten, and in consequence is one with him.[43]

Since this study is arranged topically, it is not possible here to treat Amarna religion as a historical phenomenon. But we may point out in conclusion that the teaching of Akhanjāti (Akhnaton) was abandoned in essence (belief in Jāti) immediately after the king's death, whereupon the gods who had been expelled were permitted to return; nevertheless the idea that there was a basic unity in plurality received a powerful impetus and was to have tremendous historical consequences. The existence after the end of the Amarna period of a trinity comprising Amon, Re and Ptah, a trinity in which there is no 'second' figure, is hardly accidental.

We have now learned to distinguish the various elements involved in the construction of trinities in Egypt. The starting-point, historically and theologically, was the idea of enhancing a god's power (as within Apis); its form was based on the notion that a triad could stand as a substitute for plurality as such (Leyden hymns); in a particular case modalism appeared along-side tritheism (the three phases of one sun attaining a relative independence); the development of plurality from unity was 'suspended' in the first act of creation (trinity comprising the primordial One and the first-begotten pair); finally, the three-in-one concept was made to cover successive generations (name given to the god of Amarna).[44]

It has not been our purpose to present the material here for its own sake, however much it merits our interest; we shall come back to it again when discussing the impact of Egyptian religion abroad (chap. 11).[45] What we have endeavoured to do is rather to demonstrate the vitality with which Egyptian theologians grappled with the problem of unity and plurality, to show the numerous innovations they made, and to indicate some of the characteristic ways in which they sought to solve this problem. One point in particular should now be self-evident: behind the countless deities in the pantheon there was a growing awareness of the existence of a single God. Ordinary believers offered their prayers to one God; the theologians provided this God, whichever one it might be, with supreme and extensive power; they gave him an appropriate identity, choosing from the wealth of forms available; and they forged a dialectical unity between the one God and the many gods in the pantheon.

Origins of monotheism

This is the right place to mention the thesis advanced by one leading scholar[46] to the effect that the Egyptians developed an original kind of monotheism, one which was never wholly discarded later. This view rests on the existence of a name given to this original single god, the 'Great One (Wr)'; he is said to have transmitted his name, and thus his nature, not only to Atum at Heliopolis but also to the great gods Ptah, Horus and Amon. The critic must first of all state that this is an ingenious interpretation of the facts, but no more than an interpretation. We should not accept it simply because it has won the support of another outstanding expert in the field,[47] but should rather try to form an opinion by proceeding from the approach to the subject followed here. We shall then see that the idea of an original monotheism is based upon two extremely important and incontestable facts: first, that unity is one pole of attraction in the dialectical relationship between unity and plurality; second, that the faithful in general tended to worship a single God and to regard him as the judge of the morality of their conduct. We have given clear proof of both facts (see, for example, pp. 135 f.), and need not repeat this evidence here. But we are convinced that one cannot postulate from these two facts an early and original belief in one single deity. On the contrary, the various local gods seem to have had from the start that extensive authority, in the sense of henotheism, or to put it better, monolatry, which men of a religious cast of mind require.[48] Not until these numerous deities came to be systematized did there evolve the kind of theology which sought to define, by drawing parallels, the nature of the single God, basing this upon the idea that there was one God with many aspects. This single unity, in our view, was not at that time visualized in personal form, but was seen as that primordial 'power' which existed before the gods and which later took individual shape. If this view was sufficient to satisfy men's religious needs, then we have to seek a different explanation of the 'Great One (*Wr*)'. It might simply be an adjective, or else it could be a taboo word or circumlocution for one of the gods. We do not wish to go into this point, but probably the first explanation fits some cases and the second one fits others.[49]

Relationship between deity and image

Egyptian theologians were chiefly concerned with the problems we have just discussed. But another task facing them, which in point of fact was just as urgent, was to determine the relationship between the deity and its image – especially, of course, the image used in cult. For only in exceptional cases did a god have no image or service to go with it. As regards these exceptional cases, we have seen above that cosmic beings, although potentially the object of a cult, usually took over the cult of deities with local ties (see p. 30), and that in the solar sanctuaries there were neither cult images nor chambers provided for this purpose (see p. 86). It is therefore not surprising to find that, in a hymn addressed to the Nile, one of the powers of nature, lack of imagery and cult is praised as one of its characteristics: '[the Nile] is not in stone, [to be more precise] carved as a statue or the White Crown placed [upon him], he cannot be seen [probably: as a divine image], he has no servants or superiors, no one can read [of him] in secret writings (read: *štȝw*),[50] no one knows the place where he is', etc.[51] The translation may be uncertain in some particulars, for this text originates from the Middle Kingdom but was handed down in the New Kingdom in faulty manuscripts prepared by pupils at school; but we certainly have here a stereotyped negation of the proposition that the Nile has first an image, then a cult. We do not by any means wish to assert that this denial was correct in this harsh form or for all times. On the contrary, there are other testimonies which show that there was a Nile cult, and even this Hymn to the Nile later mentions offerings (*wdn*) and a great festival of sacrifice (*ȝbt ȝt*) for the river.[52] Yet the powers of nature may indeed not have had images, as this text suggests.

The gods of the Egyptian pantheon, however, as a rule did
have such images, which were cared for daily, as we have seen
(pp. 87 f.). In chapter 5 we deliberately left open the question of the
relationship between the image and the deity. This matter is best
discussed here, because the processes of thought employed had
much in common with those described in the foregoing pages.
For we have here another instance of the phenomenon of 'habitation'; indeed, only in this context is this notion clearly defined
and made comprehensible. It will be remembered that the notion
of one god taking up his abode in another was the basis on which
numerous deities merged, and that behind the plurality of deities
there was thought to be a unity. Both facts are attested in formulae
such as that used of Amon: 'His form (*šbwt*) is each god',[53] i.e.
Amon lives in all divine beings. Or, more specifically: 'Thy
[Amon's] form (*ḫprw*) is the Nile flood.'[54] Now just as Amon is
incarnate in other gods or forces of nature, so also he takes up
habitation in his image. This problem finds expression in the
Leyden hymns: 'His [Amon's] soul (*bꜣ.f*) is in heaven, his body
(*ḏt.f*) is in the West, and his statue (*ḫnty.f*) is in Hermonthis [the
Upper Egyptian Heliopolis] bearing his crowns.'[55] Thus one
aspect of the god's nature, his *ba*, is in heaven; another one, his
body, rests in the realm of the dead (cf. here the concept of the
gods dying, pp. 24 f.); finally, his image is located at his place of
worship;[56] when it bears the divine crowns, we may recall the
passage from the Hymn to the Nile, cited a moment ago, in which
the wearing of a crown is depicted as an essential part of the
image. In these sources the problem is formulated but left dangling
in the air, as it were; for a solution we must look to numerous
statements of the Late period. In the rite known as the vigil for
Osiris there is an exact description how the *šḥ* (actually the
transfigured spirit) of the god and the *bꜣw* of his attendants
descend from heaven and enter the images in the chambers of his
sanctuary. 'Osiris...he appears as a spirit (*šḥ*) to join his form in
his sanctuary. He comes flying out of the heavens like a sparrow-
hawk with glittering plumage, and the *bꜣw* of the gods are together with him. He soars like a falcon to his chamber at Dendera..
He beholds his sanctuary...In peace he moves into his magnificent
chamber with the *bꜣw* of the gods which are about him. He sees
his secret form (*sštꜣ*) painted at its place (*sš*), his figure (*bs*) en-

graved upon the wall; then he enters his secret aspect, instals himself upon his image (*sḫm*)...The *bȝw* take their places at his side.'[57] Of such texts, which leave nothing to be desired, there are many in the temples of the Greek and Roman period. At the entrance to the sanctuary in the Horus temple at Edfu we find, in varying phraseology, an inscription to the effect that the god, as a winged sun-disk, takes a delight in his temple and his images, and that he 'comes daily from Naunet [the under-world] to see his image (*bs*) at his great seat. He descends (*hȝi*) to his image (*sḫm*) and joins (*snsn*) his falcon idols (*ᶜḥmw*).'[58] At Dendera attention is naturally concentrated on Hathor, the principal goddess there: 'She coalesces (*smȝ*) with her form (*smn*)',[59] or – in greater detail: 'She flies (*ᶜpi*) from heaven... to enter (*ᶜḳ*) the horizon of her ka upon earth, she flies upon her body, she coalesces (*snsn*) with her form (*bs*).'[60] Finally, the place is identified exactly: 'She coalesces (*ḫnm*) with her form (*ḫprw*), which is engraved (*ḥti*) in her sanctuary (*ḥm*)',[61] or: 'She settles (*ḫni*) upon her form (*bs*), which is engraved (*ḥti*) upon the wall.'[62] Of Horus, too, we read here: 'After his *bȝ* came from heaven to the house of Re, it coalesces (*sḫn*) with his form upon the wall (*ḥr sȝt*)';[63] and of Re-Harakhti, the falcon-headed sun-god, we are told: 'After his *bȝ* came from heaven [to see] his monuments, his heart coalesced (*snsn*) with his falcon idols (*ᶜḥmw*).'[64] To the observer it seems only logical that a kind of priestly title came into being, known as 'unifier of the form' apparently from the rite whereby the priest united the god with his image.[65]

Common to all these testimonies is the concept that the god, in the manifestation of a bird (often = *bȝ*), and at any rate able to fly, descends from the heights of heaven and settles upon his temple, where he unites with his images. The terminology varies: different words are used for 'unite' and 'image'. The linguistic usage would merit closer examination, and in undertaking this one would also have to ascertain which images in the temple are referred to in each case. Often images carved in relief are meant, and not only the sculpted cult image. This is clear from the use of the verb 'engrave (*ḥti*)' and the location 'upon the wall (*ḥr sȝt*)'. In the meantime we may at least draw the conclusion that the temporary habitation of the god in his image was not restricted to the sculpted cult image in the sanctuary, at any rate during the Late period.

We may conclude our discussion of the theological notions concerning the relationship between the god and his image by mentioning the point that the king – who has long since ceased in practice to be an incarnation of the cosmic god, let alone identical with him – is referred to as the 'image' or the 'living image' (in Greek rendered by εἰκὼν ζῶσα) of Re or of Amon, for example.[66] By virtue of this quality he is placed on the same level as numerous divine images. Here we have, at one level lower, the same development which occurred with the title 'son of Re' (see p. 34). If one looks at this from the vantage-point of Egyptian conditions, one will recognize that it signifies a dignity accorded to the king, although one of relatively low status.[67]

Initial assumption of identity between image and object

Our investigation has taken us deep into the relationship between god and image; we have looked at the pertinent theological problems (habitation) and the relevant cult practices (the ritual of uniting the two). It would be wrong to leave out of account the ancient Egyptian conviction that the image (or the word) was identical with the person or object represented. This view is characteristic of all primitive thought.[68] In Egypt it becomes particularly palpable in the custom of mutilating those hieroglyphic characters which represented living beings; this was done from the time of the Pyramid Texts onward and was especially frequent in them. Men were afraid that the images, being identical with what they represented, were alive and might cause harm. For this reason this precautionary measure was adopted especially in regard to texts inscribed in the vicinity of the dead.[69] It is interesting to note that the modern German word for 'image', *Bild*, is also derived from a term used in magical practices, i.e. it denotes exactly what Egyptians thought lived in the image.[70] As religious ideas developed in Egypt, a distinction came to be drawn between the image and the object represented. The idea that they were identical thus prevailed only at the outset, although admittedly we do not know how far ordinary people continued to believe in this, since the evidence to the contrary comes wholly from the priesthood.[71] Educated persons who were not priests, i.e. those who read these teachings, were familiar with the distinction between image and object, as is clear from the well-known words of the sage Ani: 'The god of this land is the sun (šw) which is on the horizon, and [only] (twt) his images are upon earth.'[72]

When this separation between image and deity was first formulated it is of course impossible to say, owing to the haphazard way in which the texts have survived. In our opinion a formulation of this kind appears in the theology of Memphis, where we hear of Ptah creating certain localities, including the gods that were worshipped there. The primordial creator-god 'had formed the gods, he made cities, he had founded nomes, he had put the gods in their shrines, he had established their offerings, he had founded their shrines, he had made their bodies like that [with which] their hearts were satisfied'. The remainder of the text continues in a way that catches our attention: 'So (šw) the gods entered (ꜥḳ) into their bodies of every [kind of] wood, of every [kind of] stone, of every [kind of] clay, or anything which might grow upon him [Ptah as the earth-god Ta-tenen].'[73] Admittedly, this passage does not seem to mention, at any rate at first glance, an ever-recurrent habitation of his image by the god such as was referred to in the later testimonies cited above. The reason is that they referred to images that were receiving regular and continuous veneration, whereas the Memphite theology is referring to the once-and-for-all act of creation. But it does at all events draw a clear distinction between the deity and its statue. First the gods are formed, then they obtain a body according to their desires, and finally they enter into this body. On top of all this the verb 'to enter (ꜥḳ)' is employed in the Memphite theology passage, and as we know this is also used to denote the temporary habitation of the image by the god.

On the further question as to whether this habitation took place once and for all, i.e. was regarded as restricted to the act of creation, or whether it was thought of as repeated, it should be pointed out that the construction šw ꜥḳ nṯrw m ḏt.sn can be construed as an iterative present: 'And so the gods enter [time and again] into their bodies.' It is therefore possible to claim that this passage wholly supports our hypothesis. How far back does this take us? The classical studies of the Shabaka text assigned it to the Archaic period or to the Old Kingdom.[74] We believe, for reasons that we cannot go into here, that the latter dating is likely, and within that period we are inclined to assign it to the turn of the Fifth and Sixth Dynasties, when for some generations the Heliopolitan Re appeared less frequently in royal names (Asosi, Unas, Teti, Pepi), allowing a free development of Memphite theology around Ptah. But we must also reckon with late interpolations. It is only our passage which seems to be out of place in the text as a whole, not only as regards its location and its subject-matter. As has long been recognized, it refers to the local gods and so on as part of the creation, although an account of the act of creation as a whole had already been given; moreover, it has nothing to say about the word of the creator, although in the main part of the text it is through this that Ptah exercises his power; on the contrary, it refers to him as the earth-god upon whom earthly materials grow.[75] For this reason one has some misgivings that this splendid piece of testimony may be of late date, perhaps even compiled under the influence of theological doctrines about the relationship between the god and his image. Such an interpolation might well have been made by the theologians of the Shabaka text themselves, who copied the badly mutilated text in a classicist spirit, in such a way that it was 'finer than before' – i.e., in the prosaic language of modern times, with all kinds of distortions.[76] If this is so, the passage would not substantiate our hypothesis; nevertheless it deserves attention for its own sake, since it poses the problem very soundly.

Ritual performed to vitalize the image

At whatever time the separation between the gods and their images took place, at the start they were thought of as identical. But we must add that from early times onward Egyptians were not satisfied with just fashioning an image, i.e. with the creation of a work of art. On the contrary, a ritual was performed on the statues while they were still in the sculptor's workshop (the 'gold house'), as a result of which the work of human hands was thought to come alive. This ceremony of 'opening the mouth' had the purpose of making all the organs serviceable and so vitalizing the image. It is moreover easy to understand that this rite was also performed on mummies. The surviving sources which mention the ritual performed on statues go on to mention acts and texts relevant to embalmment, sacrificial ritual and certain temple rituals.[77] This sacred act of animating the image, if nothing else, entitles us to exempt the Egyptians from the charges hurled at them by Old Testament writers for pagan idol-worship, which the Israelites themselves often copied, to the effect that the heathen were praying to inanimate material or the work of human hands.[78] The ancient Egyptians would have agreed that the material and the sculpture fashioned from it were inanimate; this was why they were given vitality by the ritual. But later, and precisely at the time when they came into contact with Israel and the Jews of the Diaspora, the deity was thought to be in the heavens, and only to take up a temporary residence in his image after the necessary rite had been performed. For this reason the long-winded reproaches directed by the author of the so-called Wisdom of Solomon, who probably wrote in Alexandria at the end of the Ptolemaic period, against Egyptian iconolatry in particular miss the point.[79] As with all such polemical controversies, one finds it difficult to say whether the propagandist distorted the truth wilfully or from ignorance. The Greeks, who lacked a theological literature on such matters like that which existed in Egypt, found themselves in a difficult situation. Plato takes refuge in the statement: 'While we are honouring [them], although not endowed with life (εἰκὼν ἄψυχος), we do not vainly imagine that the gods who are endowed with life (ἔμψυχος), feel a great goodwill on this account, and gratitude toward us.'[80] An Egyptian might have argued, in a less convoluted and more convincing way: 'We believe that in what appear to be statues not endowed with life we do in fact worship the power of the gods present in them, who are endowed with life.' Similarly, those Greek writers who defended heathen iconolatry against the attacks of those Christian polemicists who simplistically identified the image and the god, used different arguments, which were much weaker than those of Egyptians would have been, with their treasury of theological writings: the Greeks pleaded, for example, that the images were not the actual deity but only reminiscent of them.[81] On the other hand, the views of the Neo-Platonist Iamblichus to the effect that sacred images were imbued with the presence of God seem to reflect the solid structure of Egyptian theology – although he may have been influenced by rather similar ideas of Syrian or Mesopotamian origin.[82]

Concept of 'ba'

It would be tempting to conclude this study of Egyptian religious thought with a historical survey. But the material does not lend itself to any rough-and-ready arrangement along simple lines. There are many contradictory features, some of which may of course be resolved on closer inspection.

Let us select one case which illustrates this: the theological content of the concept ba (*bꜣ*). (For its anthropological connotations, see pp. 205 f.) It will be recalled that it is usually the ba of the god which descends from heaven and enters the image. This conveys the impression that the ba, in the guise of a bird and therefore quite free to move about, represents the living substance of the deity which is imparted to the inanimate image. Such an impression is bolstered by the fact that the chief characteristic of ba was its divine nature: 'Thou seest with thine eyes, hearest with thine ears, speakest with thy mouth, walkest with thy feet; thy ba is divine in the duat [nether world]' – this is what we are told about the dead in the so-called Book of Breathings.[83] As seeing is to eyes and hearing to ears, so is its divine quality to ba. In fact the ba is not a kind of inferior deity; on the contrary, great gods are readily referred to as ba, and for a king contemplating the hereafter the desire to become ba outweighs even that to become god.[84] On the other hand, and this completes the circle, in late testimonies we find earthly beings – as a rule living animals – called the ba of a god. The phoenix is the ba of Osiris; the ram the ba of Re, Shu and Osiris; the crocodile the ba of Sobek; the Apis bull the ba of Osiris, etc.[85] Thus on one hand the ba of a god represents its divine substance and vitality, which it imparts to the image; yet on the other hand it denotes precisely inferior earthly creatures and raises them to the level of forms of the sublime God.

This apparent contradiction can be explained without 'salto mortale'. Let us take a spell from the Book of the Dead which serves to make the dead man appear as a divine falcon, thereby giving him both its power and its mobility. There we are told first of all: 'I have appeared (*ḫꜥ.kwi*) like a divine hawk.' But the continuation runs: 'Horus [i.e., the falcon-god] has endowed (*sꜥḥ*) me with his ba.'[86]

Here, in our opinion, we have the vital link. Like the images we heard about earlier, the dead received Horus's ba, his most sublime divine substance; consequently he is now, as a falcon, an aspect (ba) of Horus in the opposite sense; that is to say, as an inferior being he embodies the ba of the superior one, and does so because (and after) he has received it. It has been well said that originally the ba was not a part of anything (and therefore not a 'soul' either), 'but on the contrary a concept of totality... designed to differentiate a divine being from human subjection to form'.[87] The analysis we have made corroborates this, for the ba is in fact the vitality and divine substance which either gives life to inanimate material or elevates from within living earthly creatures.

It is obvious what significance such an open-ended concept could have for the central concern of Egyptian theologians: incarnation. This deserves thorough investigation, in which due attention would have to be paid to the linguistic evidence. In brief, in Egyptian sentences which express an equation between subject and predicate noun, besides the simple juxtaposition ('my sister = Sothis', i.e. my sister is Sothis), one occasionally finds a construction with the preposition m. This preposition has the basic meaning of 'in', and is used here to express identity, e.g.: 'He whom we serve [is] in him', meaning 'he is the one we serve'.[88] Such constructions are apparently the philological equivalent of what takes place theologically when a god takes up his abode in another and unites with him. We do indeed find an m used to express the identity of the gods concerned in such unions. This occurs where the personal names of the partners are given and some kind of statement is made: e.g., 'Ptah [is] in Amon', meaning 'Ptah is Amon'; 'Min [is] in Anubis,' meaning 'Min is Anubis'.[89] This also shows that theological speculation enters even into private names, although apparently only rarely. But by this we do not wish to suggest that Egyptian theology had a popular quality. It was certainly not popular in the sense that the common people could follow the theologians' train of thought. But it did provide for the needs of the faithful because it helped to give the Egyptian gods a living presence. It could do so because it could enhance the power of the gods whom men worshipped and in the last instance because it revealed, as well as concealed, the one God who stood behind the numerous deities of the pantheon.

8 · Egyptian cosmogonies and doctrines of evolution

In the foregoing chapters we have seen that Egyptians saw men's thoughts and actions on earth as subject to the will of the gods and that they lived out their allotted span of years as *homines religiosi*. We have only mentioned in passing such questions as how they thought the world began and would end. We learned, for example, that in hymns God was praised as creator and preserver, and that as lord of fate he held sway over life and death (see pp. 72 ff., 80). We may now turn to the two marginal areas of earthly existence, birth and death, beginning with the former.

It may appear unsystematic to consider the world's origins after having discussed matters concerned with the world that exists. But this is not really so. For *homo religiosus* – which is to say all men on earth, for here our existential experience accords with the findings of scholarship – the relationship with the divinity throughout the course of this life is the most important thing; this is certainly the starting-point of religion as such. We tend to be held in thrall by the arrangement of the Old Testament, which begins with the creation. But we then realize that this arrangement is deliberately topical rather than chronological. Chronologically, the classical account of the creation compiled by the priestly writers (Genesis i–ii. 4a) is preceded by legal maxims based upon Yahveh's authority, as well as numerous sayings which God spoke through the mouths of the prophets concerning Yahveh's earthly purposes and deeds and, finally, traditional accounts of historical events, like the exciting tale of the succession to David's throne (2 Samuel vi ff.; 1 Kings i–ii), which portray God's direction of mundane affairs.[1] The second and earlier account of the creation, that of the Yahvist (Genesis ii. 4b ff.), is likewise by no means the earliest literary document concerning the religion of Israel. Its anthropocentric tendency already points distinctly to the relationship between God and man, which is given full expression in the subsequent story about the Fall of Man. Thus the religion of Israel also dealt first with life on earth, not the creation, and we are within our rights in treating Egyptian teachings about the creation and evolution of the cosmos at this point, after discussing the relationship between God and man in the world. Our use of two terms, creation and evolution, may seem like a clumsy paraphrase, but in fact the two phenomena are distinct in Egypt; it is precisely this distinction (and also of course the evidence of links between them) that will chiefly concern us here. The creation of the world belongs to the realm of faith. To say that God has created the world is to make a profession of belief. The evolution of the world, on the other hand, is something open to scientific investigation – even when, as in Egypt, it always remained within the domain of myth.

The fairest and most expedient course would be to introduce the reader to the principal sources, but unfortunately their character and condition militate against this. We do have a kind of composite doctrine on the creation in the Shabaka inscription frequently cited above, but this has not been handed down in a reliable form: one suspects that this relatively ancient text has had quite a history of its own, i.e. that interpolations have been added to it (see p. 155). On the other hand we have an abundance of more or less scanty references in the most varied texts which give us some very disjointed information about Egyptian notions concerning God the creator and the evolution of the world (and of life on it). In view of this it seems advisable to proceed from the main aspects of the phenomena in question and to see what the sources have to say about them.[2]

Creation

So far as the creation of the world is concerned, we must first of all look at the question of the way in which the creator acted. In part of the so-called Berlin Hymn to Ptah God is praised as the creator in the following terms: 'He who has made (*nbi*) all gods, men and animals; he who has created (*iri*) all lands and shores and the ocean in his name "fashioner of the earth" (*ḥmww tꜣ*).'[3] Naturally there are some specific features here which we shall leave out of account for the moment: the references to God as a craftsman – for the verb *nbi* denotes melting and casting, and a 'fashioner (*ḥmww*)' means simply any sort of artisan. Let us therefore go on to quote the testimony of the owner of a writing-palette from the Nineteenth Dynasty, which says in general terms of Ptah that it was he 'who created (*iri*) things that be; who made (*km*s) that which exists'.[4] This general concept of God as creator is corroborated by a mass of testimonies.[5] It deserves pride of place because it expresses the phenomenon of God's creation of the world with embryonic purity, and attests undeniably the existence of such an idea in Egypt. Other variants appeared later; but this expresses the idea in a concise form that may seem natural to us because of the parallels in neighbouring Israel; it is, however, entirely absent in early Greece, where we hear only of the evolution of the world and the gods.[6]

The creator-god as craftsman

It will be simplest first to look at the various ways in which the creator worked. Ptah, as we have seen, was depicted as an artisan or more precisely as a smith and metal-worker.[7] It would of course be wrong to link particular crafts historically with certain deities, and to argue, for instance, that Sokaris was by origin a goldsmith and that his function was merely transposed to his great Memphite neighbour Ptah.[8] Only one craft is an exception and may be singled out here: that of the potter, which had a very strong association with Khnum, who forms living creatures upon his potter's wheel; this activity is regarded as so characteristic of him that elsewhere it is said of Ptah, as a self-procreated primordial god: 'Thou art thine own Khnum.'[9] So far as we are aware, Khnum's creative role as potter is confined to living creatures. If this god is mentioned as creating the earth, a different kind of imagery is employed. For instance, Khnum is 'the very great God who has fashioned (*ḳd*) [as potter] gods and men, who has moulded (*grg*) this country with his hands'.[10] If the objects created are to be referred to, then it is said, for example, that Khnum was the god 'who fashioned with his hands all that exists'.[11] In both cases Khnum is a craftsman, one who works with his hands; but the first quotation clearly shows the tendency to limit his work as potter to the fashioning of living creatures.[12] We shall return later to this particular aspect of the creation (see pp. 183 ff.).

MER

God as procreator

In the second place, and in a very different way from his activity as craftsman, God functions as procreator. These two processes are not mutually exclusive, as is apparent from what is said about Khnum. This ram-shaped, or at least ram-headed, god is for the Egyptian the embodiment of virility: 'he who begot (*wtt*) gods and men', etc.[13] A god who possessed such natural generative power was predestined to be the creator. He became the subject of various mythical images (probably limited to particular localities) relating to his procreative role (see pp. 183 f.). The classical doctrine of the procreation of the world was formulated in the Heliopolitan system. Its main features were set down in the Pyramid Texts; it must have taken shape during the Fifth Dynasty at the latest. According to this doctrine the procreator is Atum as the primeval god, and his work is presented as a theogony. The primeval god begets first air and moisture (Shu and Tefnut),[14] and these in turn bring forth earth and sky (Geb and Nut); the beings who comprised the next generation – Osiris and Isis, Seth and Nephthys – evidently represent the political powers of the terrestrial world, naively identified with Egypt. The link between nature and history is represented by Geb, who as earth-god is at the same time primeval king, so that later the ruler of the earth is seated 'upon the throne of Geb'.[15] In his quality as ruler he also settles the conflict between his sons Osiris and Seth. The text we have makes his judgement appear as a triumph for Osiris over Seth. 'Geb has seen your nature and has set you in your place... Geb has put his sandal on the head of your foe, who flinches from you' – these are the words used to portray Osiris's victory and Seth's humiliation.[16] The judgement can, however, also be represented as the verdict of a court presided over by Geb. This occurs when Seth is exhorted to remember 'this word which Geb spoke, this threat which the gods made against you in the Mansion of the Prince at Heliopolis,[17] because you threw Osiris to the earth'.[18] Here we can merely note the vivid transition from the creation of the world to the political powers within it.[19]

To return to our main theme, it was thought that the first act of creation was effected by the primeval god without sexual intercourse (since there was as yet no partner for him): 'Atum who masturbated in Heliopolis. He took his phallus in his grasp that he might create orgasm by means of it, and so were born the twins Shu and Tefnut.'[20] Atum thus performed the first procreative act by onanism. The first couple was thought to have been begotten out of his mouth. This led to another concept, based upon one of those plays on words we are already familiar with. By this Shu is derived from 'spitting out (*išš*)' and Tefnut, moisture, from 'expectorating (*tf*)' on the part of the primeval god.[21] This idea was translated into various myths, which we cannot examine here. Evidently Shu and Tefnut played a secondary role in the construction, and the Heliopolitans' primary interest lay in the earth-god and his celestial partner.[22] On the other hand it should be emphasized that this theogony is really a cosmogony, since the couples first created embody natural forces which immediately assume the form of the ordered realm of Egypt.[23]

Finally, the fact that procreation was one of the chief ways in which the world was thought to have been brought into being is reflected in the broad meaning attached to the word *msi*, 'to bring forth'. This is used mainly to denote the bearing of a child by its mother, but in relation to the gods it is employed also for procreation by the father (e.g., in regard to Re in the name of Ramses, literally: 'It is Re who has brought him forth'); it can thus have the general sense of 'to create'.[24] In this context it may also be noted that this classical Heliopolitan concept of procreation need not by any means be described in this grossly sensual way, as onanism, but may be referred to simply and briefly as 'bringing forth (*msi*)'; it was Atum who 'brought forth' Shu and Tefnut.[25]

Creation through God's word

A third mode of creation, again completely different from the foregoing ones, is through the word of the creator. This, too, was turned into a classical doctrine in Egypt, which centred not on Atum of Heliopolis, as the previously mentioned one did, but on Ptah of Memphis. The sequence we have chosen is in accord with the chronological sequence of the sources. Although there is much uncertainty about dating the Heliopolitan system,[26] and especially the theology of Memphis,[27] one thing is certain: the treatise on the nature, rank and role of Ptah is related *expressis verbis* to the theogony of Atum, as described above. The Ennead into which the Heliopolitan group finally developed is expressly mentioned by name: 'Whereas the Ennead of Atum came into being by his semen and his fingers, the Ennead [came into being according to Memphite theology by][28] the teeth and lips in this mouth, which pronounced the name of everything, from which Shu and Tefnut came forth, and which was the fashioner of the Ennead.'[29] With this sentence we have arrived at the quintessence of the doctrine of creation through the word. It is 'the mouth which pronounced the name of everything (*r mʒṯ rn n iḫt nbt*)' from which Shu and Tefnut came forth, followed by the world of nature and ordered human history, embodied in the Ennead. It is consistent with this idea that later the word of the creator-god should be said to have established the means for sustaining life in the physical sense and the principles of order which regulate man's social and moral existence: 'Thus the *kʒw* were made and the *ḥmwswt* were appointed, they who make all provisions and all nourishment, by this speech. Thus justice was given to him who does what is liked and injustice to him who does what is disliked. Thus life was given to him who has peace and death was given to him who has sin', etc.[30]

The theology of Memphis also tells us how the creative words come about: they are 'what the heart thought (*kʒi*) and the tongue commanded (*wḏ*)',[31] i.e., they are produced by the deity in that part of his body which is the seat of life and thought, and are then made known as an utterance. Thus it is certainly no coincidence that in Memphite theology sentences are inserted which are concerned with the role the heart and tongue play in the living organism. It remains in doubt whether, according to Junker's ingenious interpretation, these sentences already existed as an independent treatise and were then erroneously and awkwardly incorporated in small units into the theological text by those who transcribed it during Shabaka's reign, or whether they were added as the result of a genuine literary development sponsored by the theologians' concern with the word of the creator-god; the latter explanation is much simpler but may therefore be more appropriate.[32]

What was the basis of this idea of creation through the word? One might make two points. First, we have here the ancient concept of identity between the word and the object it describes; for this reason the mouth which 'pronounced the name of every-thing' (l. 55) was thought capable of really creating things; on the other hand, things do not exist unless they are named, and thus the primeval condition may be termed 'when the name of any thing was not yet named'.[33] Secondly, we must realize that in a sacrosanct monarchy people automatically carried into effect the commands given to them – and it was a 'command (wḏ)' that issued forth from the god's tongue in our text (l. 56).

We cannot leave this subject without recalling at least one more important example of this. It is found in a Heliopolitan derivation of 'Utterance (Ḥw)' and 'Perception (Siȝ)', two concepts personi-fied as gods, from the primeval god Atum. Their meaning alone suggests that they are simply parallels to the tongue and heart of the god who creates through the word. They are indeed incorpo-rated into the theology of Amon and given these locations: 'Per-ception (Siȝ) is [Amon-Re's] heart, Utterance (Ḥw) is his two lips.'[34] They had chronological precedence over the gods whom they themselves formed, i.e. by bringing forth the thought in the mind of the primeval god; this is made clear by an annotation in the Coffin Texts: 'These ancestral gods (nṯrw imyw bȝḥ) – this is "Utterance" and "Perception".'[35] The Egyptologist naturally asks whether the Heliopolitan terms Ḥw and Siȝ were devised in imitation of the role which the tongue and heart played in Mem-phite theology, or whether, on the contrary, the latter were based on an existing Heliopolitan term. In either case the choice of these terms ('utterance' and 'perception'; 'tongue' and 'heart') can be explained by the fact that the two doctrines had to compete with each other, as so often happens in the history of religion. In our view the primacy of Memphis seems more likely, because here there was a consistent teaching about creation through the divine word. In Heliopolis, where the theogony was based essentially upon the idea of procreation, the elements concerned were foreign bodies, which may, like so much else here, have been drawn on in a secondary capacity.[36] For the historian of religion it is enough to have ascertained that the splendid idea that the world was created through God's word, by speech and thought, definitely existed in Egypt during the latter part of the Old Kingdom. Its dual form is naturally based upon a single conception, the like of which one would not expect to find twice within such a tiny compact area. We ourselves are familiar with the idea of creation through the word from the Old Testament. In conclusion it may therefore be noted that the points of contact between the Biblical account and ideas in Egypt, and also in Mesopotamia, have long since been recognized; this has been treated very fully in L. Dürr's monograph on the subject.[37]

Time of the creation; 'the first time'

Thus Egyptians saw the world as created by fashioning, by pro-creation and by the word. The question now arises: *when* did this creation occur? To most people this seems a misleading question, since either we can simply say that the creation of course took place at the beginning of time, or else we can give a philosophical answer and say that time cannot be relevant until a world has come into existence. Yet we may abide by our question without abandoning this philosophical insight. For to this question of 'when' the Egyptians gave a most characteristic answer which leads us deep into their way of thinking. The creation took place at 'the first time (*sp tpy*)'. This does not just mean the beginning. It only means the beginning of an event. For 'time' means an event: 'First time defeat of the east', we read in a First-Dynasty source, describing an outstanding event.[38] On the other hand 'time' does not exclude the period after the event; on the contrary, it implies that other 'times' followed, in principle times without number. Indeed, Egyptians did at first measure the passage of time by regularly recurring events, especially the taking of the census, i.e. 'time' was a paradigm to denote periodicity.[39] We shall see in a moment what importance attaches to the simple phrase *sp tpy* and the summary interpretation of it offered here for our understanding of all that follows. For if the concept of beginning is restricted to an event, there can be an eventless existence prior to the creation. Chaos is therefore to be thought of not only as confused but also as monotonous.[40] On the other hand, in so far as the first event was a real beginning, which had to be followed by repetitions of that event, this logically led to the idea, either of a world eternally striving after the *telos* of perfection, or else of periodicity as a continuum of repetitions of the creation. We shall see that the Egyptians did think there was chaos prior to the creation, and that although they did not develop a teleology of a world striving every upwards, they were familiar with the idea that the creation was being continually re-enacted in nature and history; indeed, they considered this idea to be most important.

To be faithful to our principles, we have now to seek the textual evidence for these statements, and in the first place a substantiation of the phrase 'the first time'. It is so common that it is used even to express the primordial time which began with the creation. The combinations 'at the first time $(m\ sp\ tpy)$', 'from the first time $(\underline{d}r\ sp\ tpy)$', 'as at the first time $(m\hat{\imath}\ sp\ tpy)$' all refer to conditions and events to do with the creation and the period immediately thereafter. To mention just one text, we shall choose the introduction to a decree enacted by Amon for the benefit of Princess Neskhon (Twenty-first Dynasty). Here the god is referred to as 'he who began $(\check{s}^3{}^c)$ the earth at the first time'.[41] In other words, the creation of the earth is mentioned both as an act of the first time and as a beginning, which by its very nature requires repetition, if not completion.

As far as such repetitions are concerned, they occur not only in the natural world but also in human history. Let us explain this. In nature the re-enactment of creation comes about daily. Many fine nuances of expression testify to this, and we may quote one that has on the whole been neglected. In the so-called 'new hymn to the primeval gods in the temple at Hibis' (l. 5) we hear of the creator Amon that 'he had directed the stars $(s\check{s}m.n.f)$. This phrase – only couched in the iterative verbal form $s\check{s}m.f$ – is to be found in a Hymn to Amon at Medamud: 'He directs the stars.'[42] In the great litany to the sun-god the same idea is likewise expressed in iterative form: '[Re] puts $(d\hat{\imath}.f)$ the stars upon his path', i.e. he does it afresh each day.[43] But, as is well known, the re-enactment of the creation is manifest above all in the fact that the sun-god emerges every morning from the primeval ocean Nun and by his daily journey ensures order in the cosmos. The account given of his twelfth nightly hour in the nether world is contentious in certain details, but it undoubtedly shows how the personified primeval ocean Nun raises the barque of the day $(m^cn\underline{d}t)$ bearing the morning sun-god in the guise of a scabbard, i.e. as the one 'coming into being'. The accompanying annotation runs as follows: 'These two arms emerge from the water so as to raise this god.'[44] The idea of a new beginning each day is expressed not only in the emergence of the sun-god from the primeval ocean but also in the idea of him as a new-born child who within the span of a single day lives out his life right up to old age and death. We have already discussed this in another context (see p. 145); we can now see that this means that each day nature starts quite afresh, as at the first time. This tallies with the fact that the unordered realms of chaos – which include, for example, as well as the primeval ocean Nun, the '[condensed] darkness (*kkw* [*sm3w*])' – are not abolished by the creation but that they continue to surround the orderly world on every side. This constitutes a constant threat, reflected above all in the much-cited myth about the periodic battle between the sun-god and the serpent Apophis, which is 'repelled' but is not killed because it is an immortal primeval force.[45] In this way each day brings both a confirmation of the order established at 'the first time' and also a forcible reconquest of it.

In the nature of things this warlike trait in the re-enactment of the creation is particularly evident in the historical sphere. Here the king functions as an incarnation of the primeval god. Just as Re, while traversing the sky, repels Apophis, so '[the king] drives out confusion (*isft*) in that he has appeared as Atum himself'.[46] The result of a battle in which the king 'drove confusion (*isft*) out of the Two Lands' is expressed tersely and authoritatively in the following words: 'Order (*m3ct*) is firmly in its place...and the land is as it was at the first time.'[47] The historical action of the king thus corresponds to the natural cycle and is designed to maintain or regain by force that which was established at the creation: the maat, manifest in human history as right political order. As we know, for mankind maat was simultaneously a gift and a duty to be fulfilled (see pp. 113 ff.). The fulfilment of this duty was the climax of the historical role which the king, as the heir to the procreator-god, had to play in the cosmic drama.[48]

We have thus proved what was said above about the need to repeat 'the first time'; it was indeed repeated in nature and in history. This illustrates the peculiar view held by the Egyptians about these two spheres. We can now attempt to understand the full import of the basic law of periodicity which permeates them and which links them in a way that seems so strange to modern man.[49]

But in this context another point deserves to be made which also concerns the Egyptian concept of time. The created world was visualized as having had a beginning in time. Would it therefore have an end in time? The answer to this must be yes. One chapter heading in the Book of the Dead contains the ominous words of the primeval god Atum that he, who himself had come up from chaos, would outlive the world he had created: 'The earth will appear again as the primeval ocean (Nun), as an infinite flood (*ḥḥw*) as in its initial state. I am that what remains...after I have changed into a snake whom no man knows, whom no god sees.'[50] Nun, the predominant power in chaos, whose nature is infinite, will at the end be All, and Atum no more than an obedient primeval serpent; if neither man knows it nor God sees it, this is simply because by that time there will be neither man nor God. *Les jeux sont faits*; the play of life is over; the 'mimetic role' in nature and history has come to an end. We have deliberately resorted to existentialist terminology, for our text deserves to be considered a contribution to the philosophical or scientific literature on evolution; it belongs to this realm rather than to the realm of religion. For a belief in God the creator leaves no room for the idea of a relapse into chaos,[51] and a belief in burial rites and the judgement of the dead implicitly grants the prospect of eternal life to terrestrial creatures and the values for which they stand. In the existentialist view creation can come to an end. Religious persons must believe and hope that it will be eternal.

This concept of the boundlessness of time brings us to the second question raised by the Egyptian phrase 'the first time'. Does eternity, the object of the beliefs, hopes and wishes of religious man, extend just as far backward, beyond the world's beginnings, as it does forward, to the future? The answer to this is no. Existence has a beginning in time but is open in the direction of eternity. We shall hear more about the latter notion in the next chapter, which deals with Egyptian ideas of death. In Egypt a grandiose and exceedingly complex effort was made to lend a quality of permanence to what is transient. Egyptian artists gave meaning to the the overcoming of death as a 'last time', endeavouring to exclude from their works the element of time, not only from their content but also from their structure (see p. 198). Here we shall mention that the words for 'eternity', *nḥḥ* and *ḏ.t* (which certainly need clarification as regards their basic meaning and mutual relationship; it is, for instance, not clear whether they are applicable to the spatial as well as the temporal dimensions)[52] were throughout Egyptian history wholly oriented towards the future: that is to say, a forward-looking view of infinity. Consequently 'the first time' of the creation contrasts with the concept of 'until eternity' (for example: *r nḥḥ ḏt*). For the Egyptian, in so far as he was religious, existence has a beginning, established by the creator-god, but no end. Individual experience corresponded to the principle underlying the conception of the creation of the universe. There is a well-defined correspondence between microcosm and macrocosm. For the individual, too, was born, or in religious language created (see pp. 183–5); but he was then eternal. Characteristically enough, this is even true of those who possessed *ka*, the hyper-physical vital force. This ka, which thus exists for ever, so that 'to go to it' is synonymous with 'to die' or 'to be resurrected', is created, like man himself (see pp. 183 f.).[35]

To this extent the Egyptian outlook differs from that found in the Old Testament or among Christians. The Egyptian is not familiar with the idea of 'from eternity to eternity', since he posits a concrete event at the beginning of creation and calls it 'the first time'.[54] This again is connected with the fact that his sense of time is oriented toward the future. (We have just looked at some unambiguous evidence of this; it also seems to be manifest in certain linguistic tendencies: to be more precise, the way in which the suffix conjugation, which is at first static and passive, is made dynamic and active.)[55]

The Egyptians' cosmogonic doctrines and their belief in 'the first time' set them apart from the early Greeks. We mentioned this point at the beginning of this chapter, and now is the moment to examine one of the reasons why this may have been so (for it cannot be proved). Was not this 'first time', one wonders, an expression of the Egyptians' pride in their own culture? They had created from next to nothing an autochthonous civilization conscious of its strength. The Greeks, on the other hand, who did not believe in creation but in evolution, may thereby have expressed the outlook of tribes who immigrated into a region which had a rich ready-made cultural heritage, so that, to use the phrase of Philippus of Opus, they only 'continued it to a more splendid end'.[56] And since we are taking refuge in speculation, may not the limitless recapitulations of 'the first time' in Egypt, as well as the belief that realms of chaos continued to exist along with the ordered world, reflect the geographical situation of the country? For time and again – even down to the present day – men in Egypt have had to struggle in order to preserve their small cultivated territory from the encroachment of the desert.

Thus what first appeared a futile question, when Egyptians thought the world had been created, has in fact taken us deep into the essence of the matter. The Egyptian concept of time in particular offers many valuable new insights. We saw earlier that a distinction was drawn between the cyclical line of periodicity, which was applied to human history, and the straight line extending onward to infinity (see p. 76). We now know that the creation itself is among those systems which are repeated periodically upon the cyclical line, and that the straight line runs from 'the first time', its fixed starting-point, into the eternal future aspired to by individual mortals.

Material of creation

We may now turn to another problem, which we have already touched upon here and there. Out of what did the creator bring forth the world? We have seen that a material chaos was thought to have existed. Nun, the primeval ocean, existed before the creation and continued to exist afterwards. This priority is clearly expressed in his common title, 'father of the gods'.[57] As their 'father' Nun simply exists before them; he is not by any means greater than the procreator-god himself, to whom he speaks as follows: 'My son Re, God, who is greater than his begetter and mightier than those who made him.'[58] As we know, each day the sun comes forth out of Nun, as it originally came at 'the first time'. It is therefore addressed in a hymn: 'Rise, rise (*wbn*), emerge from Nun by being rejuvenated in the condition thou didst find thyself in yesterday';[59] the sun-god is a 'hawk who rises [i.e. comes] from the Nun', and so on.[60] But the relationship between the creator and the primeval ocean never got beyond this spatial and temporal relationship.[61] The chaotic ocean could be left to evolve on its own plane; this we shall discuss very shortly. But this leads to cosmic evolution, not to creation. So far as we are aware, it is never said that the creator has created the world *out of* the chaotic material, in the sense of being dependent on it.[62] One exception which will spring to the mind of the specialist reader proves on closer examination to be deceptive. We have in mind the passage in the Berlin Hymn to Ptah: 'What thy mouth produced, what thy hands produced, thou hast taken it out (*šdi*) of Nun.'[63] At first glance, considered in isolation, it looks from this as though Ptah took out of Nun the material he needed for the creation. But, as has been rightly pointed out,[64] in its context this actually contains an allusion to Ta-tenen, 'the land rising [out of the primeval ocean]', which is equated with Ptah; if Ptah took it out of Nun, this does not mean that he fashioned the world out of this material, but on the contrary that he separated what he created from it – which is something quite different, as we shall see in a moment.

The principal feature turns out to be this: the creator-god 'who begot himself (*wtt sw ds.f*)'[65] or 'who came into being by himself (*ḫpr ds.f*)'[66] does indeed rise up from the chaos that existed before the world was created – a chaos into which he, like Atum, may return again one day (see pp. 25 f.), but he does not create anything out of this material. Let us illustrate this point by taking the three main methods of creation. When the creator functions as a craftsman, the material out of which he fashions man is not called 'Nun'. If a substance is mentioned at all, it is some material like clay or straw, taken from the real milieu of the craftsman.[67] In the second method the creator naturally relies on his own procreative power. Finally, when the creation comes about by speech and thought, logically enough objects are generated by the names they are given. The Memphite theology, that hymn to the creative word, does not contain the least suggestion that the word of God needed any ready-made material. Instead of this something quite different happened: the creator Ptah was made one with Nun and his partner Naunet, the material and cosmic primeval powers, as 'Ptah-Nun the father who [begot] Atum, Ptah-Naunet, the mother who bore Atum'.[68] In other words the creator seizes the powers latent in the primeval material and incorporates them into his own being. This occurs because (or occurred when), as a result of cosmic evolution, these powers had become given quantities which a doctrine of creation could not ignore even though it was of an entirely different structure, because it was a basic principle of Egyptian theology that no essential substance should be allowed to lie about unused. The Instruction of Ptah thus swallowed up some heterogeneous matter. If Nun and Naunet are brought into the process of creation in this way, they can only function in or through Ptah, who is the really decisive personage.

Let us again try to make the matter clear by pointing up the contrast with ideas current outside Egypt. According to the great Akkadian creation epic, Marduk of Babylon fashions the world out of Tiamat, the primeval animal he has killed.[69] Ptah, on the other hand, incorporates the primeval powers into his own substance; he thereby becomes All and creates the world through his word, by his own efforts alone. The price the Egyptians had to pay for this was of course the continuation of chaos around the orderly realms of creation (see p. 25).[70]

After these considerations we can go on to assess properly that activity of the creator-god which one may call 'ordering' (in the sense of organizing), but which is referred to in our sources as 'separating'. Everywhere on earth the essential feature of creation is probably differentiation. The Egyptian primordial god is therefore called 'the one who makes himself into millions'.[71] This idea is thought of genealogically, and is therefore seen as taking place in time and in human history. On the other hand, the differentiation of the world in terms of nature is presented as an act which is unique and spatial. The creator separates heaven and earth, which had at first been an undivided whole.[72] (This idea was not confined to Egypt.) Already in a Pyramid Text we hear of the time 'when the sky was separated from (wpi) the earth, when the gods ascended to the sky'.[73] The primeval beings attested to this; it is they 'who saw the separation (wpt) of the sky from the earth'.[74] The theogonic doctrine of Heliopolis took over this idea and gave it a classical formulation. The air-god Shu, son of Atum, separates the sky-goddess Nut from the earth-god Geb, by raising her up. This is said to have been done in obedience to an order by the Heliopolitan primeval god.[75] The role of separator is not, however, confined to Shu. It is also ascribed to Ptah, in his association with Sokaris and Osiris; he is 'the great God who has separated the sky from the earth'.[76] The same role is also conferred upon Upwawet of Assiut (and Abydos), who is praised as the one 'who has separated the sky from the earth'.[77] The idea of a separation of the sky from the earth is also implicit where we hear that a deity 'raises up the sky', which had therefore originally been beneath. On this point, among other things, there are testimonies bearing upon Ptah which in a most remarkable way take us right into the heart of his activity as creator, by equating him with Shu:[78] 'Ptah, Lord of maat...who lifted up the sky and created ($\mathit{\mathit{iri}}$) things that be...; who made (iri) the human beings and gave birth (msi) to the gods'; or: 'Ptah, Lord of maat, who raised the sky, who found (gmi) that which exists and gave birth (msi) to all that is.'[79] Here it is clear from the context that Ptah is not a god limited by his function of separating the sky from the earth, but that he is free to act and that he creates as he separates. The same is true of Khnum of Esna, of whom we are told that he raises up the sky.[80] At the end of this line of development stands Isis, as depicted in Greek aretalogies. This Egyptian figure, risen to the rank of an almighty Hellenistic goddess, is here made to say: 'I have separated the earth from heaven.' In this case, too, the arrangement of the text shows that the creation of the world is meant, for the next sentence runs: 'I have directed the course of the stars.'[81] Thus in Egypt the separation of natural phenomena is another expression of the creative act. To be sure, a strong influence is exerted here by the idea of cosmic evolution, and it is time for us now to discuss this other basic aspect of Egyptian cosmogony.

Mythology of creation and scientific thought

When discussing Egyptian ideas about when the creation occurred and out of what the world was made, we came upon the notion of primeval matter, which was deemed to have existed already prior to the event of 'the first time' and which could serve the creator as a substance to work with. We have seen how the creation, visualized as an event, led to a weakening of the idea that the creator needed to have some raw material to order what already existed. We have noted that Nun was the cardinal concept denoting primeval matter, and that he embodied the primeval ocean. Nun was not the only substance that existed before the creation: he became the embryo of a body of mythology, drawn from nature, concerned with the evolution of the world.[82]

This mythological system was based first of all upon the provision of a female partner for Nun (who grammatically was male). This was Nunet, or as the Greeks called her, Naunet. Nunet was the name given to the counter-heaven beneath the primeval ocean. The myth-makers went on to form two pairs, which to all appearances emphasized and personified the qualities of the primeval ocean: Huh and Hauhet, Kuk and Kauket. The former meant boundlessness, the latter darkness. To round off the myth, there appeared another pair, Amon and Amaunet, representing the air, which as we shall see directly added a characteristic new element to the boundless and dark primeval ocean.[83] Nun and Naunet, Huh and Hauhet, Kuk and Kauket, Amon and Amaunet together form a group of four pairs, commonly called the Ogdoad. The town where this mythological system was apparently devised was called 'the [town of] eight' (*Ḥmnw*) – a name which has survived down to the present day: the Copts called it Shmun (perhaps indicating the two parts of the town) and the Arabs used the dual form Ashmunayn ('the two eights'). This place, situated in central Egypt, which had such historical and spiritual significance, is generally known as Hermopolis, following the Egyptian and Greek tradition; according to this the local god was Thoth, whom the Greeks equated with Hermes.[84]

In this system three points are worth mentioning. First of all, it is concerned with cosmic matter, not with organic life; secondly, this cosmic matter is personified as mythical figures; finally, the stress laid on the physical qualities of the primeval substance testifies to the existence of a scientific spirit. As far as the first point is concerned, we have to keep an eye open for other sources which do cater for the evolution of life within this framework of inorganic matter; we shall come back to this later. The second point makes us conscious that for all the interest in science, the idiom employed was that of myth, so that physics never became secularized in Egypt (see pp. 8 f.). Finally, the third point makes it clear where the borderline lies between cosmic evolution and cosmic creation, for here there is keen interest in the quality of the primeval substance, which is merely hinted at in the doctrines of the creation. Certainly, and this again underlines the unbroken link between science and religion in Egypt, no hard and fast borderline was drawn between the primeval material and the creator or what he created. On the contrary, at the point where existence became evolution the phenomena of chaos acquired a double aspect: they then appear simultaneously as substance and energy and set the inert mass in motion. For this is just what happens when the air, which is itself a kind of matter, becomes a storm over the primeval ocean. 'At first calm and motionless, hovering over the sluggish primeval ocean Nun, invisible as a nullity, it [the air] could at a given moment be set in motion, apparently of itself, could churn up Nun to its depths, so that the mud lying there could condense into solid land and emerge from the flood-waters, first as a "high hillock" or as an "Isle of Flames" near Hermopolis.'[85] This primeval hillock took shape by itself, without any act of creation, by means of the elements (which admittedly were conceived of as deities); out of it were formed the elemental gods of the earthly world and, by creating light, the order within it. 'They step upon the primeval mound ($k\dot{3}\dot{i}$) and "create ($km\dot{3}$) light ($\check{s}w$)".'[86] For this reason they are called 'fathers and mothers who made the light ($i\dot{r}\dot{i}$ $\check{s}w$)' or 'men and women who created the light ($km\dot{3}$ $\check{s}w$)'. In one text which elucidates the process of creation the elemental gods are referred to as those 'who made the light as [i.e. through] the radiance (m $m\dot{3}wt$) of their hearts'. If this last-mentioned testimony remains restricted to the scientific plane, by making light develop out of radiance, the scanty formulations of the former point to the personal creation of something entirely new. It is cast in the imagery of birth, for mention is made of fathers and mothers; indeed it is said plainly that these male and female gods 'gave birth ($ms\dot{i}$) to the sun-god'.[87]

We trust that these sources have shown in a sufficiently intelligible way that the borderline between cosmic evolution and cosmic creation is a fluid one and that scientific and religious ideas interpenetrate one another. Let us attempt to give a brief systematic interpretation. The cosmic matter condensed into divine figures *a limine*. The doctrine that they evolved through motion (air) is cast in terms of myth. It can thus make contact with the religious phenomenon of creation, the appearance of the totally Other at a particular moment in evolution: primeval matter brings forth the light of the sun and with it life and order in the world. The immanent process of development is interrupted by the act of creation.

Let us single out one more fact which may show us how matters looked to a believer – say, a theologian of the god Amon, who in his manifestation as air had been one of the primeval gods but had long since become God in the broadest sense of the word (see pp. 104–6). What does the theologian do in order to provide his god with the maximum possible amount of power? Naturally, as is well known, he equates him with the sun (Amon-Re), but he also includes in his substance, *inter alia*, the primordial ocean Nun. This again takes place in a most remarkable way, in that Amon, the junior god, is ranked ahead of Nun, the senior one; Amon is then referred to as 'Nun the Old One, who evolved first', or 'Nun the Old One, the primeval one of the Two Lands, who created the primeval ones, the king of the gods', or else 'Nun the Old One, who issued forth at the first time (*ḫpr m sp tpy*)'.[88] This implies nothing less than that Nun, by being equated with Amon, is remoulded into a primeval being in the style of the creator-gods, who come into being by themselves 'at the first time'. To put it another way, among the worshippers of Amon the doctrine of evolution was absorbed by a belief in creation; Nun was absorbed by Amon-Re. Pious people prefer to have a power that creates rather than a process of evolution that is comprehensible in scientific, non-religious terms; they want the creator and universal god Amon, not the primeval substance Nun. Since this is so, one cannot rule out the possibility that more thorough thought may have been given to evolution in Egypt than is apparent from the fragmentary tradition which has been preserved for us by the theologians – men who were not concerned so much with the evolution of the world but with its creation, not with Nun and his qualities but with Amon, creator of the world and of life, lord of history, refuge of the afflicted heart (see pp. 105 f.).

Origin of life from an egg

Just now we stressed the point that the conception of cosmic evolution evident in the Hermopolitan doctrine of the eight primeval gods was concerned with cosmic matter, not with organic life. This raises the problem whether the doctrines of evolution inquired into the origin of life itself. This was indeed the case. We can identify at least two concepts from the fragmentary evidence scattered about in numerous different texts. As is only to be expected, these are again mythological notions, but they do justice to the facts in so far as they derive life from life.

First of all there is the myth of the origin of life from an egg.[89] Here the idea is that at one time life as such was brought forth from that mysterious substance which appears to be solid matter[90] but which nevertheless brings forth a young living being. It finds expression especially in the belief that the sun-god in his manifestation as a falcon sprang from an egg, whereupon, by virtue of his importance, life began upon earth. The Book of the Dead, in which man is equated with the most supreme gods, magically usurping their role, has the falcon-shaped god say: 'I am the great hawk which cometh forth from his egg.'[91] A direct relationship between the falcon and the sun is drawn already in the Middle Kingdom Coffin Texts; 'O Re, who is in his egg.'[92] In working through the material touching on the origin of life, one naturally comes upon the inevitable question 'which came first, the chicken or the egg?' For the primordial egg is occasionally referred to as having been laid by a primeval bird: 'the egg of the great cackler (*ngg*)'.[93]

Thereby, incidentally, the doctrine of the primordial egg can be linked to the theology of Amon – both to the doctrine of cosmic evolution (Amon as one of the eight primeval gods) and to the belief in creation (Amon as the creator of the world). Once even Amon is called the 'great cackler',[94] and on another occasion we are told of the sun-god that he 'emerged from the hidden egg as the child of the eight primeval gods'.[95] Here the egg becomes the means whereby life began, an intermediate position between material evolution and divine procreation. It cannot be ascertained for certain whence the concept originated and whether it was confined to a particular locality. The first traces can be authenticated in the Pyramid Texts, where a union with the ibis Thoth takes place in the marshy area of the Delta: 'Go, go to the two [halves of the] egg, go to Pe, to the Abode of Thoth.'[96] But it is quite certain that finally the concept became localized in Hermopolis, where the primordial egg, the origin of all living creatures, was even preserved as a relic. In the inscriptions of Petosiris at any rate we hear about this town that 'it is there that the two halves of the egg lie, together with all the [beings] which emerged from it'.[97] One may wonder whether Thoth, in the manifestation of an ibis, took the concept of the primordial egg from the marshes, paradise of birds, to Hermopolis, where it could become associated with the local doctrine that the world had evolved from eight primordial gods; for this was later held to be the place where the world and life had originated.[98] Of greater importance for us here is the line of development we have just indicated by referring to the egg's intermediary position between primeval matter and the creation. It leads, in late Theban inscriptions, to a characteristic combination with Ptah, who is given the predicate: 'Ptah who created (*ḳmȝ*) the egg which [or: who] emerged (*prỉ*) out of Nun.'[99] Here the doctrine of evolution centred on the egg has clearly been incorporated into the theology of the creator-god Ptah, and furthermore this is linked with the teaching of the world having evolved around Nun, whence the egg or the creator Ptah is said to have issed forth.

Origin of life from a lotus

The development of life out of the egg leads us into the animal world, even though the ornithological species involved is either concealed behind a mythical creature such as the 'great cackler' or else is derived from the falcon or ibis, and thereby from the sun and from Thoth. But we also encounter another embryonic source of organic life, this time in the plant world. This is the lotus, which again is said to have brought forth the sun-god and thereby life itself. In this case our fragmentary literary sources are supplemented by a wealth of pictorial testimony, mainly of late date.[100] We shall omit the question whether this doctrine was localized, in particular whether it was originally applied to the god Harsaphes of Herakleopolis, who as his name suggests is 'the One to be found upon his pond', and is thus most probably a lacustrine plant.[101] What is certain and also of significance for our theme is the circumstance that the doctrine of the primeval lotus, like that of the primeval egg, was associated with the sun-god and in this way acquired far-reaching importance. In the simplest form the sun-god is called 'great lotus who appeared (*ḫʕỉ*) from Nun'.[102] Here the god who creates life is equated with a primeval plant which is said to have emerged at some time or other from the primeval ocean. Much more common was the development of this idea into that of a god seated or standing in the flower, whom we may therefore call 'the god on the flower'. From the wealth of testimony to this we may single out one text which, although it does not mention the primordial substance, does mention a primeval location as its place of origin: '[the sun-god], who emerged from the lotus upon the "high hillock", who illuminates with his eyes the Two Lands'.[103] Here the primeval plant emerges in the same locality where the earth appeared as a hillock out of the primeval ocean; consequently one may claim that this is impressive evidence of the way the evolution of life was associated with the origin of solid matter. To coin a term, we have here a biogony alongside the cosmogony. The actual process whereby the sun-god emerges from the flower is described as a birth: the sun-god is a child, who 'opens his eyes' in the lotus, etc.[104]

Relationship between doctrines of creation and evolution

With this we have illustrated from Egyptian sources the mythological yet scientific view of evolution – to be more precise, of the evolution of cosmic matter and life. We hope we have done justice to it vis-à-vis the religious view that the world and life were created. Nevertheless the division between evolution and creation should not be drawn too sharply. For the testimonies available frequently make doctrines of evolution serve belief in the creation by ascribing them to the creator-gods Re, Ptah or Amon. One may risk the following assertion: most of what is said about Nun and almost everything that is said about the primeval egg and lotus only clarify or describe the notion that something was there prior to the actual creation; over and above this the egg and the lotus are occasionally the medium between the primeval substance and the first procreation or creation. In this respect the doctrines of evolution may be regarded as a kind of aid to the theology of creation. They supplemented from myths about the natural world such phrases about God as that he 'came into being of himself' or that he 'brought himself into being': he could emerge from an egg or a plant, and these principles of organic life themselves originated from the primeval ocean. We think it possible that the formulae just cited about a self-made God are actually a protest against the doctrines of evolution and that they were intended expressly to distinguish the creator-god from the independent course of nature. Since there are only exceptional cases in Egypt of *rabies theologorum*, we have no trace of a direct polemic, and the scientific view was harmoniously subordinated to the religious one.

The faithful could learn something about the evolution of the world in the statements about God the creator. They were in much the same situation as worshippers of Yahveh who listened to the priestly account of the creation; the parallel extends also to the fact that the first words of the Bible, according to the archetypal text, may not have contained a *creatio ex nihilo*. For as is known, these words may be construed as an asyndetic relative clause, and may be translated thus: 'In the beginning, when God created heaven and earth, the earth was without form...'[105] We cannot mention here all the abundant relationships, both phenomenological and historico-genetic, between Egyptian traditions and the Biblical account of the creation. Only one point ought to be made. Our study of the Egyptian material should convince the Christian, whether he is a theologian or not, that the scientific doctrines of evolution were not detrimental to the idea of a creator-god or to faith in him. On the contrary, the creation can be represented in just as sublime a way when account is taken of earlier or current scientific concepts, and when, instead of being given a *creatio ex nihilo*, one is told how, after an eventless existence, an event occurred which brought forth something quite new: order and life. For that 'first time' with which the creation begins in Egypt is, it will be recalled, an event. If the lack of a dogmatic *creatio ex nihilo* should really lead to a loss of religious substance, this is reintroduced a thousand times over by the chance of reaching an honest and authentic reconciliation with the scientific aspects. This does not mean that the scientific aspects ought to be recast in mythical form, as was the case in Egypt.

Finally, we may raise a question which, although it leads to a negative finding, takes us back again to the central concern of the Egyptologist, and thus to the point mentioned at the outset of this chapter: can the religious and scientific aspects be separated chronologically – at least in the sense that certain periods were particularly congenial to scientific inquiry? It might be pointed out that during the First Intermediate period men asked themselves questions of an anthropological nature, such as the evolution of the ba ('soul'), and this led them to make and note down empirical observations.[106] One might also recall that it was during the Hermopolitan period that this 'city of eight' acquired a wider significance, so that at this time the doctrine of the eight primeval gods (although formulated earlier) probably acquired a relevance for the entire country. But this is for the time being mere conjecture. We have so little hard and fast information about the dating and textual history of the doctrine of creation centred on Ptah of Memphis presented in the Shabaka inscription that it would be risky to say which city has precedence in the matter.

Let us therefore be content to state, first that the two aspects exist, and second that the tradition which has been handed down to us, concerned as it is with cult and theology, has de-emphasized natural evolution in favour of divine creation. The idea of the creator was constantly reformulated in new hymns of praise; the emphasis is put upon the act of creation at 'the first time'; the glorified creator is represented as coping masterfully with the pre-existent force of Nun; the creator becomes progressively the guardian and finally the lord of the king, and thus the patron of the Egyptian state. All these themes are beautifully expressed in one of the hymns to Ptah, which we shall conclude by quoting extensively: 'Hail to thee, thou who art great and old, Ta-tenen, father of the gods, the great god from the first primordial time who fashioned mankind and made the gods, who began evolution in primordial times, first one after whom everything that appeared developed, he who made the sky as something that his heart has created, who raised it by the fact that Shu supported it, who founded the earth through that which he himself had made, who surrounded it with Nun [and] and the sea, who made the nether world [and] gratified the dead, who causes Re to travel [thither] in order to resuscitate them as lord of eternity (*nḥḥ*) and lord of boundlessness (*ḏt*), lord of life, he who lets the throat breathe and gives air to every nose, who with his food keeps all Mankind alive, to whom lifetime, [to be more precise] limitation of time and evolution (*ỉ ŝŝỉ rnnt*) are subordinate, through whose utterance (*prỉt m r .f*) one lives, he who creates the offerings for all the gods in his guise the great Nun (here = Nile), lord of eternity (*nḥḥ*), to whom boundlessness (*ḏt*) is subordinate, breath of life for everyone who conducts the king to his great seat in his name, "king of the Two Lands".'[107]

9 · Death and the dead

Creation of man

In the last chapter we pointed out that the Egyptians thought the world that God had created would come to an end. Even in a cosmic dimension, therefore, the concept of death is a correlate to creation and evolution. But of course one thinks of death primarily in the context of individuals. It casts a great shadow over men's minds and has a decisive effect upon their lives. It therefore seems essential to introduce the subject with a few words about the creation of man, to which his death comes as an antithesis. It stands to reason that in our context we shall be concerned with the religious aspects of this problem; whether and to what extent Egyptians may have disregarded the religious aspects of birth and death is something that cannot be given consideration here. The creation of man is part of the creation as such; in that respect the following sentences constitute a supplement to the last chapter.

Let us begin with the notion, frequently authenticated during the Middle Kingdom, that mankind was created out of the tears of the creator-god, especially the sun-god. This myth is based upon one of those ancient popular plays on words that were so pregnant with meaning. The terms used to denote man (*rmṯ*, later *rmt*) and tear (*rmit*) are almost identical in their consonantal structure; consequently, according to an old belief, this verbal identity must indicate a connection between the objects referred to. So far as we are aware, the relevant testimonies are all of a general character; if an allusion was made to man's evolution (as tears) from God's eye, it was common practice to say that they 'came forth from his eye', i.e. the preterite form was chosen in preference to the constant iterative.[1] Thus this myth, based as it is upon an etymological parallel, appears to be organically connected with the process of creation; it evidently does not apply to each new-born child.

It is quite another matter, however, with the idea that the god Khnum fashions man (and his ka) upon his potter's wheel. Here, too, the mythical character is as plain as can be, but the legend is clearly relevant to individuals, and does not merely represent the continuous activity of the creator-god Khnum. We may recall the well-known representation in the mortuary temple of Hatshepsut at Deir el-Bahari, where Khnum is shown actually moulding Hatshepsut (and her ka) on his wheel.[2] It is worth while dwelling on this matter. Khnum (or the ram-gods who eventually are found combined under his name) owes his function as creator of living beings to the ram's virility. This animal, like the bull, was regarded by Egyptians as the very quintessence of fertility.[3] The process whereby this vital energy was transformed into the potter's power to fashion things upon his wheel seems to have taken place at one particular site where Khnum was worshipped: the town of Antinoë. At any rate, the god who fashions Hatshepsut is called 'Khnum, the potter, the lord of Hr-Wr (= Antinoë)'. On this point an appealing hypothesis, as yet unproved, has been put forward to the effect that this may have come about because Antinoë had once been a centre of pottery; such centres of craftsmanship did and do exist.[4] However this may be, the idea undoubtedly became strong as time passed and acquired such force that it became common currency throughout the land.[5] In so far as the myth was just an impressive way of representing the god's activity as creator, it will not surprise us that the Egyptians did not turn it into a dogma but kept it versatile; they even managed to adapt it to the natural process of procreation. In the same account about the procreation and birth of Hatshepsut in which Khnum acts as potter, the god says that he has created the royal child 'in this body of God, the first lord of Karnak', i.e. in the body of Amon, who according to royal dogma was the real father of the king. Consequently Khnum, as he moulds the clay (or because he does so), is deemed to be actually creating the semen in the body of the procreator.[6]

With this we have reached a plane where other gods besides Khnum need to be considered, and this in turn leads to some very important statements about religious matters. Thus we read in the Hymn to Aton from Amarna in respect of Jāti (Aton): 'Thy rays..., creating issue in women, and producing seed in mankind, giving life to the son in his mother's womb.'[7] Another application of this idea is that God created male and female beings in order to carry out his procreative purpose. Precisely this idea is found also in relation to Khnum, of whom we are told, in a text from the Greek and Roman period: 'He made the bulls to make the cows pregnant.[8]' We find corresponding sentences relating to mankind in the approximately contemporary Greek aretalogies to Isis, whose peculiar characteristics will be discussed later (chap. 11). Finally, God may be seen as simultaneously the creator of the genital organs and the first to perform the sex act. At any rate Amon is the one who 'faciens vulvam, creans phallum. Primus injecit semen (*ndmmyt*) in vaccas [?].'[9] In other words, the Egyptians were by no means content with mythical images, but traced the evolution of man back to God in the most natural way, by regarding and representing him as the creator of the genital organs and as the initiator of the sexual instinct. This idea found its way into a large number of personal names which expressed the faith of those who bestowed them by referring to the deity as the creator or donor of their child: 'He whom Ptah has made (*iri*)', 'he whom Osiris (Petosiris) has given', etc.[10] Properly understood, we have here an authentic demythologized religious statement. We should not imagine that the myth of God the potter was earlier than the formulations taken from nature: both sprang from the same belief in God the creator and lord of life. This belief does not wane, nor does it cease – either logically or chronologically. What the Egyptian said about God as the creator of life, either privately or in public worship, in hymns or in personal names, is basically no different from what a Christian mother might tell her little son about God having put him beneath her heart so that she might bring him forth according to the natural process of childbirth.[11]

God as lord of death

If God was the creator of life, he was naturally also lord of death. This is clear from our sources; he performs this function in a general way and also in particular cases. Let us first recall our investigation of the Egyptian concept of fate (see pp. 72 f.), where we learned that fate is understood primarily in the sense of man's allotted span of life. For the Egyptian, as we know, God was lord over fate and thereby also over death. God was seen as wholly sovereign, in a way alien to the Greeks, over the lives of particular individuals: '[Amon] makes a lifetime long or shortens it. He gives more than that which is fated [= lifetime] to him whom he loves;[12] or: 'I caused them [my messengers] to reach Egypt in order to ask from Amon fifty years of life for myself, over and above my fate',[13] and so on. This insight into God's mastery over death, which we have gained from the detailed exposition above and which needs no further elaboration here, is of fundamental importance for what follows. We may add here that, as was widely believed, the gods effected their power over life and death by sending messengers.[14]

Death part of cosmic order

The first point to be made here is that death, fixed by God separately for each individual, was simultaneously visualized as part of the cosmic order. This is already evident from the fact that it is one of those phenomena which did not exist before the creation, and is therefore among those negative elements which were introduced afterwards and which go to make up the world order. It is said of one primeval act of creation (of the dead king by Atum) that it took place 'before the sky existed, before earth existed, before men existed, before the gods were born, before death existed'.[15] Logically, therefore, that being which was there before the creation will 'escape (*nh*) his day of death'.[16] Just as logically, however, even the gods, in so far as they are created beings, are subject to the fate of death. We have already come across ample evidence of this (see pp. 24 f.), and need only add here that this aspect is naturally enough ignored in divine worship. It forms part of the myth of the creation, but is omitted when individual gods are the object of veneration. Theoretically, these positions can be reconciled by making each god a primeval god, so that he no longer counts as a creature and is therefore exempt from death. In practice, matters are simpler: when he prays to God, the pious man does not think at all of these mythical doctrines of creation, but has before his eyes and in his heart God as the quintessence of that power he believes to be effective.

Egyptian attitude to death

This is to say that death is very properly a human problem, and our next task is to consider how the Egyptians responded to it. Here we may first of all make a point which, although it cannot be proved, is very convincing. The Egyptians must have been constantly aware of death, for the Nile valley is a long thin strip of cultivable territory surrounded by lifeless desert; no one in central or Upper Egypt could ever forget the sharp dividing-line between fertile land and desert. For economic reasons burial-places were situated not in the fertile belt but on the edge of the desert, which contributed to the idea that desert and death were linked. All this will have eloquently pointed the lesson taught by our ancient liturgical text: 'In the middle of life we are encompassed by death.' Indeed, the Egyptians made provision for death during their lives on a scale hardly paralleled anywhere else on earth.

This preoccupation with death is something we shall leave until later; we shall deal first with what has been called 'the attitude of the ancient Egyptians to death and the dead' and 'the Egyptian concept of death'.[17] It will be best to begin with the simple question whether there is any evidence in Egypt for man's animal fear of death and the resulting repulsion. The question may be answered by a clear-cut affirmative. In the fragment of the earliest instruction we know, that of Hor-dedef (prior to that of Ptah-hotep), we find the following sentence: 'Lowly [probably: depressing (*dḥ3*)] for us is death; life we hold in high esteem.'[18] The sage recommended men to guard against the misery of death by furnishing their tombs on a lavish scale. One formula which was commonly used from the Middle Kingdom onwards as an appeal to the living runs as follows: 'O ye who love to live and hate to die, speak [the prayer for the dead]...'[19] During the New Kingdom and later there are to be found extremely pessimistic descriptions of the condition of the dead, some of which are worth quoting. In the tomb of Nefer-hotep, from the end of the Amarna period, women lament: 'Thou who [wast] rich in people, thou art in the land that likes solitude. He who loved to spread his legs in walking is bound, enwrapped and obstructed. He who liked to dress himself in rich fabrics sleeps in yesterday's cast-off garment.'[20] Death thus places man in solitude, immobility and outward poverty. It is noteworthy that this lamentation belongs to a portrayal of the ceremony of opening the mouth. This suggests that this outpouring of animal emotion could not be restrained by a ritual which had, after all, been intended to render serviceable the various organs of the dead man's body and to resuscitate him as a whole (see p. 155). One object of the ceremony is to enable the dead man to walk again, but a thrice-repeated phrase in the lamentation maintains that the man's legs are immobile.[21]

A little later, in the time of Ramses II, when the dead Mose is crossing the Nile, men and women cry out: 'He who liked to drink is in the land which hath no water; the lord of many granaries, he hath hastened thither', and the mourners in the funeral procession bewail him in the words: 'Woe for thee who [wast] rich in people. He passeth by all his kinsmen, he hath hastened to the land of eternity and darkness, in which is no light.'[22] Thus, to the short-comings already mentioned in the land of the dead, thirst and darkness are now added. We may point out here that the lack of water is deplored even in the spells in the Book of the Dead, where they are characteristically given a theological interpretation.[23] Four centuries later, during the Bubastite period, Nebneteru, priest of Amon, confesses to his merry enjoyment of life and substantiates his *carpe diem* with the following vision of the con-ditions awaiting the dead: 'The end of life is sorrow, [it] means the inadequacy of that which was with thee formerly, and emptiness in thy possessions, [it] means sitting in the hall of unconsciousness (*nhm-ib*) at the dawn of a morning which does not come..., [it] means not knowing, [it] means sleeping when the sun is in the east, [it] means being thirsty at the side of beer.'[24] To the summary list of the earthly goods lacking we now find added the intellectual deprivation represented by a state of existence akin to sleep, which completes the misery of death. The final reference to being thirsty although some beer is at one's side again indicates doubt as to the efficacy of the ritual to revive the dead man, who was provided with beer but could not drink it.

At the end of the Ptolemaic period the priest's wife Taimhotep describes the fate of the dead in even greater detail. Having recommended the enjoyment of life, she claims: 'The West [i.e., the realm of the dead], that is the land of slumber, a heavy dark-ness, the dwelling-place of those who are there [euphemism for 'the dead']. Sleeping is their occupation. They do not awaken to see their brothers. They cannot behold their fathers and their mothers. Their hearts are deprived of their wives and their children.[25] The water of life, which contains the sustenance of every life, is for me thirst. It falls [only] to him who is upon earth. I am thirsty although water is beside me, I do not know the place where I am [?] since I have come to this valley.'[26] This is followed by phrases which attest to death and men's fear of it; we shall deal with these directly. What we have read does not add any particularly new ideas to the earlier passages, but it does bring out the fear of missing the members of one's family;[27] as for the rest, we need single out only one another note of scepticism about the serviceability of a libation.

All these texts may naturally serve as testimony to the fact that the Egyptians had doubts about the concepts, doctrines and customs concerning the hereafter; for example, doubts about a spiritual existence and about rites intended to revive the dead. We shall come back to this point later. But these passages also demonstrate the very thing that led us to cite them first: man's animal aversion from the event which deprives him of the advantages of earthly existence that can readily be experienced: food and drink, freedom of movement, light, loving kinsmen, and intellectual faculties. It is therefore not surprising if, in the words cited above, 'one hates to die'; or that, in the lapidary formula of Memphite theology, maat is linked to life and injustice to death (see p. 116). We can see that the Egyptian loves life. Only in exceptional times of distress and daily danger does he cry: 'Great and small say: "I wish I might die" '[28] – a regular perversion of the normal formula which expresses the desire to live. Here one must disregard the much-quoted so-called 'One who is Tired of Life' and his conversation with his ba: the old interpretation of this as implying a readiness to commit suicide is now regarded as suspect; it is probably a discussion of the anthropological question raised by death concerning the relationship between the mobile (bird-like) ba and the dead man's body which is bound to his tomb (see p. 206).[29]

To bring out once more the basic motif of these passages, we may cite the wistful confession of a contemporary of Nebneteru, priest of Amon (Twenty-second Dynasty): 'The fleeting moment when one receives the rays of sun stands for more than eternity, since one is ruler of the nether world.' This statement, in which the dead man by inference equates himself with Osiris, king of the beyond, has quite justly been compared to the well-known lamentation of Achilles, where he repels, in the Nekuia, the consolation of Odysseus.[30] In all these testimonies, ranging in date from the beginning of the Old Kingdom to the end of the Ptolemaic period, and with varying degrees of restraint, we can hear the voice of men tortured by fear of the end – less of death itself than of the end of their happy existence and the beginning of something infinitely lengthy and disagreeable. We would not wish to maintain that only in Egypt do we find such voluminous and detailed descriptions of the privations of the dead in the tomb. But the undoubted large number of statements to this effect in Egypt has to be seen as the inevitable antithesis of another concept which survived until after the end of heathen times: the idea of the living corpse, and its impressive but gruesome symbol, the embalming of the body as a mummy.

If there was a life after death, envisaged as a continued corporeal existence; if consequently the body was preserved, a house was built for it and it was furnished after death with everything needed, then sooner or later this life after death had to appear inadequate; the rituals designed to bring about resuscitation came to seem an imperfect substitute; and men came to question the magical reification of offerings through the liturgy that accompanied them. In fact the lamentations about existence in the tomb do read like a list of privations, and are in this respect the antithesis of lists of offerings.[31] The link between them lies in the mention of things which, like beer or water, are indeed there but which the unfortuntate deceased cannot consume. Weighed down in this manner, the Egyptian – despite his anticipation of the hereafter based on equation with Osiris – never seems to have been seized by a yearning for death in joyous hope (not despair) such as was experienced by the early Christians during the age of the martyrs, and which found its classical expression in one of the epistles written by St Paul from prison: 'For to me to live is Christ, and to die is gain...My desire is to depart and to be with Christ, for that is far better' (Philippians i. 21, 23). At any rate we must be careful not to place on the same footing as the word of the Apostle such positive-sounding circumlocutions for death as 'the good fortune'[32] or even the use of its opposite, 'life' (coffin = 'lord of life', etc.). These are but euphemisms which demonstrate precisely the emotion we have described, i.e. an aversion even to pronouncing the word 'death'.[33]

The act of dying

The testimonies we have mentioned did sometimes refer to death and dying as oppressive or hateful, but they were primarily concerned with the conditions prevailing after death. Now we must take a closer look at what was said about the act of dying itself. We shall not be surprised to find it evaluated negatively. Admittedly, this does not seem to be true of its common description as sleep, which comprises the possibility of being awakened or waking up. For instance, a son addresses his dead father: 'O my father,...arise! Take to thyself this water...raise thyself upon your left side and support thyself upon your right side';[34] and then simply: 'This Great One [the dead Osiris] slept, after he had fallen to sleep; awake, raise thyself.'[35] It is, by the way, because of this call to awake that the offering of provisions for the dead was called 'emergence from the call (prt [ḥr] ḥrw)'. Osiris, the ideal of salvation, first of the king and then of all the dead, is called 'he who wakes healthy (rs-wḏꜣ)', etc.[36] No doubt this rests upon a very ancient concept of death, of which traces can be seen in the Neolithic, long before the written tradition began, when the dead were buried in a contracted position, with the head raised, which probably shows that they were laid to rest as if they were asleep.[37] This was directly linked with the offering ritual, which then for its part absorbed the myth: the deceased became Osiris, with all the destinies that befell the latter (see p. 83).[38] But just as this basic concept was maintained as a sort of characteristic guiding line through the service performed for Osiris, so the lamentations cited above show clearly that everlasting sleep was thought of as unsatisfying and undesirable. It was seen as linked with life in darkness. When Taimhotep expressly denies that the dead awake and have contact with their families, it is apparent that, later at any rate, the ritual had lost its power even in this respect. In the dim and distant past men had uncomplainingly accepted death as a kind of sleep; by ritual and myth (which assumed classical form in the belief in Osiris) they had made death bearable as sleep; however, during the period when men awakened to consciousness, the Egyptians, who as a people were intimately bound up with the earth and with the light that shone upon it, broke out in lamentations about the darkness of death; for them sleep now became merely a negative metaphor. There are also linguistic idioms which exclude any positive interpretation, even one limited in time. The most impressive of these is the characterization of death as the despoiler. This has long since been recognized and studied:[39] we now know that it was used particularly in regard to the death of young persons and that it was widely disseminated from the Middle Kingdom onward.[40] The passage in the Instruction of Ani which caused scholars to turn their attention to the matter runs as follows: 'When death comes, he steals away (read *ḫnp* instead of *ḥrp*) the infant which is on its mother's lap like him who has reached old age.'[41] In accord with this negative picture is the speech on the inexorability of death, whose messengers men would gladly seek to turn back by offering them bribes. 'There is no messenger of god who receives gifts in order to neglect [the cause why] he was dispatched', says the father of Petosiris of Hermopolis.[42] These statements are in contrast to the words: 'May death forget you (*smḫ*)',[43] which seems to us pointless and somewhat foolish. Finally, the feelings which animate the victim during his encounter with death are expressed by Taimhotep in an unmistakable way: 'Death, "Come" is his name, he summons everyone to himself. They come immediately to him, although their hearts shudder with fear of him.'[44] Enough has been said on this subject, for a monograph is now available entitled *Death as an Enemy* which takes much further the points made here.[45]

Egyptians' lifelong consciousness of death

If death became increasingly unwelcome to the Egyptian, it was an ever-present menace throughout his life and impinged to a greater or lesser extent upon his earthly existence. Its presence, as we argued above, was driven home upon him by the surrounding landscape. His oasis of culture was embedded in a lifeless waste, and his tombs were located on the edge of the hostile desert. These sentiments were expressed in words and actions. We may begin with the former, for they are so unequivocal as to need hardly any explanation. The scribe Ani includes among the basic principles of his doctrine the warning: 'Go not forth from this house (= die) to one that thou knowest not where [thy] body is to rest. Let every place that thou favourest be known so that [thou] mayest be buried. Set it before thee as thy business...Embellish thy place which is in the desert-valley, the pit which will hide thy corpse. Set it before thee (*imi r ḥȝt.k*) as thy business, which is of account in thy eyes, like unto the great elders, who rest in their sepulchre.' This is followed as a justification by the above-mentioned sentence about death as the despoiler who comes irrespective of age.[46] In short, the choice and preparation of one's tomb is one of the tasks befalling every mortal. The priest Petharpokrates, probably from the Ptolemaic period, praises himself as follows: ' I was one who foresaw (*swn*) at the time when he was strong, who kept in mind (*rdi m ib*) his dying at a time when he was strong.'[47] The context is not given, but we may assume that he took his performance of the mortuary service, so keeping alive the memory of others, as the occasion to express his own *memento mori*. At the end Petharpokrates hopes that in time he too will be covered by the maxim: 'One does [something] for him who [himself] has done [something].' According to this maxim the presence of death causes one concern both about one's own burial and about performing the mortuary service for others. What the wise Ani with remarkable psychological insight formulated as a maxim during the New Kingdom is to be found expressed succinctly in the earliest known Book of Wisdom. Hor-dedef calls on his listeners and readers to 'embellish thy [house] of the necropolis, and enrich thy place in the West'.[48]

Having examined these sentences, we may now pass on to consider men's actions. These speak for themselves, with impressive volume – in the extreme case with the massive bulk of the Great Pyramids at Giza. To be sure, these vast complexes are unthinkable without the royal dogma and the cult of the divine ruler (see pp. 84 f.). But they are equally unthinkable – and this is particularly true of the pyramid itself, as a geometrically stylized gigantic burial mound from ancient nomadic times – without men's lifelong knowledge of death, without their constant reckoning with a reality that only later they could analyse. For the building of such complexes naturally took up a great deal of the king's efforts during his reign. He did exactly what Hor-dedef, or later Ani, demanded: he concerned himself during his lifetime with his abode after death. What is true of the kings holds good for the great lords of the kingdom; the amount of effort was propor-

7

tionately reduced, but the principle was exactly the same. Here mention may be made of an extremely characteristic fact which to the historian of economic and legal institutions illustrates the king's duties towards the feudal lords, but to the historian of religion is of interest because it shows the tremendous impact of death upon the Egyptian mode of life. A successful grandee of the Sixth Dynasty by the name of Uni, who eventually became 'domain supervisor of Upper Egypt', boasts in his biography that the king furnished his tomb for him, and gave him 'a limestone sarcophagus from Tura',49 i.e. one of particularly fine material. What to modern man would seem like a broad hint is quite proper for the Egyptian, who had an intense preoccupation with death and believed that his tomb must be well furnished so that he might be assured of continued existence in the hereafter. Thus a subject of the king can actually ask to be provided with furnishings for his tomb, as the court physician Nenekhsekhmet did to his lord Sahure.50 That it was the king who ensured the sustenance of the dead is also clear from the so-called mortuary offering formula, which (as can be seen from its grammar) calls the king the provider of supplies in perpetuity – a formula based on the actual situation during the early part of the Old Kingdom, but which was still employed after rulers had ceased to make such donations.51

In all this it is worth noting that the relevant measures were of course taken during the lifetime of the person who erected the tomb, and for this very reason could find their way into his biography. It may be added that both the pyramids and the vast private tombs (mastabas) of that period were often rebuilt or expanded on the builder's orders later during his lifetime.52 The inscriptions sometimes contain prayers such as a supplication to be buried in old age, which imply that they were written when the occupier of the tomb was still alive.53 Later the Theban 'feast of the valley' joined the living and the dead in common and bibulous festivities: the families of the dead, in the retinue of Amon, would come to visit this necropolis in the West. Our sources characteristically leave it vague whether those who built tombs and are represented as taking part in this feast did so alive or dead. In any event this annual celebration made death something almost familiar to the people.54 It may therefore be said with certainty that the Egyptians were aware of its presence not only outwardly, from the desert which surrounded their fertile land, but also inwardly. To a considerable extent death prescribed their conduct and accomplishments.

The facts we have just cited might convey the impression that they concerned the upper class alone. However, this is most unlikely, for a variety of reasons. For one thing we must assume that even in ancient times poor people also were anxious to furnish their modest pit-graves with simple offerings of the most vital kind and to prepare at least what was most essential in good time while they were alive.[55] In the second place, we know that in the course of time all the Egyptian dead were mummified and became Osiris, and that the rites necessary for this were performed. Indeed, we know from legal testaments that anxiety to have the right kind of burial determined ordinary people's outlook on life. From the Ptolemaic period we have contracts in which a man making over his property would attach the following condition: 'Thou providest for me when I am alive, thou providest for me when I am dead. Thou attendest to my mummy and my burial.'[56] The entire law of inheritance, no doubt from the earliest times, was founded on that compensatory principle which made acquisition of the legacy mainly dependent upon giving the testator an appropriate burial.[57] Here we are clearly dealing with circumstances that prevailed throughout all levels of society. In conclusion: death was present to every Egyptian in his lifetime, to king and commoner alike; for all men the thought of it governed much of their earthly actions.

There is also impressive negative testimony to this consciousness of death. We hear of a custom which later aroused the surprise of the Greek historian Herodotus, who drew his information in part from personal observation. When the Egyptians are seated at a banquet, he writes, they pass around a deceased person in a container (i.e. no doubt a mummy-like statuette) so as to remind themselves of death and to encourage each other to enjoy life: 'Gaze here, and drink and be merry; for when you die, such will you be.'[58] A genre of banquet songs authenticated from the Middle Kingdom onwards, the so-called Songs of the Harpers, strikes the same note of *carpe diem*, motivated by the inexorability of death.[59] From this it is apparent that even when enjoying a banquet the Egyptian was aware of death, and that he responded appropriately in word and deed; he was evidently sceptical about certain expectations of the life hereafter. Such thoughts are more readily comprehensible on those occasions when the Songs of the Harpers were sung at a banquet celebrated in a tomb, at a great funerary festival, such as the 'feast of the valley'.[60] However this may be, here the Egyptian consciousness of death emerges in high relief, as it were: the sceptical spirit displayed is the very reverse of the confident belief that the supply of provisions to the dead and funerary rites will ensure everlasting life.

In evaluating this material, let us once again draw a comparison with other countries. In his discourses on the Resurrection St Paul cites a phrase from Isaiah: 'Let us eat and drink, for tomorrow we die.'[61] The Old Testament prophet was apparently referring to the utter frivolity of self-indulgence, of giving no thought to the end. The Apostle employs it in a purely negative sense as an antithesis to belief in the Resurrection: if the dead are not raised, this is the only alternative. Neither of these Biblical authors combines the principle of sensual enjoyment of life with a consciousness of death among their disciples; they are merely inveighing against their shallow frivolity and scepticism. But the Egyptian could not free himself from the consciousness of death even when he was calling on his fellow-men to enjoy life; this, we believe, is a hallmark of his character.

To keep to the metaphor we used above: the Egyptian consciousness of death emerges in high relief, both in a positive and in a negative sense, in faith and in scepticism. Such a pronounced trait, whether help or hindrance, could not fail to make itself felt in the way they lived. One might at first think that this consciousness of death would have led the Egyptian to asceticism in practice and to pessimism in thought. True, there is certainly no shortage of pessimistic and sceptical utterances in Egypt, and we have seen some of them (e.g., pp. 189 f.). But they scarcely go beyond what one would expect from any man who grows older and wiser with experience. We do not find any significant traces of asceticism until the Hellenistic period (leaving out of account ritual injunctions to purity and the occasional instance of prudery, which are to be expected).[62] Contemplation, in the sense of passive meditation, was never a feature of life in Egypt. The latter point is perhaps best illustrated by the fact that during the Christian era, when Pakhom, one of the fathers of monasticism, who came from Esna in Upper Egypt, drew up rules to guide his monks in their work, this *vita activa* was subsequently taken over by the Western monastic tradition; in this way Egypt was linked with the West in opposition to the *vita contemplativa* of the Greek ascetics. To put it in a more positive way: in spite of his intense awareness of death the Egyptian also made an active contribution to the affairs of this world. Indeed, without him there would not have existed the great accomplishments of Egyptian civilization in all its varied richness.

Creative consequences: the pyramids and Egyptian art

Our question must therefore be rephrased as follows: does the Egyptian's consciousness of death make an impact upon his mode of action? It does indeed, in his urge to attain everlasting life – something that is very familiar but has only rarely been understood in all its profundity. One thing is immediately evident: an awareness of death which does not lead to a sense of resignation creates a desire to achieve everlasting life. We need not be ashamed to take mummies and pyramids as symbols of this urge to eternity in ancient Egypt, even though they have become something of a cliché. The mummy, as one expression of this desire for everlasting life, may be considered later.

The pyramid gives us an insight into Egyptian art as well. A towering monument of stone, it testifies to the Egyptian love of stone as such for its durable qualities. It may indeed be argued that the Great Pyramids at Giza, as gigantic monuments to Cheops and Chephren, have in fact survived relatively undamaged for approximately four thousand five hundred years, and so far as man may judge will stand for many millennia to come. But this argument is superficial. Time is not eternity. When the author of the Instruction for Merikare said that 'the council which judges regards a lifetime as an hour',[63] he would have considered a thousand years as but a day. Who can guarantee that Egypt's monuments, now preserved by dry sand, will not at some time or other perish during another great pluvial age, such as occurred thousands of years ago when Europe went through its ice age? As it is they are sinking into the water as a result of human action. Thus we shall have to look into the deeper artistic significance of the pyramid, not just at the material it is built of and its dimensions but at the concept of its form and the way in which it expressed a certain view of the world and of life. We shall then see that through his art the Egyptian endeavoured to overcome time. As is well known, Egyptian paintings and sculpture contain no reference to time; they represent a state of being, not becoming. 'Never does a wall-painting choose a moment from the eternal stream of time which could be grasped by a single act of vision...No Egyptian painting suggests a certain time of day...With astonishing consistency a world is constructed that contains only completed objects. Everything exists, nothing evolves. Everywhere there is a rigid timeless existence.'[64] In the two-dimensional image everything that is organic and bound up with time is transferred to the plane, seen mathematically as the space in which objects exist. 'Straight lines run sharply against one another, verticals clash with horizontals, alternating with diagonals. This is the character of crystalline bodies. A maximum of unyielding processes is manifest in these lines, which turn the living organism into an abstract structure and thus translate it into a sphere of timelessness.' The same tendencies are evident in three-dimensional works. Forms with spatial qualities are preferred to those which express time. The student of Egyptian art comes to the conclusion, which is true *cum grano salis* (see pp. 210 f.), that it was 'the most remarkable attempt to overcome death'.[65]

It is our belief that this attitude of Egyptian artists to time is governed by their awareness of death, reflected in an urge to achieve eternity. The Egyptian was not crushed by death, which he experienced so pervasively and to which he attached such negative connotations. Instead he was inspired by it to splendid creative achievements. To borrow a germane phrase: *Hic gaudet mors succurrere vitae.*

Burial customs; mummification

Less has been written about the Egyptian view of death than about the dead themselves, or about burial customs and concepts of the hereafter. On such matters there is much more information, and we may therefore concentrate on the essential points.[66] A link with the foregoing analysis is provided by the idea of the living corpse, which was basic to Egyptian thought and was tenaciously maintained. For it was precisely this which lay behind the constant awareness of death, the often costly concern for a proper burial, and the feasts in common with the dead in the tombs. As we see, there was an interaction between the awareness of death, which had such an influence upon the Egyptian way of life, and the massive faith in the hereafter. The idea of the living corpse is by no means peculiar to Egypt, but is found all over the world. Even those civilizations whose literature indicates that faith in a life beyond the grave was watered down and very weak, as was the case in Israel, where Sheol, the abode of the dead, was conceived of as far removed from the presence of God (e.g., Psalms vi. 6), and also in Greece with its idea of Hades (*Odyssey*, xi), at least had the residue of a belief in an afterlife similar to life on earth; this is clear from archaeological evidence.[67] Of all the Mediterranean lands it is in Egypt that this idea was preserved most tenaciously and where it had the greatest consequences.

In this connection one naturally thinks first of mummification. As is well known, this is a means of preserving a corpse: anhydrous agents (especially natron) cause the flesh to shrivel, but it continues to exist and the body of the deceased remains covered by the skin. This state, where parts of the body, in the first instance the bones, are held together as an integral whole, was sought after by the Egyptians even before they knew of mummification. 'Your head is knit to your bones for you, and your bones are knit to your head for you', runs an ancient ritual utterance; it was later incorporated into the Pyramid Texts, where it was regarded, as we shall see, as a prerequisite of resurrection.[68] This anxiety to preserve the wholeness of the body was no doubt rooted in the knowledge that in prehistoric burials in a flexed position the head could only too easily become severed from the trunk. During the Second Dynasty, when mummification began, there was a transition to burial in the extended position: the body was enwrapped by bandages,[69] which were later impregnated with resin and occasionally modelled over the features of the deceased; one purpose of these bandages was to bind all the parts of the body together.[70] This aim was especially evident in the ancient and consistently followed custom of interring the viscera together with the mummy in four jugs (erroneously called canopic jars by earlier Egyptologists). The viscera (apart from the heart, which later was usually left in the body)[71] had to be taken out if the body was to be preserved; they were removed by a specialist, who was known as a 'paraschist', who made an incision in the left side. Thus the organs which had to be separated for natural reasons were reunited with the body by an appropriate technical method, so that the essential parts might be interred together.

This was sometimes taken to an extreme. It is attested that female deceased were not only given regular wigs, which could be regarded as an ornament, but also artificial hair, which was worked into their natural hair, either as a cue or as loose padding.[72] Recently a case came to light where the dead man, whose nose was mutilated for reasons unknown (possibly damaged during mummification), was given an artificial nose of wood to make him complete again.[73] Consequently the purpose of mummification was to keep the body intact; it was this which underlay the Egyptians' preoccupation with the dead throughout their history, and was still practised by monks in Christian times, though less intensively and using different methods.[74] In this way Egypt is the exact opposite of India, where the body was destroyed by cremation and by casting the bones into water, since in India importance was attached only to the soul's migration from existence to existence and its final salvation by entry into nirvana.[75]

We cannot here give further details about the actual process of mummification (evisceration, conservation and bandaging),[76] but must point out briefly that the dead man so preserved in the closest approximation to his bodily state was given a dwelling: this term was in fact used. 'I have made this tomb as my dwelling', an Egyptian of the Old Kingdom says without embarrassment, speaking of the building of his tomb.[77] It may of course also be called 'the house of the necropolis (*pr n ḥrt-nṯr*)', as we know from the ancient Instruction of Hor-dedef (see p. 128); it is also frequently referred to as 'the house of eternity', indicating both its function and the durable material of which it is built, whereby it is distinguished from the houses of the living, built of perishable material.

Nor can we give even an outline history of the tomb, but must leave this, like that of the temple, to students of archaeology and architecture. We can only single out the facts that are essential in the context of the history of religion. Let us first recall the

Neolithic custom of interring the dead in the settlement. This was naturally practised by a settled peasantry, and the dead man was still a part of his family.[78] The nomadic tribes, on the other hand, developed the independent grave, indicated by a mound and other signs so that the dead might continue to receive provisions. When the original community of the living and the dead breaks up, the sedentary population also take up the idea of an independent grave, and establish necropolises as accessories of their settlements;[79] the form and concept of such tombs are derived from the dwelling-house. Thus the burial-mound and the domestic sepulchre may be regarded as the basic types of Egyptian funerary architecture.[80] Again we must leave it to the archaeologists to explain the relationship between these formal elements, which results from the merger of peasant and nomadic populations that occurred in Egypt in historical times. What is of immediate interest to the historian of religion is the following: although the burial-mound prevailed as an architectural form, the domestic sepulchre prevailed as a concept. The only thing was that the idea of the dead man dwelling in the house was superseded by the idea that he had a dwelling of his own;[81] this was the result partly of nomadic influence and partly of an intellectual evolution. That the tomb served as a house may best be demonstrated by the feasts of the valley, held conjointly with the dead in the tombs of the Theban necropolis, to which incidentally the living brought their household utensils (see pp. 194 f.).

Funerary gifts and supply of provisions

This latter fact leads on to the question of funerary gifts. In Egypt the dead were provided for eternity with food, clothing and ornaments. In simple graves of the late Archaic period these may have been no more than a couple of clay or stone vessels, some spoons, combs, hairpins and cosmetic palettes; [but they attained great magnificence in the tombs of kings or wealthy private persons in the 'Egyptian baroque' period (as we know through the fortuitous discovery of the tomb of Tutankhamon in the Valley of Kings or that of the architect Kha at Deir el-Medina).[82] Such differences of scale do not affect the role of such funerary gifts, as seen from the vantage-point of the history of religion. This ancient custom, far from abating, became stronger with the spread of luxury in dynastic times; it survived the period of paganism and is encountered even in Christian (Coptic) burials.[83]

Funerary gifts in the strict sense of the word, located as close as possible to the dead (buried below ground), may be differentiated from the decorations in the upper chambers of the tomb, designed for provisions. These reliefs and paintings represent to the dead in his tomb the chief features of his earthly environment: scenes of hunting, fighting, farming and handicrafts, later also banquets, association with the king etc., which vary according to the period and the social status of the deceased. As images they are *eo ipso* identified with what they represent (see p. 153); or, as we shall learn directly, they acquire vitality by the performance of certain rituals. How seriously the identity of image and object was still taken during the efflorescence of the Old Kingdom is shown by the custom of leaving the mortuary chambers themselves without any representations, in order to protect the peace of the dead; later objects but not human beings were rendered, until finally, during the Sixth Dynasty, the fear of the living image slowly disappeared. In the tomb of Kaemankh at Giza all the scenes which elsewhere decorate the upper cult chambers – manned ships, tilling the fields, cattle-raising, work in the kitchen etc. – are painted on the walls of the sarcophagus-chamber.[84]

If we draw this distinction between funerary gifts proper and the lavish provisions made in the upper chambers, which unlike the closed sepulchral chamber were accessible to the living, we do so because of the difference in function. These upper chambers do indeed serve as a dwelling for the dead, and are accessible to the latter through a false door, but they are designed in particular for the supply of provisions, rendered daily or on the occasion of certain festivals. This is clear from the dining-table scene in the cult niche (in the last instance linked to the false door),[85] which was the starting-point of the pictorial decoration, and from the list of provisions, which was read out in the ritual, so that the object listed might materialize. This 'calling out of the supplies needed (*nis dbḥt-ḥtp*)'[86] indicates the religious purpose of decorating the cult chambers all over. These pictures summed up the content of the dead man's life on earth. They had to be at his disposal in the same way as the offerings of food and clothing.

This is not to deny the possibility that even during the late Old

Kingdom, as a result of the development of religious ideas, these images may have come to be seen as memory aids for the dead, indeed as memorials for their descendants.[87] The Old Kingdom mastabas reflect in their imagery the worldly ideals of the feudal aristocracy; but this is no argument against the validity for all classes of society of the underlying concept that earthly forms continued to exist beyond the grave. We are dealing here again with Goethe's 'conditions under which phenomena appear', quite comprehensible from a sociological viewpoint. On the collapse of the Old Kingdom ever larger groups appropriated for themselves the highest social rank, that of the king, as the images upon their sarcophagi show. In the so-called 'frieze of implements' on coffins from the First Intermediate period and the Middle Kingdom, private persons usurp the royal insignia, although with obvious hesitation.[88] They are seeking, through the medium of belief in the afterlife, to attain a certain well-defined position here on earth; and in so doing they proclaim upon their sarcophagi that such a course is open to everyone. Naturally, this appropriation of a higher status implied a belief that life in the beyond would be superior to that which these persons had enjoyed on earth; but this is something we shall come back to later (see p. 230). For the moment it is enough to underline the fact that the fundamental idea of the living corpse led to the preservation of the body by mummification, to the construction for it of a permanent dwelling, and to the provision of lavish funerary gifts for it; it also led to the regular performance of the rites accompanying the supply of such provisions, which were thought capable of turning lists or images of objects needed by the dead into the real thing.

The inner connection between the gifts buried with the dead and the provision of supplies in the upper chamber of the tomb is made clear by the history of the dining-table scene. We now know that this composition is to be found in First-Dynasty tombs near Helwan, in the lower sarcophagus-chamber, and that only later did this become the principal item of decoration in the upper ritual chamber. In view of this scholars have abandoned, in my view rightly, the attempt to distinguish in principle between the concept of the dead man resting in the tomb and that of the dead man ascending for his meal.[89] It may be possible to link the relative freedom of movement which he enjoyed with the concept of the ka, and also to link the supply of provisions with the funerary statue. The latter is all the more likely in that the ka is in the habit of taking up its abode in the statue,[90] and that the statue benefits from these supplies at least as much as the corpse itself does. It was often erected in a separate statue chamber (*serdâb*) behind the ritual chamber, sometimes even directly behind the false door, and participated directly in the ritual through the so-called '*serdâb* slits'. But we cannot really say any more about this, or the complex and scarcely definable concept of ka, as the necessary preliminary studies have yet to be undertaken.[91] Our final point in this connection is that the expenditure involved in Egyptian burials and their religious significance made every man want to be buried in his homeland and in the correct form. To bring home the body of one's father who had died in a foreign land and to bury it in one's own country were regarded as meritorious deeds.[92] When the king promised an emigrant a good Egyptian burial, instead of an unsatisfactory interment among the barbarians, this exemplified his quality of mercy.[93]

In the foregoing we have deliberately avoided the terms 'sacrifice' and 'cult of the dead', to rule out the idea that the Egyptians venerated their dead as divine, for this happened only in exceptional circumstances. Instead we have spoken of equipping the dead with gifts, and of the regular supply of provisions, to enable them to enjoy earthly life in perpetuity. Both these practices are closely linked to the grave or tomb. The question now arises: did Egyptians visualize life in the beyond as taking place solely in the tomb (through the conservation of the body or the presence of the ka as the life-force)? The answer is in the negative. The departed were also seen as living in heaven and in the realm of the dead. Let us take a brief look at each of these regions, beginning with heaven.

Concept of heaven

This was at first accessible only to the deceased king, but then became 'democratized', as it were, and opened up to commoners. If we take another look at the text we have already cited to illustrate the desire to keep the body an integral whole, we see that physical intactness in the tomb does not exclude ascent to heaven, but is rather a prerequisite for it. The sentence which runs: 'Your head is knit to your bones for you, and your bones are knit to your head for you' is followed by: 'The double doors of heaven are open for you...you sit upon his throne; you command the spirits.' To exclude all doubt, the whole passage has a heading, which is very rare in the Pyramid Texts: 'The double doors of heaven open.'[94] Logically, and as a rule, ascent to heaven and existence there are linked with the Heliopolitan doctrine and are a counterpart to the dominion of Osiris over the dead. This is expressed most distinctly in an address of the sky-goddess Nut to the dead king: 'Open up your place in the sky among the stars of the sky, for you are the Lone Star...; look down upon Osiris when he governs the spirits, for you stand far from him, you are not among them and you shall not be among them.'[95] Accordingly the desire is voiced that the king should not die, or his death is simply denied: 'Rise up..., for you have not died',[96] or: 'My father has not died the death, for my father possesses a spirit [in] the horizon.'[97] Other texts have already been cited above (see p. 39): 'You have not departed dead, you have departed alive',[98] or 'Grasp [the king] by his hand and take [him] to the sky that he may not die on earth among men'.[99] The denial of death was later appropriated by private persons, as we learn from the Coffin Texts, where we repeatedly come across phrases such as the following: 'Rise alive, you did not die; rise to life, you did not die.'[100]

But in the Coffin Texts – and with this we return to our theme – we find not only a denial of death but also the idea of an existence of the dead in heaven; moreover, this has a characteristic form, in combination with the ba as the 'soul'. There is one group of spells which contains a kind of doctrine on the soul: on a man's death his ba is separated form his body, by 'coming out of the discharges of his flesh and the perspiration [probably = foam secreted by the corpse] of his head.' Then '[the grain-god] Nepri is to take it away', so that the ba may see the primeval god Atum and may finally accompany him on his journey in the sun-barque.[101] In all this the ba seems simply to embody the man's earthly vital powers, which achieve immortality without the aid of any ritual.[102] After this the mortuary texts take one of two courses. One separates the dead man's soul from his body and assigns the former to heaven: 'The ba belongs to heaven, the dead body to the nether world.'[103] The other expresses the desire: 'May thy ba not be separated from thy body.'[104] This idea incidentally recurs in the well-known images of the soul perched like a bird in the shadow of the sycamore-trees by the tomb or fluttering down to the mummy through the shaft of the grave. [105] Here one must also mention the construction *bꜣ ḥr ẖꜣt*, 'soul on dead body', which etymologized the name of the bull-god Buchis;[106] it, too, is authenticated in images.

Let us return to the so-called Dispute with his Soul of One who is Tired of Life. Earlier we suggested that this dispute between a man and his ba concerned the anthropological problem of how body and soul are related to one another after death (see p. 189). We may now appreciate the actuality of such a question, having become acquainted with the divergent solutions offered to it during the subsequent period. But there is another problem as well. Unless our tradition is deceptive, the soul (ba), as distinct from the vital force (ka), was during the Old Kingdom the property of the king alone; during the First Intermediate period and during the Middle Kingdom it remained almost completely confined to the Coffin Texts, in which private persons usurped what had previously been reserved to the king (see pp. 226 f.). In other words, in the earlier period Egyptians apparently did not possess a ba.[107] Accordingly, during the First Intermediate period they became aware of their need for a ba and this produced a new situation which subsequently led to diametrically different solutions (whose logical incompatibility was barely understood). If this is so, one can immediately see why this burning anthropological and existential question should have become the object of a dispute. However this may be, it is our opinion that the Egyptians secured access to the realm of the dead in heaven, previously reserved to the king, and that for private persons the (bird-like) 'soul' (ba) was associated with heaven. In this way the preservation of the body in the tomb became the prerequisite for ascent to heaven. In conclusion it may be added that the two spheres, tomb and heaven, were linked in another way: the sarcophagus- and burial-chamber were interpreted as heaven. Figures of the sky-goddess Nut embellish the ceiling of the sarcophagus-chamber, which is also decorated with stars and thus turned into a canopy of heaven; contrariwise, Nut is called 'sarcophagus' or 'tomb'.[108]

Realm of the dead

If the idea of the dead going to heaven was linked with the Heliopolitan doctrine and occasionally led to a denial of death, the
realm of the dead was naturally coupled with chthonian deities,
i.e. in the last resort with Osiris. For Osiris himself had died; of his
kinsman Nepri, the grain-god, we are told: 'He lives after he has
died.'[109] Thus the death was not denied of those who stood in
succession to Osiris.[110] The titles to spells in mortuary texts
describe their purpose as: 'To live after death in the beautiful
West';[111] or one desires that 'NN shall live after his death'.[112]
What men fear and seek to avoid on this plane is that second death
mentioned in the titles of so many spells in the Coffin Texts and
the Book of the Dead, e.g.: 'Spell of not Dying a Second Time in
the Realm of the Dead (*ḥrt-nṯr*)'.[113] We shall hardly go wrong in
assuming that this second death could be inflicted by a decision
of the court of judgement; the texts sought to avert by magical
means such a negative decision, and its execution by the devourer
(see p. 127). We may also imagine this second death as that complete
destruction of body and soul wrought by the setting sun-god, who
is related to Osiris, through his messengers, who 'destroy (*dr*) the
souls and bodies of the dead (*bȝw ḫȝwt*)...which are at the [place
of execution]'.[114] Thus the second death may apply in particular
to the soul, since the body has already died during the first death:
'Not to die a second time on the part of the ba of a man.'[115]

All this leads us to the realm of Osiris, upon which the king
who has been raised to heaven looks down: 'Look [down] upon
Osiris when he governs the spirits, for you stand [high up] far off
from him', etc. (see p. 205).[116] This inevitably raises the question
as to the whereabouts of the realm of the dead. It is not easy to
answer, because the Egyptian term *dwȝt* (or *dȝt*) originally meant
something like 'twilight zone', 'nocturnal sky', and at any rate
belonged to the upper region.[117] To trace the subsequent development of this term, let us first gather a few simple facts. The realm
of the dead is the aggregate of the necropolises located on the
edge of the desert, mostly in the West. It is characterized by the
darkness of the tombs, from which one so readily 'comes forth
by day' to see the sun.[118] But it is likewise characterized as 'the
West' because it is there that the sun sets. This of course provides

a ray of hope: that during its nightly journey the sun traverses the realm of the dead and so brings light to its inhabitants. This hope was given very precise expression; we have books which describe pictorially and verbally the sun's journey through the nether world – as we may now call it – and divide the route into the twelve hours of the night: the (later so-called) Book of that which is in the Underworld (Amduat), the Book of the Gates, the Book of Caverns, and also a large number of free compilations.[119] On its journey the sun does more than bring light: its rays cause the dead Osiris, and with him every mortal, to be re-created and to rise from the dead.[120] If we now return to our question of the whereabouts of the realm of the dead, we may say that it came to be visualized as lying under the earth, like the tombs, and that the sun was thought to traverse it after it had set and before it rose again over the mountains of the horizon. We find the characteristic formulation that this nether world is 'made deep (*smḏ*)' for Osiris (and the dead), just as heaven was raised high up for his ba.[121] The nightly journey of the sun gave a unity to the realm of the dead, which was more than just a vast mass of individual graves. This unity is also characteristic of Osiris's royal domain, which has at its centre the place where justice is meted out to the dead; it had its own geography, with routes one could follow, or on which one could be impeded,[122] etc.; but this lies outside our frame of reference.

Let us summarize our survey of Egyptian funerary customs and concepts of the beyond. The basic idea of the living corpse led to mummification, the view of the tomb as a dwelling for the dead, and the furnishing of funerary gifts. Then came the provision of supplies, both for the body and for the vital force (ka) present in the statue. The tomb, we found, was not the only abode of the dead; an existence in heaven was claimed as well, especially for the soul (ba); its counterpart was a uniform nether world illumined by the sun on its nocturnal journey. Although our exposition has been topical, the reader will have sensed that a process of historical development took place. We need only recall the democratization of royal privileges, the transposition of the Duat from the nocturnal sky to the nether world, and finally the coexistence of the Heliopolitan and Osirian conceptions, which cried out for a compromise.

Historical development

A historical survey would allow one to make the connections clearer, and there are at least two lines of inquiry we must now pursue. The first concerns a mood of scepticism, fraught with great consequences, about whether an Egyptian's descendants could be relied upon to provide supplies for the dead. After men discovered that the regular funerary services were discontinued after a certain time (see p. 228), the dead were furnished with the equipment with which to carry out the ritual themselves. We have already seen that during the Sixth Dynasty the fear of images lessened to such an extent that the sarcophagus-chamber itself was decorated with representations which previously had been reserved for the upper chambers (see p. 202). Now we may add that this development was in part due also to the need to ensure that the deceased person had the images he required. He was to become self-sufficient. Characteristically enough, the provision of supplies was not suspended, e.g. in favour of increased funerary gifts, but was left to the dead man in person. This is to be understood literally: the liturgical list of provisions was accorded pride of place next to the sarcophagus, first in royal tombs and soon afterwards in those of private persons as well.[123] Close by were other spells which were likewise deemed essential for existence in the beyond (not confined to the grave), so that the dead could recite them personally for their own benefit, instead of needing a priest to do so. In this way the mortuary texts which are so characteristic of Egypt were preserved. They are to be found in the mortuary chambers of the pyramids (Pyramid Texts), upon coffins (Coffin Texts), and finally on scrolls (Book of the Dead), which were placed upon the mummy or even wrapped up with it. We shall discuss this literature in the next chapter. Here it may merely be pointed out that this custom, too, continued *mutatis mutandis* into the Christian era.[124]

The second line of inquiry which needs to be pursued in a historically oriented sketch must be an attempt to place the judgement of the dead in its proper historical setting. We have already done so in a different context, by pointing out that during the Fifth Dynasty a breach occurred between this world and the next (see p. 129). We now have to link this idea to funerary customs and concepts of the beyond, upon which it had an impact. Logically, one might think that the judgement of the dead, which measures a man's actions upon earth by the criterion of maat, would have a fatal effect upon funerary customs. For if a man's ethical conduct conformed to the standards of maat, everything else was immaterial, even a ritual burial with one's body intact and fully provided for. But the Egyptians did not draw such logical consequences; on the contrary, they adhered to their burial customs and used magical means to outflank, as it were, the judgement of the dead. We have already pointed to a likely reason for this: they did not dare make their everlasting existence dependent upon a moral evaluation – not because they were arrogant or immoral, but because they were so self-critical (see pp. 130 f.).

This is the place to mention a solution to the problem which admittedly is only attested from a very late period, although this may be just a matter of chance. In the so-called Setna Story, written in demotic, the hero of the tale looks into the realm of the dead and there sees (or learns) how, in accordance with a divine judgement, the pompous furnishings of a rich but unjust man's tomb are assigned to a poor but just man, who is buried in simple fashion; the latter achieves happiness next to Osiris, while the rich man suffers the torments of hell.[125] This tale probably embodied the best solution which the Egyptians were capable of devising: both dead men received their deserts, yet funerary furnishings remained the vehicle of salvation.

Finally, it seems worth recalling briefly the religious basis for this reliance on magic to avoid the judgement of the dead: this was the belief in equation with Osiris, the king of gods and god of vegetation, the first to rise from the dead, who encompassed within himself every person buried with the proper ritual.[126] This belief, restricted to the king in the Old Kingdom, was later extended to every Egyptian.

Significance: overcoming death

It has not been easy to make the simplifications necessary to present this account of Egyptian funerary customs and concepts of the beyond; there are so many facts to be considered, and the relationship between these is not clear. Our aim has been not to set forth all these facts but to try to interpret them as a whole. Just as we have attempted above to describe the Egyptian attitude toward death, so we must now endeavour to comprehend the customs, concepts and hopes associated with it. We have noted that doubts were sometimes expressed about whether it was worth while preserving the dead, and whether the rituals were really effective in resuscitating them (see pp. 188 f.); nevertheless, as we have seen, both customs were adhered to throughout Egyptian history. Was this just due to inertia, a form devoid of content? Or were there only a few who voiced such doubts? What is the significance of the fact that during the Late period death was widely seen as the end of life; or that men ceased to believe in the beyond, and even in the judgement of the dead; and that they pinned their hopes upon earthly *gloria*, upon their reputation with posterity?[127]

To see all this in proper perspective, let us recall what was said above (see pp. 196 f.) about the Egyptians' awareness of death and their urge to achieve everlastingness. This accounts for the ability of Egyptian art to overcome time and – we quote literally – 'to overcome death'. We must now take this point further. In our view, art cannot actually conquer death, but only translate into visual terms the attempt to conquer it. What *can* in fact conquer death is the placing of human existence upon a religious basis, which makes it independent of death. How do matters stand in this respect in Egypt? The question may surely be answered easily: Egyptian religion, in so far as it was related to death, preserved ancient ways of ensuring everlasting life and kept on discovering new ones. In the first place, it always held to the original idea of prolonging life in the tomb, and developed it on an impressive scale in reality. In the second place, it inspired the custom of resuscitating the dead man, his images and everything in his tomb, by the performance of certain rituals. When the judgement of the dead was conceived, decisions were established which were deemed valid for all eternity, not just for a man's earthly lifetime; this is why such care was taken to avoid a verdict which spelled everlasting perdition. The idea of 'becoming Osiris' was the antithesis of the idea of divine judgement upon the dead. According to this the dead person was absorbed into the substance of the deity; the (Heliopolitan) idea that he ascended to heaven and that he accompanied the sun-god on his journey had the effect of elevating him to a plane as durable as the created world itself.

Finally, equation with or filiation to a primeval god even raises the dead above the created world, and thus above any danger of an end (see p. 186).

In the light of this, let us now attempt to trace Egyptian funerary customs to their core, and to demythologize the very abstruse concepts held about the beyond. We arrive at the following simple statements: the individual is preserved in his own particular form; he enters into God or is with God.[128] This formulation conveys exactly the religious basis of the idea that man can overcome death. The Egyptians, always conscious of death, never ceased their endeavours to conquer it, as their funerary beliefs bear witness. Naturally, these beliefs underwent modifications of form, and in critical periods were weakened; yet this was historically inevitable. The consciousness of death, such a basic motif in the Egyptian outlook, and the desire for everlasting life, had as a necessary corollary doubt as to whether this high aim would be achieved. Men who longed for permanence, yet could not quite believe in it, had themselves mummified or else advocated an intensification of life on earth. When doubt triumphed, Egyptian civilization was doomed; its victory was perhaps the deepest symptom of its end. Its final outpouring of creative force flowed into the art of realistic portraiture; this began with the Ethiopian period and had not the least quality of timelessness about it. Even the inner tension that afflicted men in this Late period can be detected in these portraits, among which (alongside lifeless idealized likenesses) were some which had a touch of Roman realism; the greatest of these was the 'Green Head' in Berlin.[129] Despite all the excellence of individual pieces, we are a long way here from the ancient idea of conquering time and death; this is the clearest evidence that the end was nigh.

As we know, Egypt succumbed to Christianity, and finally to Islam. Since both these major religions spread widely throughout the world, there is no reason to seek a specific reason for their success in Egypt. Yet they were in agreement with the basic outlook of the ancient Egyptians in that they also promised eternal life; they could therefore appeal to a very ancient attitude of mind. Who can say whether Egyptian mummies may not have had something to do with the Christian concept of 'resurrection of the flesh', which belongs neither to the Old Testament religion nor to that of the earliest Christians, let alone to that of the Greeks?[130] To the Christian it may seem natural that man's everlasting life should be based upon God. But other religions, such as those of the Israelites and of the ancient Greeks, teach that God's power does not extend beyond the limits of this earthly existence: it cannot penetrate the dark realms of Sheol[131] or the gates of Hades.[132] This makes the Egyptian phenomena all the more important and specific. And one final point may be added. If the Egyptians of the Late period became sceptical towards the belief in the beyond, which had once been so strong, this does not mean that they became complete unbelievers. They retained their faith that God acts in the world of the living, that he caters for justice within it, and also that he is lord of fate, and in particular is supreme over life and death. All this was still a vital credo in Egypt during those centuries when its great civilization was moving towards its close. For all their scepticism about the immortality of the dead, they were anything but lacking in reverence.[133]

10 · Sacred writings

The subjects treated in the foregoing chapters had a common source and were connected with each other. We began with the Egyptians' gods and their worshippers, moved on to the vital relationship between God and man, and came finally to their ideas on creation and evolution, death and eternity – ideas which, though they had an enduring quality, were nevertheless real to the men who lived in each period of Egyptian history. It cannot be denied that our next field of inquiry is, in a sense, independent of what has gone before. By sacred writings we mean the religious literature of the Egyptians. Even to provide a brief account of these texts and to single out their chief characteristics would be a major task. But if we are to keep to our aim of evaluating various religious phenomena, we must ask ourselves what function such sacred writings served and what significance they had. This will enable us to see them, not in isolation, but in their relationship to other aspects of our subject. To anticipate, they can tell us much about Egyptian religion, dominated as it was by cult, and thus also about popular piety and the workings of God.

Cult religion and scriptural religion

We must now ask the reader to accompany us on what may seem to be a detour. Once again, for the last time, we shall approach the subject by contrasting diametrical opposites, and attempt first to paint a picture of the antithesis of cult religion, which we propose to call 'scriptural religion'. We of course are familiar with this kind of religion – indeed, we are prone to see in it the only form of religion because for us, whether we are Jews, Christians or Muslims, it is a characteristic of our own faith. In a scriptural religion sacred writings, deemed to be the word of God, occupy a focal point in the divine service and, what is more, are supposed to determine the way in which the faithful lead their lives. The underlying notion is of a God who speaks to man, who has created the world through his word, who directs its course through his admonitions and promises, and issues commands and laws to govern the conduct both of society as a whole and of the individuals who compose it. It may be demonstrated that scriptural religion in this form, at any rate within the area covered by the ancient cult religions of the Mediterranean lands, had its origins in a particular set of historical facts. We are alluding to the chain of events extending from Josiah to Ezra, by way of the kingdom of Judah and the birth of Judaism. It was at this time and in this region that the area over which traditional ritual had an impact was reduced, that it became concentrated upon the Deuteronomy, and that religious communities came to concern themselves very largely with written records: laws, words of the prophets, and directives by the priests. In other words, as cult became drained of its content the resulting vacuum was filled by the forceful presence of the word of God, revealed to man on frequent occasions. Above all, the law, which affected so profoundly the daily life of pious Jews, had to be proclaimed, and also elucidated. Beside the place of worship, confined to a single location, there appeared everywhere places of scripture; beside the temple there appeared the synagogue. It is as plain as can be that here we have the origins of the practices of reading the scripture and of delivering sermons, which Judaism bequeathed to Christianity.

It follows logically that Judaism was aware of all those elements which in retrospect appear to be indispensable components of scriptural religion: above all the canon, which determined what was and what was not Scripture, and which guaranteed the correct wording of the texts, right down to each individual letter.[1] Thus arose what already in the time of Jesus was called the Scripture, a term which expressed an awareness that the texts it contained formed an integral, authoritative whole. This development can be traced historically; it is a legitimate subject for research; and one cannot but ask oneself whether this momentous legacy of Israel was not deeply rooted in the very substance of the Judaic religion. We believe that this was so. This ancient people of the desert had the great gift of hearkening – that is to say, a genius for perceiving profound spiritual truths – which led them to obedience to God, as well as to the powers of reasoning. This genius enabled the Israelites to hear God when he spoke to them; it led them to place his word, rather than his image, in the centre of the divine service. Although continually challenged by the custom of all their neighbours, the Israelites developed a cult that was devoid of images, one based solely on the word of God, on the Scripture.[2]

Those who have followed our interpretation from the beginning will readily conclude that Egyptian religion had no part in this development of scriptural religion, which was peculiar to the Judaeo-Christian tradition, and never experienced a similar evolution. We may recall that in Egypt ritual was of central importance; that there was a place for it in every Egyptian settlement; and that personal piety was closely connected with the temple and its images (see pp. 101 ff.). We may also call to mind that God's command was not made explicit but was confined to the establishing of maat, so that there was no place in Egyptian religious literature for that Law which played so great a role in Israel. Finally we may recollect the related fact that the teachings concerned with right conduct and maat as its criterion were based expressly upon human experience, and did not claim to be the word of God (see p. 117).

This, however, by no means exhausts the problems involved in Egyptian sacred writings. On the contrary, it will now be our task to compile an inventory of them and to single out their characteristic features. Without losing sight of the points just made, we shall endeavour to show that certain characteristics of the Scriptures are to be found in Egyptian texts just as they are in those texts which, through contact with the Scriptures, acquired a completely different value upon Israelite soil.

Range of religious literature

Any attempt to inventory Egyptian religious literature runs up against the difficulty, not that there is too little of it, but that there is such a wealth of texts.[3] Since much manuscript material has been lost, whereas texts have been preserved that were carved on stone and wood, one cannot attempt a thorough classification of the materials used, but must concentrate on the content. Consequently we must include in our subject-matter the vast mass of texts inscribed on temple walls and the numerous coffins bearing spells for the dead. At a rough estimate the areas covered with hieroglyphs, especially in late Upper Egyptian temples from Dendera to Philae, would measure several acres in extent. Incidentally, the different writing substances exerted an influence upon one another: stone was occasionally given the yellowish-brown colour of early papyrus,[4] while the columns of religious papyri were separated by rows of lines, as in stone inscriptions.[5] That the texts we know only as inscriptions were copied from papyrus, and that this more perishable material was exposed to the ravages of time, is expressly mentioned in the introduction to the Shabaka inscription: 'Then [his majesty] copied [it] anew...His majesty had found [it] as [something] which the ancestors had made but which was worm-eaten'; then follows the dubious phrase that the copy 'is better than its state formerly'; the problem this raises has also been discussed in another context.[6]

It would of course be an undertaking in itself to make a full inventory of this material. This task, by the way, need not stop at simple registration, but could involve a systematic arrangement according to genre, and in particular a classification of the rituals or hymns, which must often have differed only slightly from one another. Let us cite one example to make this clear. Scholars have long been accustomed to take inscriptions on sarcophagi or manuscripts of mortuary papyri as different items of evidence referring to one and the same text and its historical evolution;[7] *mutatis mutandis*, we would often be able to discover a similar state of affairs in regard to rituals and hymns, several versions of which are recorded on temple walls or on papyri. To put it differently, in many cases what one at first glance would take to be a separate work turns out on closer inspection to be a copy, or more usually a variant, which differs from the basic type in some local feature or by mentioning the local deity.[8]

We have had to confine ourselves here to pointing out these basic types, and the textual evidence for them; but we cannot omit a brief list of the genres of religious literature in Egypt. These are, essentially: ritual books of various kinds, hymns of a cultic or literary character which may or may not be intended for use as prayers, theological treatises without any visible ritual purpose,[9] and finally the peculiar phenomenon of the so-called 'mortuary literature'.[10] This order is most characteristic. The main emphasis is upon cult, carried out as laid down in the ritual books; most of the hymns are likewise employed in cult, and the mortuary texts, too, serve a special form of cult, namely the provision of supplies for the dead.[11] On the other hand, as has already been mentioned, there is a complete lack of any literature laying down religious laws, and the teachings of the sages are so obviously based on human experience rather than the word of God that as a matter of principle they must be kept separate from religious texts.

Finally, myths play a unique and significant role, about which something must be said. Most of the genres which we have listed contain allusions to myth: for instance, it is used (mostly in individual quotations) to elucidate certain ritual acts (see pp. 82–4), or it makes itself heard in hymns of praise (see p. 94), or else serves the dead as a magic means of identifying themselves with a deity. But myths do not seem to have been written down in literary form for their own sake. Where we encounter one as a composite whole, it serves an alien purpose: in the crudest form, it is pressed into the service of magic, as in the tale of the great name of Re, which has come down to us as the prototype of magic acts, or at least into the service of the dead, as in the myth about the destruction of mankind (the so-called 'Book of the Heavenly Cow'), recorded in the royal tombs at Thebes.[12] From this one point may be deduced with certainty. Myths, as tales about deities and their activities, were not written down so that they should of themselves proclaim God; instead, they were a medium used in the cult to make God manifest to the faithful as well as proclaiming him (see p. 94). This explains why myth could so easily sink down to the level of a magic tool and could also form a bridge to narrative literature. We have aready given an example of the former; in regard to the latter we may mention the famous Late Egyptian Tale of Two Brothers, whose names alone, Anubis and Bata, indicate that they belong to the divine realm.[13] All this underlines the fact that Egyptian religion was centred upon cult, whose pride of place was challenged neither by religious laws nor by wisdom literature – nor indeed by myth, which was an independent medium for transmitting the sacred word.

Our inventory, however, would be incomplete without some consideration of the complex of ritual books. We use the term 'complex' deliberately. For in fact these comprise a large number of writings which differ as much in content as the ritual acts themselves. We have, firstly, in the divine cult the precepts governing performance of the daily service (which incidentally were recorded both on papyri and on temple walls, the former being

a primary, the latter a secondary source);[14] secondly, in the
funerary service we have the ritual of embalming[15] and that of
opening the mouth (see pp. 155, 187). The spheres of divine cult
and concern for the departed are linked in the 'vigils' of the Osirian
services: these were observed in order to help the god in his helpless state, poised between death and resurrection, to attain new
life; they were likewise carried out according to a certain ritual.[16]
Finally, a text, instead of justifying, by means of a myth, some action that had occurred in ancient times, and thus having a secondary
character, could spring freely and directly from the persons of
the myth and their history. In such cases the ritual may acquire
the form of a dramatic scenario, with roles being allotted and directions given about staging (see p. 84); it was according to such
texts that men celebrated the festivals which originated from the
worship of Osiris, as well as those which centred upon Horus and
the king.[17] But the factor which unites all ritual books is the function they fulfil in cult: they do not exist for their own sake but are
subordinate to the ritual action whose rules they prescribe. They
have no life of their own and are consequently not really
literature at all, but cult preserved in textual form. The vast
difference between them and the Old Testament, in which men
hearkened to the word of God, is as plain as can be.

Characteristics of religious literature; divine authorship

As we have already dealt at some length with hymns and their
role in cult, and shall discuss mortuary literature separately
below, we may now move on from listing the genres of Egyptian
religious literature to some consideration of its characteristics.
The first question concerns the origin of a religious text: who wrote
it, how it was made available to others, or simply how old it is.
As regards authorship, this is occasionally attributed to a deity:
above all Thoth, god of scribes and 'lord of the word of God'.[18]
Thus we are told in one spell in the Book of the Dead: 'The
majesty of Thoth made [him] for the majesty of the king
Osiris', i.e. for the prototype of every Egyptian dead person.[19]
This idea is expressed with even greater precision by a phrase in
what is likewise a mortuary work, the Book of Breathings: '[Thoth]
has written for you with his own fingers the Book of Breathings.'[20]
But in this late text Isis is given as the author, or at least as the

scribe; she 'makes [the book] for her brother Osiris'.[21] In Egypt this mighty concept of divine authorship seems to displace completely that of the human scribe being divinely inspired, which was so highly developed by the Greeks and later by the early Christians. So far as we are aware, there is no evidence of God stimulating men to write,[22] although we know that God could inspire various human actions (see pp. 64–6). With some reservations one could cite sporadic passages in later texts where writings are called 'souls of Re (*bꜣw Rꜥ*)', or 'souls of the gods (*bꜣw nṯrw*)', which has been interpreted as 'emanation'[23] and according to common linguistic usage may in fact mean something like 'manifestation'.[24] It is similarly only with the utmost caution that one may point to images of a scribe with the god Thoth in the form of a baboon perched on his shoulders – a type which is remarkably reminiscent of the well-known ancient potraits of the king with the falcon. Just as these latter illustrate the Horus aspect of the sacrosanct ruler (see p. 34), so on a different level the scribes with Thoth could represent the Hermopolitan god inspiring the content of the work being written.[25] In other cases importance is especially attached to the statement that the writings in question were discovered in unusual and rare circumstances. A chapter in the Book of the Dead, according to its rubric, is said to have been 'found at Shmun [Hermopolis] under the feet of the majesty of this sublime god [Thoth] upon a slab of Upper Egyptian granite in the script of the god himself, in the time of...Mycerinus, by Prince Hor-dedef. He found the spell when he was engaged in inspecting the temples.'[26] Finally, a detailed account from the age of Augustus describes the discovery of the mortuary Book of Breathings mentioned above, which a priest copied from the mummy bandages of Psammetichus I and was acknowledged by the new pharaoh. Möller, who brought this matter to light, suggested that this demotic text might have been dependent upon the well-known Biblical tale of the discovery of Deuteronomy (II Kings xxii. 8 ff.).[27]

Divine authorship elevates religious literature from present day existence; similarly, the accounts about the discovery of such works ascribe them to a more or less distant past. This exemplifies the tendency to emphasize the antiquity of sacred writings, which is particularly evident in the retention of ancient linguistic forms or the deliberate choice of archaistic expressions.[28] Egyptians could also adopt the customs of bygone ages in their mode of writing.[29] This of course does not rule out the possibility – which may have occurred quite frequently – that material from the living language of the faithful entered into the words used in cult. For example, humble participants in the divine service could join in singing the hymns.[30] There are also examples in Egypt of pseud-epigraphic antedatings – that is to say, ascriptions to authors or other authorities of the past, such as are so familiar from the Jewish and early Christian literature. They are found on the periphery of religious writings. The prophecy of Neferti, in which Amenemhet I (early Twelfth Dynasty) is glorified as the donor of salvation, is inserted into a tale ascribed to the time of King Snefru, of the early Fourth Dynasty; the prophecy is that 'justice (*maat*) will come into its place, while wrongdoing (*ìsft*) is driven out', and has the familiar religious-cum-political aspect.[31] Certainly not too much ought to be made of the names of the authors, which at any rate cannot be compared to those of Enoch, Moses, Elijah or others to whom pseudepigraphic writings related to the Bible are attributed; whereas a great deal of importance attaches to antiquity itself and the securing of a *vaticinium ex eventu* which could be useful to the new ruler. This propagandist intention is as plain as can be in the case of a work which is put into the mouth of the murdered Amenemhet I but was in fact written in the milieu of his son Sesostris I.[32] But here we have already left the sphere of religious literature, even in the area of divine kingship. Likewise on the very periphery of our material are texts of a legal nature, in which donations to temples are antedated. The best-known example, and also the one that goes furthest back in time, is in the so-called Famine Stele, from the Ptolemaic era, where a donation of land to Khnum of Elephantine is documentarily attributed to Zoser, the founder of the Third Dynasty and builder of the famous stepped pyramid (see p. 33). The best analogy to this is to be found not in the Bible but in the history of Christian ecclesiastical law: the so-called Donation of Constantine, which was made the documentary basis of the Church's claim to temporal power.

Unity and variety in religious literature

Thus Egypt offers us materials which describe the origin of sacred writings in terms of divine authorship, remarkable circumstances of discovery and great antiquity. We may now turn to the question whether Egyptian religious texts were homogeneous or not. In the first place, it is to be expected that in the Egyptian cult religion and its pantheon there was no such unity as we find in Biblical scripture (γραφή). This is indeed so: neither this unity nor even the concept of it exists in Egypt. Where ritual books are used in cult, and where hymns vary according to the peculiar characteristics of the god concerned and the place where he is worshipped, we cannot expect homogeneity, either in the composition of a corpus of writings or in the way these works were regarded throughout Egypt. There is a particle of truth in the statement of Clement of Alexandria[33] that the Egyptians had forty-two sacred writings by Hermes (Thoth), in so far as these texts, which include geographical and medical works among others, constitute the entire range of material available for the education of priests.[34] The reference to Thoth's authorship, as we know, is based on ancient tradition; the figure forty-two probably stems from the number of Egyptian nomes, and thus conveys the notion of completeness.[35] All this of course does not imply that literary compilations were totally unknown in Egypt. Characteristically enough, such compilations are to be found among mortuary literature, which tended towards uniformity throughout the land. Here the spells from the Book of the Dead, which at first appeared under individual rubrics and had a heterogeneous character, finally secured a common title, 'Coming Forth by Day'.[36] This was written on the outside of these scrolls.[37] Accordingly the first chapter of the collection is referred to as 'Here begin the chapters',[38] and finally the sense of unity is so strong that supplements are referred to as such, namely: 'The chapters which are taken from another work and are added to the Book of Coming Forth by Day'.[39]

Textual changes

Thirdly, with regard to the text, we need not expect in a cult religion such as the Egyptian one the punctilious adherence to

literalness which developed in the land of the Bible. Let us take
one simple and impressive fact. The Book of the Dead, the textual
history of which has been fairly well studied, underwent extensive
change during the half-millennium between the end of the First
Intermediate period (earliest inscriptions on coffins) and the New
Kingdom (classical manuscripts), as a result of which the original
was often distorted beyond recognition.[40] This is by no means only
due to errors by scribes but has deeper reasons. In so far as the
texts comprise mythical material, their meaning came to be forgotten once the age of mythology was past. Secondly, and this
is of particular importance to us here, the Egyptians were not afraid
of altering the text. They did so, for example, when there was an
opportunity to devise some play on words. The phrase 'I am Orion
(*s3ḥ*) who has mercy upon you in what he does...' is transformed
in the Middle Kingdom into an entirely different sentence for
the sake of indulging in a play on words prompted by the name
Orion: 'I am Orion (*s3ḥ*) who sets foot (*s3ḥ*) upon his Two Lands
...'[41] The Greeks, and following them the Christians, corrected
the interpretation where necessary, but the Egyptians corrected
the text![42] Thus we need not be surprised at such less radical
practices as inserting into manuscripts marginal glosses, which
on occasion are developed into a regular interrogatory technique;
sometimes these have several versions or meanings. We have
already pointed to the root of such explanations in connection
with the statements about *Ḥw*, *S3* and Nun (see pp. 165, 171); we
may now quote these in full: 'Ye ancestors, raise up your arms to
me...[gloss:] Who are they, these ancestors of the gods? They
are *Ḥw* and *S3*.'[43] Or: 'I am the great god who came into being
by himself...[gloss:] What does that mean? The great god who
gave birth to himself, that is Nun – that is Nun, the father of the
gods. Other version [or meaning]: that is Re.'[44] Nor need one be
surprised that texts were added to or abridged. The so-called 'great
solar litany' seems to be an expanded version of the small one; on
the other hand, the so-called 'small Amduat' (Book of that which
is in the Underworld) appears to be an extract from the larger one;
at any rate it is called 'compendium [or extract: *sḥwy*] of this
[larger] book'.[45]

By contrast it seems strange if, in this milieu where religious
texts were treated so freely, one comes across a formula which

urges with classical explicitness that the original wording be preserved. We may have an example of this in an admonition that occurs towards the end of the Instruction of Ptah-hotep and has been translated as follows: 'Take no word (*mdt*) away (*iti*), and add nothing (*ini*) thereto, and put not one thing (*kt*) in the place of another (*kt*).'[46] But in the meantime study of linguistic usage has shown that the verbs *iti* and *ini*, traditionally translated as 'take away' and 'add', may when juxtaposed have the sense of confused movement; *mdt* may mean 'things' as well as 'word'; the two expressions *kt* need not be related to *mdt* but may stand independently. Accordingly the translation should read: 'Do not say now this and now that [and] confound not one thing with another.'[47] This removes the crux from a testimony which seems to be mocked by the later history of the much-amended text, and which would have had no factual basis in a cult religion like that of Egypt.[48] Nevertheless the possibility remains that Egyptians of later periods and their neighbours may have understood the sage's admonition in the same sense as we Egyptologists at first did; they may well have interpreted it simply as an admonition to copy correctly. For we do indeed have ambiguous wordings in the Instruction of Ptah-hotep (see p. 128); and here too we may be dealing with one such, made unintentionally.[49] If so, it would be conceivable that the formula, understood as an admonition to preserve the original wording, found its way to Israel, together with Egyptian wisdom literature, and that it bore rich fruit there, upon the alien soil of a scriptural religion – with consequences that made themselves felt from Deuteronomy to the Revelation of St John and beyond.[50] But this is admittedly no more than a hypothesis, given the present state of our knowledge.

Recitation of religious literature

How did matters stand in Egypt in regard to the reading of religious literature? The Egyptologist will immediately think of the official whom we have become accustomed to call a 'lector priest', but whose title is literally 'bearer of the festival roll (*ḥrw ḥbt*)'.[51] This is the man who recites from a scroll both in the divine cult and in the mortuary service, and whose image is often represented. That this is a ritual document is evident, *inter alia*, from the designation given to the document he bears.[52] This does not mean that the

lector priest can be compared to the reader of holy writ in the
Judaeo-Christian world; nor does his rank in the Egyptian priesthood give him a central position in the divine service. For the
so-called lector priest comes beneath the priest proper, who
performs the actual ritual and for this reason does hold such
a central position. He belonged to the *clerus minor*; and if he is at
the top of this class, this is simply because he had mastered the
difficult art of reading, which was for the select few.[53] The only
evidence that points to the reciting of texts having an independent
function in the divine service seems to be the custom (which is
admittedly authenticated only very late, at Edfu and Thebes) of
giving an interpretation of the text after the ritual had been
performed.[54] Here we have the phenomenon of a translation which
is a kind of interpretation – a translation from an earlier linguistic
form into the contemporary one, which modernizes the text both
linguistically and intellectually. This is something we find again
in Palestine, in the shape of the so-called Targums: translations,
sometimes quite free, of the basic text from the sacred ancient
Hebrew tongue into the living Hebrew and Aramaic language,
which thereby standardize its theological content in accordance
with present concepts.[55] The question must be asked whether this
cult practice, which resembles the customs observed by the early
Christian communities and by those who worshipped at the
Hellenistic mysteries in its combination of ritual performance and
instruction,[56] did not develop until the Late period. At any rate it
testifies to two things: first, that an address was delivered to the
assembled faithful – a kind of profession of faith, whose nature we
can grasp by comparing it with the hymns recited in the cult
(see pp. 90 ff.); secondly, that it had a functional purpose within
the structure of the cult, in that it offered an interpretation of the
rituals that were performed. Thus we may say that reading texts
was an essential component of the ritual, which helped it to run
smoothly and if need be elucidated it.

Secret texts

But in Egypt it was not always thought desirable to read texts;
in some cases they were kept secret. This is not surprising in
a country where the public were excluded from certain divine
services, such as the daily care of the cult image (see pp. 87 f.).

This secrecy is occasionally described in strong terms: '[Amon], thou most mysterious of the mysterious, whose mystery is unknown',[57] etc. It stands to reason that rituals which were recited in a secluded chamber of the temple were in practice neither heard nor seen by any unauthorized person; at any rate, so far as we are aware, no injunctions were given about the need to keep them secret. Another factor is that these manuscripts had already been removed from the profane sphere when they were compiled, since they were as a rule written exclusively in the 'house of life', which was administered by priests.[58] But mortuary literature, which was at everyone's disposal after the democratization of funerary beliefs, teems with such instructions. There we are told, for example: 'Let none who is outside know [this spell]; not thy father or thy son; it is for thyself alone.'[59] According to this it is even forbidden to pass the text on directly from one generation to another within a single family, a method which elsewhere – the classical example is in the wisdom literature – was regarded as ideal and traditional. Of the content it is said: 'No one knows [it] who is outside; it is his [the dead's] mystery; the profane know [it] not (*ḫꜣw-mr*).'[60] Even in the late Book of Breathings we read: 'Hide it, hide it, do not let anyone read it!'[61] Writers deplore the fact that certain texts are profaned at a time of upheaval and confusion: 'Forsooth, magical spells (*ḥkꜣw*) are divulged (*šḥꜣ*).'[62] In our view this provides the key: it is magical spells which are particularly affected by such secrecy. For in the last resort it would be harmful if they were to come into unauthorized hands. Where a magical book, so we are told, comes into someone's possession illegally, it wreaks death and destruction. This was the case with Noferkaptah and his family, who according to a demotic tale appropriated a carefully concealed secret document of Thoth.[63] Mortuary literature, as we shall see directly, is in essence magical literature, and to an ever increasing extent took on its characteristics. This was why it was enveloped in the veil of secrecy in which magicians kept their spells. There is ample testimony to this in Greek magical literature on Egyptian soil.[64]

Mortuary literature

Enough has now been said about the characteristics of religious literature in Egypt. We hope it has become clear that these facts

about the homogeneity of the texts, and whether they were recited
or kept secret, have substantiated our main point about the nature
of the Egyptians' outlook, shaped as it was by their cult religion.
It stands to reason that there were also features, like the divine
origin of the sacred writings and their venerable antiquity, which
are not fundamentally different from those encountered in scriptural religion. For in all religions God is seen as the ultimate
Cause, and his ordinances – whether they be of a juridical or ritual
nature – were written down from the earliest times. What we still
owe the reader in this context is a brief description and analysis
of a curious phenomenon which we have often mentioned but
have yet to treat systematically: Egyptian mortuary literature. It
is fairly easy to sketch the range of its content.[65] There are first
of all inscriptions in the chambers and upon the sarcophagi of
the pyramids from the late Old Kingdom, starting with Unas, the
last ruler of the Fifth Dynasty. We call these the Pyramid Texts.
The spells intended for the king live on in some texts of the First
Intermediate period inscribed inside the coffins of private persons,
which incorporated local and non-royal traditions.[66] These are
referred to appropriately as the Coffin Texts. These spells were
handed down to the New Kingdom and beyond, although they
underwent the radical textual alterations just mentioned (see
p. 223). Since they were usually inscribed upon a papyrus scroll
and interred with the mummy, they are referred to as the Book of
the Dead; this term must be understood in a general sense, for
these heterogeneous spells by no means formed a book. We have
already seen that later the Egyptians tried to give this collection
a uniform character by adding headings and rearranging the
material (see pp. 222 f.). In later times several compilations were
made of these texts, among them the Book of Breathings, the
Rhind mortuary papyrus, the Book of Traversing Eternity, as well
as various others we have mentioned.[67]

Outside this main line of development are writings which concentrate upon certain themes and whose interest, on account of
their geographical subject-matter, often seems to lie less in the
text than in the cartographic representations, or at least the
descriptions arranged by regions. These are the so-called 'guides
to the beyond' which, as their name suggests, guide the dead
along their way through the hereafter and afford them protection

there; they also contain an account, divided into hourly sections, of the sun's journey through the nocturnal realm of the dead, i.e. the event which offered the dead the greatest hope of salvation (see pp. 207 f.). The first-mentioned function is particularly characteristic of the Book of the Two Ways, but also of several spells in the Book of the Dead which treat of the deceased's sojourn in and movement about the sacred realm, the fields of offerings or rushes,[68] or more especially (7, 14, 21) deal with the gates of the nether world and thus with access to the Fields of Rushes.[69] The Amduat (Book of that which is in the Underworld),[70] the Book of Gates and the Book of Caverns all serve the second of the two functions indicated.[71]

Reasons for development of mortuary literature

This phenomenon of Egyptian mortuary literature is almost unique, at any rate in the ancient Mediterranean world; the so-called Orphic Passes of the Dead, which in their subject-matter are close to it, probably did not develop independently, either as a whole or in points of detail, but derived from Egyptian custom.[72] But this inevitably poses the question how this strange phenomenon came to pass. We are not thinking in chronological terms, for it seems to be definitely established that it commenced with the texts found in the Unas pyramid.[73] But why was it that religious texts were inscribed in mortuary chambers or buried with the dead? On this point Egyptologists at first simply thought that the Egyptians had had unfortunate experiences with the reliability of the regular provision of supplies for the dead, and that for this reason they '[came] upon the idea of making themselves independent of the goodwill of an impious posterity by taking into their tombs, for their own personal use, the texts which the priests were supposed to read for them but would presumably cease to read'.[74] But beyond that some scholars have recently taken the bold step of seeing the Pyramid Texts, given their content and arrangement, as the quintessence of the rituals carried out when the ruler was interred; the actual course of this event, which took place in the chambers of the temple complex of the Pyramid area, was then, as it were, reflected in the inscriptions in the corridors and chambers of the actual pyramid, the royal burial-place.[75] This bold, learned and ingenious interpretation can properly be assessed only by one who has examined it in terms of the vast and diverse material. When this is done, it appears that quite serious objections may be levelled against numerous points in the argumentation and thus against the thesis as such.[76] Without losing sight of this new perspective, we are led back to the simple but plausible idea of the autarky of the dead, in the first place by the mortuary offerings. We have already pointed out (p. 209) that the spells of the so-called sacrificial ritual, i.e. the texts used in the provision of supplies, were inscribed in a prominent place where they could be seen by the dead person resting in his sarcophagus. Even if they are placed there in pursuance of some general concept of ritual as such, as would follow from the theory just mentioned, one can hardly deny, in our opinion, that they were placed next to the dead in order to ensure their continued existence in the beyond, and were therefore the source and starting-point of all the spells recorded. In other words, texts were written down so that the dead themselves could 'proclaim the provision of supplies (*nis dbḥt-ḥtp*)' instead of this being done by unreliable priests. This was the nucleus around which the texts crystallized; if others were added which were concerned with the preservation of the body of the deceased, or with the king's ascent to heaven, these were no doubt derived from the respective ritual acts performed. They may be explained by the simple fact that the conservation of the body and the king's ascent to heaven belong to the general picture which men had of existence in the nether world, as linked both to the tomb and to heaven. When in the course of time the realm of the dead became more generally identified with the nether world (see pp. 217 f.), mortuary literature with its guides to the beyond became increasingly oriented toward this goal.[77]

Magical significance of mortuary literature

We hope that these remarks have explained sufficiently clearly the cause and purpose of mortuary literature, and that we have given the traditional interpretation its due without ignoring recent scholarship. What still remains to be done is to provide an interpretation of this phenomenon which would lead to a fundamentally correct understanding of the spells. To put it in a nutshell, mortuary texts are magical texts. Admittedly, this does not hold good for all periods to the same extent, but becomes more marked with the passage of time. When texts are inscribed in the king's tomb, the recitation of which is intended to guarantee his royal existence for all eternity, and whose statements about his divinity have a real analogy in the terrestrial concept of sacrosanct monarchy, the magical character of the sentences is confined to the fact that the written word is imagined as efficacious, i.e. is made effective through recitation by the dead. True, here powers are already ascribed to the king which he did not have in real life, at least at the time when the texts were written. An extreme example of this occurs in the so-called Cannibal Spell of the Pyramid Texts,[78] which elevates the king *inter alia* to the plane of an absolute and arbitrary lord of fate 'in this his dignity of: "If he wishes he does; if he dislikes, he does not", '[79] but then reveals its cloven hoof when, at the end, the dead king is shown as quite helpless, for after the earlier bombast he is made to utter the very modest hope: 'And the doers of [ill] deeds have no power to destroy the favourite place of NN [i.e. his tomb] among those who live in this land for ever and ever.'[80]

Moreover, after the Pyramid Texts pure magical spells, such as those designed to ward off snakes, scorpions, crocodiles, etc., frequently found their way into mortuary literature.[81] In them we encounter magical words such as *hi ti ti bi ti*,[82] composed just like our word 'hocus-pocus'. The magical character of mortuary literature is enhanced very substantially when texts intended to immortalize the king's existence are usurped by private persons, and the mere identity of word and reality is thereby transformed by a form of words, being given a strange or non-existent reality. This is precisely what magic seeks to do, and this is precisely what happens with the Coffin Texts; moreover, not only the spells designed for the king are taken over but also the royal insignia, in the so-called frieze of implements found on the sarcophagi (see p. 203). Consequently it is not surprising that when we discussed the injunctions to keep texts secret we came across testimonies in mortuary literature which are also found in magical texts (see pp. 225 f.).

This basic insight into the nature of mortuary literature should always be kept in view when interpreting individual statements. We may illustrate this by a single example. If one were to seek

them out and collect them, one would probably find well over
one hundred pieces of evidence to show that the dead man, when
he is imagined as a speaker, puts himself on the same level as the
gods: 'I am Atum, for I was alone. I am Re at his first appearance',[83] etc. The dead person seeks to climb high: by equating
himself with the primeval god, he enters into his creative power.[84]
But it would be a fateful mistake if one were to deduce from such
sentences that the Egyptians regarded themselves as God. This
was not so; on the contrary they prostrated themselves before the
deity in all humility, cognizant of his lordship over them, and this
we have set forth in detail earlier (e.g. pp. 62 ff.). What may be
inferred here is something that is best understood in the light of
the ultimate purpose of this literary genre. We may formulate it
thus: the Egyptian, faced with death, sought the best possible way
in which he could become immortal; used as he was to magical
practices in his life on earth, he went on to usurp divine powers
by employing magical verbal formulae.[85] Of course one must also
guard against the error that verbal magic was the basis of
Egyptian funerary beliefs: it was in fact no more than a mode of
approach, just like ritual, or the judgement of the dead (although
this latter was something completely different and of course
fraught with anxiety). The basis of the funerary belief seems to
me to be – at least in the dynastic period[86] – the inspiring belief
in the reality of God. This led the faithful to try to enter into this
reality, and to regard all magic as a gift of God, granted 'as
weapons to ward off what might happen'.[87] Thus the work done
on Egyptian mortuary literature is a classic example of the truth
of the maxim that interpretation must proceed from a thorough
understanding of the genre as such. The Egyptian mortuary texts
are a lucrative source of information on mythology and rituals,
and also on theological doctrines. But they would lead to a seriously
distorted picture of Egyptian piety if one took them in isolation
from their context.

11 · Egyptian religion and the outside world

The last chapter, as was pointed out in the introductory remarks, formed an independent section. The same is true, only more so, of the present chapter: an examination of alien influences on Egyptian religion and the impact which it had upon foreign lands, both at the time and later. We are dealing here with a wide range of problems, and in particular with a large amount of detail, which has to be identified, systematized and evaluated. The course of historical development governs the arrangement of this material. But we must ask the question whether the nature of Egyptian religion, as explored above, lies behind this mass of details. We are convinced that this is so, and that the insights we have so far obtained will stand us in good stead when approaching this topic.

If Egyptian religion, as we have seen, is a national religion, this fact must determine the limits and scope of its influence, as well as that of the influences exerted upon it. Yet if it was more than just a national cult, and contained elements of personal piety, it must have been receptive to external stimuli and also capable of having an impact on non-Egyptians. These brief introductory remarks have, it is hoped, indicated some of the methodological principles we are following here; they may in addition have thrown some light on the train of thought which unites the several themes discussed in this volume. Nevertheless this last chapter, as will become apparent again and again, has an independent character, and this has its grounds in the nature of the subject-matter, which leads us beyond the physical boundaries of Egypt.

Beginning of contact with foreign lands

Let us first look at the historical and geographical background. We have already seen in chapter 3 that the Egyptians were conscious of being surrounded by neighbours: Libyans in the west, Nubians in the south, Asiatics in the north-east; to these were then added the inhabitants of the Aegean world to the north, who only later attained real significance. In principle we shall have to explore the contacts that existed in each of these directions. But when did these contacts begin? This is not so easy to answer. We may exclude on principle the early period in the development of Egyptian culture – one in which the Libyans to the west played a significant role. We do so not only because information is scarce about these early centuries, but also because such influences should not be accounted as foreign borrowings: we are dealing here rather with an integral part of the process whereby the Egyptians constructed their own cultural forms. For these Libyans may be called 'Egyptians outside the Nile valley', who had ceased to participate in the cultural development of their kinsmen in the fertile territories watered by this river.[1] Thus the supposedly Libyan elements in the costume of the Egyptian king – animal tail, possibly also the uraeus serpent as a successor to the characteristic Libyan forelock – are probably in fact nothing other than archaic forms common to the Libyan–Egyptian group, which later were preserved only by tribes outside the civilization of the Nile valley.[2]

It is from this angle that one should approach the question of the Libyan origin of Egyptian deities. This question particularly concerns Neith, who as goddess of Saïs in the western Delta was in any case close to the tribes in the west; however, in her manifestation as mistress of bow and arrow, i.e. as goddess of hunting, Neith was neither of Egyptian nor of Libyan origin, in the sense of an ethnic attribution, but was simply derived from the ancient hunter culture as such.[3] In those cases where a deity, like Ash, is clearly associated with the western desert, including its fertile areas, and is called 'Lord of *Tḥnw* [Libya]', he appears falcon-headed or in completely human form, and thus as a wholly Egyptian god. This is most emphatically corroborated by the function this lord of Libya fulfils, in bringing to the pharaoh 'all the good things' of the hilly country which he represents.[4] Ash is to the Egyptian the numen appertaining to the western desert, who in his way looks after Egyptian society, embodied in the king; he therefore does not introduce any alien features into the Egyptian pantheon.[5] In this capacity he is, by the way, later equated with Seth, the lord of the desert and of foreign lands in general, and so is fully integrated into the Egyptian pantheon.[6]

Old Kingdom

We began by asking at what point in time the Egyptians came into
contact with the religion of their neighbours and decided to exclude
their relationship with the early Libyans. By speaking of Ash, who
was simultaneously lord of the western desert and an Egyptian
god, we have thus imperceptibly approached the Old Kingdom.
The same pattern is to be found in relations with Nubia, to the
south. Here it is Dedun whose territorial allegiance and other
characteristics are given in his title 'The youth of Upper Egypt
who came out of Nubia'; he bears incense, which comes from the
south.[7] Originally a bird of prey, of indeterminate species, in
Egypt he became assimilated to the Horus falcon.[8] The most impressive testimony illustrating his incorporation into the Egyptian
pantheon seems to be an utterance in the Pyramid Texts in which
the king is equated with the deities of remote territories, among
them 'Dedun who presides over Nubia'.[9] As the bearer of incense,
he serves the needs of Egypt and its king, like Ash; it may be
noted here that he kept to this role and expanded it fundamentally
when he later brought to the Egyptian ruler, as his subjects, the
peoples of the south.[10] Consequently Dedun, too, is the god of
a certain region who became a pillar of the Egyptian national
religion, but in doing so made no more of a change in the Egyptian
pantheon than his neighbour to the west did. In our view this
circumstance seems characteristic of Egypt's situation during
Old Kingdom times: as a matter of course it is regarded as the
centre of the earth; its neighbours have no rights of their own,
but their gods are members of the Egyptian pantheon, as lords of
certain regions; in this capacity they serve the Egyptian sacrosanct
ruler and may indeed even be encompassed by his nature.

Middle Kingdom

We have no cause to assume that this picture changed in any
essential way during the Middle Kingdom. What was new was
the greater intensity of contacts with adjacent areas in the north-
east, such as Palestine, Phoenicia and Syria. Military campaigns
brought Egyptian troops at least as far as Sekhmen;[11] from Egyptian
archaeological finds in Phoenicia and the Syrian interior it may
be inferred that the land of the Nile exerted at least a commercial

and cultural influence in areas considerably further to the north, such as Ugarit and Alalakh.[12]

During the Middle Kingdom the native princes of the port of Byblos (Gebal), which had always had close links with Egypt, even bore Egyptian titles which only the pharaohs were able to confer;[13] finally, extensive areas of Palestine and Phoenicia are identified as belonging to the Egyptian sphere of influence by the fact that in certain texts their rulers and peoples are outlawed as enemies of the pharaoh.[14] In the available testimonies we do not find any mention of a god who represents the whole area of these regions in the same way as Ash represented the western desert or Dedun the south; the reason for this lies in the territory's political structure, which was predominantly one of city states. Thus we must rest content with the information, which takes us beyond the sphere of religious policy, that the Egyptian Hathor, who was equated with the town-goddess of Byblos (at some moment which at first was very difficult to determine), is called in Egyptian mortuary literature 'Hathor, Lady of Byblos'.[15] Two points are worthy of note here. In the first place this testimony goes beyond the limits of historical documents (or at least those written for the king, such as the Pyramid Texts); it is also, as indicated above, more than a mere document of religious policy. Hathor, 'Lady of Byblos', acquired a significance for every Egyptian mortal. In the second place it is worth emphasizing the way in which she acquired this prominence: she was thought of as 'steering the ship [of the dead]'. This was a feature which, it appears, is not recorded anywhere else in connection with Hathor, but which can be derived quite naturally from her character as the 'lady' of an important port. If this is the case, we could speak here of a Syrian goddess exerting an influence upon an Egyptian one.[16] Unfortunately the origin of the equation of Hathor with the 'Lady of Byblos' remains obscure, both as regards its date and the circumstances which led to it;[17] partly for this reason we cannot say for sure whether this is an *interpretatio Aegyptiaca* of the Syrian goddess with a retroactive effect upon her Egyptian partner, or whether the Egyptians simply gave their goddess a Syrian territory as her sphere of influence. One point is, however, certain: if the former holds good, one may speak of an enrichment of religion in comparison with the Old Kingdom:

contact with Syria would have led an Egyptian deity to acquire a new trait. At any rate, whatever the exact circumstances were, they were felt beyond the limits of the official cult and affected the attitude of individual believers. For 'the Lady of Byblos', like 'Hathor', now appeared as a girl's name in Egypt.[18] On the other hand, we must evidently reject what purports to be a second testimony pointing to the presence of a Near Eastern goddess in Egyptian mortuary literature. In the Coffin Texts[19] attempts have been made to find Ishtar.[20] But in fact this seems to be the designation of a bird demon, whose name should not be read as *ištrt* (= Ishtar), but in the light of parallel passages as *ištt*.[21]

New Kingdom

During the New Kingdom Egyptian religion maintained its basic characteristics and played a part in political history. Even the variations which occur between those areas where it was disseminated are accounted for by differences in their historical experience. As far as Syria is concerned (and this area may be taken for our purposes here as including Palestine and Phoenicia as well), although the pharaohs did have temples erected or expanded, these were as a rule dedicated to native deities.[22] Where Egyptian deities were granted a temple, as Amon was in Gaza and Ptah in Ashkelon,[23] it was apparently built and maintained for reasons of a political and legal character: Syrian places were required to pay tribute to the respective sanctuaries of the great Egyptian deities (see pp. 52 f.). This state of affairs is quite natural, given the pattern of Egyptian authority in Syria. As is generally known, the petty states there were allowed to keep most of their traditional rights, and this led logically to the pharaohs worshipping the local deities.[24] In Nubia, on the other hand, which was incorporated into the Egyptian empire as a colony, a whole number of huge sanctuaries were built by the pharaohs, above all the vast rock-cut temple at Abu Simbel; most of these were dedicated to the principal gods, Amon, Re and Ptah. Moreover, it was here that the cult of the dead and living rulers flourished. This started with the service (apparently established or revived by Thutmosis III) for the ἥρως κτίστης Sesostris III, as organizer and preserver of the province. Later this led to the worship of the current ruler, especially of Amenophis III and Ramses II, whose images in

Nubian temples were habitually placed on the same level as those of the national gods.[25]

Thus we may say that in Syria the negative aspect of the national religion was dominant, in that there the pharaohs worshipped the local gods of the tributary states, whereas in Nubia the positive aspect prevailed, since here they enlarged the territory in which the Egyptian deities were venerated. We have deliberately used the word 'dominant', for we have seen that the Egyptian rulers also worshipped Egyptian gods in Syria, and on the other hand that the Nubian god Dedun brought his peoples to the pharaoh. Finally, it may be added that Dedun played a distinctly political role when he was worshipped as the guardian of the fortress of Semna on the southern border of Lower Nubia.[26] Moreover, it was here that he assumed the role of sky-god, lord of the Egyptian royal throne and father of the pharaoh: 'In this land thy [Dedun's] beloved son Mn-ḫpr-Rᶜ seats himself upon thy seat; he inherits thy throne; he becomes king of Upper and Lower Egypt, the like of whom will not be seen again', etc.[27]

Popular character of this influence

Nevertheless the full correspondence between religious and historical events during the New Kingdom would not be apparent if we were to confine ourselves to the chief aspects apparent in the national religion, which is more political than religious. Did the local population already take part in the divine service before any Egyptian temple existed in Syria? This was certainly so in the case of the temple of Ptah at Ashkelon, for our knowledge of this temple comes from the testimony of a female 'singer' of this god, who bears the name of *Krkr* (or *Klkl*): certainly not an Egyptian name, and written syllabically as was customary with foreign words.[28] But if non-Egyptians did participate in the divine service, one must allow for the possibility, indeed the probability, that the actual content of Egyptian religion had an influence upon foreigners, as a result of the political and legal factors we have mentioned. If a singer sang hymns, she can hardly have escaped being influenced by their religious content to which we have referred earlier (see p. 92).

This leads us beyond the external aspects of religious history to its inner essentials: we have to consider the worshippers who, as they took part in the divine service, were surely affected by its forms, and probably by its content as well. This was not the only way in which Egyptian religion exerted an impact upon neighbouring peoples. Those who travelled about the eastern Mediterranean world – whether in groups as prisoners of war, mercenaries or colonists, or individually as diplomats, merchants etc. – brought with them their traditional religion. People from Near Eastern lands, especially of course Syrians, found their way to Egypt, voluntarily or by coercion. Among those in the former category were the Hyksos, who during the Second Intermediate period gained a footing first of all in the eastern Delta (capital: Avaris) and then penetrated to varying distances into the interior of the country. Their god is said to have been Seth: '[The Hyksos king] Apophis took to him Sutekh [Seth] for lord and served not any god that was in the whole land save only Sutekh [Seth].'[29] Here it may be assumed that Seth stands for the Syrian god 'Baal', because of all foreign deities Baal alone is designated in later Egyptian texts by Seth's animal (its species cannot be determined with certainty).[30] As the ancient god of foreign lands[31] Seth was a natural candidate for an *interpretatio Aegyptiaca* of the god of the Hyksos; his function as thunder-god[32] may have been an additional reason, but this is not certain, since the original nature of the Hyksos' god Baal can no longer be made out. Besides Baal–Seth a significant role must at that time have been played by Anath, who is attested by several theophorous royal names of the Hyksos.[33] However, when the Egyptians turned the tables on the invaders, expelled them, and sent their own armies across the Euphrates, masses of foreigners from the territory they passed through reached the banks of the Nile – at first involuntarily, but later no doubt often of their own free will.

Zenith of Syrian influence

This was the beginning of the period when foreign, especially Syrian, deities were worshipped on a large scale in Egypt; it came to an end only toward the close of the Ramesside period,[34] and is worth our attention for its own sake. We cannot go into detail about individual deities,[35] and may merely note that in addition to Baal, who is almost completely absorbed by Seth, there were Resheph and Hurun, and among the goddesses Anath, Astarte and Kadesh.[36] We may rather confine ourselves to some features of outstanding interest to the historian of religion and try to define the nature and significance of these phenomena. In the first place we must admit that these gods, which at first sight seem to be a mass of 'displaced persons', became integrated into the national religion. Recent research has shown that the Syrian deities were included in the official cult, or to be more precise were associated with the kings, while at the same time they also found favour among non-Egyptians, especially those living in the Asiatic quarter at Memphis and possibly also the workers settled at Deir el-Medina.[37] The former circumstance can be explained by the historical factor mentioned above, namely that the pharaohs showed respect for the deities of those states that were allowed to retain their political autonomy and went on to incorporate them into the pantheon. What we are dealing with here is thus a particular case of the general phenomenon of *evocatio*: the god is not summoned to Egypt from his alien realm after its conquest, but his power is absorbed into that of the Egyptian pantheon after his territory has been taken over. This is done primarily through the intermediacy of the king, who adopts some such epithet as 'beloved of [the Syrian god] Hurun', just as Hurun is in turn beloved of the national god Amon etc.[38] In all this the point to note is that the adopted Syrian deities are numbered among those whose power is of a martial kind. Pugnaciousness is a characteristic of the goddesses Anath and Astarte as well as of the gods Baal, Resheph and Hurun. This is shown by their titles no less than by their physical attributes. Thus Resheph is called 'lord of strength',[39] is merged with the Theban war-god to become Month-Resheph,[40] or appears performing model acts of valour, which the king emulates 'like Resheph'.[41] Astarte (or one of her Syrian comrades-in-arms, possibly Anath) is known to us as a horsewoman brandishing her bow and arrow, so that her warlike function apparently overshadows that of a goddess of fertility and love.[42]

We may sum up by saying that the national structure of Egyptian religion asserted itself actively in connection with the official cult; one might say that the gods in the Egyptian pantheon expanded their radius of activity in a way that corresponded to the expansion of their influence at home which may have occurred at this time (see pp. 50, 53). On the other hand the unmistakable connection between the worship of Syrian gods and immigrant communities from this area indicates a certain passive resistance to these foreign deities on the part of the Egyptians, who remained faithful to their national traditions. Admittedly, this reserve was by no means universal, and we may regard the public worship by these immigrants of Syrian gods as giving the latter entry into the Egyptians' hearts.[43] We may explain this by pointing to the fact that these gods were not only seen as warlike – which logically was useful to the national cult – but were also popularly regarded as having healing powers.[44] Resheph, Astarte and her companions became known to the Egyptians at a time when they were liberating themselves from the accepted ideas and asserting their individual needs in terms of their attitude to personal piety. Since the Syrian deities were considered by their original worshippers to be gods of healing, it was only natural that Egyptians with the same needs should seek aid from them as well.

We have two long-familiar items of evidence which show that simple private persons besought 'Ishtar of Syria' to grant them a cure for all their ills; this goddess may be distinct from Astarte and may be identified as Ishtar of Mitanni.[45] One of these testimonies quite definitely points to a family born in Syria, on account of the personal names mentioned in it. The other one concerns a servant of a high priest of Ptah with the Egyptian name of *Ptḥ-ꜥnḫ* (or *ꜥnḫ-Ptḥ*). In this case the donor may have originated from Syria, but this rests on indirect evidence: the important role played by the temple of Ptah at Memphis in the cult of Asiatic deities. We would prefer to see in this an example of the fact that Syrian gods were invoked by the Egyptians to aid them in their sufferings. The lead was taken in this, as we know, by someone as important as King Amenophis III, who in the last year of his reign, i.e. apparently during his last illness and consequently without success, got his father-in-law, the Mitanni prince Tusratta, to send him on loan an image of Ishtar of Nineveh.[46] This also shows that Syrian deities were regarded in Egypt as gods in the full sense of the word. The king, who was associated with them *ex officio* through his role in the national cult, also expected salvation from them as a human being in need. To be sure, this was not a foreign innovation in Egyptian religion. What both

Syrians and natives expected from these gods was nothing other than what was solicited from Amon and other Egyptian deities at that time: help in personal distress (see pp. 104f.). But one should not rule out the possibility that the worship of Syrian deities enhanced their health-giving functions and helped to determine their form.[47]

It is now time to return to the starting-point of this section. We have been concerned to show how the coming together of different religions, each of which had developed in its own milieu, affected ordinary people, and to this end our investigation has focused on the veneration of Syrian gods in Egypt. Our conclusion is that, despite the ambiguities inherent in national structure, the influence of foreign gods extended down to the level of plain people, for whom they had a certain attraction. Just as the native, or at any rate non-Egyptian, singer of Ptah of Ashkelon could hardly be indifferent to the appeal of the Egyptian god whose praises she sang, so Egyptians encountered in their own homeland Syrian deities from whom they implored and anticipated salvation. How much alien influence was actually transmitted in this way it is impossible as yet to say. For foreign gods like Resheph (see p. 239) acquired the attributes of their Egyptian equivalents; we even know that they were equated with one another by Egyptian theologians, who in this ignored the native tradition: e.g., 'Kadesh–Astarte–Anath'.[48] Here, too, to use an old Egyptian phrase, 'the barbarians everywhere became Egyptians'. They wore Egyptian costume and so concealed their alien origin.

Contacts with the south in the Ethiopian period

If we are to continue in chronological sequence we may now go on to consider the state of affairs among Egypt's southern neighbours. We are mainly concerned with the period after the end of the New Kingdom, especially the so-called Ethiopian period. If in regard to Syria we may speak of a reciprocal relationship in which the Syrians had a slight advantage,[49] in regard to the south it is clear that Egyptian influence prevailed. This corresponded to political realities, and is evident above all in the fact that even on Nubian soil Nubian deities are put into the strait-jacket of an *interpretatio Aegyptiaca* by Egyptian testimonies – for example, we hear of various 'Horus gods in Wawat' (Lower Nubia) and of

'Hathor, Lady of '*Ibšk* [Abu Simbel]';[50] yet we do not find them being worshipped in Egypt itself, even in this Egyptian costume. The balance of forces in this respect becomes quite plain about the middle of the eighth century B.C., after the collapse of the New Kingdom and the end of Libyan rule, when the southerners for their part advanced triumphantly as far as the Delta and held sway as the Twenty-fifth Dynasty from their capital of Napata, situated on the Gebel Barkal below the Fourth Cataract. For the conquerors did not raise their shields in honour of any native deity but rather worshipped the Theban god Amon. In their own capital the Ethiopian kings spent enormous sums of money restoring and enlarging New Kingdom temples and building sacred edifices in a purely Egyptian style dedicated to Amon.[51] They made constant references to 'Amon of Napata' who 'guides the king on all his noble undertakings', etc.[52] The enormous influence exerted by Amon and his priests upon the government of the country is also shown by their role in the selection of the Ethiopian king.[53] It is a peculiarly piquant historical fact that the Ethiopians surpassed the Egyptians in the orthodoxy of their worship of Amon, for it often happens that ideas are taken to an extreme by those who receive them at second hand in a foreign country. A famous testimony illustrating devotion to Ptah at this time is the preservation of his ancient teaching in the inscription made for the Ethiopian Shabaka, to which reference has been made above (see p. 154 and *passim*).[54] We also hear of King Harsijotef arranging processional ceremonies at various places for Osiris, Isis, Horus, Re and Onuris, in addition of course to Amon.[55] This makes it plain that the Ethiopians by no means preferred a monotheistic cult of Amon to the profusion of the Egyptian pantheon, whose various members are frequently encountered in their temple reliefs. They adhered to the basic structure of the Egyptian pantheon as much as they adhered to the individual figures which it comprised.

The influence of Egyptian forms is also quite obvious on funerary customs. To single out just two characteristic features, ancient Egyptian Pyramid Texts are to be found in the small steep pyramids of the tomb complexes at Napata,[56] and the so-called negative confession of sins from the ancient Book of the Dead, dating from the New Kingdom (see p. 130), occurs in an inscription of the Ethiopian prince Chaliut.[57] Mention may also be made of donation plaques which often bore an offering formula of the Egyptian type (see p. 194), and of the large number of heart scarabs and *ushabtis* included among offerings. These afford proof that the Ethiopians took over from the Egyptians their ideas about the nether world: the preservation of the body of the deceased, the judgement of the dead, and the continuance of agricultural work. Later, when the centre of the kingdom was moved to the south and the capital was located at Meroë (Begerewiyeh), above the mouth of the Atbara, the influence of Egyptian religion by no means diminished on the Upper Nile. On the contrary, massive monuments were erected to Amon in the new capital as well.[58] Of the other Egyptian deities worshipped, Isis in particular stands out.[59] Her cult radiated into Nubia from her sanctuary at Philae, on the Egyptian southern border, whose fame spread far and wide, right up to the close of antiquity.[60]

This leads us to the funerary beliefs of the Meroites. On the rear wall of chapels in front of the pyramids at Meroë the deceased is usually represented as Osiris between Isis and Nephthys. The names of Isis and Osiris later found their way into the texts written down in Meroitic, a distinct language which at present occupies an isolated position. These names are also found on offering-tablets, the form of which provides further evidence of Egyptian influence.[61] On the other hand, the conspicuous lion gods seem to denote a native tradition. We may soon gain a clearer idea of the god Apedemak, since recently archaeologists succeeded in excavating the 'Lion Temple' at Mussawarat es-Sufra.[62] In view of this we may desist from speculation on this subject for the time being, and may merely mention the association of the lion with the south in Egyptian mythology and theology, with regard to Onuris-Shu and Tefnut. [63] In this area, shortly after the birth of Christ, a god was worshipped who was portrayed with a nimbus of rays about his head, and holding his arm in a posture characteristic of Mithra – i.e., a Helios-Mithra.[64] This is evidence that Meroitic civilization (approx. 300 B.C.–A.D. 350) belonged to the world of Hellenism and Roman imperial rule.

Contacts with the Greek world: earliest period

This brings us to the final and at the same time most important theme to be treated in this chapter, which we can deal with only briefly: the relations between Egypt and the Greek world in matters of religion. With regard to the length of time during which such contact took place, one should put out of one's mind the common preconception that it was limited to the period after Alexander the Great's liberation of Egypt from the Persian yoke, i.e., after the foundation of Alexandria in 332–331 B.C. (to choose a symbolic date). No doubt the relationship between Egypt and the Hellenic lands – more concretely, between Egyptians and Greeks, i.e. persons of Greek culture – were greatly intensified once Ptolemaic Egypt had come under the sway of Macedonia. Political and economic developments brought numerous Greeks into the country, where a bilingual social stratum evolved and intellectual exchanges of every kind were bound to take place.[65] But one has to reckon with a reciprocal relationship between Egyptian and Greek religion already prior to the beginning of the Hellenistic age. We shall not pursue here the difficult questions of Egypt's link with early Cretan culture (for example, the influence of the Osirian service upon the subject of the friezes on the sarcophagi at Hagia Triada, which may be connected either with the Osiris cult or with Osirian funerary processions).[66] But we cannot overlook the events leading up to the Hellenistic age. The three centuries from the appearance of Greek mercenaries in Egypt (under Psammetichus I) to Alexander's military and political feats[67] laid the foundations for the extensive cultural contacts that were to follow. If we consider the important phenomenon of the *interpretatio Graeca* of Egyptian deities, we shall see that we are not always dealing with a mere mechanical transposition. When a Greek writer such as Herodotus tells his readers that the Egyptian king of the gods (Amon) has the same form as Zeus, or that the Egyptian god of artisans (Ptah) corresponds to Hephaistos, we can see traces of Greek influence upon the Egyptian god and *vice versa*. The equation of Ptah with Hephaistos, which occurred during the fifth century at the latest, seems to have brought to a head earlier attempts to evolve a dwarf figure. By contrast in Samos a bronze cat of Egyptian origin was dedicated to Hera although the cat has no relation to this deity; this was no doubt done because it was associated with the Egyptian god analogous to Hera: Mut, the consort of Amon, who was equated with the cat Bastet.[68] Besides this mention may be made of Egyptian influence upon the cosmogonic doctrine and the pre-occupation with the dead characteristic of Greek devotees of Orphism. In our view such influence is evident in their peculiar doctrine of the cosmic egg fertilized by the wind,[69] which needs further clarification, as well as in their use (in the so-called Orphic Passes of the Dead) of mortuary literature; this was unheard of elsewhere in the Greek world, whereas it was common currency in Egypt (see p. 228).

The Hellenistic age

These examples from the prehistory of Hellenism, which could easily be augmented – incidentally, a worthwhile scholarly task – have probably led the attentive reader to the hypothesis that the national character of Egyptian religion had begun to lose its vigour in this period by comparison with the New Kingdom. For neither the *interpretationes Graecae* nor the totally private and non-political borrowings by the Orphic communities had any noticeable effect upon the respective national cults. Let us see whether this assumption is verified when we come to examine the Hellenistic age itself.

It cannot be denied that the Macedonian kings of Egypt also kept the ancient national cult in being, thereby manifesting their loyalty to the pharaonic tradition. It is also generally known that the Ptolemaic rulers, like the Roman emperors who succeeded them, restored, enlarged and built Egyptian temples on a grand scale, and that they associated with the royal and local deities according to ancient ritual, as is clear from these gods' images and inscriptions. Further evidence of this is to be found in the Ptolemaic ruler cult, which was eventually extended to the living king. (We cannot discuss here the related problems of the Greek and Egyptian roots of this phenomenon, or its historical development, whereby Egyptian forms came to the fore; nor can we consider the question, important in its own right, of the relationship between the apotheosis of deceased rulers and those still living.)[70]

Also relevant in this context are the measures taken to institute or transform cults, clearly undertaken in the interest of the state, or to be more precise for reasons of religious policy, in order to unite Greeks and Egyptians. We are referring to another well-known phenomenon, the creation of the god Sarapis, who combined Egyptian and Greek elements in exemplary fashion. His name is Egyptian, admittedly in a Grecianized form. According to the more probable hypothesis it is a mutilation of 'Osiris–Apis', based upon a misunderstanding;[71] it therefore refers to the Apis bull who was worshipped at Memphis and who, after his death, on becoming an Osiris, was interred together with his companions in a huge tomb complex. His appearance, by contrast, is Greek, admittedly in a barbarized form: he is seated upon a throne, bearded and clad in a chiton. Tradition has it that the figure was brought to Alexandria from Sinope in Asia Minor, probably already during the reign of Ptolemy I.[72] On stylistic grounds, which seem well founded, it has been attributed to the Carian master Bryaxis.[73] In saying that the god Sarapis was created, we wish to bring out the conspicuous point that he owes his form and role to the Macedonian ruler's need for a deity who could be worshipped jointly by Greeks and Egyptians and who for this reason could serve as a national god in the same way as Horus, Re, or Amon had once met the needs of the Egyptians.[74] Unfortunately we cannot even indicate here the numerous problems which Sarapis presents.[75] We must rest content with the laconic remark that the Ptolemies' plan failed. For although Sarapis did win the allegiance of people all over the ancient Mediterranean world and went on to play an important part in imperial Roman times, he did not appeal to the Egyptians themselves, who instead kept to the traditional figures of the Osirian group.[76]

Now we can at last answer the question with which we began: was the national structure of Egyptian religion weakened from this moment onward? Put in these terms, it can be unhesitatingly answered in the affirmative. True, traces of a national structure can still be seen, in the incorporation of the Ptolemies into the ancient divine service and in the attempt to create a national god that would be acceptable also to the Egyptians. But on the other hand Sarapis's very failure in Egypt shows that the Greek rulers were unable to find a new form that would fit the old content. Sarapis did *not* become what Horus or Amon had been. The subjects of the Ptolemies did not have a living god who, like Horus during the Archaic period and Amon during the Old Kingdom, would have been in their eyes the lawful representative of order. Thus national structure asserted itself only in a petrified form (in the king's performance of sacerdotal functions in the national sanctuaries) and in a negative form (the rejection of the Sarapis cult by the native population). How could it have been otherwise, one is driven to ask, in view of the fact that Egyptian history had run its course and self-assertion was synonymous with self-defence?

We have to look outside the realm of the official cult to find something that did not become petrified but, as we shall see later, remained vitally alive and was consequently able to exert an influence upon other lands. This was the Egyptians' unbroken belief in the vast number of divine forms which they had created – in that divine reality which the Greeks had largely lost; the fact that it survived among the Egyptians and other oriental peoples led them and the Romans to the dictum, given various forms, that the barbarians were more pious than the Hellenes.[77] This sense of piety is manifest in those inscriptions of the Late period which regarded God as the lord of fate, drew an increasingly close connection between God and ethical norms, and were unaffected by the growing spirit of scepticism in regard to traditional mortuary customs and concepts of the hereafter (see pp. 72 ff., 213).

This finally yields an answer to our cardinal question. We may say that the more the national structure of Egyptian religion weakened, the stronger became the impact of personal piety. It is predominantly this fact[78] (and only initially and marginally reasons of religious policy)[79] that explains the impact which Egyptian religious forms exerted all over the Hellenistic–Roman world It is not an exaggeration to state that this had repercussions of world-historical importance.

Turning now to this phenomenon, which again deserves more space, we may first illustrate the interplay of forces that naturally resulted when the two realms encountered one another – as had occurred before the Hellenistic age, when the Greeks and Egyptians had first met. The Greeks left their mark on the Egyptian deities and *vice versa*. Thus Anubis, the Egyptian god of death, who according to ancient native tradition never carried a key, now frequently takes on the function of a key-bearer, apparently because he is mentioned in one and the same breath with Aiakos, the Greek judge of the dead, who did carry a key.[80] Contrariwise, in Egypt Asklepios in his manifestation as saviour (σωτήρ) must look after the Nile flood, so acquiring a trait he did not have in his homeland.[81] To avoid becoming lost in detail, let us follow the encounter between Egyptians and Greeks, and the influence of Egyptian deities abroad, by looking at the fortunes of Isis – the most impressive example and the one most thoroughly studied. By contrast with Sarapis, she was of purely Egyptian origin. Her form and characteristics were adapted to suit Greek requirements and the Greek imagination. Her form was not difficult to modify. The goddess, who even in the latest Egyptian temple images was depicted as wearing the ancient robe with shoulder-straps, and thus remote from current fashion,[82] was for the Greek worshipper represented as clad in contemporary Egyptian costume.[83] Her drapery was Greek; her Egyptian attributes (headgear) were reduced in size; and certain new characteristics were added (e.g., the cornucopia). In this way a typology was produced which – whether austere or benign – could have an immediate appeal for the Greeks.[84] The cornucopia attribute was a most significant addition by the Hellenistic theologians and provides a clue to their view of the goddess's nature. For the cornucopia was the property of the almighty Tyche, from which she dispensed her gifts in arbitrary fashion; and it is Tyche who is now assigned to Isis.[85] This symbolizes a very fundamental process: fate, which in the Greek world had emancipated itself fully from the power of the gods and had even posed a threat to their existence,[86] is here placed under the guiding hand of Isis; it is therefore an explicit movement in the reverse direction to the Grecianizing tendency evident elsewhere.[87] This is brought out very clearly in the final sentences of Greek Isis aretalogies. We have already quoted the relevant sentences and may repeat them here: 'I [Isis] conquer Heimarmene. Heimarmene obeys me.' We may now also repeat our conviction that it was preeminently this consoling power over fate which accounts for the Egyptian (and oriental) gods' triumphal progress through the Greek and Roman world, where men were languishing in such trepidation before fate (see p. 74).

These literary works about Isis to which we have already

referred on several occasions, must now be characterized rather more closely in the present context. They are a series of predications spoken by Isis in the first person singular about herself, her nature and activity. We have just heard the final sentences; the initial formula, in corresponding style, runs as follows: 'I am Isis, the ruler of each land (M 3 a).' One naturally wants to know if this is a Greek translation of an Egyptian original or if the initial text, upon which the various forms (some of which are metrical) are based, was a Greek one. The most recent research has shown that the latter is the case. For in addition to sentences which could be Egyptian in form and content we find others which convey an Egyptian content in a Greek manner, and yet others which are purely Greek in content. One is therefore compelled to conclude that a Greek worshipper of Isis in Egypt, who was familiar with native concepts about his goddess and also no doubt had a command of Egyptian, composed the text in his mother tongue for his fellow countrymen on the Nile and in other foreign places.[88] To illustrate the direction in which the Grecianizing of the Isis cult was moving, we give here a few characteristic sentences which cannot be derived from the Egyptian Isis image: 'I have overthrown the governments of the tyrants (M 25)' – a characteristic Greek political national ideal; 'Together with my brother Osiris I have put an end to cannibalism (M 21)' – a glorification of the Greek concept of the culture hero; 'I am the lady of seafaring (M 49)' – a clear and succinct confirmation of the archaeological evidence that Isis was related to navigation,[89] which in former times was obviously not part of her sphere.[90] This latter activity helped to make her an all-encompassing deity, just as Sarapis likewise assumed such comprehensive functions. In this Grecianized form, Isis penetrated to the furthermost extremities of the Greek and Roman world. As is known, she is to be found in the Danubian lands, in the province of Germania, and even as far north as Hadrian's Wall in Britain.[91] This was the final result of a mission whose function consisted of composing Greek texts to advance an Egyptian goddess.[92] As such it symbolizes the breaching of national barriers. That regular translations were also undertaken of Egyptian texts, with the object of winning Greek-speaking devotees for an Egyptian deity, is attested by the fact (alluded to briefly above) that upon the instruction of the god a manuscript about the Egyptian saviour hero Imhotep was translated into Greek. The account of this culminates in the characteristic words: 'The entire Greek language will relate thy tale and every Greek will worship Imouthes [Imhotep], son of Ptah.'⁹³

In conclusion we may single out from the overwhelming material at least one other point which in its way also demonstrates the main lines of religious development: Grecianizing influence, dissemination abroad, and the bond with the individual in need of salvation. In this case we are thinking not of a deity but of an institution: the mysteries associated with Isis and Osiris, or to be more precise their form and function in the Hellenistic world. These afford impressive proof of the radical transformation which took place in Egyptian custom, despite the many formal parallels between the ancient Egyptian burial ceremonies (in which the deceased becomes Osiris and enters into God by the performance of the funerary rites) and the Hellenistic mysteries (which sought to elevate the mystic to the divine plane by associating him with Isis and Osiris). This transformation consists in the following: in Egypt it was the *dead*, whereas in the Hellenistic world it was the *living* who were so consecrated and thereby saved from their state of worldly terror.⁹⁴ Admittedly, it will probably be no coincidence, but rather the effect of Egyptian tradition, that even in the hellenized Isis mysteries the person to be initiated has to traverse the realm of the dead symbolically.⁹⁵ As regards the dissemination of the Isis–Osiris mysteries, our chief witness Apuleius suggests that such celebrations took place in Rome as well as Corinth (Kenchreai);⁹⁶ indeed, the worship of Egyptian gods is corroborated by many other sources. Finally, the bond with the individual in distress becomes evident from the rite itself, which endeavours to bring the person to be initiated into communion with the deity through acts of a most personal kind.⁹⁷ The peculiar charm of the history of these Egypto-Hellenistic mysteries lies in the curious fact of their revival at the time of classical freemasonry – as will be familiar to those who are well acquainted with Mozart's *Magic Flute*. It has remained alive up to the present time, so that one can draw a line connecting Egypt, through Antiquity, with the modern West.

Contribution to Old and New Testaments

The impact of a historical phenomenon may thus be temporal as well as spatial, as our last example shows. The influence of Egyptian religion on posterity is mainly felt through Christianity and its antecedents. Egypt's contribution to the Old Testament is actually a product of that country's relations with Syria; its contribution to the New Testament, indeed even to early Christian theology, must be seen as a special instance of that general influence exerted by Egypt upon the Hellenistic world. It was only when these two religions became established that the Egyptian influences contained within them could be transmitted to later generations. We know that there were major differences between Egyptian religion on the one hand and Judaism and Christianity on the other, since both the latter were scriptural religions, deemed by their adherents to have been revealed by God (see pp. 31 ff., 214 ff.); we therefore cannot expect the Egyptian influence to be very marked. It is rather a matter of certain details which were taken over ready-made by the younger and less developed neighbours of the land on the Nile. Yet such details are not to be despised; the transmission and adoption of minor details accounts for much of the historical continuity between different peoples and ages. In expounding this principle it is to be hoped that we have left no room for any suspicion on the reader's part that in what follows we are either depreciating the role of Judaism or Christianity in the history of religion or overestimating the importance of trivia.

Let us begin with the Old Testament. In the first place we may refer once again to the possibility that a sentence in the Instruction of Ptah-hotep was conceived in a later period of Egyptian history in the following way: 'Take no word away, and add nothing thereto, and put not one thing in the place of another',[98] and that this sentence found its way to Palestine together with Egyptian wisdom literature. There it may have led to the formulation, in an admittedly most effective way, of the central concern of a scriptural religion: the safeguarding of the text against omissions, additions or alterations.[99] Keeping to such rigorous interpretation of the evidence, we may go on to recall the doctrine of creation through the word, which as we know (see pp. 163–6) was one of the principal elements in the Egyptian cosmogony; this was not published again until the eighth century, and so became relevant for the Late period. It had an effect upon the account of the creation contained in the priestly writing, and thus upon one of the chief elements in the concept of God entertained by the Jews – and passed on by them to the Christians.

Less important, but more readily comprehensible, is the influence of the Egyptian court chronicle upon the literary form of the Israelites' chronicle account of David and Solomon.[100] Here we may mention the traces left by Egyptian royal ritual upon the courts of Israelite rulers,[101] which affected even Isaiah's famous list of appellations for the Prince of Peace. For this, although mutilated, is probably derived from the fivefold titulary of the Egyptian king.[102] The similarity of genres in this case extends even to Mesopotamia. It is also found in the familiar parallels between Egyptian and Israelite wisdom literature, which in general may be regarded as a gift of Egypt. From the standpoint of subject-matter, i.e. judged with an eye to specific points of Old Testament religion, we have here another instance of texts losing some of their significance in transmission. For the Chokma literature, which has a supranational character because it is located in the general area between the Nile and Tigris, does not take us to the heart of Old Testament prophecy. The best known links of this character are those between the Instruction of Amenemope and the Biblical Book of Proverbs. However, in this one case we may not be dealing with an original Egyptian work; the sentences attributed to Amenemope may have been composed in Hebrew or Aramaic, in which case the verses in the Book of Proverbs would be derived in the last instance from Semitic tradition.[103] Other passages can, however, be claimed as Egyptian in inspiration: for instance, the Egyptian (and Mesopotamian) lists of knowledge, which were the basis of the proverbs which King Solomon spoke on all manner of things, ranging from the cedar to the hyssop,[104] or the various Egyptian influences upon the mood, concepts and diction of the so-called 'preacher of Solomon' (Koheleth). We may recall here only the *carpe diem*, recommended on the Nile from the time of the Songs of the Harpers onward (see p. 195), and the concept of καιρός, which we now know to have been common currency in Egypt (see pp. 76 ff.).[105] Finally, examples may be mentioned which show that Biblical texts had 'local colour' from Egypt, without this involving any borrowings from Egyptian religion. These passages are naturally to be found most frequently where the Old Testament story takes place upon Egyptian soil and where it relates to Egyptian conditions: most notably in the narratives about Joseph.[106]

Here we can do no more than point out the range of influences transmitted, from major religious values down to minor matters of merely cultural interest. Unfortunately the degree to which this influence is perceptible stands in indirect proportion to the significance of the facts.[107] A few words may be added on the Greek translation of the Old Testament made at Alexandria and known as the Septuagint on account of the seventy translators employed on it. This eventually became almost a kind of holy writ for Christians. It can be demonstrated that the place of translation left its mark on many passages. Certainly these were not of crucial importance; nevertheless it is in the Septuagint that we find an invocation unknown to Israelite or Judaic theology: 'Lord, lord, king of the gods.'[108] In my view this may be explained without difficulty if one assumes that the translators had in mind a designation of God which combined two proper names (κύριος also renders the proper name of Yahveh) with the title 'king of the gods'. This is precisely the case with Amon-Rasonther, i.e. 'Amon-Re, king of the gods', who at that time was still important.[109]

Egypt's links with the religion of the Old Testament have been known and studied for a long time. But hardly any consideration has been given to the fact that the religious forms of the land of the Nile also had an effect upon the New Testament and so upon early Christianity. Such lack of interest can scarcely be due to dogmatic reservations, for if this were so such a ban would also have affected investigations into the contributions of Greek philosophy and the Hellenistic mystery religions, which have long since been recognized. It is rather the case that scholars have failed to appreciate the influence which Egypt had exerted upon the entire Hellenistic world in which Christianity was destined to take shape. By putting matters in this way we wish to make it clear that the contributions which Egypt made to Christianity in its formative stage of evolution should not be seen simply as direct contacts between a particular form developed in Egypt and some-

thing morphologically akin in Christianity. It is most important
that this point should be properly understood and appreciated.
In one of the few cases where a concept that figures in the New
Testament has been taken to be ultimately of Egyptian origin,
Jesus's parable of Dives and Lazarus, it has quite correctly been
assumed that this transmission took place by way of Jewish
material.[110] How complex the process may be within the Egyptian
tradition itself, and how large a part was played by Greek elements
(Stoic diatribes), emerged some years ago from an analysis of the
association between ship and tongue in the Epistle of St James,
which was originally Egyptian.[111] The way in which Egyptian
influence made itself felt is fairly clear in those cases where it first
affected images in the Old Testament (including the Apocrypha)
which were later taken over by New Testament writers. This
seems to me to be the case with two passages in the Epistle to the
Romans: the proverbial 'coals of fire' which were to be heaped
upon one's enemy – derived from a Late Egyptian penitential
rite[112] – and, much more significantly, the Apostle's words on
the absolute power of the Creator to confer honour and dishonour,
so making a quite arbitrary distinction between his creatures; here
St Paul is giving universal currency to a formula that we first hear
of with Amenemope.[113]

Finally, the path taken by Egyptian influence can also be followed
where the Christian form can be traced back first to an Egypto-
Hellenistic one, and this in turn traced back to Egypt itself. This
is the case with the acclamation εῖς θεός ('God is One'), used by
the earliest Christian communities: this is derived from one
employed in the service of Sarapis ('One is Zeus-Sarapis'), and
this in turn comes from the early Egyptian theologians' form
('One is Amon', etc.).[114] In most cases, however, intermediary
stages cannot as yet be identified. Attempts to establish the lines
of transmission must be based upon the fundamental principle
which we have formulated above: namely, that Egyptian religion
passed on its forms to the Hellenistic world and so enlarged the
range of expression available to the latter. In our view this influence
makes itself felt, for example, in the much-cited 'second death'
in the Revelation of St John, which may owe something to the
widely disseminated Egyptian concept of a second mortality.[115]
It is also present in the notion of a 'crown of life', or in those of

righteousness and glory; in elucidating these concepts one must draw not only upon Greek material but also upon the 'crown of righteousness' to which there were so many references during the last centuries of Egyptian paganism.[116]

Egypt's significance for early Christian theology

These few examples must suffice.[117] The remainder of this chapter will be devoted to a cursory examination of Egypt's significance for early Christian theology. When considering Egyptian religious thought we learned of the phenomenon whereby three gods were combined to form one. Various motives led to the evolution of this concept, which allowed for many shades of interpretation between the two poles of monism and triadism; as we have seen, the trinity was a major preoccupation of Egyptian theologians (see pp. 142 ff.). The evidence quoted above extended down to the Late period; here we may add that we also find such evidence in Greek only one generation before the beginnings of Christian theological speculation on such matters. An amulet dating from the period around A.D. 100, now in the British Museum, bears a distich which forms the accompanying text to a rendering, on the reverse side, of three Egyptian deities: a falcon-headed Bait,[118] a frog-headed Hathor and a winged serpent by the name of Akori.[119] It runs, in prose translation: 'One is Bait, one is Hathor, one is Akori – to these belongs *one* power. Be greeted, father of the world, be greeted, God in three forms (τρίμορφος θεός).'[120] This distich contains the εἷς θεός acclamation just mentioned, which goes back at least to the Amon theology of the Ramesside period; the one God (father of the cosmos) has as his attributes (to use the Egyptian terminology) three *ḫprw* or *bȝw*, 'forms' or 'appearances'; thus three gods are combined and treated as a single being, addressed in the singular. In this way the spiritual force of Egyptian religion shows a direct link with Christian theology.

In order to avoid any gross misunderstanding, we must at once emphasize that the substance of the Christian Trinity is of course Biblical: Father, Son and Holy Ghost. The three are mentioned alongside one another in the New Testament, probably for liturgical reasons.[121] But one essential point is still lacking for the Trinity in the proper sense: the concept or notion of such a combination. Indeed, there is no sign as yet of an awareness of the problem of three-in-one, or of the complex theological pre-requisites for this awareness, i.e. the attitudes of mind inculcated by a certain type of education and the existence of appropriate trends of thought. This compels the scholar to look outward to neighbouring lands: not directly to Egypt, but to the whole surrounding area. If such a search is undertaken, it will yield a negative result for all territories except Egypt. Mesopotamian theologians, who faced the same problems as their opposite numbers in Egypt, because they had to reconcile local gods with national deities and cosmic beings, apparently did not arrive at trinitarian formulae.[122] Nor is any such evidence forthcoming from Syria, even after the amount of original literature increases considerably. On the contrary, the Syrian goddesses Kadesh, Astarte and Anath apparently only coalesce into a triune deity on Egyptian soil (see p. 143). One would not expect such a development to occur in Israel, with its consistent henotheism. Charac-teristically, the Yahvist tale of the three divine beings who called on Abraham at the sacred tree of Mamre does not lead to any effort to resolve the theological problem raised by the presence of three persons; instead the narrator simply omits the two who are superfluous.[123] It is a thinker *from Alexandria*, Philo, who inter-prets the text in terms of the Trinity and thereby opens up a fruit-ful line of argument for Christian exegetes. His comment runs: 'To those who are able to distinguish [Moses] represents it as something absolutely natural that one can be three and three can be one, because according to the higher reasoning they are one.'[124] Finally, on Greek soil in the sixth century theology becomes completely sterilized by the emergence, out of the religious do-main, of philosophy. Prior to that, it is true, Hesiod classified the gods genealogically, but nowhere did he discuss problems of religious thought such as those known to Egypt.

Thus only Egypt remains. Philo's remarkable exegesis points to this, and this may be taken as a hint that we are on the right road. Further encouragement may be drawn from the succession of great Christian thinkers (and their Gnostic forerunners) who originated from Egypt or lived there, starting with Valentine and Basilides (c. A.D. 135), followed by Clement and Origen, and leading to Alexander, Athanasius and the presbyter Arius. Only two data may be singled out here, which testify to the emergence in

Christian Egypt of the problems we are interested in. Basilides seems to have been the first to use the concept ὁμοούσιος, which was later to attain such importance.[125] According to the Egyptian Gospel Jesus is supposed to have said to his disciples that 'the same was the Father, the same was the Son and the same the Holy Ghost'.[126]

Without abandoning our principle that Egyptian influence made itself felt as an undercurrent throughout Hellenism, we may nevertheless claim pride of place for Alexandria and so consider Alexandrian theology as the intermediary between the Egyptian religious heritage and Christianity. The Trinity is not the only subject-matter at issue here. Also Christology, which is closely linked to it – the doctrine concerning the nature of Christ and especially his pre-existence before the creation and time – revolves around questions which had been posed earlier by Egyptian theologians and which they solved in a strikingly similar way. These questions are discussed in the doctrines concerning Shu, the son of the Heliopolitan primary god Atum, which the Coffin Texts have preserved for us; here the deceased is equated with the son of God: 'I am Shu whom Atum has made the day when he [himself] came into being.' The idea is expressed still more clearly in an address by Atum: 'When I was alone with the [primordial ocean] Nun [and when the creation] did not yet exist, Shu [and his sister Tefnut] were with me.'[127] In this particular case, admittedly, the path of contact with Christian theology has not yet been explored.[128] But in view of what we have been able to show in regard to the Trinity, this ought to be regarded as a stimulus to further research, not as a stumbling-block.

The multifarious links between Egypt and Judaeo-Christian scriptures and trinitarian theology can already be traced with some degree of plausibility. The same is true of many other matters that we have been unable to consider here, such as the relationship between the Isis cult and Mariolatry[129] or between the exclusiveness of Late Egyptian temples and the monasticism that sprang up in the Nile valley.[130] All this entitles us to the opinion that Egypt played its part in the efforts of Christians to achieve an understanding of God and his works, which are eternal.

The characteristics of the gods

In a book on Egyptian religion the ordinary reader will naturally expect to find at least the most important data about the gods of the country. Since our survey is not designed in such a way as to record these data systematically, the following list has been compiled by Dr Müller-Kriesel. It is based by and large on the relevant articles by Bonnet in *Reallexikon der ägyptischen Religionsgeschichte*, to which reference may be made for further details. The reader will see from the index whether and where the individual gods listed here are mentioned in the text of this volume.

Aker

Earth-god, first represented as a strip of land with a human head, later with two lion heads or as a double sphinx. In the belief in the hereafter he is occasionally a helper of the dead. As a rule he is overshadowed by Geb.

Amaunet

Female counterpart to Amon among the primordial gods of the Hermopolitan Ogdoad. Regarded occasionally as the mother, at Thebes also as the consort of Amon in addition to Mut. Worshipped in cult only when assimilated with Neith; like the latter, interpreted as Athena by the Greeks.

Amon

'The Hidden One', originally the wind-god and thus frequently called 'soul of Shu'. Together with Amaunet forms one of the couples of the Hermopolitan Ogdoad. Closely associated with Min of Coptos as Min-Amon, when Thebes flourishes he becomes the national god Amon-Rasonther ('Amon-Re, king of the gods'); combined with Mut and Khons, forms the Theban triad, but also appears as the helper of any pious person in need. Usually represented in human form (possibly ithyphallic) with a plumed crown. His sacred animals are the ram and the goose. There are a large number of separate forms, including Khamutef (*q.v.*).

Amon-Rasonther

See Amon.

Amset

See Horus' children.

Anath

Western Semitic goddess, apparently introduced by the Hyksos
and then worshipped particularly at Tanis. Appears as war-
goddess; is regarded as daughter of Re and consort of Seth. In
human form; her attributes include the shield, battle-axe and a tall
crown encircled by plumes.

Andjeti

See Osiris.

Antaios

Actually ꜥ*ntyw*, the 'two falcons'; in the New Kingdom combined
to form one deity and then equated with Horus; the identification
with Antaios is based upon the similar sound of the names.

Anubis

Jackal-headed god of the necropolis. As grave-digger *par excellence*,
it is his duty to glorify the deceased; he is thus depicted with
black skin; later has a place in Osirian cycle (for example as the
son).

Anuket

In the area of the First Cataract, a human-shaped goddess;
together with Khnum and Satis, she is regarded as dispenser of
'cool water'; is worshipped at Elephantine; her sacred animal is
the gazelle.

Apis

Earliest and best known (fully theriomorphic) Egyptian deity in
the form of a bull; especially associated with Ptah (Apeum at
Memphis) and Osiris; ensures fertility; is rendered as a bull with
solar disk and uraeus between its horns.

Astarte

In the Near East, goddess of love and war; worshipped in Egypt from the Eighteenth Dynasty to the Ptolemaic period; frequently equated with Sekhmet or Hathor and regarded as a consort of Seth.

Aton

A designation of the sun as a constellation which develops in the Middle Kingdom and becomes a special aspect of the sun-god. During the reign of Amenophis IV there appears the so-called 'Aton of rays' in the form of a solar disk with rays terminating in hands. Worshipped at Akhet-Aton (Tell el-Amarna); his nature is determined by his creative omnipresence and his paternal role vis-à-vis the king. The name was probably pronounced as Jāti during the Amarna period.

Atum

Primordial and creator-god, in human and serpent form, supreme in the Heliopolitan Ennead; begat Shu and Tefnut; coalesced with Re to form Re-Atum.

Bastet

Goddess of Bubastis in the form of a cat; is regarded as a benevolent counterpart of the lion-goddess Sekhmet.

Bes

Group of demons, predominantly male, with grotesque face and dwarf-like stature, with a head that often looks like a lion's mask. They provide protection in birth and are regarded as dispensers of virility.

Buchis

Sacred bull of Hermonthis; like Apis, is rendered entirely in animal form; equated with Month and Re.

Dedun

God represented in human form; worshipped at Philae as Arsnuphis; entered the Egyptian pantheon as Lord of Nubia and thus *inter alia* as dispenser of incense.

Dewamutef

See Horus' children.

Edjo (Uto)

A goddess of Buto, worshipped in the form of a uraeus serpent; tutelary goddess of the prehistoric Delta kingdom; with the papyrus plant, the symbol of Lower Egypt and mistress of its crown; counterpart to the Upper Egyptian vulture-goddess Nekhbet; with the latter protectress goddess of the king.

Geb

Earth-god; in the Heliopolitan Ennead consort of Nut (sky) and begetter of Osiris, his brothers and sisters; solely in human form; a primordial god who is usually benevolently disposed towards the dead. Note the male gender (by contrast with 'mother earth' elsewhere).

Hah

Personification of infinity, represented as the sky-bearer; equated with Shu and Amon.

Hapi

See Horus' children.

Harakhti

See Horus.

Harendotes

See Horus.

Harmakhis

See Horus.

Harmerti

See Horus.

Haroeris

See Horus.

Harpocrates

See Horus.

Harsaphes

Ram-headed god of Herakleopolis, equated by the Greeks with Herakles. After the end of the Old Kingdom, assimilated with Osiris and especially with Re and later Amon. As 'He who is on his lake', also the god who appears on the lotus flower (primeval god).

Harsiesis

See Horus.

Hathor

Sky-goddess, depicted as a cow, at times in human form with cow's ears and horns. Goddess of love, dance, alcohol, also mistress of foreign lands; at Thebes, goddess of the dead. She was equated with Isis and the town-goddess ('Lady') of Byblos; as Hathor of Dendera, she was the consort of Horus of Edfu and mother of Harsomtus. The Seven Hathors, probably associated with Hathor as goddess of death, correspond to the Greek *moirai*.

Hatmehit

'First of the fish', goddess of the nome of Mendes, ultimately humanized; soon ousted by the ram of Mendes and assigned to him as consort.

Heket

Primordial goddess at Antinoë, in the form of a frog, regarded as assistant at the birth of Khnum and his consort.

Horus

Sky-god in the form of a falcon; his eyes are the sun and the moon. Earliest royal god, who is incarnate in the ruler of the day. At Heliopolis coalesced with Re, resulting in a god of composite form Re-Harakhti (Re 'Horus of the Horizon'). Separate forms: Harsiesis, 'Horus, son of Isis'; Haroeris, 'Horus the Elder'; Harendotes, 'Horus, avenger of his father' (of Osiris); Harpocrates, 'Horus, the child' (of Isis); Khenti-irti (assimilated with the falcon-god of Leontopolis); Khentekhtay (ancientcroco dile-god on whom Horus impressed his name and shape); Harmakhis, Horus on the horizons (the Sphinx of Giza is considered as his aspect); Harmerti, 'Horus of the two eyes' (falcon-god of Sheden). During the Late period worshipped in particular at Edfu.

Horus' children

Four lesser deities, Amset, Dewamutef, Hapi and Kebehsenuf, who are regarded as representatives of the cardinal points of the compass and lords of the canopic jars.

Hu

1. At Heliopolis, probably a personification of the divine utterance; embodies, in addition to Sia (cognizance), the divine creative power.
2. Embodiment of nourishment.
These two occasionally coalesce.

Ihy

Son of Hathor of Dendera, youthful god depicted with menat (neck ornament) and sistrum.

Imhotep (Imouthes)

Architect and adviser of King Zoser who was deified during the Late period. Represented in sacerdotal dress, he is regarded as son of Ptah. At Memphis, worshipped as a god of healing and identified by the Greeks with Asklepios.

Isis

Goddess in human form, of unknown origin, possibly a personification of the throne; regarded as the daughter of Geb, consort and sister of Osiris and mother of Horus. During the Late period she becomes a universal goddess by assimilation with Astarte, Bastet, Hathor, Nut, Sothis, Thermuthis and others; most important place of worship was at Philae. Equated with Demeter by the Greeks; during the Hellenistic and Roman Imperial periods, worshipped to the furthest limits of the Roman Empire.

Kadesh

Goddess of love, usually represented naked, authenticated from the New Kingdom; introduced from the Near East; with Resheph and Min combined to form a triad; occasionally equated with Hathor but also with Syrian equivalents (Astarte, Anath).

Kebehsenuf

See Horus' children.

Khamutef

One of the separate aspects of Amon, 'who has completed his moment'. He is represented as a serpent and may be the basis of the Kneph authenticated by the Greeks.

Khentekhtay

See Horus.

Khenti-amentiu

See Osiris.

Khenti-irti

See Horus.

Khepri

Primordial god in the form of a scarabaeus; coalesced with Re and Atum; usually denotes the rising sun.

Khnum

God in the form of a human being with ram's head; the most important localities include Hypselis, Esna, Antinoë and Elephantine, where he figured as donor of the Nile waters. At Antinoë and Esna he is worshipped as the primordial creator-god, who forms mankind on his potter's wheel. At Antinoë his consort is Heket, the goddess of birth, while at Esna this role falls to Neith.

Khons

Moon-god; in the Theban triad, son of Amon and Mut. In human form with a moon disk suggesting headgear; the main temple at Karnak is dedicated to him.

Maat

Personification in human form of the concept maat; became the daughter of Re; is closely associated with the administration of justice and vouchsafed a cult of her own.

Meskhenet

Personification of the tile upon which a woman kneels in child-birth; usually rendered as a tile with a human head. Regarded as protectress of the newly born and goddess of destiny.

Min

Ithyphallic god of virility and fertility, and thus creator-god; coalesced with Amon and Horus, especially as Harendotes and Harsiesis. Principal places of worship: Coptos and Akhmim.

Mnevis

Sacred bull of Heliopolis, assimilated to the sun-god and designated as his herald.

Month

Before Amon the principal god of Thebes; originally in the form of a falcon and approximated to Horus: 'Horus with the strong arm.' He appears chiefly as a war-god.

Mut

Consort of Amon in the Theban triad; originally represented as a vulture, later completely humanized. As an 'eye of the sun' she came to be closely linked with the sun. Assimilated with Hathor, Bastet, Sekhmet and Edjo.

Naunet

Female counterpart to Nun, the primordial waters; in combination with the latter, forms the first pair of the Ogdoad in Hermopolitan cosmology. Personification of the counter-heaven. Like all female members of the Ogdoad, Naunet possesses a serpent's head.

Nefertem

A youthful god represented seated upon a lotus blossom; sometimes regarded as the youthful sun; in the Memphite triad, son of Ptah and Sekhmet.

Neith

Warlike goddess in human form, worshipped chiefly at Saïs; equated by the Greeks with Athena. Later a primeval bisexual goddess. Mother of Sobek, also mistress of the primeval waters.

Nekhbet

Upper Egyptian counterpart to the Lower Egyptian Edjo, with whom she is usually linked; Mistress of the White (Upper Egyptian) Crown and protectress of the king.

Nephthys

Youngest child of Geb and Nut and last member of the Heliopolitan Ennead. Appears as consort of Seth, but in the Osirian legend as a wailing woman alongside Isis. Apparently not the object of a cult.

Nepri

Personification of corn and equated with Osiris; also, as the son of Thermuthis and in combination with him, considered as parallel to Isis and the Horus child.

Nut

In the Heliopolitan Ennead, sky-goddess, consort of Geb and mother of the Osirian family; also regarded as mother of the sun, moon and other heavenly bodies, which she daily devours and bears again.

Onuris

Town-god of This, with warlike features and therefore interpreted by the Greeks as Ares. Equated with Shu; regarded especially as a god who brought the solar eye back from distant lands, as his name suggests.

Osiris

Presumably a deity from Busiris incorporated into the Heliopolitan Ennead, but also combined with Isis and Horus to form a family. Osiris is regarded as the dead king who rules over the nether world (judgement of the dead) and is rejuvenated in his son Horus. As a symbol of eternal life he becomes god of the dead *par excellence*; at the same time, as the god who dies and rises again, he becomes the symbol of all vegetation; therefore closely linked to the waxing and waning moon. Equated with Ptah, Sokaris, Khenti-amentiu ('First of the Westerns' at Abydos), and Andjeti. Mainly worshipped at Abydos and Philae. His destiny is represented in mysteries.

Petbe

God of revenge, authenticated only in Greek and Roman times; corresponds in function to the Greek Nemesis and is identified by the Greeks with Kronos.

Ptah

Town-god of Memphis; coalesced with the Memphite earth-god Ta-tenen as well as Sokaris and Osiris; represented in human form with a close-shaven head. Primordial and creator-god (creator through the word) as well as lord of artisans; equated with Hephaistos by the Greeks.

Re

Sun-god of Heliopolis, where he coalesced with Atum and Horus to form Re-Atum or Re-Harakhti. In combination with Atum, Re becomes the primordial god; as god of the earth and sky he is lord of the cosmic order and father of Maat. As a cosmic god Re is treated in human form; as Re-Harakhti he is represented with a falcon head. His cult symbol is the obelisk. From the Fifth Dynasty onward he becomes the national god. His essence enters into many local deities (Sobek-Re, etc.) and is also combined with the supreme deity Amon (Amon-Re).

Resheph

Canaanite–Phoenician god of thunder, worshipped in Egypt from the New Kingdom onwards; his attributes include the battle-axe, spear and shield.

Sarapis

Hellenistic hybrid god, whose main cult centre was in Alexandria; later worshipped by the Greeks as Helios or Zeus. The name is a combination of Osiris and Apis; accordingly he has Isis as his consort and is regarded as god of the nether world and fertility, but also becomes physician and general helper in distress. He never became fully accepted by the Egyptian element of the population in the Ptolemaic kingdom.

Satis

Goddess of Elephantine; consort of Khnum and companion of Anuket. As 'dispenser of cool water coming from Elephantine', she is equated with Sothis. During the Late period, depicted in human form wearing an Upper Egyptian crown and two horns of gazelles.

Sekhmet

With Ptah and Nefertem she forms the Memphite triad; is regarded as mistress of war and sickness. Usually rendered as a woman with lion's head; her benevolent counterpart is the cat-goddess Bastet, with whom she is closely linked.

Selket

Upper Egyptian scorpion-goddess, but humanized. As mistress and guardian of life, she is equated with Neith, Isis and Thermuthis. In the belief in the hereafter she plays a vital role as a protectress of the dead.

Seshat

Goddess of writing and books; sister or daughter of Thoth; equated with Isis during the Late period; interpreted as a Muse by the Greeks.

Seth

Powerful god whose peculiar sacred animal has no zoological equivalent. In the Heliopolitan Ennead, son of Geb and Nut and brother of Osiris, whom he murders; is regarded as god of the desert and the storm, and therefore becomes lord of foreign lands and the deity loathed by foreigners. In the Osirian myth Nephthys appears as his consort. As the god of foreign parts, he has Anath and Astarte as his companions.

Shay

'That which is decreed', originally the lifetime appointed at birth; later also fate in the broader sense of the word; rendered by the Greeks as Agathodaimon. At Hypselis, associated with Khnum and the object of a cult.

Shed

'The Saviour', a youthful god intimately connected with Horus; destroys noxious animals, but also in general personifies the deity's succouring aspect.

Shu

In the Heliopolitan Ennead, son of Atum and consort of Tefnut. An ancient cosmic power, he is regarded as god of the air and bearer of heaven, at times also as the sun. By himself found exclusively in human form; but he and Tefnut are equated with the two lions of Leontopolis.

Sia

Personification of divine cognizance and thus approximated to Thoth; in conjunction with Hu (q.v.), the expression of divine creativeness through thought and speech.

Sobek

Crocodile-god, disseminated throughout Egypt; has cult centres at Ombos and in the Faiyum, where in the Middle Kingdom he coalesces with Re, becomes Sobek-Re and is worshipped as primordial deity and creator-god.

Sokaris

Ancient god of artisans and the dead at Memphis, in the form of a falcon, who by virtue of his functions (or localization) is associated with Ptah and also with Osiris.

Sopdu

Upper Egyptian god in the form of a falcon; coalesced with Horus; is regarded in particular as the lord of the eastern border and of foreign lands.

Sothis

Egyptian name of female gender given to Sirius, who is regarded as responsible for the Nile floodwaters and as lord of the beginning of the year. At an early stage Sothis coalesces with Isis (the consort of Osiris who was thought of as Orion); later fused with Satis by virtue of the similarity in the sound of their names; worshipped as Isisothis during the Late period.

Ta-tenen

See Ptah.

Tefnut

In the Heliopolitan Ennead, daughter of Atum and consort of Shu; probably personifies the element of moisture.

Thermuthis

'The provider of nourishment', goddess of fertility and harvest, in the form of a serpent; as mother of Nepri, effects a parallel with Isis and the Horus child. She is also regarded as goddess of fate and is associated with Shay and Meskhenet; during the Late period equated with Isis (Isermuthis).

Thoth

God of unknown origin (probably from the Delta), worshipped as an ibis or baboon. In historic times Hermopolis is his main cult centre. In the Osirian myth Thoth is the vizier of Osiris; in general he is lord of wisdom and particularly of laws and sacred writings. Furthermore he is regarded as the moon or the lunar eye, and therefore as the master of chronology. He is also the messenger and was interpreted by the Greeks as Hermes.

Thoueris

The most common figure in a group of hippopotamus goddesses; is worshipped as a goddess of fertility in the form of a hippopotamus with young. Together with her partner Bes she protects women in labour. Iopet (Opet) of Luxor has a form identical to that of Thoueris.

Unut

Originally goddess of Hermopolis, in the form of a hare, later by and large displaced by other deities. Occasionally regarded as a demon of the nether world.

Upwawet

'Opener-of-the-Ways'; jackal-headed god of Assiut with warlike features; equated with Horus, but especially with Anubis. At Abydos, god of the necropolis.

Chronological table

Note

The discussion of Egyptian religion has been arranged topically. This arrangement has not entirely excluded a historical approach, but this had to be given a secondary place. We cannot hope to present historical developments at all adequately in the form of an appendix: this would require a second volume. Here we merely offer the reader a list of the chief events in Egyptian history coupled with the basic facts and sources relevant to the history of Egyptian religion. This table is drawn up with some reluctance, since it involves presenting the dates and formulations given with proper reserve in the text as apparently firm and definite statements. Only by consulting this table in conjunction with the text can one avoid the risk of excessive schematization, which results from the margin of uncertainty inherent in the sources and the fact that most religious phenomena are gradual developments. If used in this way, it may provide an outline frame of chronological reference. The dates are based on details in E. Otto, *Ägypten. Der Weg des Pharaonenreiches*, 3rd ed., 1958. The beginning of the Archaic (Thinite) period may be dated up to one hundred years later; for the prehistoric periods only rough approximations are possible.

Periods, dynasties, names of rulers	Developments in religious history	Selected sources
NEOLITHIC (approx. from 5000)	Age of 'powers'. Interment in settlements (agriculturalists) and necropolises (primarily nomadic). Afterlife regarded as prolongation of life in this world	Settlements. Necropolises
ENEOLITHIC (post-Neolithic)	Conception of personal god begins	
ARCHAIC PERIOD (so-called Thinite period) I–II Dyn., *c.* 3000–2780	Discovery of writing indicates formation of historical consciousness	Stelae, small plaques recording annals, seals (with concise inscriptions)
Narmer, Menes-Aha, Zet ('serpent'), Udimu (Den) and others	'God' appears as a concept and adopts forms and names Development of many rites and myths	N.B. Henceforth archaeological sources will be mentioned only in exceptional cases

Chronological table (*cont.*)

Periods, dynasties, names of rulers	Developments in religious history	Selected sources
	Personal names begin to indicate relationship between God and man. The king, at first perhaps identical with the cosmic god, appears as his incarnation ('Horus NN')	
OLD KINGDOM III–VIII Dyn., *c.* 2780–2250 III Dyn.: Zoser and others IV Dyn.: Snefru, Cheops, Chephren, Mycerinus etc. V Dyn.: Userkaf, Sahure, Neferirkare, Neuserre, Unas etc. VI Dyn.: Teti, Pepi I, II and others, then decline	Major theological systems: Heliopolis (evolved under III–V Dyn.) and Memphis (origin of its doctrine probably under V–VI Dyn.) Doctrine of the king's two bodies (as a person = human being, as office-bearer = god; identifiable from IV Dyn.). King as god degraded to 'son of Re', i.e. responsible to his father; Re cult becomes national religion Linked with this: growing differentiation between this world and the hereafter. Idea emerges of the generally binding judgement of the dead (early V Dyn.?) First tangible statements about maat as a norm in this world and the beyond, in nature and society. Recording of essential funerary supplies (burial rituals) for the deceased king to read in his tomb (end of V Dyn.) Lessening of fear of images based on the equation of image and object (VI Dyn.)	Pyramid Texts (recorded from Unas onwards) Memphite theology Shabaka inscription (nucleus V–VI Dyn.?) Instruction of Hordedef (IV Dyn.?) Instruction of Ptahhotep (V Dyn.)
FIRST INTERMEDIATE PERIOD (so-called Herakleopolitan period) IX–X Dyn. of Herakleopolis, early XI Dyn. of Thebes, *c.* 2250–2040 Achthoes, I–III Merikare and others (Herakleopolitan) Antef and Mentuhotep (many rulers of this name)	Rise of bourgeoisie: scientific and ethical concerns are introduced into religion Royal mortuary texts and religious privileges (divinity in death) are acquired by private persons. (Beginning of development whereby every deceased Egyptian becomes an 'Osiris')	(Early) Coffin Texts Admonitions of Ipuwer (soon after end of Old Kingdom) So-called Discourse between a man weary of life and his ba

Chronological table (*cont.*)

Periods, dynasties, names of rulers	Developments in religious history	Selected sources
(Thebans)	Doctrine of the ba ('soul') and assignment of a ba to everyone. Consideration of relationship between the ba and the body after death Cosmogonic doctrine of Hermopolis gains importance for all Egypt (eight primordial gods, incl. Nun and Amon) The deity criticized for the imperfect course of world events; justification (theodicy) of the creator-god Doctrine of the judgement of the dead gains in importance. God seen as pastor of mankind	Instruction for King Merikare (X Dyn.)
MIDDLE KINGDOM late XI, XII and early XIII Dyn., 2040–*c.* 1730 XI Dyn.: Mentuhotep Neb-hepet-Re unites Upper and Lower Egypt XII Dyn.: Amenemhet I–IV, Sesostris I–III	King seen as political redeemer, yet as a lonely human being Continuing crisis over ideas of the hereafter (scepticism); but the notions of becoming Osiris and attaining proximity to the sun-god gain ground, affording the hope of salvation Amon attains a privileged position (royal name Amenemhet = 'Amon is supreme') Widening of political horizons makes foreign deities relevant to Egyptians for the first time ('Lady of Byblos' equated with Hathor)	(Late) Coffin Texts Book of the Two Ways (earliest cartographic work) Prophecy of Neferti (period of Amenemhet I) So-called Instruction of Amenemhet (composed after his death) Earliest record of Songs of the Harpers Large number of stelae at Abydos (incl. that of Ikhernofret on Osirian festivals at Abydos) Recording of the so-called Ramesseum Dramatic Papyrus (probably part of an ancient Sed festival rite)
SECOND INTERMEDIATE PERIOD (Hyksos period) (late XIII, XIV Dyn., partly running parallel to Hyksos as XV–XVI Dyn.;	Hyksos introduce Syrian gods into Egypt. Their principal god is Baal (interpreted as Seth); Anath appears in royal names	Pap. Sallier I (Book of Apophis and Sekenenre)

Chronological table (*cont.*)

Periods, dynasties, names of rulers	Developments in religious history	Selected sources
contemporaneous with their late phase: XVII Dyn. of Thebes, *c.* 1730–1562) Apophis, Sekenenre, Kamose and others		
NEW KINGDOM XVIII Dyn., 1562– 1308 Ahmose, Ameno- phis I–IV, Thutmosis I–IV, Haremhab etc.; included in this: Amarna period (Amenophis IV = 'Akhnaton', 1361– *c.* 1340)	Amon becomes patron of the empire. Kings claim a per- sonal link with him; his national temple at Karnak is, however, also a place of private piety Gods acquire universal traits. Mortuary literature (books) provided to accompany the dead Guides to the beyond (nightly journey of the sun) recorded in royal tombs Proclamation of the belief in Jāti (= 'Aton') during reign of Amenophis IV – Akhanjāti ('Akhnaton') Breakthrough and formation of elements of popular piety (concept of fate) during Amarna period Invasion of Israelite tribes (?)	Book of the Dead, Book of Amduat, later also Book of the Gates, and Book of Caverns Instruction of Ani Hymns and other testimonials of religious belief in the rock-cut tombs at Amarna
XIX–XX Dyn. (Ramesside period) 1308–1085 Ramses I–XI, Seti I–II, Merenptah etc.	Amon theology and church (possessions and power) reach their zenith. Increase of personal piety. Foreign, esp. Syrian, cults gain in importance Oppression and exodus of Israelite tribes (both probably under Ramses II)	Hymns to Amon at Leyden (recorded during reign of Ramses II) Pap. Harris (Ramses III–IV) Memorial tablets from Deir el-Medina (Western Thebes)
LATE PERIOD XXI Dyn. (rulers at Thebes and Tanis) 1085–950 Herihor, Paynozem, Psusennes etc.	Theocracy of Amon as final political consequence of his material and spiritual power	
XXII–XXIII Dyn. (Libyans, so-called	As the sense of national unity wanes, local deities win	Biographies, mainly in form of inscrip-

Chronological table (*cont.*)

Periods, dynasties, names of rulers	Developments in religious history	Selected sources
Bubastids) 950–730, finally overlapping with Ethiopians	increasing prominence Growing interplay between religion and ethics	tions on statues Instruction of Amenemope (possibly a little later)
XXV Dyn. (Ethiopians, simultaneously short-lived XXIV Dyn. in Delta) 751–656 Piankhi, Shabaka, Taharka etc.	Reception of Egyptian pantheon (esp. Amon) and cult of the dead in Napatan kingdom in the south (continuing to affect people of Meroë during the Hellenistic and Roman periods)	Memphite theology translated into stone, possibly final interpolations (Shabaka) Temples at Napata, Gematen (Kawa) etc.
XXVI Dyn. (Saites, restoration of Egyptian independence) 663–525 Psammetichus I–III, Necho, Apries, Amasis	Contact with the Greeks brings first consequences for Egyptian and Greek religious beliefs	Tombs near Napata
XXVII Dyn. (Persians) 525–332 Cambyses, Darius I–III, Xerxes etc. Included herein: XXVIII–XXX Dyn. (last native kings) 404–341 Amyrtaeus, Nectanebo I–II etc.	Increased contact between Egyptian and Greek religion	Herodotus, Book II (*c.* 450)
GRECO-ROMAN PERIOD Dynasty of Alexander and Ptolemies 332–30	Wholesale encounter of Egyptian and Greek religion; Hellenism as a sum larger than its parts Creation of Sarapis (during reign of Ptolemy I) Hellenized Egyptian gods (Isis and her associates) In Egypt itself temple architecture in ancient style, continuation of traditional ideology of sacrosanct monarchy (titularies, association with the gods)	Inscriptions of Petosiris, (demotic) instructions of Onchsheshonqy and of the Insinger Papyrus (both possibly a little earlier) Bulk of texts (incl. the rite in which the deity enters into the image and of the Osirian vigils) recorded in Upper Egyptian temples

Chronological table *(cont.)*

Periods, dynasties, names of rulers	Developments in religious history	Selected sources
		(esp. Dendera, Thebes, Esna, Edfu, Kom Ombo, and Philae) Compilations of mortuary literature (Book of Breathings, Rhind mortuary papyrus etc., MSS not until Roman period). Greek Isis aretalogies
Romans (Egypt an Imperial province) 30 B.C.– A.D. 395 Augustus to Theodosius I	Continuation of tendencies that appeared in Hellenistic age, incl. missionary activity abroad and maintenance of the traditional ideology of sacrosanct monarchy within the country. Final democratization of cult of the dead becomes evident. Penetration of Christianity (by way of Alexandria), which under Bishop Demetrius (*c.* 180) enters history in developed form Bible translated into Egyptian dialects (Coptic) Hermits and monasticism (with *vita activa*) spread in Egypt Sarapeum at Alexandria destroyed (391) Preservation of ancient funerary customs (mummification, funerary gifts, a kind of Book of the Dead)	Later inscriptions in Upper Egyptian temples mentioned above Representations on coffins and shrouds Oxyrhynchus Papyrus 1380 (Isis litany) and 1381 (translations for Imhotep–Imouthes) Apuleius, *Metamorphoses*, Bk. 11 *Christian sources:* Athanasius, *Life of St Anthony*, Rules of Pakhom
Byzantines 395–640 Arcadius to Heraclius	Paganism in Egypt mainly current among Greeks in the cities and neighbours to the south Justinian (527–65) closes oracle of Amon at the oasis of Siwa and later the Isis temple at Philae, but even monks are mummified during the 6th century	

Notes

INTRODUCTION

1 Herrmann, *Untersuchungen.*
2 E. Otto, *ZDMG*, 102, 1952, pp. 192 ff.
3 W. Helck, *ZDMG*, 102, 1952, pp. 39 ff. This development is already found during the Middle Kingdom. Sinuhe describes the princely house in which he is received as furnished with 'images of the horizon (*ᶜḥmw nw ꜣḫt*)', by which he no doubt meant images of the gods. Sinuhe B 287.
4 L. Klebs, *ZÄS*, 61, 1926, pp. 105 f.
5 H. Junker, *Pyramidenzeit. Das Wesen der altägyptischen Religion*, Einsiedeln–Zurich–Cologne, 1949.
6 The terms are listed in *Wb.*, vi, 250; a characteristic example is an invocation addressed to Isis at Aswan, which after a long hymnic eulogy of the goddess ends in a short prayer for the king: J. de Morgan, *Catalogue des monuments...de l'Égypte antique*, i, Vienna, 1894, p. 55.
7 S. Morenz, *ThLZ*, 75, 1950, cols. 709 ff.; see chap. 10.
8 The prayer was usually enriched by the addition of hymnic elements (see n. 6) and thus made more obscure to the modern reader; on this whole topic cf. the entries for 'piety' and 'prayer' in Bonnet, *RÄRG*, pp. 196 ff., 204 ff.
9 In his stimulating and profound *Magie und Religion* (photographic reprint Gütersloh, 1955) C. H. Ratschow writes (p. 130): 'Egyptian religion in fact never found the way to religion.' I was reminded of this after I had finished this work, and I hope that it may help to convince readers of Ratschow that in the minds of the Egyptians, once they had attained the stage of historical consciousness, one finds precisely that realization of God, with all the characteristics which Ratschow (pp. 125–47) deems essential for the existence of true religion, i.e. one which has outgrown the limits of an *unio magica.*

CHAPTER 1

1 Wolf, *Kunst*, pp. 31 f.; 'cosmic concept and artistic form'.
2 Cf. the chapters in Wolf, op. cit., on the 'meaning' of these works of art, where more attention is paid than is possible here to their wide range.
3 A. Hermann, 'Beiträge zur Erklärung der ägyptischen Liebesdichtung', *FS. Grapow*, pp. 118 ff.; idem, *Altägyptische Liebesdichtung*, Wiesbaden, 1959, pp. 124 ff.

4 On this see the numerous studies by É. Drioton, such as: 'Le Théâtre dans l'ancienne Égypte', *Revue d'histoire du théâtre*, 6, 1954, pp. 7 ff., and 'La Question du théâtre égyptien', *Comptes Rendus de l'Académie des Inscriptions et Belles-Lettres*, Paris, 1954, pp. 51 ff.

5 Bonnett, *RÄRG*, pp. 440 ff.

6 Latest study: O. Firchow, 'Die Boten der Götter', *FS. Grapow*, p. 85.

7 It is noteworthy that in the Edwin Smith Papyrus, a surgical handbook, hardly any of these sayings are to be found; this work was evidently 'secular' in origin: Firchow, op. cit., p. 85.

8 But what does this term mean in art and literature? Who would dare claim that 'progress' has been made since Phidias or Rembrandt, Homer, Shakespeare or Goethe?

9 Grapow, *Grundriss*, III, pp. 92 ff.

10 Junker, *Stundenwachen*; Kees, *Ägypten*, p. 303.

11 Kees, op. cit., p. 304.

12 J. v. Beckrath, 'Der ägyptische Ursprung unseres Kalenders', *Saeculum*, 4, 1953, pp. 1 ff.

13 The Egyptian inscription with the greatest number of lines is Ramses III's calendar of festivals on the southern outer wall of Medinet Habu, which has more than 1400 lines: H. H. Nelson et al., *Medinet Habu*, 3, 1934 (*OIP*, no. 23).

14 Where the earth appears as a circle with the nomes of Egypt forming an inner ring, this is not a departure from the basic type but simply a variant reading (possibly a late one); on this point cf. J. J. Clère, *Fragments d'une nouvelle représentation égyptienne du monde* (*MDAIK*, 16, 1958, pp. 30 ff.).

15 This was the case, for example, in the ethnic and geographical parts of the encyclopaedic lists: Sir Alan Gardiner, *Ancient Egyptian Onomastica*, London, 1947, esp. I, pp. 113* ff.

16 Kees, *Totenglauben*, pp. 287 ff. and Fig. 7; Grapow, *HO* I 2, pp. 47 ff.

17 *ASAE*, 49, 1949, pp. 337 ff.; *JEA*, 4, 1917, Pl. 29; G. Daressy, *Ostraca*, Cairo, 1901, Pl. 32.

18 On this entire problem cf. S. Morenz, 'Wortspiele in Ägypten', *FS. Johannes Jahn*, Leipzig, 1957, pp. 23 ff., esp. 27 f.

19 Morenz, op. cit., pp. 24, 27; for an appreciation of the literary form: S. Schott, *Mythe und Mythenbildung im alten Ägypten* (*Unters.*, 15, 1945), pp. 59 ff.

20 Ranke, *Personennamen*, I (1935), p. 78, nos. 21 ff.; II (1952), p. 220.

21 At first the juxtaposition of two contradictory terms expresses totality in Egyptian. For examples, see A. Massart, *Mélanges bibliques rédigés en l'honneur de André Robert*, Paris, 1957, pp. 38 ff.

22 In connection with the king's accession and the establishing of the

duration of his reign, we may point to the ceremonies performed at the *Išd* tree, discussed by H. W. Helck, *ZÄS*, 82, 1958, p. 117; on the king's actions as the celebration of a ritual designed to ward off enemies and to preserve order, cf. E. Hornung, *Zur geschichtlichen Rolle des Königs in der 18. Dynastie* (*MDAIK*, 15, 1957), pp. 120 ff.

23 Instruction for Merikare: Pap. Erm. 1116A, ll. 70 f., also 119 ff.; translated in Volten, *Pol. Schriften*, pp. 37, 65.

24 Further details, especially on the role of priests in Egyptian scholarship, in S. Sauneron, *Les Prêtres de l'ancienne Égypte*, Paris, 1957 (trans. A. Morrissett, *The Priests of Ancient Egypt*, New York–London, 1960), pp. 111 ff.

25 J. Fränkel, *Dichtung und Wissenschaft*, Heidelberg, 1954, pp. 28 ff.

26 S. N. Kramer, *From the Tablets of Sumer*, Indian Hills, 1956, p. 271 (plan of Nippur); it may admittedly be pointed out that, in contrast to Greek cities, the Sumerian ones are known to have had a sacred character: E. Kornemann, *Die Antike*, 8, Berlin, 1932, pp. 105 ff. Thus the ancient town-plans in Mesopotamia may also have been religious in origin. On the theological foundations of Mesopotamian geography see B. Meissner, *Babylonien und Assyrien*, II, Heidelberg, 1925, pp. 377 ff.

27 E. Otto, *Ägypten. Der Weg des Pharaonenreiches*, Stuttgart, 1953, p. 48.

28 A convincing picture of the origins of this practice is given by H. W. Helck, *Untersuchungen zu den Beamtentiteln des ägyptischen Alten Reiches* (*ÄgFo*, 18, 1954), pp. 11 ff., 129 ff.

29 On the latter see W. Spiegelberg, *Ägyptische Verpfründungsverträge mit Vermögensabtretung* (*SHAW*, 1923, 6), p. 12; see also below, p. 204.

30 Lucid expositions in Otto, *Prolegomena zur Frage der Gesetzgebung und Rechtsprechung in Ägypten* (*MDAIK*, 14, 1956), pp. 150 f.

31 Helck, op. cit., p. 74, with ample evidence in n. 53.

32 That ritual acts in the proper sense of the term were performed for the personified goddess Maat is clear from the references in *Wb.* II, 20, 12; besides *ḥm-nṯr Mꜣꜥt* there also existed *wꜥb n Mꜣꜥt*.

33 These oaths have been collected and studied by J. A. Wilson, 'The Oath in Ancient Egypt', *JNES*, 7, 1948, p. 129; cf. also J. Vergote, *Joseph en Égypte*, Louvain, 1959, pp. 162 ff.

34 Otto, op. cit., p. 159; on the external phenomena connected with oracles, see Bonnet, *RÄRG*, pp. 560 ff.; see also above, p. 103. On the oracle as a means of judicial determination, in this instance during the Late period, cf. O. Kaiser, *Zeitschrift für Religions- und Geistesgeschichte*, 10, 1958, pp. 193 ff.

35 G. Roeder, *Ägyptische Bronzewerke*, Glückstadt, 1937, §§623 f., 678a and e; idem, *Ägyptische Bronzefiguren*, Berlin, 1956, §§710 ff.

36 Material in Grapow, *Grundriss*, III, pp. 137 ff.; on the attribution
to the Late period: Otto, *ZÄS*, 78, 1943, pp. 37 f.

37 An impressive statement about the permanent vitality of religion
forms the conclusion to J. H. Breasted's *Development of Religion
and Thought in Ancient Egypt* (New York, 1912), as noted by J. A.
Wilson in his introduction to the second edition (New York, 1959,
p. xii).

CHAPTER 2

1 *Phänomenologie der Religion*, 2nd rev. ed., Tübingen, 1956, p. 103
[Eng. tr. of 1st ed. by J. E. Turner, *Religion in Essence and Manifestation*, London, 1938].

2 Wolf, *Kunst*, pp. 30 ff.; I regret having to depend on the work of
art historians for the time being: an examination of prehistoric
Egyptian religion, particularly in order to throw light on what one
may call 'the development of the concept of God', is one of the
most urgent, although also the most complex, tasks facing Egyptologists, involving as it does a synthesis of empirical investigation
and skilful interpretation.

3 On the discovery of writing and the link with the development of
historical consciousness: S. Schott, *Hieroglyphen. Untersuchungen
zum Ursprung der Schrift* (*AMAW*, 1950, no. 24), esp. p. 35.

4 Still valuable on this concept is F. R. Lehmann, *Mana. Der Begriff
des 'ausserordentlichen Wirkungsvollen' bei Südseevölkern*, Leipzig,
1922. W. Baetke, *Das Heilige im Germanischen*, Tübingen, 1942,
pp. 10 ff., with good reason pointed to the necessary link between
mana and concrete objects and persons. Mana cannot exist in
detached form. But even though it makes itself manifest in persons,
a mana-bearing person is by no means a god, as will emerge from
the discussion in this chapter.

5 G. v. d. Leeuw, *Godsvoorstellingen in de oud-Aegyptische Pyramidetexten*, Leyden, 1916, pp. 22 ff.; link between *sḥmw* 'powers',
and the dead: e.g., *Pyr.*, 895d and Sethe, *Kommentar*, IV, pp. 169 f.;
also Kees, *Totenglauben*, p. 43.

6 It occupies a place beside the ka of the deity concerned, e.g. Horus;
Edfou, II, p. 47.

7 *Wb.*, IV, 244, 13 ff.

8 Stele (*wḏ*) alongside ka, *šꜣy* (fate), etc., in the tomb of Amenemhet:
N. de G. Davies and A. H. Gardiner, *The Tomb of Amenemhet*,
London, 1915, Pl. XIX.

9 Survey and details in Kees, *Götterglaube*, pp. 4 ff.

10 Discussion and bibliography in Kees, op. cit., pp. 1–3; Bonnet,
RÄRG, esp. pp. 822 f.

11 Egyptologists are again willing to employ the concept of power, and

to good effect: cf. the study by Helck on the sacral monarchy mentioned on p. 280, n. 28.

12 K. Goldammer, *Tribus. Zeitschrift für Ethnologie*, 4–5, 1956, pp. 13 ff.

13 This theory was most recently advanced by F. W. v. Bissing, *Versuch zur Bestimmung der Grundbedeutung des Wortes NUTR für Gott im Altägyptischen* (*SBAW*, 1951, 2).

14 S. Morenz, *OLZ*, 49, 1954, cols. 123–5.

15 S. Schott, *Mythe und Mythenbildung im alten Ägypten* (*Unters.*, 15, 1945), pp. 97 ff.; cf. later also *CT*, III, 276a and *passim*.

16 Sethe, *Urgeschichte*, § 31.

17 E. Otto, *Beiträge zur Geschichte der Stierkulte in Ägypten* (*Unters.*, 13, 1938), p. 5.

18 v. Bissing, 'Ägyptische Kultbilder der Ptolomaier- und Römerzeit', *AO*, 34, 1–2, Figs. 12–13 and pp. 24 f.

19 We are glad to find ourselves in agreement with H. Frankfort, *Kingship and the Gods*, Chicago, 1948, p. 378, n. 5, and *Ancient Egyptian Religion*, 2nd rev. ed., New York, 1949, chap. I.

20 E.g., attribution of the sycamore and papyrus to Hathor, and of the *ben-ben* stone to Re, etc.

21 On the methods used see Wolf, *Kunst*, p. 47.

22 In the same way as they also belong to images of (deceased) human beings, either to make them complete or to differentiate between them: latest study of the subject: Wolf, op. cit., p. 193, also p. 74.

23 H. W. Helck, *ZÄS*, 80, 1955, p. 145 – where the formulation is incorrect in so far as it is stated that the names bore no relation to the beings concerned.

24 Turin Papyrus, from the close of the New Kingdom, trans. Roeder, *Urk.*, pp. 138 ff.

25 Kees, *Götterglaube*, pp. 171 f.

26 E.g., Leyden Hymns to Amon (Papyrus Leiden I 350), IV 20.

27 Helck, op. cit., and W. Till, 'Zum Sprachtabu im Ägyptischen', *FS. Grapow*, pp. 322 ff.

28 With regard to Egypt, cf. Ranke, *Personennamen*, II, pp. 177 ff.

29 We shall of course have to explain references to names that were kept secret. But these can easily be understood partly in terms of magic and partly in terms of a mystification of cult.

30 Kees, *Götterglaube*, p. 172.

31 W. Wessetzky, *AÄS*, 82, 1958, pp. 152 ff.

32 On this subject see Sethe, *Urgeschichte*, §102; on the form of the name beginning with Aleph, see Grapow, *ZÄS*, 46, 1909, pp. 107 ff.

33 For a discussion of other possibilities, see R. Anthes, *ZÄS*, 82, 1958, pp. 1 ff.

34 Kees, *Ägypten*, p. 299. Phases of the moon were the main festivals in Heliopolis, the 'sun's town'; on the other hand the moon is

regarded merely as the 'representative of Re': P. Boylan, *Thoth, the Hermes of Egypt*, London, 1922, p. 81.

35 M. Sandman-Holmberg, *The God Ptah*, Lund, 1946, pp. 8 ff.; the difficulty becomes greater when one considers that the function of the sculptor originally seems to have been attached to Sokaris, who was later identified with Ptah: op. cit., pp. 55 ff.; Morenz, 'Ptah-Hephaistos, der Zwerg', *In memoriam Johannes Stroux. FS. Fr. Zucker*, ed. W. Müller, Berlin, 1954, p. 282.

36 Sethe, *Urgeschichte*, §94; for critical views, W. Westendorf, *MIO*, 2, 1954, pp. 165 ff. A useful compilation of deviant forms was given long ago by Erman, *ZÄS*, 46, 1909–10, pp. 92 ff.

37 Kees, *MIO*, 6, 1958, p. 160.

38 This accords with the creative meaning given to the word in Egypt: tongue or teeth and lips, the means of speech, were regarded as organs of the creator-god, e.g. in Memphite theology (see above, p. 163).

39 In the way intended by the classical philologist, W. F. Otto, who in his studies on Greek religion does not divide the gods into classes but assumes the totality of their nature so that one can speak of their existence.

40 Old Kingdom; Shabaka inscription 59.

41 Later Ramesside: Pap. Berlin 3049, 16, 2.

42 *LD*, IV, 58a.

43 *BD* 154 [E. A. Wallis Budge, *Book of the Dead*, II, London, 1901, p. 518]; cf. Sander-Hansen, *Tod*, p. 8.

44 E. Hornung, *ZÄS*, 81, 1956, p. 32; on the equality between Re and Osiris in suffering the fate of death there is ample material in A. Piankoff and N. Rambova, *Mythological Papyri* (Bollingen Series, XL), 3, New York, 1957.

45 Sethe, *Amun*, §§102 ff.

46 *Edfou*, I, 173, 382.

47 Thus C. J. Bleeker, *Die Geburt eines Gottes. Eine Studie über den ägyptischen Gott Min und sein Fest*, Leyden, 1956.

48 Chap. 21; and also Hopfner, *Plutarch*, I, pp. 161 f. containing further material.

49 Important ideas on this point in Hornung, op. cit., pp. 28 ff.; see also above, pp. 168, 172.

50 Pap. BM 10188, 26, 2 (Book on the Destruction of Apophis); cf. Grapow, *ZÄS*, 67, 1931, pp. 34 ff.; [E. A. Wallis Budge, *From Fetish to God in Ancient Egypt*, London, 1934, p. 433].

51 *BD* 175; translation: Kees, *Lesebuch*, p. 28; [E. A. Wallis Budge, *Book of the Dead*, II, London, 1901, p. 564]; see above, p. 169.

52 Several items of evidence in Kees, *Götterglaube*, pp. 162 f., 256, 353; on the phenomenon as such cf. H. Baumann, *Das doppelte*

Geschlecht. Studien zur Bisexualität in Ritus und Mythos, Berlin, 1955.

53 Shabaka inscription 50a–51a, and also Sethe, *Dram. Texte*, p. 48.

54 *Pyr.*, 1656, and also W. Spiegelberg, *ZÄS*, 65, 1930, pp. 120 f.

55 Pap. Erm. 1116A, ll. 136 f.; for the translation see A. Volten, *Demotische Traumdeutung (Anal. Aeg.,* III, 1942), p. 40.

56 E.g. *Pyr.*, ut. 539; cf. Kees, *Totenglauben*; further details now in S. Schott, *Altägyptische Vorstellungen vom Weltende (Analecta Biblica*, Rome, 12, 1959), p. 329.

57 According to letters in Greek from Roman Egypt; C. H. Roberts in S. R. K. Glanville (ed.), *The Legacy of Egypt*, Oxford, 1942, p. 280.

58 Pap. Berlin 3038, 8, 1, and also Grapow, *Grundriss*, III, p. 33; it may perhaps be translated as follows: 'elimination of the shadow of a god, of a deceased man, of a deceased woman' – thus Grapow, op. cit., IV, 1, 1958, p. 262; for the Egyptian a man's shadow also forms part of his person.

59 Correct interpretation in G. Posener, *Les Empreintes magiques de Gizeh et les morts dangereux (MDAIK,* 16, 1958), pp. 252 ff., esp. p. 267, contrary to Sethe, *Die Ächtung feindlicher Fürsten, Völker und Dinge auf altägyptischen Tongefässcherben (APAW,* 1926, 5), p. 32 (dubious text Pl. 10).

60 On the general principle: Sethe, *Urgeschichte*, §4, later also Bonnet, *ZÄS*, 75, 1939, pp. 42 f., and *RÄRG*, p. 218, as well as Kees, *Götterglaube*, p. 130; on the secondary character of local gods, cf. S. Mowinckel, *Religion und Kultus*, Göttingen, 1953, p. 42.

61 The invocations of Ptah by artisans in distress owing to illness indicate a synthesis between specialized and universal power: here the god is undoubtedly the patron of artisans and also has comprehensive powers of action: Erman, *Denksteine aus der thebanischen Gräberstadt (SPAW,* 1911), pp. 1101 f. Alternatively, amidst statements which simply characterize Ptah as the creator one finds a reference to his specific character: 'He who has created the kinds of craft (*ḥmww*)' (e.g., group of statuary, Berlin 6910).

62 That specialization did not develop as far as it did in the Greek pantheon was correctly emphasized by H. Bonnet, *ZÄS*, 75, 1939, p. 42. On this see above, p. 141.

63 S. Morenz, 'Die Erwählung zwischen Gott und König in Ägypten', *Sino-Japonica. FS. A. Wedemeyer*, ed. H. Steininger et al., Leipzig, 1956, p. 136; cf. also personal names of the types: 'He (she) appertains to god NN', 'The man of god NN', 'Man (s) of god NN': Ranke, *Personennamen*, II, p. 226.

64 In *CT*, II, 41a Pet appears beside Geb: '[I am] he for whom width was made by Pet and breadth by Geb', etc.

65 Sethe, *Urgeschichte*, §70.
66 For example, the personified concept of Shay, 'fate' (see below, chap. 4) and especially Maat (see below, chap. 6).
67 Bonnet, *RÄRG*, p. 626.
68 H. Stock, *Saeculum*, I, 1950, pp. 620 ff., esp. p. 622, who attaches great importance to local (and ethnic) ties.
69 A beginning of this kind need not be linked to Menes but may have taken place some generations earlier; cf. W. Kaiser, *ZÄS*, 86, 1961.
70 We have a late pre-Dynastic slate palette from Gerzeh featuring an ox head decorated with stars (W. M. F. Petrie, *The Labyrinth, Gerzeh and Mazguneh*, London, 1912, Pl. VI, 7) which has been confirmed by the representation on a First-Dynasty porphyry vase from Hierakonpolis: A. J. Arkell, *JEA*, 44, 1958, p. 5, and E. M. Burgess and A. J. Arkell, ibid., pp. 6 ff. This shows that at that time a cosmic aspect was already to be found among animal deities who were regarded from a typological standpoint as tribal numina, i.e. as local gods.
71 This naturally does not exclude a secondary assimilation to animal gods and the assumption of elements of their form: Re as falcon-headed, by equation with Horus; Shu and Tefnut as a pair of lions, by being localized at Leontopolis.
72 Text: J. Couyat and P. Montet, *Les Inscriptions hiéroglyphiques et hiératiques du Ouadi Hammâmât (MIFAO, 34)*, p. 97 (no. 191). The process need not be imagined visually: mȝȝ ḫprw may also denote 'to perceive the nature'; on the miracle of rain cf. G. Posener, 'À propos de la "pluie miraculeuse"', *Revue de Philologie...*, 25, 1951, pp. 162 ff.
73 Translation in, e.g., Erman, *Egyptians*, p. 31.
74 G. Lanczkowski, *ZDMG*, 103, 1953, pp. 360 ff. (containing further bibliography), has the merit of having commented upon the Story of the Shipwrecked Sailor from the standpoint of the history of religion but in our view has erred in the way in which he has classified the genre.
75 Text now in *Urk.*, IV, 1539 ff.; translation in Erman, *Die Sphinxstele (SPAW*, 1904), p. 11; [Eng. trans. by J. H. Breasted, *Ancient Records of Egypt*, II, Chicago, 1906, p. 323].
76 A. Hermann, *Die ägyptische Königsnovelle (LÄSt, 10, 1938)*.
77 Text, translation and most recent treatment in P. Barguet, *La Stèle de la famine à Séhel (Bibl. d'Ét.*, XXIV, 1953); earlier German translation in Roeder, *Urk.*, pp. 177 ff.
78 For more specific details see E. Schweitzer, 'Ego eimi' (dissertation, Basle), 1939.
79 Naturally these do not include the numerous cases in which the deceased, in order to enhance his power, is identified with a god

and which likewise lead to the phrase 'I am the god NN'; these are 'formulae of identification', which R. C. Bultmann, in *Das Evangelium des Johannes*, Göttingen, 1937, p. 167 [Eng. trans. by G. R. Beasley-Murray et al., Oxford, 1971], has distinguished from other types which can lead to revelation (see above, p. 231).

80 E. Chassinat, *Mammisi d'Edfou*, Pl. 116.

81 On this see Müller, *Iris-Aretalogien*.

82 In a suggestive review (*JAOS*, 74, 1954, pp. 35 ff.) R. Anthes speaks in this sense of a 'religion of revelation': 'It was Horus who manifested himself as the living king', etc. (p. 38). In employing this terminology one must, however, realize that, as stated above, revelation has to be understood both more broadly and in a less precise sense.

83 Cf. U. Schweitzer, *Das Wesen des Ka im Diesseits und Jenseits der alten Ägypter* (*ÄgFo*, 19, 1956), p. 53, and H. Brunner, *ZÄS*, 83, 1958, pp. 74 f.

84 Cf. J. Leclant, *MDAIK*, 15, 1957, p. 166, who refers to the female counterpart 'who appears upon the throne of Tefnut' as the title of the so-called '[female] worshippers of God'.

85 H. Müller, *Die formale Entwicklung der Titulatur der ägyptischen Könige* (*ÄgFo*, 7, 1938); important modifications by S. Schott, *Zur Krönungstitulatur der Pyramidenzeit* (*NAWG*, 1956, no. 4); the fivefold title is the basis of a famous saying by Isaiah (ix. 51): A. Alt, *FS. A. Bertholet*, ed. W. Baumgartner et al., Tübingen, 1950, pp. 42 f.

86 E. Otto, *Die Lehre von den beiden Ländern in der ägyptischen Religionsgeschichte* (*Anal. Or.*, 17, 1938), pp. 10 ff.

87 In *ZÄS*, 86, 1961, E. Otto makes a plausible case for the view that in the case of *bȧty*, i.e. the second part, this was originally the primeval kingdom, and that the expression as a whole only became attributed to a particular locality in later times. The other title, 'Golden Horus', cannot be interpreted for certain: Bonnet, *RÄRG*, pp. 216 f.

88 So-called Berlin Leather MS; translation in Erman, *Egyptians*, p. 50.

89 Thutmosis Annals; *Urk.*, iv, 649 and *passim*.

90 H. Stock, op. cit., pp. 628 f.; we speak deliberately only of a 'centre' since we do not rule out the possibility that the conception of a sun-god existed also in the south.

91 Wolf, *Kunst*, pp. 109, 215 f.

92 Translation in Erman, *Egyptians*, pp. 44 ff.

93 On the appearance of the cycles, cf. U. Schweitzer, op. cit., p. 65.

94 *LD*, iv, pp. 60–1, from Hermonthis, now destroyed.

95 Brought to notice by J. Spiegel, *ZÄS*, 75, 1939, pp. 112 ff.; the derivation of *maiestas* from *maius* has been established in the reverse direction by study of the linguistic usage in the Roman ruler cult.

96 H. Goedicke, *Die Stellung des Königs im Alten Reich (Ägyptologische Abhandlungen*, II, Wiesbaden, 1960); *nìswt* is in this case set off graphically against the abbreviated form in the title *nìswt-bìt* by being spelled more completely: Goedicke, op. cit., p. 17.

97 According to his custom, Goedicke bases his study upon Old Kingdom documents, disregarding the familiar picture given in the Pyramid Texts about the rank held by the divine king after his death.

98 *Pyr.*, 410a, 411a–b; on this see Sethe, *Kommentar*, II, pp. 168 f.

99 *Pyr.*, 221 and hymns to the crown in Erman, *Hymnen an das Diadem der Pharaonen (APAW*, 1911), p. 23; translations also in Erman, *Egyptians*, pp. 10 f.

100 H. Ricke and S. Schott, *Beiträge zur ägyptischen Bauforschung und Altertumskunde*, 5, 1950, pp. 105, 160 f., 186 ff.

101 According to an ancient play performed to celebrate the accession of the new ruler and his coronation, preserved in a Middle Kingdom MS and intended for Sesostris I (Sethe, *Dram. Texte*, pp. 203 ff. (scene 31)): 'Securing the crown [by] the keeper of the huge feather.'

102 S. Schott, *Altägyptische Festdaten (AMAW*, 1950, no. 10), pp. 60 ff.

103 Pap. Erm. 1116A, l. 135.

104 Sinuhe B 69; [Erman, *Egyptians*, p. 19; cf. Sir Alan Gardiner, *Notes on the Story of Sinuhe*, Paris, 1916, p. 170].

105 Goedicke, op. cit., p. 61.

106 *Pyr.*, 134d; death is denied also to private persons in the same way: *CT*, I, 190a–b (Spell 44). On this democratization of the cult of the dead, see Chap. 9.

107 *Pyr.*, 604e–f.

108 H. Ricke and S. Schott, op. cit., distinguished clearly between the architecture and function of 'temples of funerary offerings' and 'temples of worship' in Old Kingdom royal tombs.

109 Admonitions VII, 2; Erman, *Egyptians*, p. 101; A. H. Gardiner, *The Admonitions of an Egyptian Sage*, Leipzig, 1909, p. 54, points out that the text refers to the pillaging of tombs. The following translation is also possible: 'What the pyramid concealed is become empty'. In this case the words refer to the mummy, coffin and funerary furniture.

110 A Song of the Harper Antef, Pap. Harris 500, VI, 4; German

translation now in S. Schott, *Altägyptische Liebeslieder...*, Zurich, 1950, p. 54; the text may also be divided differently: 'The gods who formerly arose repose in their pyramids' – cf. M. Lichtheim, *JNES*, IV, 1945, p. 192.

111 *Urk.*, I, 42; also Goedicke, op. cit., p. 55.

112 Pap. Millingen, I, 3–5; text and translation in Volten, *Pol. Schriften*, pp. 106 f.; see also E. Otto, *HO* I 2, pp. 117 f.; [Eng. trans. based partly on J. A. Wilson, *The Burden of Egypt*, Chicago–London, 1951, p. 131 and partly on B. Gunn, *Instruction of Ptahhotep*, London, 1906, p. 67].

113 Rituals in the temple of Seti I at Abydos in Pap. Berlin 3055, 3014, 3053; text and translation in A. Moret, *Le Rituel du culte divin journalier en Égypte*, Paris, 1902, pp. 56 ff. The daily ritual does admittedly throw an ambiguous light on the position of the royal priest: in addition to words of humility we find those expressing assuredness vis-à-vis the cult image, for which the ritual is performed and which is dependent upon the priest for its care: Bonnet, 'Die Symbolik der Reinigungen im ägyptischen Kult', *Angelos*, I, Leipzig, 1925, p. 120.

114 H. G. Fischer, 'Prostrate Figures of Egyptian Kings', University Museum *Bulletin*, Philadelphia, 20, 1, 1956, pp. 27 ff.; ibid., 21, 2, 1957, pp. 35 ff.

115 On this point see Bonnet, *RÄRG*, p. 387, and U. Hölscher, 'Medinet Habu', *Morgenland*, fasc. 24, Berlin, 1933, p. 8 (Seti I at Qurna).

116 Abu Simbel, stele in the niche north of the colossi; text: *Les Temples immergés de la Nubie*, I, Pl. 166 and p. 163.

117 J. Spiegel, 'Der "Ruf" des Königs', *WZKM*, 54, 1957, pp. 191 ff.

CHAPTER 3

1 We have chosen this term in preference to 'popular religion', because the latter puts the accent on the social factor: 'religion of the simple people'. We are quite aware that the ancient Egyptians were scarcely at any time a 'nation' in the modern sense.

2 Judg. ix. 37, as a designation of Gerizim, where the Samaritans' temple was later regarded as the navel of the earth; Ezra xxxviii. 12, with reference to the land of the Jews.

3 Jub. viii. 19; En. xxvi. 1; on a map of the world dating from 1280 Jerusalem is located in the middle of the cosmic circle: *The Jewish Encyclopedia*, 7, p. 128.

4 A. J. Wensinck, *The Ideas of the Western Semites concerning the Navel of the Earth* (*Verhandelingen der Koninklijke Akademie van*

Wetenschappen te Amsterdam, pt. XVII, no. 1), Amsterdam, 1916; W. G. Roscher, *Der Omphalosgedanke bei verschiedenen Völkern* (*BSAW*, 70, 2, 1918); cf. now also R. Meyer, *Theologisches Wörterbuch*, NT, III, p. 43, and M. Eliade, *Der Mythos der ewigen Wiederkehr*, 1953, pp. 24 ff. [original published in French as *Le Mythe de l'éternel retour*, Paris, 1949; Eng. trans. by W. R. Trask, *Myth of the Eternal Return*, London, 1955].

5 A. de Buck, 'De egyptische voorstellingen betreffende den oerheuvel', Leyden, 1922; this is an important dissertation by the famous Dutch Egyptologist and historian of religion.

6 *Pyr.*, 1587c; a similar phrase occurs in 1652a.

7 On Thebes cf. Sethe, *Amun*, §§ 250 ff.

8 Bonnet, *RÄRG*, pp. 847 f.

9 S. Morenz, 'Ägypten und die altorphische Kosmogonie', *FS. Schubart*, esp. p. 96.

10 Theban Temple 49k; on this see Morenz, op. cit., p. 100.

11 Hymns to Amon (Leyden Papyrus I 350), II, 12; translation in Kees, *Lesebuch*, p. 3; [A. H. Gardiner, 'Hymn to Amon from a Leiden Papyrus', *ZÄS*, 42, 1905, p. 21].

12 Said of Dendera: *Dendérah*, III, 78n.

13 One must guard against identifying the *ḥꜣw-nbwt* automatically with the Aegean peoples, and thereby completing the circle to the north; on the complex history of this designation, see J. Vercoutter, *Les Haour-nebout* (*BIFAO*, 48, 1949), pp. 107 ff.

14 H. Brugsch, *Reise nach der Grossen Oase El Khargeh in der libischen Wüste*, Leipzig, 1878, Pl. 13; while these words are addressed to the Persian Darius, they refer of course to his qualities as king of Egypt.

15 H. Gauthier, *Les fêtes du dieu Min*, Cairo, 1931, p. 215; Bonnet, *RÄRG*, p. 398; C. J. Bleeker, *Die Geburt eines Gottes. Eine Studie über den ägyptischen Gott Min und sein Fest*, Leyden, 1956, pp. 90 f.

16 H. Schäfer, *Ägyptische und heutige Kunst und Weltgebäude der alten Ägypter*, Berlin, 1928, pp. 86 f.; on this now see J. J. Clère, *MDAIK*, 16, 1958, pp. 30 ff.; see above, p. 279, n. 14.

17 μέση τῆς οἰκουμένης: 1, 21 end: he adds as a comparison: 'like the pupil in the centre of the eye' (cf. Fr. Sbordone, *Hori Apollinis Hieroglyphica*, Naples, 1940, p. 64).

18 1, 49, 45; cf. C. Wachsmuth and O. Hense (ed.), *Joannis Stobaei Anthologium*, Berlin–Leipzig, 1884, I, p. 412.

19 Th. Hopfner, *Fontes Historiae Religionis Aegyptiacae*, Bonn, 1922–5, p. 620; in ancient Egypt, on the other hand, the country's physical circumstances were deemed to be reflected in the sky: one spoke of the 'two skies' just as of the 'Two Lands' (Pyr. 406c, possibly also 541c); cf. later, e.g., *Urk.*, VI, 125. Both of these expressions are Egyptocentric.

20 *Wb.*, VI, 183.

21 E. Hornung, *ZÄS*, 81, 1956, pp. 28 ff.; cf. also H. Brunner, 'Zum Raumbegriff der Ägypter', *Studium generale*, Oporto, 10, 1957, pp. 612 ff.; on the whole question see above, p. 173.

22 *Wb.*, V, 220, 7–8.

23 Ptolemy's decree conferring benefactions on the priesthood (Rosetta Stone); the translator of the inscriptions on the obelisk of Ramses II in the Circus Maximus later regularly chose the term οἰκουμένη, but this idiosyncrasy should not by any means prompt the conclusion that the Egyptians rendered οἰκουμένη by 'the Two Lands': on this see A. Erman, *Die Obeliskenübersetzung des Hermapion (SPAW,* 1914, no. 9), p. 271.

24 *Urk.*, IV, 85 (Thutmosis I) [J. H. Breasted, *Ancient Records of Egypt*, II, Chicago, 1906, p. 28]. Later (under Ramses III–IV) the Red Sea is called 'the large sea of the inverted water'. This clearly shows that the Egyptians knew that the Euphrates could be reached from the Red Sea by way of the Persian Gulf: Otto, *Ägypten*, p. 186.

25 Text: Davies, *Amarna*, VI, Pl. 27, l. 10; translation: Sethe in H. Schäfer, *Amarna in Religion und Kunst (Sendschrift der Deutschen Orient Gesellschaft*, no. 7), Leipzig, 1931, p. 68.

26 Sir Alan Gardiner, *Ancient Egyptian Onomastica*, I, London, 1947, pp. 98* ff.

27 Ibid., p. 110*.

28 Here in my view Gardiner's account and interpretation (ibid., p. 100*) fails to do justice to the matter.

29 I, 9; text in A. H. Gardiner, *The Admonitions of an Egyptian Sage*, Leipzig, 1909, p. 20; translation, e.g., in Erman, *Egyptians*, p. 94; here Gardiner and Erman have both correctly recognized the problem of *rmṯ*.

30 Book of the Gates, II, 4–5; Grapow, *HO* I 2, p. 54.

31 Wolf, *Kunst*, p. 211: Sahure, Fifth Dynasty.

32 Sinuhe B 33; [A. H. Gardiner, *Notes on the Story of Sinuhe*, Paris, 1916, p. 169].

33 *Urk.*, IV, 698 (Thutmosis III, dealing with the spoils of a battle on the Euphrates).

34 II, 143.

35 A more detailed study of these facts would be desirable, taking account of those passages in which a private person who has risen in the world confesses that the ruler made him 'a man' (*m rmṯ*): Davies, *Amarna*, II, Pl. VII, p. 29 (Panehesy), discussed by Erman, *Religion*, p. 121; also Louvre C 213 (XIX Dyn.). This would shift the emphasis from the national to the social plane and illustrate even better the link with καλὸς κάγαθός. Was this statement perhaps first made by foreigners?

Let us recall that '[every] young nation regards itself as the best
and most distinguished, the chosen one among all others, which are
regarded as inferior by comparison'; F. Solmsen, *Indogermanische
Eigennamen als Spiegel der Kulturgeschichte*, Heidelberg, 1922,
pp. 99 f. A well-known example is Ārja = 'the illustrious', 'the
noble'. G. Fecht, *ZDMG*, 106, 1956, pp. 50 f., compares the
Egyptian *ḥꜣtyw-ꜥ*, probably meaning 'the first ones', 'the most
privileged'.

36 Text and translation: H. W. Helck, *ZÄS*, 83, 1958, Pl. III, ll. 10–11
and p. 35.

37 We do not know of any parallel for the expression *tꜣ wꜥty*.

38 Cairo 34025, ll. 12 f.; text: Spiegelberg, *ZÄS*, 34, 1896, p. 4; most
recent translation by J. A. Wilson in *ANET*, p. 377.

39 If a limitation of this kind applies to the national gods, it is of
course still more applicable to local deities; see above, p. 28.
Cosmic gods, too, who in accordance with their nature have the
greatest freedom of movement, took on political aspects – e.g., by
being equated with national or local gods. Thus the sun-god is
even among the patrons of Egyptian army units (poem to the battle
of Kadesh: Erman, *Egyptians*, p. 263).

40 Gardiner, *Ostraca*, Pl. XI.

41 Correspondingly in a hymn to Osiris (Bib. Nat. 20, l. 20) we are
told of the corn-god Nepri: 'he let saturation ensue and gave it to
all lands (*tꜣw nbw*)'.

42 Davies, *Amarna*, VI, Pl. 27, ll. 8 f.; translation: Sethe in Schäfer,
op. cit., p. 67; I prefer the division of meaning which Sethe here
relegates to the notes. [Eng. trans. also in *ANET*, p. 370.]

43 Evidence, including in the first place the Leipzig Ostracon which
has now been made available again, in J. Černý, 'Thoth as Creator
of Languages', *JEA*, 34, 1948, pp. 121 f.; alongside the testimonies
about Thoth and Aton we may place the so-called Song of the
Primordial Gods of the Temple at Hibis: 'The creator has distinguished (*stny*) between their tongues.' The material has been
reworked by S. Sauneron, *La différentiation des langages d'après la
tradition égyptienne (BIFAO*, 60, 1960), pp. 31 ff. On the general
history of linguistic differentiation, see A. Borst, *Der Turmbau zu
Babel*, I, Stuttgart, 1957.

44 Sethe, 'Kosmopolitische Gedanken der Ägypter des Neuen Reiches
in bezug auf das Totenreich', *Studies presented to F. Ll. Griffith*
London, 1932, pp. 432 f.

45 Together with many previous scholars we believe that at least some
affinity existed between the innovative Aton religion and the general
trend toward universalism: cf., e.g., H. Schäfer, op. cit., p. 36, and
Otto, *Ägypten*, p. 161.

46 Poem to the Battle at Kadesh, in which Ramses II defeated the Hittites and their allies: Erman, *Egyptians*, pp. 263 f. Even more impressive, since it is more general in scope, is the (somewhat earlier) phrase in which the king is referred to as '[he] who protects Egypt, [but] who stamps out (*ptpt*) foreign peoples (*ḫ3styw*)'. It is to be found upon the rock-cut tombs erected in honour of Seti I near Qasr Ibrim; the inadequate publication of it by A. H. Sayce, *Rec. de trav.*, 16, 1894, pp. 170 f., has been superseded by F. Hintze, Die Felsenstele Sethos' I bei Qasr Ibrim', *ZÄS*, 87, 1962.

47 On Nubia see Kees, *Ägypten*, pp. 349 f.; Erman, *Religion*, pp. 351 ff.; T. Säve-Söderbergh, 'Ägypten und Nubien' (Lund, 1941), pp. 200 f.; on Syria, cf. A. Alt, 'Ägyptische Tempel in Palästina und die Landnahme der Philister', *ZDPV*, 67, 1944–5, pp. 1 ff. (now in *Kleine Schriften zur Geschichte des Volkes Israel*, 1, 2nd rev. ed., Munich, 1953, pp. 21 ff.).

48 Alt, op. cit., pp. 6 f.

49 Evidence in Säve-Söderbergh, op. cit., p. 201.

50 Pap. Salt 825 VII, 5; on the other hand the use of mortuary literature, for example, by foreigners was apparently not subject to such restrictions even in pre-Greek times: some details in Morenz, *FS. Schubart*, pp. 69 f.

51 Esna 197, 20; from the edition by Sauneron, to whom I am indebted for allowing me to use this information prior to publication; [cf. S. Sauneron, *Les Fêtes religieuses d'Esna...*, Cairo, 1962]. If on the other hand access by 'foreigners' (*rwtyw*) was prohibited at Philae, which as a sanctuary on the border was open to aliens from the south, and was even designed to attract them, importance no doubt attaches to the (partly destroyed) addendum that nothing is known about these 'foreigners': H. Junker, *Analecta Biblica*, 12, 1959, pp. 156–8.

52 Herodotus, II, 39 and 41; Plato, *Laws*, XII, 953e; further details in B. H. Stricker, *De Brief van Aristeas (Verhandelingen der Koninklijke Nederlandse Akademie van Wetenschappen te Amsterdam, Afd. Letterkunde, Nieuwe reeks*, pt. 62, no. 4, 1956), pp. 36 ff.

53 L. Klebs, *ZÄS*, 61, 1926, p. 105.

54 Ample material from the Pyramid period in Ranke, *Personennamen*, II, pp. 230 f.; H. Junker, *Pyramidenzeit. Das Wesen der altägyptischen Religion*, Einsiedeln–Zurich–Cologne, 1949, was probably the first to draw conclusions from this in the sense given here.

55 Junker, *Gîza*, XII, pp. 151 ff., distinguishes personal names from the Giza tombs which he dates by adding *GB* (*Grabbesitzer*, i.e. 'tomb owner', in contrast to *MB*, *Mastababesitzer*, 'mastaba owner') in cases when such persons are the owners of these unpretentious complexes.

56 *Pyr*, 337a–d.

57 *Pyr.*, 574d.

58 *Pyr.*, 575e.

59 Fundamental on this point: Kees, *Totenglauben*; see below, chap. 9.

60 S. Morenz, *Die Zauberflöte*, Cologne, 1952, pp. 75 ff.

61 Brought to notice by É. Drioton, 'Cyrille d'Alexandrie et l'ancienne religion égyptienne', *Kyrilliana*, Cairo, 1947, p. 9; further material in Morenz, 'Anubis mit dem Schlüssel', *Geschichte und Altes Testament. FS. Alt*, Tübingen, 1953–4, pp. 61 f.

62 S. Morenz, 'Das Werden zu Osiris', *Forschungen und Berichte*, 1, (*FS. Justi*, Berlin, 1957), p. 57.

63 J. A. Wilson in H. and H. A. Frankfort, J. A. Wilson and T. Jacobsen, *Before Philosophy*, Harmondsworth, 1949, pp. 117 f. This passage is not yet to be found in the CT; for the text, see provisionally P. Lacau, *Sarcophages antérieurs au Nouvel Empire*, Cairo, 1901, p. 220 (Cat. gén. no. 28085). The importance of the text was realized already by J. H. Breasted, *The Dawn of Conscience*, New York–London, 1933, p. 221.

CHAPTER 4

1 Zeus addressing the gods: [*The Odyssey*, trans. R. Fitzgerald, London, 1962, Book 1, 32].

2 *Urk.*, III, 112.

3 Pap. Erm. 1116A, ll. 133 f.; the connection was noted by Erman, *Egyptians*, p. 83, n. 3.

4 So-called Book of the Celestial Cow, translated in Erman, op. cit., pp. 47 ff.; cf. Ranke, in *AOT*, pp. 3–5.

5 Pap. Erm. 1116A, ll. 70 f.; translation based on Volten, *Pol. Schriften*, p. 37; [*ANET*, p. 416].

6 A. Götze, *Die Pestgebete des Muršili* (*Kleinasiatische Forschungen*, 1, 1930), pp. 161 ff.

7 Ibid., pp. 119–23; Volten, op. cit., p. 65; [*ANET*, p. 417].

8 Erman, *Denksteine aus der thebanischen Gräberstadt* (*SPAW*, 1911), pp. 1089 ff., esp. pp. 1090, 1094, 1098, 1101 f., 1103.

9 Coffin of Ankhpekhrad, Late period: text, translation and commentary in E. Lüddeckens, *Totenklagen*, pp. 164 f.

10 G. Posener, *MDAIK*, 16, 1948, p. 268, incl. nn. 6, 7.

11 Pap. Erm. 1116A, ll. 46 f.; Volten, op. cit., p. 23; one may also point to the identical idea in the final sentence and in the fourth commandment of the decalogue. (Incidentally, piety and kindness toward one's father and mother also counted as an Egyptian virtue: *Urk.*, I, 199, 6; 204, 8; on this see E. Edel, *Untersuchungen zur Phraseologie der ägyptischen Inschriften des Alten Reiches* (*MDAIK*, 13, 1944), p. 43.)

12 The words in square brackets may also be missing: the material, grouped according to variant readings, has been compiled by Edel, op. cit., pp. 34 f.

13 Discussion of the question of the significance of the 'Great God': Junker, *Gîza*, II, pp. 54 ff. Ample material on divine reward for right conduct is to be found also in late biographies: Otto, *Biogr. Inschr.*, *passim* (see also below, chap. 6).

14 Shabaka inscription 57; text (partly restored) and translation: Sethe, *Dram. Texte*, 64; cf. also Junker, *Götterlehre*, pp. 59–61, who correctly emphasizes that the formulation was derived from the divine word; [Eng. trans.: *ANET*, p. 5].

15 Cf. the tales in the tract Taanith in the Babylonian Talmud.

16 *Pyr.*, 436a–b; the fact that this is an extract from the Horus myth was recognized by Sethe, *Kommentar*, II, p. 21.

17 *Pyr.*, 1295a.

18 Possibly *Pyr.*, 1292b ff.

19 *Pyr.*, 657a–d; Sethe also regards the text as a command to the bereaved: op. cit., III, p. 207.

20 *Urk.*, IV, 223 f.

21 *Edfou*, I, 301, 309; also O. Firchow, *FS. Grapow*, p. 91.

22 Otto, *MDAIK*, 14, 1956, pp. 154 ff.

23 *Urk.*, IV, 565.

24 *Urk.*, IV, 184. A noteworthy peculiarity of such divine commands to undertake a campaign seems to be present in the account of Kamose's campaign and the events preceding it. In this the king's counsellors first advise against the enterprise, but Kamose proceeds with it since he feels strong enough to attack 'through the command of Amon, the just of counsels (*mtr sḥr.w*)'. The commanding god thus appears as the better counsellor (Carnarvon tablet, l. 10); text: Gardiner, *JEA*, 3, 1916, p. 104; latest translation: *ANET*, p. 232.

25 *Urk.*, IV, 730.

26 In this respect the account by E. Hornung of the historic role played by the king (*MDAIK*, 15, 1957, p. 150) needs to be supplemented and corrected.

27 Pap. Harris I, 3, 10.

28 *Urk.*, III, 22; [Frankfort, *Kingship and the Gods*, Chicago, 1948, p. 42].

29 *Urk.*, III, 91.

30 Text, translation and commentary: Junker, *Götterdekret*, pp. 7 ff., 60.

31 [*ANET*, p. 8.]

32 We are deliberately using cautious language here, for no preliminary studies have yet been undertaken. There is an urgent need for a study of divine commands in Egypt. Isolated pieces of evidence

would hardly suffice to refute the construction given here; those cited below are exceptions, and distinguishable as such. But we should not exclude the possibility that the material at our disposal is inadequate, and some of it may have escaped our notice.

33 *wdt prt m r.k*: G. Daressy, *Rec. de trav.*, 35, 1913, p. 126; translation: Otto, *Biogr. Inschr.*, p. 150.

34 Text: H. Brugsch, *Thesaurus inscriptionum aegyptiacarum*, V, Leipzig, 1891, p. 923: *imi ir.tw*: 'bring about that one does', etc. Translation: Otto, *Biogr. Inschr.*, p. 192.

35 Otto, op. cit., esp. pp. 100 f.; cf. also *HO* I 2, p. 109 (Brunner) and p. 151 (Otto).

36 Evidence (for Amon) is provided by Grapow, *Ausdrücke*, pp. 156 f. Much further detail in A. H. Gardiner (ed.), *Papyri in the British Museum*, 3rd series, I, 1935, p. 32 (Pap. Chester Beatty, IV).

37 Pap. Erm. 1116A, l. 131; further extracts in F. Hintze, *ZÄS*, 78, 1943, pp. 55 f.; in the Old Testament, too, the documentation for God the shepherd begins with the indirect testimony of God the shepherd distinguishing between men's souls: I Sam. xxv. 29; on this, see now O. Eissfeldt, *Der Beutel der Lebendigen: alttestamentliche Erzählungs- und Dichtungsmotive im Lichte neuer Nūzi-Texte* (*BSAW*, 105, 6, 1960).

38 I, 350, IV, 14 or V, 20 f.; [*ANET*, pp. 368 f.].

39 On the sun-god as guide see Zandee, *Hymnen*, p. 79.

40 *Urk.*, III, 110.

41 Text: G. Daressy, *Rec. de trav.*, 16, 1894, p. 56 (XXII Dyn.): cf. Erman, *Religion*, p. 164.

42 Amenemope XX, 4–6; for the understanding of figurative speech, cf. S. Herrmann, *ZÄS*, 79, 1954, pp. 106 ff.; [*ANET*, p. 424; cf. F. Ll. Griffith, 'The Teaching of Amenophis the Son of Kanakht', *JEA*, 12, 1926, p. 216].

43 Sinuhe B 228–30; trans. in H. Grapow, *Sinuhe*, p. 85; [Eng. trans.: A. H. Gardiner, *Notes on the Story of Sinuhe*, Paris, 1916, p. 174].

44 W. Wreszinski, *OLZ*, 13, 1910, Pl. IV; translation: Otto, *Biogr. Inschr.*, p. 160.

45 Berlin 7798; further details below, chap. 6.

46 Wreszinski, *Ägyptische Inschriften aus dem K.K. Hofmuseum in Wien*, 1906, p. 160 (Ptolemaic).

47 Bonnet, *RÄRG*, pp. 225 ff.

48 E.g., statue Louvre A 90 (XXVI Dyn.); text: G. Maspero, *ZÄS*, 22, 1884, p. 89; translation: Otto, *Biogr. Inschr.*, p. 163; see also Canopus decree 11 in *Urk.*, II, 133 among many others.

49 *Urk.*, IV, 198 or 134.

50 *Urk.*, IV, 261; [J. H. Breasted, *Ancient Records of Egypt*, II, Chicago, 1906, p. 99].

51 Text: *Urk.*, IV, 1282: *ìn nṯr dd m ìb.f*; translation: S. Schott, *Altägyptische Liebeslieder*, Zurich, 1950, p. 93.

52 Text: G. Legrain, *Statues de rois et particuliers*, Cairo, 1914, p. 65 (Cat. gén. 42226k); translation: Otto, *Biogr. Inschr.*, pp. 148 f.; on inspiration (ἐπίπνοια) and conduct of life in Greek times (Chairemon) see below, p. 336, n. 22.

53 G. Daressy, *ASAE*, 1916, p. 2 (XXX Dyn.).

54 Prisse 550 f.; text and translation in Žába, *Ptahhotep*, pp. 59, 101; on the concept of the 'hearkening heart' in Israel (I Kings iii. 9) and possible reference to Egypt, cf. S. Herrmann, 'Die Königsnovelle in Ägypten und Israel', *Geschichte und Altes Testament. FS. Alt*, Tübingen, 1953-4, pp. 38 f., and H. Brunner, *ThLZ*, 79, 1954, cols. 697 ff.; on the heart as the seat of foolish disobedience to God's commandment: Jer. v. 23; [*ANET*, p. 414].

55 Text: Lefebvre, *Petosiris*, II, p. 91 (inscription 127, l. 6).

56 Impenitence of the heart: e.g., Isaiah vi. 10; infatuation (ἄτη): e.g., *Iliad*, XIX, 88, 137; also οὖλος ὄνειρος: ibid., II, beginning.

57 I base my statement here on earlier detailed studies; for additional evidence and discussion, see S. Morenz and D. Müller, *Schicksal*.

58 Prisse 545 f.; Žába, *Ptahhotep*, pp. 58 f. or 101; [*ANET*, p. 414]; H. Frankfort, *Egyptian Religion*, New York, 1948, p. 74].

59 Prisse, 216 f.; Žába, op. cit., pp. 33, 80; [*ANET*, p. 413].

60 Prisse 301 f.; commentary by G. Fecht, *Der Habgierige und die Maat* (*ADAIK*, I, 1958), pp. 36 f.; [Erman, *Egyptians*, p. 60].

61 Texts and translation: H. Brunner, *Die Lehre des Kheti, Sohnes des Duauf* (*ÄgFo*, 13, 1944), pp. 204 ff., 24; [*ANET*, p. 434].

62 Amenemope XXIV, 13-17; translation and latest treatment: Morenz, *ZÄS*, 84, 1959, pp. 79 f.; [*ANET*, p. 424].

63 Romans ix. 21; also Morenz, op. cit.

64 This thesis, based upon linguistic evidence, is presented by É. Drioton, *Mélanges bibliques rédigés en l'honneur de André Robart*, Paris, 1957, pp. 254 ff.; but see below, p. 348, n. 103.

65 1, 7; text and translation: A. H. Gardiner, *The Admonitions of an Egyptian Sage*, Leipzig, 1909, p. 20.

66 Poseidonios, Cicero, etc.: Morenz and Müller, op. cit., p. 11.

67 1, 10; Gardiner, op. cit., p. 21.

68 Pap. Erm. 1116A, 68 f., 71 f.; text and translation: Volten, *Pol. Schriften*, p. 37; [*ANET*, p. 416].

69 Pap. Erm. 1116B r, l. 26; translation: Erman, *Egyptians*, p. 113.

70 Pap. Erm. 1115, 30-2, 97 f.; translation: Erman, op. cit., p. 30.

71 *Urk.*, IV, 390; translation: Gardiner, *JEA*, 32, 1946, p. 48.

72 Pap. Harris I, 22, 5.

73 On the form (three radicals tert. inf. and not two radicals, as assumed hitherto), cf. Morenz and Müller, op. cit., pp. 23 f.

74 Prisse 480; Žába, *Ptahhotep*, pp. 54 or 98; [*ANET*, p. 414].

75 Sinuhe B 156; translation: Grapow, *Sinuhe*, p. 62; [A. H. Gardiner, *Notes on the Story of Sinuhe*, Paris, 1916, p. 172].

76 Sinuhe B 229; Grapow, op. cit., p. 85; [*ANET*, p. 21; Gardiner, loc. cit.].

77 *Urk.*, IV, 5; in *Urk.*, IV, 29 f., we call in question, in common with other scholars, the interpretation of *šȝw* as 'fate', which has become customary: Morenz and Müller, op. cit., pp. 17 f.

78 E.g., Davies, *Amarna*, I, Pl. 34.

79 There are two terms derived from *šȝ*, 'to determine': masc. *šȝw* (later usually spelled *šȝy*) and fem. *šȝyt*; on this duality, cf. Morenz and Müller, op. cit., pp. 24 f.

80 Leyden I, 350, III, 17; on this see Zandee, *Hymnen*, p. 58; [*ANET*, p. 369].

81 Pap. Golénischeff, 2, 57 f.; translation: Erman, *Egyptians*, p. 183 (10,000 should be corrected to 50).

82 III, 16; Zandee, *Hymnen*, p. 56; [*ANET*, p. 369].

83 W. Spiegelberg, *ZÄS*, 57, 1922, pp. 70 f.

84 Pap. Harris 500, VI, 3.

85 Pap. Harris 500, V, 4, 3; translation: Erman, *Egyptians*, pp. 161 f.

86 Morenz and Müller, op. cit., pp. 20 f.

87 Leyden I, 350, V, 23; Zandee, op. cit., p. 103; [*ANET*, p. 369].

88 Pap. Anastasi v, 17, 2 f.

89 Morenz and Müller, op. cit., p. 24.

90 This is said frequently, and is akin to a formula: e.g. *LD*, IV, 58a; cf. Morenz and Müller, op. cit., p. 28.

91 Helck, *ZÄS*, 82, 1958, pp. 117 ff.; on the ceremony around the Ished tree.

92 W. F. Otto, *Die Götter Griechenlands*, 3rd ed., Frankfurt, 1947, p. 257, 5th ed., 1961; [trans. M. Hadas, *The Homeric Gods. The Spiritual Significance of Greek Religion*, London, 1955, p. 264].

93 A. Abt, *ARW*, 18, 1915, pp. 257 ff.

94 W. Peek, *Der Isishymnus von Andros und verwandte Texte*, Berlin, 1930, p. 124.

95 Material in Morenz and Müller, op. cit., p. 31.

96 [*Metamorphoses or Golden Ass of Apuleius of Madaura*, trans. H. E. Butler, II, Oxford, 1910.]

97 H. Junker, *Der grosse Pylon des Tempels der Isis in Philä* (*DWAW*, special vol., Vienna, 1958), p. 76.

98 On other vital questions – personification of the concept of destiny, function of the Seven Hathors, and their roots in fertility deities – cf. Morenz and Müller, op. cit., pp. 25, 32–4.

99 Text: J. Černý and Sir Alan Gardiner, *Hieratic Ostraca*, Oxford, I,

1957, Pl. I–IA; translation by Gardiner, *WZKM*, 54, 1957 (*FS. Junker*), pp. 43 ff.

100 Pap. Berlin 3049, XIII, 2.

101 Classical examples of representing the course of life as a *cursus honorum* are, in the Old Kingdom, the biography of Uni (*Urk.*, I, 98 ff.); in the Eighteenth Dynasty that of Ahmose of El Kab (*Urk.*, IV, 1 ff.).

102 On the cyclic notion of time see W. F. Otto, 'Altägyptische Zeitvorstellungen und Zeitbegriffe', *Die Welt als Geschichte*, 14, 1954, pp. 135 ff., esp. pp. 139 ff.; on the general principle of periodicity: J. A. Wilson, *The Burden of Egypt*, Chicago, 1951, pp. 13 f.; on the lineal notion of time, see Morenz, 'Ägyptische Ewigkeit des Individuums und indische Seelenwanderung', *Asiatica: FS. Fr. Weller*, ed. J. Schubert and U. Schneider, Leipzig, 1954, pp. 414 ff. These three works, which appeared simultaneously, hardly refer to other aspects of time than those they are directly concerned with.

103 Stele Leyden V, 55 (Ptolemaic); translation: Otto, *Biogr. Inschr.*, pp. 187 f.; on the meaning of *tr*, see Otto, op. cit., pp. 136 f.

104 The expert will be quick to note that by citing Koh. and Ps. civ we have mentioned works of literature that have always been suspected of Egyptian connections; we must resist the temptation to reformulate these suspicions here.

105 Pap. Sallier III, 3, 8 f. or 10, 9 f.; [Erman, *Egyptians*, pp. 264, 269].

106 H. E. Naville, *Textes relatifs au Mythe d'Horus...*, Basle, 1870, Pl. XIV.

107 This point was made already by H. Gressmann, 'Hadad und Baal', *Abhandlungen zur semitischen Religionskunde und Sprachwissenschaft* (*FS. Baudissin*), ed. W. Frankenberg and F. Küchler, suppl. fasc. to *Zeitschrift für die alttestamentliche Wissenschaft*, 33, Giessen, 1918, p. 201.

108 Taken from the late Apophis Book: Pap. BM 10188, 24, 1 f. or 33, 5; similarly, e.g., *Urk.*, VI, 67.

109 Pap. Berlin 3050, 3, 6 or 3, 1.

110 *Urk.*, VI, 60 f.

111 Naville, op. cit., Pl. XVIII.

112 Prisse 60, 68, 74; Žába, *Ptahhotep*, pp. 21 f., 72 f.; [Erman, *Egyptians*, pp. 54, 56].

113 *Urk.*, IV, 498.

114 *Dendérah*, III, 25.

115 Philae photo 891.

116 K. F. Piehl, *Inscriptions hiéroglyphiques*, II, Stockholm–Leipzig, 1890, p. 112.

117 Lefebvre, *Petosiris*, II, p. 21, in inscription no. 48, 4.
118 Ibid., p. 21, in inscription no. 48, 5.
119 Dümichen, *Geogr. Inschr.*, III, 74, from Dendera.
120 *Pyr.*, 1929, after Neit, 759 f.
121 J. de Morgan et al., *Kom Ombos*, Cairo, 1909, III, p. 127, no. 699.
122 'Stele of Chaliut': G. Reisner, *ZÄS*, 70, 1934, pp. 40, 42.
123 W. Wreszinski, *OLZ*, 13, 1910, Pl. IV; translation based upon Otto, *Biogr. Inschr.*, p. 159.
124 *Urk.*, VI, 124 f.; in the late Egyptian (almost demotic) translation of the text, *ꜣt* is rendered by *wnwt*, 'hour'; according to this the two words were approximately synonymous. In practice *wnwt* is also found used with a suffix in reference to persons (cf. Amenemope, IX, 13: 'Every man is [destined] for his hour (*tꜣy.f wnwt*)', and ibid., XXIV, 18: 'when [the creator-god] is in his hour of life'; [F. Ll. Griffith, 'The Teaching of Amenophis, the Son of Kanakht', *JEA*, 12, 1926, p. 206]). Also *rk*, which is commonly used in assigning dates, may acquire the meaning of καιρός; e.g., Pap. Leyden I, 350, III, 21. On this see Zandee, *Hymnen*, p. 61 and Posener, *Mélanges J. Lévy*, 1955, p. 471 incl. n. 3. On the other hand, like *tr*, *sw* and *nw* may refer to objects. In the case of *sw*, an example was given above; for *nw*, cf., for example, F. A. F. Mariette, *Abydos*, Paris, 1869–80, I, 51, 33–4, and *Edfou*, I, 162. The dividing line is normally quite clear; it runs not just between two words (*ꜣt* and *tr*) but between two groups. Beyond this point, it is essential that the entire material should be analysed in a special study.
125 *LD*, III, 207d; with an even more precise concept of time, *hrw*, 'day', one may also refer to the 'day of death' assigned to someone ('his day of death'): *Pyr.*, 1467a.

CHAPTER 5

1 S. Mowinckel, *Psalmenstudien*, Kristiania, 1922, pt. II, p. 16; Mowinckel dealt with the whole problem later in *Religion und Kultus*, Göttingen, 1953.
2 E. Würthwein, 'Amos V: 21–27', *ThLZ*, 1947, cols. 143 ff.
3 Among those initiating the discussion was K. Th. Preuss, *Der religiöse Gehalt der Mythen*, Tübingen, 1933; cf. also the general tenor of the collective work: S. H. Hooke (ed.), *Myth, Ritual and Kingship*, Oxford, 1958.
4 In particular those buried in secluded cemeteries; when interment took place within the settlement the deceased was not provided with any funerary gifts, but it may be assumed that at mealtime he was accorded hiss hare; this is a particularly good analogy to the

offerings to supernatural forces or to the gods. On this point see H. Junker, *Vorläufiger Bericht über die Grabung...von Merimde-Benisalame* (*SWAW*, 1929), pp. 194 f.

5 Summarized in Porter and Moss, v, pp. 193 ff.

6 W. M. F. Petrie, *Royal Tombs*, II, 1901, Pl. X, 2.

7 On this basic distinction cf. Mowinckel, *Religion und Kultus*, Göttingen, 1953, p. 29.

8 *Pyr.*, 105a; further evidence may be found, e.g., in O. Firchow, *Grundzüge der Stilistik in den altägyptischen Pyramidentexten*, Berlin, 1953, pp. 223 ff.

9 On the 'Eye of Horus': Bonnet, *RÄRG*, pp. 314 f.; on its interpretation: G. Rudnitzky, *Die Aussage über 'Das Auge des Horus'* (*Anal. Aeg.*, Copenhagen, v, 1956).

10 S. Morenz, 'Wortspiele in Ägypten', *FS. J. Jahn*, Leipzig, 1958, pp. 23 ff.

11 *Pyr.*, 614a.

12 Honesty requires us to point out that we have drawn general conclusions from limited material – the so-called offering spells; some sceptics may question the validity of this.

13 Ancient and varied examples are provided in the so-called Ramesseum Dramatic Papyrus: Sethe, *Dram. Texte*, pp. 103 ff., also the list on pp. 99 ff., and Rudnitzky, op. cit., pp. 25 ff.; on the content and the order of the ritual acts, cf. H. W. Helck, *Orientalia*, 23, 1954, pp. 383 ff.

14 On the symbolism of sacrifice cf. H. Junker, *ZÄS*, 48, 1911, pp. 69 ff., and H. Kees, *NAWG*, 1942, pp. 71 ff.; on that of ablutions and the burning of incense cf. H. Bonnet, *Angelos. Archiv für neutestamentliche Zeitgeschichte und Kulturkunde*, I, 1925, pp. 103 ff., or *ZÄS*, 67, 131, pp. 20 ff., and *RÄRG*, pp. 624 ff. or 633 ff.

15 E. Otto, *Das Verhältnis von Rite und Mythus im Ägyptischen* (*SHAW*, 1958, 1), pp. 5 f.

16 The older generation of Egyptologists would hardly have approved of this mode of reasoning. For Sethe the Pyramid Texts originated in the earliest times, long before the discovery of writing. The first to emphasize that myths were not created until historic times was S. Schott, *Mythe und Mythenbildung im alten Ägypten* (*Unters.*, 15). It is to him that we also owe representations of the relationship between ritual and myth, both in regard to the underlying essentials and to the historical development: e.g., *Die Deutung der Geheimnisse des Rituals für die Abwehr des Bösen* (*AMAW*, 1954, no. 5), pp. 16 ff. The discussion is continued on a different plane by E. Otto, *Das Verhältnis von Rite und Mythus im Ägyptischen* (see n. 15). We may spare the non-specialist reader an exposition of these important questions of principle and method, but should like to point out that

these problems exist and that we prefer to adopt a well-established view.

17 Lately Wolf, *Kunst*.

18 H. Brugsch, *ZÄS*, 9, 1871, p. 44; we interpret *sšm* as 'plan', not as 'guidance', in accordance with its frequent meaning of 'design'.

19 Brugsch, *ZÄS*, 10, 1872, p. 4; K. Sethe, *Imhotep, der Asklepios der Ägypter* (*Unters.*, II, 1902), pp. 107 f.

20 Bonnet, *RÄRG*, p. 779.

21 *Dendérah*, III, Pl. 77a–b.

22 H. Ricke and S. Schott, *Beiträge zur ägyptischen Bauforschung und Altertumskunde*, fasc. 5, 1950.

23 Wolf, *Kunst*, pp. 117 f.

24 Bonnet, *RÄRG*, pp. 735 ff.

25 U. Hölscher, 'Medinet Habu', *Morgenland*, 24, 1933, pp. 41 f., Figs. 19, 33 ff. (now: *Die Wiedergewinnung von Medinet Habu im westlichen Theben*, 1958, p. 51 and Fig. 16b).

26 Cf. the description by G. Steindorff in K. Baedeker, *Egypt*, Leipzig, 1929, p. 372.

27 *Urk.*, II, 154, 226.

28 H. Brugsch, *ZÄS*, 9, 1871, p. 138.

29 J. Dümichen, *ZÄS*, 7, 1869, Plate at p. 104; on the entire subject, see also Erman, *Religion*, p. 369.

30 A. Moret, *Le Rituel du culte divin journalier en Égypte*, Paris, 1902.

31 Bonnet, *RÄRG*, p. 640. The mythical interpretation becomes clear in examples given by Erman, *Religion*, pp. 174 f.; unfortunately the pages dealing with cult, though excellent as description, are spoiled by facetious value judgements which show that this great philologist and cultural historian was not familiar with religious phenomena.

32 That of the *ḥm-nṯr* (προφήτης). In the Book of Rites the great Wêb priest (ᶜwbᶜꜣ) is mentioned as the one who performs the ritual (Moret, op. cit., p. 7; also Junker, *Götterdekret*, p. 19), but this is due to the practice whereby ritual duties were progressively delegated to others. 'Vicars' of this kind came to be as essential as they were in the European Middle Ages, for one reason because the great holders of permanent established posts had other (political) commitments and were not available for the cult. (Information kindly supplied by H. Kees.)

33 *ḏsr* originally meant 'to isolate' (see above, pp. 99 f.).

34 *Urk.*, IV, 99; further details in H. Grapow, *Ausdrücke*, p. 26; [Engl. trans. based upon J. H. Breasted, *Ancient Records of Egypt*, II, p. 39].

35 For this reason its ceiling is adorned with stars and from its floor plant-like columns and shrubs grow like vegetation; cf. also the linguistic phrases mentioned by Grapow, op. cit., pp. 26 f.

36 On this cf. J. Černý, *JEA*, 34, 1948, p. 120.

37 We have already mentioned the vast calendar of festivals at Medinet Habu: see above, p. 279, n. 13; according to this every third day would have been a feast-day. The calendars of festivals from the temple at Edfu, on which we have drawn, were edited by H. Brugsch: *Drei Festkalender des Tempels von Apollinopolis Magna...*, Leipzig, 1877 (this includes translations of the calendars of Dendera and Esna). On Edfu cf. now M. Alliot, *Le Culte d'Horus à Edfou au temps des Ptolémées* (*Bibl. d'Ét.*, 20, 1949, 1954), esp. pp. 197 ff.

38 Thus Isis as Sothis (Sirius) brings the Nile: J. de Morgan, *Catalogue des monuments et inscriptions de l'Égypte antique*, I, Vienna, 1894, p. 55 (from Aswan): 'Isis, thou who bringest the Nile that it may flood the Two Lands, in thy name Sothis.' This goddess, like many others, is 'ruler of the stars' (Philae 543, photo 164–5). Re is 'the lord of the sky and lord of the earth' (*BD* 15, A 3, 6), etc.

39 We may mention here some characteristic phrases from late temples. About Isis we hear: 'Without her one does not stand upon the throne' (*Dendérah*, III, 83g). Or: 'The king stands upon his throne according to her word' (J. Dümichen, *Kalenderinschriften*, 49, from Dendera). Hathor is 'the one who raises the one she loves to be ruler in the palace; there is no accession to the throne ($ḥꜥt$) without her' (*Edfou*, I, 291), etc.

40 Bonnet, *RÄRG*, p. 185, in his attempt to provide a welcome analysis of the festivals, correctly emphasizes the differences; but he also realizes that all the streams coalesce in the heart of the pious person 'who takes everything from the hands of God'.

41 W. Wolf, *Das schöne Fest von Opet* (*Veröffentlichungen der E. v. Sieglin-Expedition*, V, Leipzig, 1931), pp. 72 f., where further evidence may be found.

42 S. Morenz, *HO* I 1, 1959, pp. 90 f.

43 *Urk.*, II, 137 (decree of Canopus).

44 Ani III, 7 f.; text and trans. in Volten, *Studien...Anii*, pp. 62 f.; [Engl. trans.: Erman, *Egyptians*, p. 235; *ANET*, p. 420].

45 Drinking as a means of partaking in the feast of the gods: Ani III, 9 in Volten, op. cit., p. 63. It is only obnoxious if it, for example, disturbs the peace and solemnity of another sanctuary: Junker, *Götterdekret*, esp. p. 84.

46 Herodotus II, 60.

47 Herodotus II, 62; during a feast of Hathor at Dendera the people welcome the image at the corners of the streets, their hands full of flowers: Erman, *Religion*, p. 368, based upon J. Dümichen, *Baugeschichte des Denderatempels...*, Strasbourg, 1877–, 39.

48 S. Morenz, *Die Zauberflöte*, Cologne, 1952, p. 78; it is not entirely true, as we stated there, that there is no authentic evidence of the

name 'secrets' (*št3w, sšt3w*) for such games; R. Anthes has drawn our attention to a stele at Abydos on which the deceased declares: 'I acted as the "son-whom-he-loves"...in the "festival (*sšt3*)" of the Lord of Abydos' (Cairo 20539 IIb 7: H. O. Lange and H. Schäfer, *Die Grab- und Denksteine des Mittleren Reiches*, II, Leipzig, 1908, p. 155. Thus here a game is referred to as a 'secret' although games of this type were at least partly public.

49 Ranke, *Personennamen*, II, p. 235.

50 We provisionally make such a hypothesis, when we suggest that certain hymns were subdivided into roles: this idea is not without some foundation of fact.

51 Egyptian hymns need the same kind of investigation given to another genre by Herrmann, *Untersuchungen*. We may expect this from a study by D. Müller, who kindly advised me in the writing of this section.

52 As did A. H. Gardiner, *ZÄS*, 42, 1905, p. 13, with reference to the Amon hymns of the Leyden Papyrus I, 350.

53 Chapters 18–19 and 37–41: Moret, op. cit., 67 ff., 121 ff.

54 Erman, *Hymnen an das Diadem der Pharaonen* (*APAW*, Berlin, 1911), p. 18.

55 On this point, see the basic remarks by H. Junker, *ZÄS*, 67, 1931, pp. 51 f., on the hymns to Haroeris and Suchos (Sobek) at Kom Ombo, recorded in the late Roman Imperial period.

56 *Urk.*, IV, 158; unfortunately the text has been partly destroyed; the word *i3w*, 'glorification', which has been supplied by Sethe, seems cogent.

57 Pap. Berlin 3048, II–XII; text, translation and brief commentary in Wolf, *ZÄS*, 64, 1928, pp. 17 ff.

58 III, 2 – IV, 2: Wolf, op. cit., pp. 22 ff.

59 Thus apparently the text is a compilation of quite different passages, and it is important to determine why they were eventually combined into a single manuscript. This cannot have been on account of the name Ptah, for it does not appear in the extracts to be discussed presently and in the second one (IX, 4a–12a) the content does not suggest a relationship to Ptah at any point. Were the reasons of an archival character? Or was this done at the behest of its owner, who may have been a priest (the text was acquired in conjunction with books on rites for the daily service, and they may have been discovered together: Wolf, op. cit., p. 17)?

60 There is ample authentic evidence of singers of this kind (*ḥsw*, later predominantly *šm3w*), more often than not apparently female, and their 'superiors'; they tended to be linked to a particular god or temple by means of a genitive pronoun. On ritual singing, see Ani III, 7; on the service position and rights of the female personnel,

see in particular H. Kees, *Das Priesteramt im ägyptischen Staat vom neuen Reich bis zur Spätzeit*, Leyden–Cologne, 1953, p. 302.

61 *Edfou*, I, 442 (represented pictorially in II, Pl. 34b; these are drums); on this point see Erman, *Religion*, p. 372; no doubt this is an ancient royal song.

62 This is followed by an extract, partly destroyed, in which apparently '[the great ones and] the low ones (*šwš*)' are enumerated; in each case the recitals are addressed to the largest possible number of people.

63 J. de Morgan, *Kom Ombos*, Vienna, I, 74, nos. 86 f.

64 The invocation tallies exactly with the hallelujah of the psalms; in each case the name of the deity invoked is added to the imperative of a verb with the meaning of 'praise', 'worship'.

65 *Urk.*, VIII, 90 f. (nos. 106, 108); for the location see p. 40. Naturally it must be borne in mind that there were only a few persons who could read the written text. Some further items of evidence: J. de Morgan, *Kom Ombos*, II, 19, nos. 39, 541, 578 f.

66 Philae photo 164 f. (Philadelphus Gate).

67 Text and translation: B. v. Turajeff, *ZÄS*, 33, 1895, pp. 121–3.

68 Pap. Anastasi III, 4, 12 ff.; translation: Erman, *Egyptians*, pp. 306 f.

69 Erman, *Religion*, p. 178, in relation to the Hymn to Osiris Louvre C 30.

70 Alternatively the words might suggest the radiance emitted by the image during the procession: *Urk.*, IV, 157 f.

71 Leipoldt and Morenz, pp. 62 f., provide material for comparison.

72 III, 16 f.; my translation is based upon Zandee, *Hymnen*, pp. 54 ff.; [*ANET*, p. 369].

73 This is in accordance with Egyptian legal thinking, to be more precise with the principle of compensation: on this see E. Seidl, *ZDMG*, 107, 1957, pp. 260 f.

74 *Urk.*, IV, 181 f.

75 Hymn of Eye: M. Sandman, *Texts from the Time of Akhenaten* (*Bibl. Aeg.* 8, 1938), p. 91, ll. 9 f.

76 *Urk.*, IV, 767; it is worth noting that this is taken from a stone memorial erected in the Ptah temple at Karnak; [Eng. trans. by J. H. Breasted, *Ancient Records of Egypt*, II, Chicago, 1906, p. 246].

77 *Urk.*, 863.

78 Text: Lefebvre, *Petosiris*, II, p. 36 (no. 61b, conclusion); translation: Otto, *Biogr. Inschr.*

79 Text: op. cit., pp. 58 f.; translation: op. cit., p. 182.

80 Pap. Erm. 1116A, ll. 129 f.; translation based upon Volten, *Pol. Schriften*, p. 69; [Eng. trans.: A. H. Gardiner, *JEA*, I, 1914, p. 34]; the setting up of inscriptions (*ḥtỉ*) might be interpreted in this con-

text as a glorification of God, i.e. hymns such as Ramses III had inscribed upon gold plaques and presented to the temple of Amon (Pap. Harris I, 6, 5): 'I made for you huge gold plaques in embossed work, inscribed (*ḥtỉ* as in the case of Merikare) in the great name of Your Majesty with my words of praise (*snsw*).' This testimony points to the composition of hymns on behalf of the king, i.e. commissioned by him, which were then assigned to the temple.

81 Op. cit., ll. 65 f.; Volten, op. cit., p. 35; [Eng. trans.: Erman, *Egyptians*, pp. 78 f.].

82 H. D. Schädel, *Die Listen des grossen Papyrus Harris* (*LÄSt*, 6, 1936), esp. pp. 68 f.

83 VII, 15 f.: Volten, *Studien...Anii*, pp. 111 f.

84 This remark should not be misunderstood as a personal profession of faith by the author but as an endeavour to assess properly the historical data about Egyptian religion.

85 Op. cit., ll. 127–9; Volten, *Pol. Schriften*, p. 69; [Erman, *Egyptians*, p. 83].

86 Cf. esp. Hosea vi. 6.

87 VII, 12 ff.; cf. also the passage cited above: III, 7 f.; Volten, *Studien ...Anii*, pp. 110 ff.

88 See above, p. 284 including n. 57; further details in Bonnet, *RÄRG*, p. 112.

89 The evidence provided by S. Mowinckel, *Religion und Kultus*, Göttingen, 1953, p. 33 (Latin *sanctus*, derived from *sancire* = 'to separate'; Hebrew *qādōš* with the corresponding basic meaning) have not yet been verified, so far as we know. We have been unable to ascertain this meaning of *sancire*; as regards the root *kdš* one can at present say only that it is inherent in it. On the other hand *templum*, according to Varro, frg. Gellius 14, 7, 7, could have originally meant a limited area.

90 In *Urk.*, IV, 157 it is described in the negative with regard to the young Thutmosis III: 'My initiation (*bs*) as priest (*ḥm-nṯr*) had not yet taken place.'

91 Sir Alan Gardiner, *JEA*, 32, 1946, p. 51.

92 A. Piankoff and N. Rambova, *Mythological Papyri* (Bollingen Series, XL, 3, 1957), Pl. 2 and text p. 76.

93 *BD* 78, 22.

94 Text: Turajeff, *ZÄS*, 46, 1909–10, p. 75; translation: Otto, *Biogr. Inschr.*, p. 173.

95 Decree on Rosetta Stone N 7 (*Urk.*, II, 172).

96 *Urk.*, IV, 157; see above, p. 1.

97 Kees, *Priestertum*, p. 1; one should distinguish the permanent function from the individual act commissioned (particularly that connected with the so-called festival ladder): Kees, op. cit.. 322 ff.

98 A profound insight into these matters is provided by the expert account of Kees (*Priestertum*), although it covers only a limited period of time.

99 Dümichen, *Geogr. Inschr.*, II, 97 (from Edfu); cf. Junker, *Götterdekret*, p. 20.

100 Pap. Leyden I, 350; III, 17.

101 Bonnet, *RÄRG*, pp. 413 ff.

102 Text now in *Urk.*, 1833 and 1835; translation based upon H. W. Helck, *Der Einfluss der Militärführer in der 18. ägyptischen Dynastie* (*Unters.*, 14, 1939), p. 12.

103 Cairo 901 (text: M. Benson and J. Gourlay, *The Temple of Mut in Asher...*, London, 1899, pp. 332) and 627; translation based upon Helck, op. cit., p. 13.

104 E. Otto, *Beiträge zur Geschichte der Stierkulte* (*Unters.*, 13, 1938), pp. 25 f., also p. 38.

105 Kees, 'Der berichtende Gottesdiener (𓏏𓏏𓏏)', *ZÄS*, 85, 1960; from this function of 'carrying the message' Kees has explained in an appealing way the Greek rendering of *ḥm-nṯr* by προφήτης.

106 Cf. the lavishly documented article in Bonnet, *RÄRG*, pp. 560 ff., and a Berlin dissertation: H.-H. Schenke, 'Die Orakel im alten Ägypten', limited to the cult oracles which are the most important ones in this context.

107 Erman, *SPAW*, 1911, no. 49, pp. 1086 ff.

108 Berlin no. 23077; cf. also Erman, *Religion*, p. 142 incl. Pl. 5.

109 Ranke, *Personennamen*, II, pp. 240, 252.

110 Erman, *SPAW*, 1911, pp. 1086 f.

111 [*ANET*, p. 380.]

112 According to Helck, op. cit., p. 13.

113 On the other hand, it is scarcely adequate to depict the mode of interpretation as conventional, as does Brunner (*MDAIK*, 16, 1958, p. 11), even though a conventional element is undeniably present.

114 Ani III, 2 f.; this passage supplements the above-mentioned Hymn to Thoth (p. 304, n. 68), in so far as it confirms the fact that the individual combined his words with an act of sacrifice in the temple; [*ANET*, p. 420].

115 É. Drioton, *Bulletin...de la Société française d'Égyptologie*, 26, (July) 1958, p. 39.

116 E. Otto, *Ägypten. Der Weg des Pharaonenreiches*, Stuttgart, 1953, pp. 214 f.; correct interpretation well formulated by Wolf, *OLZ*, 42, 1939, cols. 732 f.: 'In point of fact due to the force of circumstances the general (Heri-Hor) was transformed into a cleric at the moment when he seized power, and thus the final result was a markedly clerical solution.'

117 Drioton, op. cit., p. 38.

118 Pap. Anastasi II, 9, 2.

119 III, 18 f.; Zandee, *Hymnen*, p. 59; [A. H. Gardiner, 'Hymns to Amon from a Leyden Papyrus', *ZÄS*, 42, 1905, p. 29].

120 One other characteristic piece of evidence may be mentioned. In a list of possible deeds of salvation by Amon we read: 'He remembers thy name upon the sea when it is rough (*khb*); at peace he lands (*s꜄ḥ*) on the shore (*dmì*)' (É. Chassinat, *Le Mammisi d'Edfou*, Cairo, 1910, 47, 6). Brunner entertains the idea of a linguistic metaphor, in the sense of the general shipwreck of one's life (*MDAIK*, 16 1958 p. 15); but in the circumstances this seems unnecessary vis-à-vis Amon.

121 Müller, *Isis-Aretalogien*.

122 Drioton, *ZÄS*, 79, 1954, pp. 3 ff.; on deciphering the Amon trigrams: idem, *WZKM*, 54, 1957, pp. 11 ff.

123 Ranke, *Personennamen*, II, p. 225; cf. also Grapow, *Ausdrücke*, p. 52.

124 [*ANET*, p. 369.]

125 Material and interpretation in S. Morenz, *Sino-Japonica. FS. A. Wedemeyer* (ed. H. Steininger et al.), Leipzig, 1956, pp. 118 ff.; since then Drioton, *Analecta Biblica*, 12, 1959, pp. 57 ff., has collected the formulae concerning mutual love between God and man, in regard to Amon and other deities. (These are of the type: 'Amon loves him who loves him.')

126 The aspect of the deity as saviour in need became more pronounced with time, but it was present from the very beginning; cf. the archaic personal name *Šd-nṯr*, 'he whom [the] god has saved' or 'the god saves' (i.e. 'may save'): A. Klasens, *OMRO*, 37, 1956, no. 122 in the list of names (later lavish in names of various deities). This aspect is naturally not confined to certain words. In the Instruction for Merikare (l. 135; Volten, *Pol. Schriften*, pp. 75 f.) it is evident in the comforting formulation that God hears those who weep: 'When they [men in trouble] weep, he hears': *ANET*, p. 417.

127 Berlin no. 19791; on this see G. Möller, *ZÄS*, 54, 1918, p. 139.

128 Thus cult and popular piety are in accord, in so far as images used in temples were equipped to express vital functions – and this may be assumed in regard to the (oracle?) bust of the falcon-headed sun-god, from the Roman Imperial period, which possessed a kind of channel through which he could speak: G. Loukianoff, *ASAE*, 36, 1936, pp. 187 ff.

129 Ch. Nims, *JNES*, 14, 1955, p. 119; further material from Medinet Habu is mentioned by H. G. Fischer, *AJA*, 63, 1959, pp. 196–8.

130 Helck, *ZÄS*, 83, 1958, p. 91.

131 In so far as these are figures at temple entrances, the reason may have been that they were within everyone's reach: Fischer, op. cit., p. 198.

132 Djedkhonsefankh the Younger, Bubastite period: Kees, *Priestertum*, pp. 218 f.; on the question of God as succourer, see the article by H. Brunner, *MDAIK*, 16, 1958, pp. 5 ff.; in points of detail it has been called in question but on the whole it is important.

133 Vienna, Stele 150 (Ptolemaic); text: W. Wreszinski, *Ägyptische Inschriften an dem K.K. Hofmuseum in Wien*, 1906, p. 87; translation based upon Otto, *Biogr. Inschr.*, p. 188.

134 J. Spiegel, *WZKM*, 54, 1957, pp. 191 ff., esp. pp. 197–9, 203.

135 Ranke, *Personennamen*, II, p. 224; names of this kind increase from the Middle Kingdom onward: Ranke, op. cit., p. 250.

136 Evidence in H. Kees, *ZÄS*, 73, 1937, p. 83; the inscriptions are in the following tenor: 'I was a poor man (*nmḥ*) through my father and my mother, but the ruler built me up' (i.e., established my brilliant existence), etc.

137 Traces of genuine popular piety are, on the other hand, to be met with in small images, some of them lacking all artistic sense, inscribed upon sherds, which have been found in houses at Amarna (representing Horus, and even Amon): E. Brunner-Traut, *Die altägyptischen Scherbenbilder der deutschen Museen und Sammlungen*, Wiesbaden, 1956, pp. 23 f., 80 f. (nos. 7, 80).

138 A. Hauck, *Kirchengeschichte Deutschlands*, IV, Leipzig, 1903, p. 869.

139 That Egyptian customs and religious beliefs could undergo a crisis is something different; it was not caused by popular piety but resulted from the experience of catastrophe and the length of their history; some details below in chap. 8.

140 Brunner, op. cit., pp. 13 ff.

141 I have suggested some key points in a critical review: *OLZ*, 49, 1954, cols. 31 ff. Here reference may also be made to the worship of earlier monuments in later periods, as was apparently the case with a boundary stele at Abydos, for example: D. Randall-MacIver and A. C. Mace, *El Amrah and Abydos*, London, 1902, p. 64 and Pl. 37.

CHAPTER 6

1 On table manners Ptah-hotep provides fairly detailed instructions: Pap. Prisse 119 ff.; text and translation by Žába, *Ptahhotep*, pp. 25, 75 f. They are still found in the rules which the monk Pakhom set down for his disciples: Dom A. Boon, *Pachomiana Latina*, Louvain, 1932, p. 172 (Greek), p. 20 (Latin).

2 Survey in Brunner, *HO*, I 2, pp. 90 ff.

3 F. Hintze, *ZÄS*, 79, 154, pp. 33 ff. Likewise close to Ani is the Instruction of Amon-nakht, the surviving parts of which have been published by G. Posener, *RdE*, 10, 1955, pp. 61 ff., mainly on the basis of Ostracon BM 41541.

4 Text: Sir Alan Gardiner (ed.), *The Ramesseum Papyri. Plates*, Oxford, 1955, Pl. 1 ff.; translated and discussed by J. W. B. Barns, *Five Ramesseum Papyri*, Oxford, 1956 (these are papyri nos. 1, 11); cf. also Posener, *RdE*, 6, 1949, pp. 38, 46 as well as 9, 1952, p. 119.

5 Text and translation: S. R. K. Glanville, *The Instructions of 'Onchsheshonqy* (BM Pap. 10508), London, 1955 (*Catalogue of Demotic Papyri in the British Museum*, 11); see also the excellent Dutch translation by B. H. Stricker, *Jaarbericht...Ex Oriente Lux*, no. 15, 1957-8, pp. 11 ff.; furthermore the remarks by Volten, *OLZ*, 52, 1957, cols. 125 ff. What were apparently disordered fragments of this instruction were brought to notice by H. S. Smith in the Demotic Papyrus Cairo 30682: *JEA*, 44, 1958, pp. 121 f.

6 A. Volten, 'Die moralischen Lehren des demotischen Papyrus Louvre 2414', *Studi in memoria di I. Rosellini*, Pisa, 1955, 11, 269 ff.

7 On the relationship between the historical and ethical elements in biographies, see Otto, *HO*, 1 2, pp. 151 f.

8 E.g., Otto, op. cit., p. 151 and *Biogr. Inschr.*, pp. 100 f.

9 Text and German translation by E. Edel, *MIO*, 1, 2, 1953, Pl. II and p. 213; comments on the dubious connection: pp. 224 f., inter alia with reference to the Tale of the Eloquent Peasant B 1, 320-2, in which are to be found echoes of the quotation mentioned.

10 Text and translation: Ch. Maystre, *Les déclarations d'innocence* (*Recherches d'Archéologie...*, 8, 1937), pp. 10 ff.

11 J. Spiegel, *Die Idee vom Totengericht in der ägyptischen Religion* (*LÄSt*, 2, 1935), p. 57.

12 The Coptic form of the word (Sahidic *mě*) reproduces the Greek ἀλήθεια.

13 J. A. Wilson, in H. and H. A. Frankfort, J. A. Wilson and T. Jacobsen, *Before Philosophy*, Harmondsworth, 1954, pp. 119 f.

14 Cf. Brunner, *Vetus Testamentum*, 8, 1958, pp. 426 ff.; he also drew parallels with Old Testament statements to the effect that justice is the base of the throne – derived from one of the Egyptian meanings of maat, socle of the throne.

15 R. Anthes, 'Die Maat des Echnaton von Amarna', suppl. to *JAOS*, no. 14, 1952, p. 2, no. 3.

16 *Pyr.*, 1775b.

17 *Urk.*, VII, 27.

18 *Urk.*, IV, 2026; so-called 'Restoration Stele'.

19 Further details in G. Posener, *Littérature et politique dans*

l'Égypte de la XIIe dynastie, Paris, 1956, pp. 57 f., and E. Otto, *MDAIK*, 14, 1956, pp. 150 f.

20 Theban temple, 95k or 90k, from the Greek and Roman period; text and translation: Sethe, *Amun*, §125 and Pl. IV.

21 Pap. Prisse 88 ff. and 312 ff.; we are here following the well-founded translation by Fecht, *Habgierige*, pp. 33 or 45; [Eng. trans. based partly upon *ANET*, p. 412 and partly upon Erman, *Egyptians*, p. 60].

22 Cf., e.g., Tale of the Eloquent Peasant B 1, 292: 'Thou art greedy ...thou robbest (*'w'j*).'

23 Edel, *MIO*,I, 2, 1953, pp. 220 f.

24 B 1, 320 f.; [A. H. Gardiner, 'Tale of the Eloquent Peasant', *JEA*, 9, 1923, p. 20].

25 According to Edel, op. cit., pp. 225 f.

26 This connection may support the fine interpretation by Fecht, op. cit., pp. 13–15, to which we are indebted for the hymnic-like substance.

27 Shabaka inscription 57; text with cogent construction: Sethe, *Dram. Texte*, p. 64; cf. also Junker, *Götterlehre*, pp. 59–61. The identical idea was also formulated similarly later: e.g., *Urk.*, IV, 492 (time of Hatshepsut); *Urk.*, V, 57 (New Kingdom annotations to the *BD* 17, section 23); [*ANET*, p. 5].

28 A. Alt, *Die Ursprünge des israelitischen Rechts* (*BSAW*, 86, 1, 1934); now in *Kleine Schriften zur Geschichte des Volkes Israel*, I, Munich, 1953, pp. 278 ff.

29 Rabbinical Judaism brought about an apotheosis of the law: it 'exists in eternity', exists before the creation of the world, is laid down by God in the 'celestial house of teaching', etc.: evidence in Leipoldt and Morenz, p. 9.

30 Mark vii. 1 ff. or ii. 23 ff.; the saying about 'making a fence to *torah*' is to be found formulated as a task of the rabbis in Aboth i. 1; cf. furthermore ibid., iii. 13 and Bab. Jebamoth 21a.

31 Evidence in C. Lange, *Amenemope*, pp. 20 f. (inter alia Am. II, 7 and VI, 7).

32 Pap. Erm. 1116A, ll. 143 f.; Volten, *Pol. Schriften*, pp. 79 f.; [*ANET*, p. 418].

33 Ani IX, 13 ff., cf. H. Brunner, *Altägyptische Erziehung*, Wiesbaden, 1957, p. 58.

34 Junker, *Götterlehre*, p. 59.

35 B 1, 318–22; [A. H. Gardiner, 'Tale of the Eloquent Peasant', *JEA*, 9, 1923, p. 20].

36 [*ANET*, p. 8.]

37 Otto, *MDAIK*, 14, 1956, p. 151; the fact that Otto draws the same conclusions from an entirely different field of legislation and judicial practice serves to corroborate the correctness of our approach.

38 Amenemope xx, 14 or xxi, 22.

39 Bab. Shabbath 31a.

40 Mark xii. 28 ff.

41 *Urk.*, IV, 384 f.; inscription from Speos Artemidos; [Eng. trans. based upon J. H. Breasted, *Ancient Records of Egypt*, II, Chicago, 1906, p. 123].

42 Text and translation: Helck, *ZÄS*, 80, 1955, p. 114 and Pl. X, l. 6; text now also in *Urk.*, IV, 2140 ff.

43 *Edfou*, I, 521 (Ptolemy IV).

44 *Dendérah*, II, 58 (Nero).

45 F. A. F. Mariette, *Abydos*, Paris, 1869–80, I, 52, 14–15.

46 Volten, *Studien zum...Anii*, p. 140.

47 Ani, IX, 14; Volten, op. cit., pp. 137, 139.

48 Amenemope, xxvII, 10; Lange, op. cit., pp. 134 ff.; [Eng. trans. based partly upon *ANET*, p. 424].

49 Pap. Prisse 575 ff.; Žába, op. cit., pp. 60 f. or 102; [*ANET*, p. 414].

50 Pap. BM 10509, parallel to Pap. Prisse 90 f.: Fecht, *Habgierige*, pp. 15 ff.

51 *CT*, III, 293c (BD 70, 10); for an explanation see Kees, *Göttinger Totenbuchstudien* (*Unters.*, 17, 1954), pp. 37 f.

52 *iwty-ḥȝty.f*, 'witless', cf. Hebrew *'ēn-leb* and in particular the context in Jeremiah v. 21.

53 A. Erman, *Denksteine aus der thebanischen Gräberstadt* (*SPAW*, 1911), p. 1098.

54 Pap. Anastasi III, 10, 7; text: A. H. Gardiner, *Late-Egyptian Miscellanies* (*Bibl. Aeg.*, VII, 1937), pp. 18 f.; [Erman, *Egyptians*, p. 307].

55 B 1, 209 f.; text and translation: F. Vogelsang, *Kommentar zu den Klagen des Bauern* (*Unters.*, 6, 1913), pp. 160–2; [A. H. Gardiner, 'Tale of the Eloquent Peasant', *JEA*, 9, 1923, p. 16].

56 6 r, 8 f; the words *ꜥkȝ n* (probably for *m*) *ḥr.k* can hardly place the action at the subjective discretion of the doer, for example 'right in your eyes', but simply refer to the doer, i.e., 'right for you', 'right in regard to you'.

57 C. F. Piehl, *ZÄS*, 25, 1887, p. 120; translation: Otto, *Biogr. Inschr.*, p. 162.

58 Text: C. F. Piehl, *Inscriptions hiéroglyphiques recueillies en Europe et en Égypte*, Stockholm–Leipzig, 1886, Pl. 37; translation: Otto, op. cit., p. 194.

59 Turin 156; text: G. Maspero, *Rec. de trav.*, 4, 1883, p. 131; on this cf. the phrase *ḥꜥ m mȝꜥt*, 'to take a delight in maat', used for the sun-god: *Wb.*, III, 40, 13.

60 The 'eudemonistic misinterpretation of Egyptian wisdom literature' which this led to has rightly been rejected; instead maat is

referred to as the foundation of the moral: H. Gese, *Lehre und Wirklichkeit in der alten Weisheit*, Tübingen, 1958, pp. 7 ff.

61 *sbꜣyt* may also acquire the meaning of 'punishment' and thus God also 'instructs' by punishment; the matter is presented from the vantage-point of the sinner who confesses, e.g. in Turin 102. A. Erman, *Denksteine aus der thebanischen Gräberstadt* (*SPAW*, 1911), p. 1098.

62 This has been correctly sensed by Gese (op. cit., pp. 17 ff.), who emphasizes the 'non-disposability of maat'.

63 W. F. Reineke realized the importance of this passage, which he discovered for me in the material gathered for the dictionary.

64 N. de G. Davies, *The Tomb of Nefer-Ḥotep at Thebes* (*PMMA*, 9, 1933), p. 54, Pl. 37; cf. also R. Anthes, 'Die Maat des Echnaton von Amarna', *JAOS*, Suppl. no. 14, 1952, p. 13.

65 A bridge between the two may be formed by some instructive maxims with an ambiguous text, in which two kinds of material are concealed at once: Fecht, op. cit., pp. 27 ff. The more profound content may be called esoteric.

66 For the effect upon living persons, see the so-called 'formula of knowledge' in Old Kingdom biographies: E. Edel, *Untersuchungen zur Phraseologie der ägyptischen Inschriften des Alten Reiches* (*MDAIK*, 13, 1944), pp. 22 ff.; on mastering one's own fate in the hereafter, see 'Spells for Knowing the Souls of Sacred Places': Sethe et al., *ZÄS*, 57, 1922, pp. 1 ff. and epilogue to *BD* 125; see above, p. 131.

67 H. W. Helck, *Untersuchungen zu den ägyptischen Beamtentiteln des Alten Reiches* (*ÄgFo*, 18, 1954), p. 74 (see above p. 13).

68 G. Möller, *ZÄS*, 56, 1920, pp. 67 f.

69 H. Donner, *ZÄS*, 82, 1958, pp. 16–18.

70 Sethe, *Amun*, §125 (see above, pp. 114 f.).

71 Bonnet, *RÄRG*, p. 334.

72 Shown in gruesome activity on the shroud Berlin 11652, 4th cent. A.D.: S. Morenz, *Forschungen und Berichte*, 1 (*FS. L. Justi*, Berlin, 1957), p. 65 and Fig. 7.

73 A survey is provided by E. Lüddeckens, *Alter und Einheitlichkeit der ägyptischen Vorstellung vom Totengericht* (*Jahrbuch MAW*, 1953), pp. 182 ff.

74 Pap. Erm. 1116A, ll. 54–6; [Erman, *Egyptians*, pp. 77 ff.].

75 G. Fecht, op. cit., pp. 26 f., 51.

76 Among other sources the Pyramid Texts are particularly important; cf. the survey in Fecht, op. cit., p. 32.

77 G. Posener, *RdE*, 9, 1952, pp. 109 ff., and Fecht, op. cit., pp. 50 f.; [Eng. trans. based partly upon *ANET*, p. 419].

78 The question of social origin is considered by Lüddeckens, op. cit., pp. 185 f.

79 J. Spiegel, op. cit., pp. 41 f.; Lüddeckens, op. cit., pp. 186 f.

80 *TR* 37 (*Rec. de trav.*, 30, 1908, p. 189; now *CT*, v, 321c–d). The passage seems characteristic, although the relationship between the god and the image as seen by the Greeks is not thereby exhausted. (On the identity which was the point of departure here also, etc., see H. E. Killy and K. Schefold, *RAC*, II, 1954, cols. 302 ff.)

81 H. Kees in F. W. v. Bissing (ed.), *Das Re-Heiligtum des Königs Ne-Woser-Re*, III, Leipzig, 1928, p. 41 and fragments no. 318, 346.

82 W. Westendorf, *MIO*, 2, 1954, pp. 172–4.

83 W. Westendorf, op. cit., pp. 180 f.; we have formulated this with greater precision to bring out the principal lines of the argument.

84 H. Gauthier, *Le Livre des rois d'Égypte*, I, 1907, pp. 62 f. or 106 f.

85 An interpretation which in my view is suggested in the case of *Pyr.*, 1520–3.

86 v, 5; translation in B. H. Stricker, *Jaarbericht...Ex Oriente Lux*, 15, 1957–8, p. 15.

87 It is rather the case that one finds a supplication being addressed to the judge: 'Mayest thou not let my wickedness ascend to this god whom you serve' (final address, 4 f.).

88 Final address, 21 ff.

89 Ibid., 28 ff.

90 Cf., e.g., Lüddeckens, op. cit., pp. 187 f.

91 Cf., e.g., J. Spiegel, *Die Idee vom Totengericht in der ägyptischen Religion* (*LÄSt*, 2, 1935), esp. pp. 46 ff.

92 Spiegel, op. cit., esp. 60–2.

93 Ibid., p. 63.

94 H. Kees, *Göttinger Totenbuchstudien* (*Unters.*, 17, 1954), pp. 37 f.; see above, p. 122.

95 *BD* 125, introduction, 1 f.; [E. A. Wallis Budge, *Book of the Dead*, II, London, 1901, p. 360].

96 XIX, 18: C. Lange, *Amenemope* p. 97; [*ANET*, p. 423].

97 The Instruction of Amenemope may have been transcribed from Hebrew or Aramaic, but its teaching is put into the mouth of an Egyptian who is provided with personal data, and the very fact of its having been translated gave it acceptance among Egyptians.

98 A. Erman, *Denksteine aus der thebanischen Gräberstadt* (*SPAW*, 1911), p. 1094 and Pap. Anastasi II, 10, 7; the fact that God 'likes to be merciful after his wrath (*špt*)' is praised later by Sobek-Re: Junker, *ZÄS*, 67, 1931, p. 55 (Kom Ombo); [B. Gunn, *JEA*, III, 1916, p. 85; Erman, *Egyptians*, p. 307].

99 The fact that somebody dies young is equivalent to his 'having no faults' (Lower Egyptian): Otto, *Biogr. Inschr.*, pp. 46 ff.; also cf. C. E. Sander-Hansen, *Tod*, p. 29.

100 Logically death as such then becomes the 'wages of sin':
Romans vi. 23.

101 Cf., e.g., H. Gunkel, *Religion in Geschichte und Gegenwart*, 2nd ed.,
v, 1931, col. 882; if Bonnet, *RÄRG*, p. 760 (also p. 175) regards the
ethical concept of God as the prerequisite for a consciousness of
original sin, it must be added that this is in itself an insufficient
basis.

102 Text: Lefebvre, *Petosiris*, ii, p. 54 (no. 81); translation: Otto,
Biogr. Inschr., p. 182.

103 More detail in H. Junker, *Christus und die Religionen der Erde*, ii,
1951, pp. 596 ff.

104 Examples in E. Edel, *Untersuchungen zur Phraseologie der ägyptischen Inschriften des Alten Reiches* (*MDAIK*, 13, 1944), pp. 39 f.

105 Edel, op. cit., p. 55.

106 Edel, op. cit., pp. 40 ff.; cf. also *BD* 125, final address, 11; [E. A.
Wallis Budge, *Book of the Dead*, ii, London, 1906, p. 360].

107 *BD* 125, introduction, 11 f.

108 Spiegel, op. cit., pp. 57 f.

109 Ani iii, 3 ff. and vii, 12 ff.; text and translation in Volten, *Studien
zum...Anii*, pp. 62 f., 110 ff.

110 Pap. Erm. 1116A, ll. 130 ff.; text and translation: Volten, *Pol.
Schriften*, pp. 73 ff.

111 Evidence in Otto, *Biogr. Inschr.*, pp. 31 ff.

112 In this sense no doubt Ani vii, 12 ff.; on the entire question cf.
also Bonnet, *ZÄS*, 75, 1939, p. 49.

113 [*ANET*, p. 380].

114 W. F. Otto, *Die Götter Griechenlands*, 3rd ed., Frankfurt, 1947;
[trans. M. Hadas, *The Homeric Gods. The Spiritual Significance of
Greek Religion*, London, 1955], pp. 169 ff. The unity of the heavenly
power which was latent in this for the Greeks was 'more than just
a person. But for the very reason that it is beyond representation,
moral ideas could be attached to it (p. 171).'

CHAPTER 7

1 An unequivocal verdict can hardly be expected, all the less so
since the concept of freedom does not exist in Egyptian.

2 Pap. Beatty iv, 6, 5–7; translation: Sir Alan Gardiner, *Hieratic
Papyri in the British Museum*, 3rd Series, i, London, 1935, p. 43.

3 Our interpretation proceeds from the fact that the sentence
'Ignorant and wise are of one piece' is clearly an error. From this we
infer that the followng sentence, too, is intended to indicate an error
and that in rectifying it the sage gives *šʒi* and *rnnt* a meaning close
to that we have suggested above.

4 Among German writers most prominently by Sethe and Kees, who agree on this principle.

5 Bonnet always kept it in view; cf., e.g., *ZÄS*, 75, 1939, pp. 42 f.

6 Wolf, *Kunst*, p. 255.

7 In *Götterglaube* (pp. 119 ff.) Kees deals with the 'principles of [theological] formation', drawing upon his earlier sketch, *Kulte und Kultstätten*, which provided the raw material for the later study.

8 In *ZÄS*, 75, 1939, pp. 40 ff., Bonnet wrote an article 'Zum Verständnis des Synkretismus' in which he threw much light upon the nature of Egyptian theology, using the example of the coalescence of deities; unfortunately he did not give substantiating evidence from the sources, but drew upon his knowledge of their immense variety of forms. Cf. also *RÄRG*, pp. 237 ff.

9 Otto, *Biogr. Inschr.*, p. 88.

10 XXIX, 4; translation: A. Volten, *Das demotische Weisheitsbuch* (*Anal. Aeg.*, II, 1941), p. 213.

11 Sir Alan Gardiner, *JEA*, 30, 1944, pp. 27 f.

12 Examples in H. G. Liddell and R. Scott, *A Greek–English Lexicon*, 9th ed., Oxford, 1966, s.v. συγκρητίζω. The hybrid *syncrescere*, upon which one might fall back, would be a purely artificial construction.

13 H. Kees, *ZÄS*, 64, 1930, pp. 108 f.

14 This cannot be put better than it has been by Bonnet, op. cit., pp. 43 ff.

15 Text and translation: H. Junker, *ZÄS*, 67, 131, pp. 54 f.

16 Pap. Berlin 3048, IX, 4a–12a; see above p. 92.

17 To be sure, it has rightly been emphasized that in cult – in sacrifice, spells and festivities – the particular character of the individual deity was more marked than in the hymns, and thus in theology: Junker, op. cit., p. 52. Thus in the daily ritual the priest says to the local deity: 'I have not assimilated (*stwt*) your colour [= individuality] to [that of] another god': Pap. Berlin 3055, 5; rightly understood by Sethe, *Dram. Texte*, p. 69.

18 Wolf, *Kunst*, pp. 297 ff.; Herrmann, *Untersuchungen*, esp. pp. 99 f.

19 In the Egyptian script, so long as it existed, the plural was indicated by writing a sign three times over or by adding three strokes.

20 For the following examples we are indebted to W. Westendorf. From the Middle Kingdom: Turin 278; Berlin 7731; Louvre C 38; Turin 98; Florence 7603; Cairo 90434; Amherst Collection 450. From the New Kingdom: Louvre C 46; Leyden D 32; Louvre C 76; Turin 28. Evidence from the Ethiopian period in J. Leclant, *Enquêtes sur les sacerdoces et les sanctuaires égyptiens à l'époque dite 'éthiopienne', XXV dynastie* (*Bibl. d'Ét.*, 17, 1954), pp. 52 f.

21 E.g., from the Middle Kingdom: Leyden v, 108; from the New Kingdom: Berlin 7272.

22 J. E. S. Edwards, *JNES*, 14, 1955, pp. 49–51.
23 F. A. F. Mariette, *Le Sérapéum de Memphis découvert et décrit*, III, Paris, 1857, Pl. 8; cf. E. Otto, *Beiträge zur Geschichte der Stierkulte* (*Unters.*, 13, 1938), p. 32.
24 W. Spiegelberg, 'Die sogenannte demotische Chronik', *Demotische Studien*, 7, Leipzig, 1914, pp. 12, 20 (= v, 72 f.); cf. Ed. Meyer, *Ägyptische Dokumente aus der Perserzeit* (*SPAW*, 1915, no. 16), p. 301.
25 IV, 21–2; [*ANET*, p. 369].
26 A. H. Gardiner, *ZÄS*, 42, 1905, p. 36.
27 Compare the somewhat later date given in the Great Harris for the period of Ramses III: H. D. Schaedel, *Die Listen des Grossen Pap. Harris* (*LÄSt*, 6, 1936), esp. the graphic description on p. 52.
28 On Re in Karnak see Kees, *Orientalia*, 18, 1949, pp. 427 ff.; on Ptah in that place see above, p. 77, n. 77.
29 C. de Wit, *Le Flambeau*, 4, 1956, p. 414.
30 [*ANET*, p. 369.]
31 *Pyr.*, 1695; partial parallels: 1449a, 1587d.
32 W. Pleyte and F. Rossi, *Les Papyrus de Turin*, Pl. 131, l. 10; translation: Roeder, *Urk.*, p. 141.
33 *BD* 64, 11.
34 E.g., *Dendérah*, I, 55.
35 Spell 80 in *CT*, II, 39.
36 Coffin of an Amon priest during the Twenty-second Dynasty: Kees, *Götterglaube*, p. 171.
37 Kees, op. cit., p. 161.
38 E.g., Hymn to Amon from Hibis; text: H. Brugsch, *Reise nach der Grossen Oase...*, Leipzig, 1878, Pl. 15, ll. 13 f.; translation: A. Scharff, *Altägyptische Sonnenlieder* (*Kunst und Altertum*, 4, Berlin, 1922), p. 89.
39 G. Fecht, *ZÄS*, 85, 1960; the king himself is accordingly not called Akhnaton but something like Akhanjāti. The name of his spouse, 'Nofretete' (Nefertiti), has been reconstructed as Naptēta by means of cuneiform, i.e. vocalized material (E. Edel, *JNES*, 7, 1948, p. 14) and was in contemporary Egyptian called something like Naftēta. Whether these well-founded forms can prevail vis-à-vis the traditional but inexact forms seems doubtful because of the amount of effort involved. But we have pointed this out in the hope that it may encourage a move along the right path.
40 Formerly fundamental: Sethe, *Beiträge zur Geschichte Amenophis IV* (*NGGW*, 1921), pp. 101 ff.; with regard to our case: pp. 109 ff., incl. n. 3; cf. also B. Gunn, *JEA*, 9, 1929, p. 174, n. 6.
41 This view is held by Fecht, op. cit., to whom we may refer the reader for further details on the interpretation of Akhanjāti's name.

42 Jāti sounds very similar to *it*, 'father', which was then pronounced as *jāt*: Fecht, op. cit., where the evidence is given for the form *itn*, meaning begetter of the king.

43 On continued existence during the Ramesside period, cf. H. Jacob-sohn, *Die dogmatische Stellung des Königs in der Theologie der alten Ägypter* (*ÄgFo*, 8, 1939), esp. pp. 56 f., and Fecht, op. cit.

44 The later form of this name eliminates Shu and thus the son, which has rightly been interpreted as reducing the initially radical claims of the king: Fecht, op. cit. This runs parallel with the adjustment to the traditional artistic form in later Amarna works, by comparison with the radical and expressionist early forms: Wolf, *Kunst*, pp. 454 f.

45 I intend to treat the material monographically in a publication of the Leipzig Academy; cf. the report of a lecture in *Deutsche Litera-turzeitung*..., Berlin, 78, 1957, cols. 373 ff.

46 H. Junker, especially in his *Götterlehre*, pp. 25–37, 76 f. Junker has elaborated his position anew in his brief survey of Egyptian religion (*Christus und die Religionen der Erde*, ed. F. König, II, 1, Vienna, 1951, pp. 570 ff.).

47 Kees, *Götterlehre*, pp. 270–8; the addenda in the second impression do not contribute anything vital.

48 This constitutes, in our view, the valuable kernel of truth in Junker's account.

49 We may be reproached for having ourselves (see above, p. 17) used an adjective, *sḥmt*, 'the Powerful One', in support of our thesis that man first believed in 'power'; but the charge that both explanations are equally uncertain would, however, be unjustified, for not only have we mentioned *sḥmt* merely as a testimony to the concept of power known from the general history of religion, but also we have been able to point to the fact that *sḥmt* as Sekhmet has an assured place as an independent deity, which cannot be said of the 'Great One'.

50 Since *šd* is ambiguous, it may also of course mean: 'secret festivals are not celebrated [in his honour]'.

51 Text in G. Maspero, *Hymne au Nil* (*Bibl. d'Ét.*, 5, 1912), p. 10.

52 Text: Maspero, op. cit., pp. 16 f.; Erman, *Egyptians*, p. 146. What the author of the Hymn to the Nile apparently had in mind was the fact that the Nile did not have a cult image or receive daily service, but that sacrifice was made to it at a festival, on the occasion of the flood (*ḥꜥpy*): further details in Bonnet, *RÄRG*, pp. 525 ff.; S. Morenz, *Die Geschichte von Joseph dem Zimmermann* (*Texte und Untersuchungen zur Geschichte der altchristlichen Literatur*, 56, Leipzig, 1951), pp. 31 ff.; A. Hermann, *ZÄS*, 85, 1960, pp. 35 ff.

53 Pap. Neskhons, III, 2, Twenty-first Dynasty; I understand the sentence *ꜣbwt.f m uṯr nb* to signify identity; see below, p. 320, no. 89.

318   EGYPTIAN RELIGION

54 H. Brugsch, *Reise nach der Grossen Oase...*, Leipzig, 1878, Pl. 27, 40.

55 IV, 16 f.; I understand *wṯs ḥ ͨw* in accordance with *Wb.*, I, 383, 3. A different view is taken by Zandee, *Hymnen*, p. 75: 'verheffende zijn verschijning', i.e. 'bearing his appearance'; [*ANET*, p. 368].

56 On the significance of Hermonthis in this respect cf. Zandee, op. cit., p. 82.

57 Texts from Dendera, translated in Junker, *Stundenwachen*, p. 6.

58 Text and translation: A. M. Blackman and H. W. Fairman, *Miscellanea Gregoriana*, 1941, pp. 398 f.

59 *Dendérah*, III, 33 s-t.

60 J. Dümichen, *Altägyptische Tempelinschriften*, II, Leipzig, 1867, Pl. 24.

61 *Dendérah*, I, 87a.

62 Ibid., 29c.

63 *Dendérah*, II, 45c.

64 Ibid., 73c.

65 Attested in the forms *smꜣ irw* and *smꜣ ḫprw*, of course not until the Greek and Roman period: *Wb.*, III, 447, 14 f.; *smꜣ irw*, e.g., in the list in *Dendérah*, III, 78k.

66 The material, which is composed of various words denoting 'image', especially *šm*, *tit*, *twt*, deserves to be collected, classified and interpreted. We may note that this state of affairs is attested from the Eighteenth Dynasty onward and is encountered most frequently in the Greek and Roman period. The early passage in *Urk.*, IV, 533 f. concerning Thutmosis III cannot be interpreted with certainty since the text is damaged.

67 The term apparently developed too late for it to be accepted as part of the royal titulary, which had already become firmly established. That it is, e.g., possible for a *šm ͨnḫ 'Imn* to appear in conjunction with the old titles for 'Horus' and 'son of Re' is, however, shown by, for example, the list of names in the decree on the Rosetta Stone: N 2 (*Urk.*, II, 170).

68 E. Cassirer, *Philosophie der symbolischen Formen*, esp. II, 1953, pp. 50 ff. [Eng. trans. by R. Manheim: *Philosophy of Symbolic Form*, II, New Haven, 1955]; on the role of words in the ancient Near East see Morenz, *FS. Johannes Jahn*, Leipzig, 1958, p. 24.

69 S. Schott, *Hieroglyphen. Untersuchungen zum Ursprung der Schrift* (*AMAW*, 1950, 24), pp. 82 f.; also Kees, *ZÄS*, 57, 1922, p. 93 (on Coffin Texts from Lisht); on its extension to the so-called concubine figures: Schott, *JEA*, 16, 1930, p. 23.

70 Th. Frings, *Antike und Christentum an der Wiege der deutschen Sprache* (*BSAW*, 97, 1, 1949), p. 28.

71 It is tempting to draw upon material from living religions for com-

parison, but we have doubts as to whether this would be successful. Catholic priests are usually excellent psychologists but in my experience they differ widely in their judgement about whether simple pious people are able to distinguish between the mother of the Lord and the image of the Virgin.

72 VII, 16; according to Volten, *Studien zum...Anii*, pp. 60 ff., 116, this text belongs to the Eighteenth Dynasty; we also see no reason for assuming that this statement reflects the Amarna religion; [*ANET*, p. 420].

73 Shabaka inscription 59 f.; [*ANET*, p. 5].

74 Sethe, *Dram. Texte*, pp. 5, 70: early First Dynasty; Junker, *Götterlehre*, pp. 6 ff.: Old Kingdom; since Ptah has entered into personal names, Helck puts in a plea for the late Fourth Dynasty: *ZÄS*, 79, 1954, p. 32.

75 For a possible explanation of the spatial displacement, see Junker, op. cit., pp. 72 f., 75.

76 Shabaka inscription 2; the use of the ancient particle *sw* would then be merely an archaism.

77 The original reference to the statue was discovered by N. de G. Davies and A. H. Gardiner, *The Tomb of Amenemhet*, London, 1915, pp. 57 f.; opening of the mouth in the Pyramid Texts: 1329b–1330b (ritual before the statue: 1968b); production of statues (possibly with the ancient opening-of-the-mouth ritual) recorded in ancient annals and no doubt celebrated as a festival: S. Schott, *Altägyptische Festdaten* (*AMAW*, 1950, 10), p. 64. On the whole question see now: E. Otto, *Das altägyptische Mundöffnungsritual* (*Ägyptologische Abhandlungen*, 3, Wiesbaden, 1960), and Bonnet, *RÄRG*, pp. 118 ff. (s.v. *Bild*) and 487 ff. (s.v. *Mundöffnung*).

78 Some references: Deuteronomy iv. 28; Isaiah ii. 8, xvii. 8, xxxvii. 19, xliv. 9 ff.; Jeremiah i. 16, ii. 27, x. 3 ff., xxv. 6 f., xxxii. 30; Psalms cxv. 4 ff.

79 Sap. Sal. 13–15, esp. 15, 4 ff.

80 *Laws*, XI, 931 a. [Plato's *Works*, trans. by G. Burges, London, 1896, v, p. 486]. This passage seems to represent the essence of his views, although Plato's contribution to Greek theology is of course a more complex subject.

81 They were ὑπομνήσεως ἕνεκα: W. Nestle, *ARW*, 37, 1941–2, p. 75.

82 This we deduce from the characterization of his position in J. Geffcken, *ARW*, 19, 1916–19, pp. 308 f. The Egyptian tradition is indicated by Greco-Egyptian theologians adopting the Egyptian position and by formulating essential points in Greek; see now R. Merkelbach, *Archiv für Papyrusforschung* (ed. Fr. Zucker), 17, Leipzig, 1960, pp. 108 f. (incl. bibliography).

320   EGYPTIAN RELIGION

83 Pap. Louvre 3284, II, 14 f.; translation and commentary: Morenz, *ZÄS*, 84, 1959, p. 136.
84 Kees, *Götterglaube*, p. 157.
85 Evidence in Spiegelberg, *ZÄS*, 62, 1926, p. 35; on Apis: E. Otto, *Beiträge zur Geschichte der Stierkulte* (*Unters.*, 13, 1938, p. 27) (apparently on this point we have only the testimonies of classical authors); cf. also S. Morenz, 'Ägyptische Ewigkeit des Individuums …', *Asiatica, FS. Fr. Weller*, ed. J. Schubert and U. Schneider, Leipzig, 1954, pp. 416 f.
86 *BD* 78, 17 f., 27 f.; for commentary: Morenz, op. cit., p. 422.
87 Kees, *Götterglaube*, p. 46.
88 *Urk.*, IV, 17; K. Sethe, *Der Nominalsatz im Ägyptischen und Koptischen* (*ASAW*, 33, 3, 1916), pp. 97 f. and *Kommentar*, II, pp. 309 f. (on *Pyr.*, 482a–b).
89 Ranke, *Personennamen*, I, 139, 16 or II, 19 (both New Kingdom); on this in general, II, 240; see also above, p. 151: *šbwt.f m nṯr nb*, 'his [Amon's] form is every god', or literally: 'his form is in every god'.

CHAPTER 8

1 Roughly contemporary with the priestly writers' account is the comprehensive (co-called Deuteronomic) redaction of the historical material, the sense of which is similar.
2 On many of the matters treated in the following pages the reader will now find a great deal of carefully selected material in S. Sauneron and J. Yoyotte, *La Naissance du monde selon l'Égypte ancienne* (*Sources orientales*, I: *La Naissance du monde*), Paris, 1959, pp. 17–91. Especially on questions relating to Khnum one may consult the translations of certain texts from Esna edited by Sauneron: ibid., pp. 72–4.
3 Pap. Berlin 3048, VIII, 2; text and translation: Wolf, *ZÄS*, 64, 1928, pp. 30–2.
4 M. Sandman-Holmberg, *The God Ptah*, Lund, 1946, p. 34 and 10*.
5 Same wording as Berlin 6764 for Amon in, e.g., the prayer to Ramses III: Pap. Harris, I, 3, 3.
6 Cf., e.g., U. v. Wilamowitz-Moellendorff, *Der Glaube der Hellenen*, 2nd ed., Berlin, 1955, I, pp. 342 f., or M. P. Nilsson, *Geschichte der griechischen Religion*, I, Munich, 1941, p. 33; not until Plato did philosophers elaborate anything comparable, in the figure of the *demiourgos*: J. Kerschensteiner, *Platon und der Orient*, Stuttgart, 1945, pp. 77 ff., 128 f.; cf also Müller, *Isis-Aretalogien*.
7 This is authenticated in numerous inscriptions in Theban temples from the Greek period: Sethe, *Amun*, §99.

8 Sandman-Holmberg, op. cit., pp. 55 f.
9 Berlin 3048 IV, 6; Wolf, op. cit., pp. 23, 26; [*ANET*, p. 367].
10 Philae photo 977; text and translation: A. Badawi, *Der Gott Chnum*, Glückstadt, 1936, p. 53.
11 H. Brugsch, *Thesaurus inscriptionum aegyptiacarum*, Leipzig, 1883–91, 651 D, from Esna; text and translation: Badawi, op. cit., p. 54.
12 Sauneron kindly drew my attention to Esna 17, 12–19 (ed. G. Daressy, *Rec. de trav.*, 27, 1905, pp. 84 f.; the edition could be improved), and in explanation of the text suggested that Khnum begins to work as a potter only after the cosmic substance had been ordered (*šꜣꜥ ḳd*).
13 Philae photo 125; Badawi, op. cit., p. 55.
14 On Tefnut as 'moisture' see Sethe, *Urgeschichte*, §§117, 124, and the pun mentioned immediately below in *Pyr.*, 1652c.
15 Kees, *Götterglaube*, p. 227.
16 *Pyr.*, 576c, 578b; ut. 356 in its entirety.
17 In his *Kommentar*, IV, p. 277, Sethe regards a subsidiary order 'in the princely house, in Heliopolis' as the original one, in which case the word of Geb pertains to the princely house and the threats of the gods to Heliopolis.
18 *Pyr.*, 957b–c.
19 On Geb as arbitrator and judge, above all between the Lower Egyptian Horus and the Upper Egyptian Seth, see Shabaka inscription 8, 10a–12a: Sethe, *Dram. Texte*, pp. 23, 27; for the revision of this decision by Geb and the unification of the Two Lands under Horus: ibid., 10c–12c and Sethe, op. cit., pp. 27 f.
20 *Pyr.*, 1248a–d; translation: Kees, *Götterglaube*, pp. 219 f.
21 *Pyr.*, 1652c; on this see S. Morenz, 'Wortspiele in Ägypten', *FS. J. Jahn*, Leipzig, 1958, p. 24.
22 Kees, *Götterglaube*, esp. p. 227.
23 That Geb formed the link has just been mentioned; in terms of religious politics, the Heliopolitans were able to gain control of these basic historical forces primarily by bringing in the Osirian cycle: Kees, *Götterglaube*, pp. 254 ff.
24 *Wb.*, II, 137 f.; thus it may unhesitatingly be used with *ỉrỉ* throughout: Junker, *Götterlehre*, p. 61.
25 E.g., *CT*, II, 39d.
26 Kees, *Götterglaube*, p. 248: period between Third and Fifth Dynasties.
27 See above, p. 154; in my view: transition from the Fifth to Sixth Dynasty.
28 On this compare Junker, *Götterlehre*, p. 57.
29 Shabaka inscription, l. 55; translation: Sethe, *Dram. Texte*, p. 57, and Junker, op. cit., p. 55; [*ANET*, p. 5].

30 Op. cit., l. 57; Sethe, op. cit., pp. 61, 64; Junker, op. cit., p. 59; on the origin of *kȝw* and *ḥmwswt* as creative and tutelary powers, cf. Helck, *ZÄS*, 79, 1954, pp. 28 ff; [*ANET*, loc. cit.].

31 Op. cit., l. 56, in l. 57 repeated twice; [*ANET*, loc. cit.].

32 Junker, op. cit., pp. 69 ff.; for a contrary view cf. S. Morenz, 'Eine "Naturlehre" in den Sargtexten', *WZKM*, 54, 1957 (*FS. Junker*), pp. 119, 128 f.; the Herakleopolitan period seems to have been a suitable matrix for elements from the world of nature.

33 Pap. Berlin 3055, xvi, 3 f.; translation: H. Grapow, *ZÄS*, 67, 1931, p. 36; there the same expression *mȝṯ rn* is used as a designation as was employed in Memphite theology.

34 Pap. Leyden I, 350, v, 16.

35 *BD* 17; text: *Urk.*, v, 30 (Middle Kingdom); one New Kingdom gloss on this text has *Ḥw* and *Sȝȝ* emerging from the blood of Re's phallus, i.e. approaches the sexual sphere.

36 In *Götterglaube*, p. 228, Kees enters *Ḥw* and *Sȝȝ* under the heading of 'transformations' of the Heliopolitan system; in *RÄRG*, p. 319, Bonnet expresses a view close to ours. One temporarily insurmountable difficulty lies in the fact that in regard to Heliopolis we do not have any literary testimony such as exists for Memphite theology.

37 L. Dürr, *Die Wertung des göttlichen Wortes im Alten Testament und im antiken Orient* (*MVAeG*, 42, 1, 1938); the material drawn upon from Egypt, esp. pp. 23 ff., 134 ff., naturally needs to be supplemented (cf., for instance, *CT*, II, 7e, 23e ff., 43d, which have appeared subsequently); if a new interpretation were to be undertaken, many points would have to be omitted or rearranged, but this work deserves credit for providing such rich and stimulating material.

38 Small plaques of annals of Udimu: S. Schott, *Hieroglyphen. Untersuchungen zum Ursprung der Schrift* (*AMAW*, 1950), 24; (1951), p. 30, Pl. 9 and Fig. 19.

39 A basic account: K. Sethe, *Die Entwicklung der Jahresdatierung bei den alten Ägyptern* (*Unters.*, 3, 1905), esp. pp. 75 ff.

40 Cf. *iners* (Ovid, *Metamorphoses*, I, 8); at this point it may be mentioned that the Egyptian concept of the primary element, Nun, is in later texts linked with a verb *nny*, 'to be inert': Sethe, *Amun*, § 145.

41 Text: G. Maspero, *Les Momies royales de Déir el-Bahari* (*Mém. de la Mission*, I, Cairo, 1889), p. 595.

42 Text and translation: É. Drioton, *Rapport sur les fouilles de Médamoud, 1926* (*FIFAO*, 4, pt. 2, 1927, pp. 38 f.).

43 H. E. Naville, *La Litanie du soleil...*, Leipzig, 1875, Pl. X, 23; cf. also Müller, *Isis-Aretalogien*.

44 On the interpretation of this imagery a debate took place between H. Schäfer, *Ägyptische und heutige Kunst und Weltgebäude der alten*

NOTES 323

Ägypter, Berlin, p. 108, and K. Sethe, *Altägyptische Vorstellungen vom Lauf der Sonne* (*SPAW*, 1928, 22), pp. 6 ff.; this latter in turn brought a response from Schäfer: *ZÄS*, 71, 1935, pp. 15 ff. On the whole question see O. Kaiser, *Die mythologische Bedeutung des Meeres in Ägypten, Ugarit und Israel*, Berlin, 1959, pp. 20 ff.

45 E. Hornung, *ZÄS*, 81, 1956, pp. 28 ff., with evidence in support of the preceding remarks.

46 *Urk.*, VII, 27, concerning Amenemhet II; see above, p. 114.

47 *Urk.*, IV, 2026, so-called 'Restoration Stele' of Tutankhamon; see above, p. 114.

48 Hornung, *MDAIK*, 15, 1957, pp. 128 f.

49 On this question cf. J. A. Wilson, *The Burden of Egypt*, Chicago, 1951, pp. 13 f.

50 Chap. 175; well-known translation: Kees, *Lesebuch*, p. 28; see above, p. 26. The beginning, *iw t3 r iim nwn*, is in my view best translated literally: 'Earth will go [again] into the Nun': in either case what is meant is that the earth will vanish into the primordial watery waste.

51 In Memphite theology one would, for example, look in vain for statements about an 'end' of the creation, just as little as one would expect any pious person to turn to his god after thinking of the 'death' of this god, for everything that has been fashioned is deemed to be of limited duration.

52 Cf. for the present G. Thausing, *Mélanges Maspero*, I, 1935–8, pp. 35 ff., Abd el-Mohsen Bakir, *JEA*, 39, 1953, pp. 110 f.; the possibility considered here that *nḥḥ* was originally related to *past* eternity seems most doubtful to us; in any case it would be replaced by *future* eternity in view of the main line of development of this word (cf., e.g., *Pyr.*, 414c); cf. also Hornung, *ZÄS*, 81, 1956, pp. 31 f. That both these concepts had a similar orientation (towards the future) is also suggested by the fact that they are frequently linked in a dualistic scheme: e.g., '*niswt*-king of the *nḥḥ*-eternity, *bity*-king of the *ḏt*-eternity' (in regard to Thoth: *Urk.*, VIII, 152; similarly in regard to the king: *Edfou*, I, 290).

53 U. Schweitzer, *Das Wesen des Ka im Diesseits und Jenseits der alten Ägypter* (*ÄgFo*, 19, 1956), pp. 45, 83.

54 S. Morenz, *Die Zauberflöte*, Cologne, 1952, p. 87.

55 Besides Morenz, op. cit., pp. 86–8, see now W. Westendorf, *Der Gebrauch des Passivs in der klassischen Literatur der Ägypter* (*MIO*, I, 1953), pp. 231 f.

56 *Epinomis* 987 D.

57 E.g., *Urk.*, V, 8 (New Kingdom gloss on *BD* 17, 2).

58 Text: Ch. Maystre, *Le Livre de la vache du ciel dans les tombeaux de la vallée des rois* (*BIFAO*, 40, 1941), p. 63; translation: H. Ranke, *AOT*, I, 1909, p. 183.

59 *r-ꜥ-n sf* can also mean 'in your place of yesterday'; *BD* 15A, II, 11 f.

60 *wbn* or *ỉw m nwn*: *BD* 71, 1; text and translation: Morenz, *FS. Schubart*, 1950, pp. 105, 77; Pap. Carlsberg I, 19 f., text and translation: H. O. Lange and O. Neugebauer (eds.), *Pap. Carlsberg no. I* ...(*Kongelige Danske Videnskabernes Selskab, Hist.-fil. Skrifter*, I, 2, 1940), Pl. I and p. 19.

61 On the spatial relationship cf. Sethe, *Amun*, §78.

62 In Amun, §99, Sethe adduces two examples from Theban inscriptions in temples of the Greek period, according to which Ptah as goldsmith fashioned the eight primordial gods 'from the Nun (*m nwn*)'. But here it is evidently only a case of representing Nun as the oldest figure among the primordial gods who sprang from him (Sethe, op. cit., §120).

63 IV, 8 f.; Wolf, *ZÄS*, 64, 1929, pp. 23, 26.

64 Wolf, op. cit., p. 28.

65 Thus of Ptah, ibid., III, 1.

66 Likewise of Ptah: e.g., *Edfou*, II, 37.

67 Amenemope XXIV, 13–17; see above, p. 67.

68 Shabaka inscription 50a–51a; Sethe, *Dram. Texte*, pp. 46 f.; Junker, *Götterlehre*, pp. 16 f.; [*ANET*, p. 5].

69 Pl. IV, 135 ff.; but translation: E. A. Speiser, *ANET*, p. 67.

70 In Israel the same continued existence is still evident in the nature of the sea which Yahveh had 'shut in with doors', for which he 'prescribed bounds and set bars and doors' (Job xxxviii. 8 ff.). But here as elsewhere in the Old Testament (Psalms lxxiv. 13 f., lxxxix. 10 f., civ. 9 f.; Proverbs viii. 28 f.; Jeremiah v. 22; cf. W. Eltester (ed.), *Neutestamentliche Studien für R. Bultmann*, Berlin, 1954, esp. pp. 214 f.) Yahveh is represented as the lord and his rule as fully realized.

71 Hymn to Amon from Hibis, text: H. Brugsch, *Reise nach der Grossen Oase*..., Leipzig, 1878, Pl. 15, ll. 13 f.; translation: Scharff, *Ägyptische Sonnenlieder*, Berlin, 1922, p. 89; see above, p. 146.

72 Morenz, *Religion in Geschichte und Gegenwart*, 3rd ed., III, 1959, col. 329.

73 *Pyr.*, 1208c,

74 *CT*, IV, 36 (spell 286).

75 Kees, *Götterglaube*, p. 226.

76 Stele Leyden v, 12.

77 P. Munro, *ZÄS*, 85, 1960, p. 64.

78 Pap. Berlin 3048, III, 5; Wolf, op. cit., pp. 20 f.

79 New Kingdom sources: text and translation: M. Sandman-Holmberg, *The God Ptah*, Lund, 1946, pp. 10*, 34; the very rare use of *gmỉ* 'to find', denoting the activity of the creator, I relate to inspiration by the heart of Ptah.

80 Esna temple, text no. 394; translation: S. Sauneron and J. Yoyotte, *La Naissance du monde selon l'Égypte ancienne* (*Sources orientales*, I: *La Naissance du monde*), Paris, 1959, p. 72.

81 M 12 f.; cf. also Müller, *Isis-Aretalogien*.

82 On the following cf. the basic Academy publication by Sethe, *Amun*.

83 Ibid., §§126 ff., 145 ff.

84 Ibid., §§65 ff.

85 Ibid., §151; on the 'Isle of Flames' as the primordial place in Hermopolis (especially as the place where the sun-god came into being) and in other functions, cf. Kees, *ZÄS*, 78, 1942, pp. 41 ff.

86 Theban temples 145b, 35c; texts and translation: Sethe, op. cit., §96.

87 Texts and translation: ibid., §100.

88 Texts and translations: ibid., §140.

89 Collection of material and interpretation in Morenz, *FS. Schubart*, 1950, pp. 74–83; some now also available in G. Roeder, *Hermopolis 1929–1939*, Hildesheim, 1959, p. 186 (v, §44).

90 In Egyptian *inr*, 'stone', is used figuratively with regard to the egg-shell: *Wb.*, I, 98, 6; on the matter itself cf., e.g., M. P. Nilsson, *Geschichte der griechischen Religion* (*Handbuch der Altertumswissenschaft*), sec. 5, pt. 2, vol. I, Munich, 1941, p. 648.

91 *BD* 77, 2; on this see Morenz, op. cit., p. 76.

92 *BD* 17, 57 (*Urk.*, v, p. 55); Morenz, op. cit., p. 74.

93 *BD* 54, 2; Morenz, op. cit., p. 76.

94 E.g., Pap. Leyden I, 350, IV, 6; Morenz, op. cit., p. 76.

95 Sethe, *Amun*, §160.

96 *Pyr.*, 1271c; on this see Kees, *ZÄS*, 60, 1925, pp. 14 f.; Morenz, op. cit., p. 78; on Thoth as 'son of the egg-shell' cf. also *BD* 134, 9.

97 Lefebvre, *Petosiris*, II, pp. 38 f. (inscription no. 62); Morenz, op. cit., p. 79.

98 On Thoth's origin from the Delta: Kees, *Götterglaube*, pp. 48, 305 f.; on Hermopolis as a cosmogonic site: Morenz, op. cit., p. 94, and S. Morenz and J. Schubert, *Der Gott auf der Blume. Eine ägyptische Kosmologie und ihre weltweite Bildwirkung* (*Artibus Asiae*, suppl. 12, Ascona, 1954), p. 47.

99 Sethe, *Amun*, §122; on the possibility that the participle *pr*, written without the feminine ending, may relate to Ptah instead of to *swḥ.t* (egg), cf. Morenz, *FS. Schubart*, p. 81, n. 4.

100 Collection and interpretation of material in Morenz and Schubert, op. cit., pp. 13–82; several points also in G. Roeder, *Hermopolis 1929–1939*, Hildesheim, 1959, p. 190 (v, §50).

101 Morenz and Schubert, op. cit., pp. 22 ff. We should stress that this is a construction which in our view is not unfounded but

inevitably rests upon a weak foundation so long as we possess such an infinitesimal amount of material about Harsaphes (as stated on p. 29 of the work mentioned). There we referred to a testimony by Tacitus (*Annals*, II, 60) according to which 'Herakles', i.e. the *interpretatio Graeca* of Harsaphes of Herakleopolis, is regarded as the oldest inhabitant of Egypt (op. cit., p. 30); now (taking up a kind suggestion by E. Hammerschmidt) we may add a Coptic tradition in which the birth of Christ is transposed to Herakleopolis, thus allotting it the rank of a source of salvation: G. Giamberardini, *Il natale nella chiesa copta*, Cairo, 1958, pp. 14 f. (There is no need, as this author does, to draw a parallel with Hermopolis, for one may refer directly to Herakleopolis.)

102 Twentieth-Dynasty ostracon: Erman, *ZÄS*, 38, 1900, p. 24; on this see Morenz and Schubert, op. cit., p. 46.

103 G. Daressy, *ASAE*, 17, 1917, p. 122; on this see Morenz and Schubert, op. cit., p. 47.

104 J. Dümichen, *Baugeschichte des Dendera-tempels...*, Strasbourg, 1877, 12; on this see Morenz and Schubert, op. cit., p. 48.

105 It is not until the Septuagint that the usual meaning is established linguistically as well.

106 E.g., *CT*, II, 95a (spell 99); see above, p. 20.

107 Pap. Harris, I, 44, 3 ff.; now translated in G. Roeder, *Die ägyptische Religion in Texten und Bildern*, Zurich–Stuttgart, 1959, I, p. 50; [partly based on M. Sandman-Holmberg, *The God Ptah*, Lund, 1946, pp. 31, 41, 45, 117].

CHAPTER 9

1 Evidence in F. Hintze, *ZÄS*, 78, 1943, pp. 55 f.

2 Text: *Urk.*, IV, 223 f.; illustration: H. E. Naville, *The Temple of Deir el-Bahari*, II, 1886, Pl. 48; other evidence of the fashioning of individuals by Khnum in A. M. Badawi, *Der Gott Chnum*, Glückstadt, 1937, p. 53.

3 On Khnum as procreator cf. Badawi, op. cit., p. 55.

4 S. Schott, *OLZ*, 42, 1939, col. 93.

5 Badawi, op. cit., pp. 52 ff.; the earliest testimony is to be found in *Pyr.*, 524a.

6 *Urk.*, IV, 223; on this see Sethe, *Urkunden der Dynastie XVIII. bearbeitet und übersetzt*, I, Leipzig, 1914, p. 104, n. 1; cf. also Badawi, op. cit., p. 45.

7 Text: Davies, *Amarna*, VI, 27, 6; translation: Sethe in Schäfer, *Amarna in Religion und Kunst*, Leipzig, 1931, p. 65; my view of course differs from that of Sethe: 'who makes water [= seed] into man'.

8 H. Brugsch, *Thesaurus inscriptionum aegyptiacarum*, Leipzig, 1883–91, 625A; from Esna, the place where Khnum was worshipped.

9 Pap. Leyden I, 350, V, 1 f.; for the comprehension of the second part see Zandee, *Hymnen*, p. 52; [A. H. Gardiner, 'Hymns to Amon from a Leyden Papyrus', *ZÄS*, 42, 1905, p. 37].

10 Evidence in Ranke, *Personennamen*, II, p. 227.

11 The evaluation of the myth constructed around Khnum in a publication of the Gesellschaft zur Verbreitung wissenschaftlicher Kenntnisse (series D, fasc. 5) by Dr H. Scheler, entitled *Der Marxismus-Leninismus über Religion und Kirche*, Leipzig–Jena, 1956, shows remarkable lack of comprehension.

12 Pap. Leyden I, 350, III, 17; [*ANET*, p. 369].

13 Wen-Amon: Pap. Golénischeff, 2, 57 f.; [*ANET*, p. 28].

14 Evidence in Firchow, *FS. Grapow*, pp. 89 ff.

15 *Pyr.*, 1466b–d; translation: Grapow, *ZÄS*, 67, 1931, p. 35; cf. also Sander-Hansen, *Tod*, p. 8.

16 *Pyr.*, 1467a.

17 We are quoting publications by Gardiner, 1935, and Sander-Hansen (*MDVS*, 29, 2, 1942).

18 G. Posener, *RdE*, 9, 1952, p. 113.

19 E.g., *Urk.*, VII, 14.

20 Text and translation: Lüddeckens, *Totenklagen*, p. 112.

21 The matter is interpreted similarly by Lüddeckens: ibid., p. 172.

22 Ibid., pp. 134 f.

23 Chap. 175.

24 Text and translation: Kees, *ZÄS*, 74, 1938, pp. 78 f.

25 Although put into the mouth of a woman, the text thus implies that the situation is that of a man; either it was indeed compiled by the consort of Taimhotep or else the formula was simply intended to be masculine.

26 Stele BM 157; text: H. Brugsch, *Thesaurus inscriptionum aegyptiacarum*, Leipzig, 1883–91, 918 ff.; we have given the translation by Otto, *Biogr. Inschr.*, p. 193; cf. also Erman, *FS. E. Sachau* (ed. G. Weil), Berlin, 1915, pp. 108 ff.

27 Here, too, there seems to be much doubt as to the efficacy of rites; anyway, the Coffin Texts contain a spell with the expedient title: 'union of relatives (*šbt*) in the realm of the dead' (*CT*, II, 160 f., title to spell 136).

28 Admonitions, IV, 2; text and translation: A. H. Gardiner, *The Admonitions of an Egyptian Sage*, Leipzig, 1909, p. 36.

29 On the history of the problem and its solution on the basis of literary and historical evidence in the sense indicated here, cf. Herrmann, *Untersuchungen*, pp. 62 ff.; work on questions relating

to this text is still in progress; cf. R. O. Faulkner, *JEA*, 42, 1956, pp. 21 ff., and A. Hermann, *OLZ*, 54, 1959, cols. 257–9.

30 *Odyssey*, XI, 489–91; for information about the Egyptian text and this impressive comparison we are indebted to the late lamented A. de Buck: cf. *Jb. d. Koninklijke Nederlandsche Akademie van Wetenschappen 1957–8*, 1958, pp. 74 ff.

31 On such lists see, e.g., Junker, *Gîza*, I, 177 ff.; II, 69 ff.; III, 98 ff.

32 Song of the Harper Nefer-hotep 2 and Pap. Harris 500, VI, 3; [*ANET*, p. 467].

33 Evidence and correct interpretation in Grapow, *Ausdrücke*, pp. 18 f., 138; cf. also Sander-Hansen, *Tod*, p. 25.

34 *Pyr.*, 1877e–1878c.

35 *Pyr.*, 735a–b.

36 E.g., *Pyr.*, 331c.

37 G. Brunton and G. Caton-Thompson, *The Badarian Civilisation and Predynastic Remains near Badari*, London, 1928, p. 18; H. Junker, *Vorläufiger Bericht über die Grabung...von Merimde-Benisalame* (*SWAW*, 1929), p. 200.

38 On the entire question cf. also Kees, *Totenglauben*, 2nd ed., pp. 14–16; also A. de Buck, *De godsdienstige Opvatting van den Slaap*, Leyden, 1939, and Sander-Hansen, *Tod*, pp. 12 f.

39 Grapow, *ZÄS*, 72, 1936, pp. 76 f. (on Ani, V, 2–4).

40 Ph. Derchain, *CdE*, 33, 1958, pp. 29 ff.

41 [*ANET*, p. 420.]

42 Text: Lefebvre, *Petosiris*, II, p. 90 (no. 127); translation: Otto, *Biogr. Inschr.*, p. 184.

43 Inscription on statue of Neshor, Twenty-sixth Dynasty; (badly damaged) text: P. Pierret, *Recueil d'inscriptions inédites du Louvre*, I, Paris, 1874, pp. 21 ff.; translation: Otto, op. cit., p. 164. This may be a final secularized form of the ancient belief that the sacrosanct king will escape death through his link with the primordial god (*Pyr.*, 1467a; see above, p. 186). There may be a link here with the request in the Coffin Texts, related to a private person: 'As regards death, mayest thou escape it' (*CT*, I, 284g).

44 Translation based upon Otto, op. cit., p. 193.

45 The study with this title by J. Zandee appeared as *Studies in the History of Religions* (supplements to *Numen*), V, Leyden, 1960. It could not be utilized here, but would have enriched our account rather than changed it.

46 Ani, IV, 11 ff.: the text was interpreted by Volten, *Studien...Anii*, pp. 72 ff.; [*ANET*, p. 420; Erman, *Egyptians*, p. 237].

47 Text: Pierret, op. cit., II, 1878, p. 21; translation: Otto, *Biogr. Inschr.*, p. 190.

48 G. Posener, *RdE*, 9, 1952, p. 113; [*ANET*, p. 419].

49 *Urk.*, I, 99; several further examples of the furnishing of private tombs by the king during the Old Kingdom: *Urk.*, I, 18, 65, 146, 203; cf. also H. W. Helck, *MDAIK*, 14, 1956, esp. p. 68 (Helck has convincingly traced the term *imȝḫw*, which was later spiritualized, back to the sense of 'the person provided for'); [Breasted, *Ancient Records of Egypt*, Chicago, 1906, I, p. 141].

50 *Urk.*, I, 38.

51 The basic source is Junker, *Gîza*, II, pp. 41 ff.

52 Cf. e.g., ibid., I, p. 218.

53 Ibid., II, pp. 45 f.

54 Great progress in understanding this festival was made by S. Schott, *Das schöne Fest vom Wüstentale* (*AMAW*, 1952, 11).

55 During the Neolithic period the tombs were invariably furnished on a modest scale. Naturally it cannot be disputed that at that time the bodies of the poorest persons were simply covered with earth or even quite deliberately destroyed, and that immortality was at first confined to the aristocracy. On this see M. S. Murray, *JEA*, 42, 1956, pp. 86 ff., although his hypothesis necessarily rests upon unproven assumptions at crucial points.

56 W. Spiegelberg, *Ägyptische Verpfründungsverträge mit Vermögensabtretungen* (*BHAW*, 1923, 6), esp. pp. 11 f.

57 Seidl, *ZDMG*, 107, 1957, pp. 272–4.

58 Herodotus, II, 78 [G. Rawlinson, *Histories of Herodotus*, II, London, 1858, p. 130]; an idea of what these figures looked like may be gained from one of the wooden statuettes published by F. W. v. Bissing, *ZÄS*, 50, 1912, pp. 63–5. Cf. also Plutarch, *On Isis and Osiris*, 17, and on this Hopfner, *Plutarch*, I, pp. 74–6.

59 On these texts cf. M. Lichtheim, *JNES*, 4, 1945, pp. 178 ff.; their relationship with the prophetic books of the Old Testament are examined by the author in *HO* I 2, 1952, p. 199.

60 This was mooted by Erman, *Egyptians*, p. 132; Songs of the Harpers are indeed recorded in Theban tombs: Lichtheim, op. cit., pp. 185 ff., 201 f., 202 ff.; translations in S. Schott, *Altägyptische Liebeslieder*, Zurich, 1950, pp. 131 ff. Schott also drew upon the Songs of the Harpers in regard to matters pertaining to the feast of the valley, hinting cautiously that they played a role in the lives of mortals: *Das schöne Fest vom Wüstentale* (*AMAW*, 1952, 11), p. 78; cf. also pp. 75, 81.

61 I Corinthians xv. 32, after Isaiah xxii. 13.

62 On the latter cf. Schott, *ZÄS*, 75, 1939, pp. 100 ff.; on priests enjoying life even during what seems the bigoted Late period, see Kees, *ZÄS*, 74, 1938, pp. 73 ff., esp. 82–5; later, e.g. Pap. Insinger XVII, 11 ff.; on the entire question see Morenz, *ThLZ*, 74, 1949, esp. cols. 427 f.

63 Pap. Erm. 1116A, l. 55; [Eng. trans. partly based upon *ANET*, p. 415].

64 Here and immediately below we are following Wolf, *Kunst*, pp. 268–71.

65 G. v. Kaschnitz-Weinberg, *Bemerkungen zur Struktur der ägyptischen Plastik* (*Kunstwissenschaftliche Forschungen*, 2, 1933), p. 24.

66 We may once again recommend the fundamental work by Kees, *Totenglauben* (2nd ed., 1956).

67 On Israel see G. Quell, *Die Auffassung des Todes in Israel*, Leipzig, 1925, pp. 17 ff.; on Greece let us recall the well-known fact that large quantities of funerary gifts were made for the deceased; characteristically, an unmarried girl who died was given bridal jewellery and a λουτροφόρος so that afterwards she could take the marital bath: E. Buschor, *Grab eines attischen Mädchens*, 2nd ed., Munich, 1941, p. 16.

68 E.g., *Pyr.*, 572c; further details in Sethe, *Zur Geschichte der Einbalsamierung bei den Ägyptern* (*SPAW*, 1934, 13), pp. 5 f.

69 G. E. Smith, *JEA*, 1, 1914, Pl. 31, where there are as yet no traces of mummification on the head.

70 Bonnet, *RÄRG*, p. 482.

71 On this see Sethe, op. cit., pp. 28 ff.; kidneys may also have been treated separately: Diodorus, 1, 91 and Sethe, op. cit., p. 28.

72 E.g., H. E. Winlock, *The Tomb of Queen Meryet-Amūn at Thebes* (*PMMA*, 6, 1932, Pl. 13); G. E. Smith, *The Royal Mummies*, Cairo, 1912, Pl. 7 (Cat. gén. no. 61055); these facts were brought to our notice by Ch. Müller, 'Die Frauenfrisur im alten Ägypten' (diss.), 1960.

73 G. Mérei and J. Nemeskéri, *ZÄS*, 84, 1959, pp. 76–8; it is certain that the nose was added to the body when mummified, since the knots of the attaching straps have left their traces on the base of the skull.

74 H. Abel in H. Ranke (ed.), *Koptische Friedhöfe bei Karâra...*, Berlin–Leipzig, 1926, pp. 15 f.; A. L. Schmitz, *ZÄS*, 65, 1930, esp. pp. 9, 19 f.; at this time the dead were wrapped several times over in shrouds, with salt and juniper berries placed between the layers.

75 S. Morenz, *Asiatica. FS. F. Weller*, ed. J. Schubert and U. Schneider, Leipzig, 1954, pp. 414 ff., esp. 425 f.

76 The basic sources are G. E. Smith and W. R. Dawson, *Egyptian Mummies*, London, 1924, and A. Lucas, *Ancient Egyptian Materials and Industries*, 2nd ed., London, 1934, pp. 230 ff.; on the religious and historical aspects see the above-mentioned Leipzig Academy publication by Sethe. One may also consult the excellent description by Herodotus (II, 86–8) which without doubt applies to the

period in question (*ca.* 450 B.C.). Some information on the history of this custom is provided by Bonnet, *RÄRG*, pp. 482 ff. and A. Hermann, *RAC*, III, 1959, cols. 799 ff.

77 *Urk.*, I, 121; [Breasted, *Ancient Records of Egypt*, Chicago, 1906, I, p. 115].

78 See above, p. 299, n. 4; on the facts and problems mentioned here and below: A. Scharff, *Das Grab als Wohnhaus in der ägyptischen Frühzeit* (*SBAW*, 1944-6, 6).

79 That the cemetery also came into existence in nomad territory is possible to the extent that other burials were made close to a prominent mound.

80 H. Ricke, *Bemerkungen zur ägyptischen Baukunst des Alten Reiches*, I, Zurich, 1944, pp. 38 ff.

81 We first arrived at this conclusion, which still seems convincing, in a review of Scharff's Leipzig Academy publication: *Orientalia*, 20, 1951, p. 212.

82 The treasures of the latter are to be found in Turin: E. Schiaparelii, *La tomba intatta dell'architetto Cha* (*Relazione sui lavori della missione archeologica italiana in Egitto*, II, 1927). The transport of such funerary gifts to the tomb is represented in, for example, the tomb of Ramose (late XVIII Dyn., Thebes, tomb 55); this is most accessible to German readers in A. Champdor, *Die altägyptische Malerei*, Leipzig, 1957, p. 163.

83 H. Abel in H. Ranke (ed.), *Koptische Friedhöfe bei Karâra...*, Berlin–Leipzig, 1926, pp. 17 ff.; A. L. Schmitz, *ZÄS*, 65, esp. pp. 13 ff.

84 Junker, *Gîza*, IV, pp. 43 ff.

85 On the question of the false door and the dining-table scene, cf. Scharff, op. cit., p. 40, and Junker, *Gîza*, XII, pp. 49 ff.

86 On the substance, development, meaning and ritual treatment of the 'large list of dishes', cf. Junker, *Gîza*, II, pp. 69 ff.

87 Wolf, *Kunst*, pp. 258 ff., esp. p. 262.

88 Kees, *Totenglauben*, 2nd ed., pp. 166 f.

89 Junker, *Gîza*, XII, pp. 49 ff., esp. p. 51.

90 Ibid., XI, pp. 226 ff.; cf. also the term '*ka* house' to denote the statue-chamber: ibid., III, p. 120; *ḥwt-kꜣ* is of course by no means restricted to this usage: U. Schweitzer, *Das Wesen des Ka im Diesseits und Jenseits der alten Ägypter* (*ÄgFo* 19, 1956), pp. 84-6.

91 Cf. Bonnet, *RÄRG*, pp. 357 ff., and the study by Schweitzer cited above. Everyone who reflects on the concept of *ka* can discern new features in it. A member of my seminar, Rev. Dr Feller, voiced the appealing idea that the *ka* denotes the ability of a man to associate with the deity, since its symbol may be regarded as a gesture of adoration. This interpretation would explain a good deal, and

certainly deserves to be discussed: this would be the positive (in the religious sense) antithesis to the interpretation of this symbol as a gesture of warding off evil.

92 *Urk.*, I, 135 ff.

93 Sinuhe B 189 ff.

94 *Pyr.*, ut. 355; ut. 373 is similar.

95 *Pyr.*, 251a–d; translation based upon Sethe, *Kommentar*, I, pp. 234 f.

96 E.g., *Pyr.*, 657e.

97 E.g., *Pyr.*, 1385b–c.

98 *Pyr.*, 134a.

99 *Pyr.*, 604e–f.

100 *CT*, I, 190a–b; further details in Sander-Hansen, *Tod*, p. 19.

101 *CT*, II, 94–111 (spells 99–104); translation and commentary: Otto, *Miscellanea Gregoriana*, 1941, pp. 151 ff.

102 Otto, *ZÄS*, 77, 1942, p. 91.

103 *Urk.*, IV, 481.

104 E.g., *Urk.*, IV, 114.

105 N. de G. Davies, *Two Ramesside Tombs at Thebes*, New York, 1927, Pl. 1; Bonnet, *Bilderatlas*, Fig. 110 (after a vignette in the *BD*).

106 Morenz, *FS. Grapow*, 1955, p. 239.

107 Ranke, *ZÄS*, 75, 1939, p. 133; L. J. Cazemier, *Orientalia Neerlandica*, Leyden, 1948, pp. 62 ff.; in *ZÄS*, 77, 1942, p. 91, Otto also obtains this result after a critical examination of the tradition. In my view its correctness depends on the fact that ba did not originally mean 'soul' but divine reality: see above, p.   , and Kees in Bonnet, *RÄRG*, p. 74. On the other hand J. Pirenne is wrong in his claim (*CdE*, 34, 1959, pp. 208 ff.) that *bꜣ* was the soul of everyone in the Old Kingdom, which he bases on the Pyramid Texts (e.g., the passage *Pyr.*, 854, clearly refers to the sun-god).

108 A. Rusch, *Die Entwicklung der Himmelsgötter zu einer Totengottheit* (*MVAeG*, 27, 1922). Kees provides detailed information about what follows, especially the geography of the beyond, in *Totenglauben*, 2nd ed., pp. 67 ff.

109 *CT*, II, 95e.

110 Sander-Hansen, *Tod*, pp. 20 f.

111 *CT*, II, 260a–b.

112 *BD* 3.

113 *BD* 175, 176; cf. also *CT*, II, 47b; *BD* 44, 64, 114, 116, 136A, 137A.

114 Great solar litany: *Mém. de la Miss.*, II, I, Pl. XI, ll. 150 f.; cf. Firchow, *FS. Grapow*, p. 90, who is scarcely correct in translating *dr* (without a preposition between objects) as 'to divide'.

115 *BD* 64, addendum.
116 *Pyr.*, 251b–c.
117 Material compiled in Sethe, *Kommentar*, I, pp. 49–51.
118 'Coming Forth by Day' is the expedient title of certain spells in
the Book of the Dead, but it is also the name of the entire collection and thus, for example, written on the outside of a Twenty-
first-Dynasty papyrus: H. E. Weinlock, *The Egyptian Expedition,
1929–30* (*BMMA*), p. 24.
119 For the first-mentioned classical guides to the beyond, see Grapow,
HO, I 2, 1952, pp. 50–6; for the later ones see A. Piankoff and
N. Rambova, *Mythological Papyri* (Bollingen Series, 40, New
York, 1957).
120 Piankoff and Rambova, op. cit., textual figs. 47, 50 ff., 58, and
translation in the volume of text, p. 114.
121 *Edfou*, I, 346; in the third place, thereafter 'the earth was created
for his image (*sḫm*).'
122 E.g., *BD* 64, addendum.
123 Junker, *Gîza*, IV, p. 44.
124 The choicest item of evidence is a mummy bandage from
Oxyrhynchus inscribed with an uncanonical saying by Jesus:
'Jesus saith: Nothing is buried which will not be raised up':
H. Ch. Puech, *Revue de l'histoire des religions*, 147, 1955, pp. 126–9,
and lately O. Hofius, *Evangelische Theologie*, 20, 1, 1960, p. 40.
125 II Setna, II, 9 ff.; text and translation: F. Ll. Griffith, *Stories of
the High Priests of Memphis*, Oxford, 1900, pp. 154–7. A fine
contrast to the Egyptian solution in the case of Setna is provided
by the dialogue between Diogenes the dog and Mausolus (Lucian,
Dialogues of the Dead, 24): the splendid tomb of Mausolus is considered just a white elephant.
126 See above, p. 131; on the 'Osiris mystery' cf. S. Morenz, *Die
Zauberflöte*, Cologne, 1952, pp. 72 ff.
127 Otto, *Biogr. Inschr.*, pp. 43 ff., esp. p. 64.
128 In the records of the trial of the assassins of Ramses III, the following sentence is put into the mouth of the murdered man, which at
this time could hardly be true of only the king: 'While I am consecrated (*ḥwi*) and exempted (*mk*) for ever, while I am among the
just kings who are with (lit.: before) Amon-Re, King of the Gods,
and with Osiris, the ruler of eternity' (Judicial Papyrus of Turin,
III, 3–5; translation: A. de Buck, *JEA*, 23, 1937, p. 154). Thus we
have here once again the quintessence of hope in the life hereafter.
129 To this interpretation from the standpoint of the history of religion
we may add the assessment of the art historian Wolf, *Kunst*, esp.
pp. 616 f., 628 f.; in our view both are wholly compatible.
130 Popular Jewish belief led in the same direction; it is, however,

doubtful whether it could gain so much influence as Egypt did upon the nascent Christian religion after Judaism had been superseded by Christianity.

131 Psalms vi. 6.

132 W. F. Otto, *Die Götter Griechenlands*, 3rd ed., 1947, pp. 257 ff.; [see chap. 4, n. 92].

133 Otto, *Biogr. Inschr.*, pp. 20 ff.; for a late example of God as lord of fate, etc.: Morenz and Müller, *Schicksal*, pp. 30 ff.

CHAPTER 10

1 The classical source is Josephus, *Contra Apionem*, 1, 8, §§ 38–42.

2 The above follows Morenz, *ThLZ*, 75, 1950, cols. 709 ff.; later the arguments developed there were forced into the Procrustes' bed of a thesis by K.-H. Bernhardt, 'Gott und Bild', Berlin, 1956, pp. 75–8. This evaluated critically 'previous attempts to derive and interpret the ban on images in the Old Testament', i.e. condemns them [the attempts] systematically. How wrong he is himself is evident from the title of the Morenz article. This reads: 'Development and Nature of Scriptural Religion', and thus is not an attempt to bring out the negative side of the prohibition of images, but rather to investigate the positive side of serving God through the written word and Holy Scripture.

We must in particular refute two points (ad p. 78, bottom): 1. By no means have we dispensed with a historical derivation of the phenomenon of scriptural religion but have derived it from the chain of events from Josiah to Ezra, in the sense of the text above. 2. If nevertheless we tried to delve deeper and to identify as the ultimate source of scriptural religion a genius for 'hearkening' (to be understood in the spiritual sense, and therefore implying the human being as a whole), we did not say that Israel was blind.

We were concerned only with the dominant feature, which Bernhardt does his best to blur. The incomprehension he shows may best be illustrated by one example. He points to the vision of grasshoppers (Amos vii. 1 f.) as evidence for the role of visions (which we do not deny, but which we place in the context of the Old Testament). When the Jews hearkened, it was not to grasshoppers, but to God, that their ears and minds were turned.

3 On the following, cf. the monograph by Leipoldt and Morenz; this gives a fairly large amount of space to Egyptian matters.

4 Grapow, *ZÄS*, 72, 1936, p. 17: Book of that which is in the Underworld (Amduat).

5 Sethe, *Dram. Texte*, p. 87; so-called Ramesseum Dramatic Papyrus; on this see Leipoldt and Morenz, p. 15.

6 Line 2; Sethe, *Dram. Texte*, p. 20 (see above, p. 155); [*ANET*, p. 4].

7 Cf. the various editions of the corpora by A. de Buck, *The Egyptian Coffin Texts*, 1934–, and E. Naville, *Das ägyptische Todtenbuch der XVIII. bis XX. Dynastie*, Berlin, 1886.

8 The ideal case of two renderings of a completely identical (hymnic) text in two different temples is provided by H. Junker, *Ein Preis der Isis aus den Tempeln von Philae und Kalabša* (*Anzeiger der WAW*, 18. Jhrg., 1957, Vienna, 1958).

9 This does not mean that such ritual purpose did not exist: so far as Memphite theology is concerned, it may be assumed that works were recited during the jubilee festivals of Memphis or of the Ptah temple.

10 Some details in Morenz, *RAC*, II, 1954, cols. 692–5.

11 Text: W. Pleyte and F. Rossi, *Papyrus de Turin*, 1869, Pls. 131–8; translation, e.g.: Roeder, *Urk.*, pp. 138 ff.

12 Text: C. Maystre (ed.), *Le Livre de la vache du ciel...*(*BIAF*, 40, 1941), pp. 53 f.; translation, e.g.: Ranke in *AOT*, pp. 3–5.

13 Pap. d'Orbiney; text: A. H. Gardiner, *Late Egyptian Stories* (*Bibl. Aeg.*, I, 1932), pp. 9 ff.; translation, e.g.: Erman, *Egyptians*, pp. 150 ff.; on Bata and his native town of Sako we now have some information in Pap. Jumilhac in the Louvre, studied by J. Vandier; cf. J. Yoyotte, *RdE*, 9, 1952, pp. 157 ff. On the fluid boundaries between myth and fictional tales, so far as Egypt is concerned, see E. Brunner-Traut, *ZÄS*, 80, 1955, pp. 12 f. and esp. p. 16. It is from this borderline area between myth and fictional literature that The Story of the Shipwrecked Sailor comes; it cannot simply be considered part of religious literature (see above, p. 32).

14 Texts: Pap. Berlin 3055 or 3014 and 3053 as well as temple of King Seti I at Abydos (A. M. Calverley, M. F. Broome and A. H. Gardiner, *The Temple of King Sethos I at Abydos*, 2 vols., London–Chicago, 1933–5); translation: A. Moret, *Le Rituel du culte divin journalier en Égypte*, Paris, 1902.

15 Manuscripts of the first century A.D. in Cairo (Pap. Boulaq 3) and Paris (Pap. Louvre 5158); text now in S. Sauneron, *Le Rituel de l'embaumement: pap. Boulaq III, pap. Louvre 5. 158*, Cairo, 1952.

16 Recorded pictorially and in writing in Osirian chambers at Dendera, Edfu and Philae; cf. Junker, *Stundenwachen*; further rituals are mentioned by Kees, *HO*, I 2, pp. 76 ff.

17 Beside the well-known texts from the Berlin memorial of Ikhernofret (H. Schäfer, *Die Mysterien des Osiris in Abydos unter König Sesostris III* (*Unters.* 4, 1905); here, of course given only in the form of an account) and the so-called Ramesseum Dramatic Papyrus (Sethe, *Dram. Texte*, pp. 83 ff.), cf. the material which has since been

studied esp. by É. Drioton: e.g., in *Revue de l'Égypte ancienne*, 2, Paris, 1929, pp. 172 ff. and *Le Texte dramatique d'Edfou* (*CASAE*, 11, 1948). We can make only brief reference to the divine dialogues in the mortuary texts (Atum and Nun: *CT*, spell 80; Atum and Osiris: *BD* 175).

18 On this role of Thoth cf. P. Boylan, *Thoth, the Hermes of Egypt*, London, 1922, pp. 92 ff.

19 *BD* 101, 11 f.

20 Pap. Louvre 3284, 11, 8 f.

21 Ibid., 1, 1; in the Greco-Egyptian tradition Isis appears beside Thoth as inventor of writing. The Memphite text of the Isis aretalogy (M 3c) runs as follows: 'Jointly with Hermes I have invented the signs for writing, sacred ones and those of the vernacular'; on this see D. Müller, *Isis-Aretalogien*. Isis attained this role by equation with Seshat, the goddess of writing; in an Edfu text (1, 378) we hear of Thoth: 'Isis is beside him as Seshat.'

22 The clear case of inspiration found in Pap. Oxyrhynchus 1381 as regards the translation of a work by Imhotep–Asklepios into Greek, apparently follows the Greek and not the Egyptian tradition: Leipoldt, *FS. Schubart*, pp. 56 ff. On the other hand an ancient Egyptian tradition seems to be present when Chairemon (in Porphyry, *On abstinence*, IV, 6: Hopfner, *Fontes*, p. 180) refers to the alleged mode of life of Egyptian priests as 'permanently in contact with divine cognition (γνῶσις) and inspiration (ἐπίπνοια)'.

23 Sir A. Gardiner, *JEA*, 24, 1938, p. 168.

24 E.g., Famine Stele, l. 5.

25 Granite statue Cairo 42162 (Ramsesnakht), now illustrated in G. Roeder, *Die ägyptische Religion in Texten und Bildern*, I, Zurich, 1959, Pl. 18; the idea of inspiration was already expressed by G. Legrain, *Statues et statuettes de rois et de particuliers*, II, 1909 (Cat. gén.), p. 29.

26 *BD* 30 B, addendum.

27 G. Möller, *Amtliche Berichte aus den Königlichen Kunstsammlungen*, 39, 1918, pp. 180 ff.; on all the points raised above cf. Leipoldt and Morenz, pp. 28–30; further details on remarkable circumstances of discovery in Schott, *HO*, I 2, p. 230. Text and translation of the tale in question now in W. Erichsen, *Eine neue demotische Erzählung* (*AMAW*, 1956, 2).

28 This is the case in the Shabaka inscription: Junker, *Götterlehre*, pp. 12 ff., or in the legend of Hatshepsut's procreation by Amon and the king's consort Ahmose (form *sw sḏm.f*: *Urk.*, IV, 291 ff.; on this see Sethe, *ZDMG*, 79, 1925, p. 315). We cannot examine the delicate question whether in each case the text is an ancient one or merely an archaized formulation.

29 As, for example, in the Ramesseum Dramatic Papyrus: Sethe, *Dram. Texte*, p. 91; Junker, *Götterlehre*, p. 14.

30 Evidence from Thutmosis III onward in S. Schott, *Das schöne Fest vom Wüstentale* (*AMAW*, 19, 1952, 11), p. 46.

31 Pap. Erm. 1116B; our quotation: ll. 68 f.; in fact earlier spells were used there: Herrmann, *Untersuchungen*, pp. 37 ff.; [*ANET*, p. 446].

32 As discovered by A. de Buck, *Mélanges Maspero*, 1935–8, pp. 847 ff. (see above, p. 40).

33 [Clement of Alexandria], *Die Teppiche–Stromateis*, VI, 4, 37, 3 (II, p. 449), Basle, 1936.

34 In my view Th. Hopfner in Bonnet, *RÄRG*, p. 291, is correct.

35 Leipoldt and Morenz, pp. 40 f.

36 *pr.t m hrw* is the heading of several early spells (already in the Coffin Texts): *CT*, I, 313, II, 67. A work by H. Grapow on the titles of Egyptian spells and books is in progress.

37 H. E. Winlock, *The Egyptian Expedition, 1929–1930* (*BMMA*), p. 24 (XXI Dyn.).

38 *BD* I, 1, based upon Nineteenth-Dynasty manuscripts; this may be modelled on other genres (wisdom literature, works on medicine); evidence of this in Schott, *HO*, I 2, p. 229.

39 *BD* 163 (heading), based upon the Ptolemaic Turin Papyrus edited by R. Lepsius: *Das Todtenbuch der Ägypter nach dem hieroglyphischen Papyrus in Turin*, Leipzig, 1842.

40 Cf., e.g., the history of chapters 69 and 70 in the Book of the Dead: Kees, *Göttinger Totenbuchstudien* (*Unters.*, 17, 1954).

41 *CT*, III, 227, on this see Kees, op. cit., pp. 6, 14; on the whole question cf. Morenz, *OLZ*, 52, 1957, cols. 124 f.

42 Leipoldt and Morenz, p. 131.

43 *BD* 17, 15 (*Urk.*, V, 30).

44 *BD* 17, 2 (*Urk.*, V, 8); other evidence in Leipoldt and Morenz, pp. 128 f.

45 Grapow, *ZÄS*, 72, 1936, p. 30.

46 Pap. Prisse 608 f.; lately interpreted in this way by Volten, *Studien zum...Anii*, p. 8, and by the author in *Heilige Schriften. Betrachtungen zur Religionsgeschichte der antiken Mittelmeerwelt*, Leipzig, 1953, p. 56; [Erman, *Egyptians*, p. 65].

47 Žába, *Ptahhotep*, pp. 104, 169 f.

48 Leipoldt and Morenz, p. 56.

49 It must be borne in mind that the language used in the Instruction of Ptah-hotep was antiquated for New Kingdom readers, who had to work hard in order to understand the text. Moreover, it must be taken into account that 'to add' and 'to take away' or 'to diminish', employed in various phrases, were familiar to Egyptians as exem-

plary lapses, and therefore this could in itself lead to a new interpretation. Thus the introduction to the Book of the Dead 125 lists prohibited additions and decreases of the corn measure, arable land and the plummet of scales: the verbs *ỉnỉ* and *ỉtỉ* are not used, but rather *wȝḥ* and *ḥbỉ*.

50 Deuteronomy iv. 2 and xiii. 1; Revelation xxii. 18 f; further evidence in Leipoldt and Morenz, pp. 57 f.

51 On the reading of the title: Sethe, *ZÄS*, 70, 1934, p. 134.

52 Bonnet, *RÄRG*, pp. 860 f.

53 Latest study: J. Vergote, *Joseph en Égypte* (*Orientalia et Biblica Lovaniensia*, 3, Louvain, 1959), pp. 80 ff.; on this see Morenz, *ThLZ*, 84, 1959, cols. 407 f.

54 S. Schott, *Die Deutung der Geheimnisse des Rituals für die Abwehr des Bösen. Eine altägyptische Übersetzung...(AMAW*, 1954, 5), pp. 13–15.

55 Schott, op. cit., pp. 38 ff.; on this see Morenz, *Deutsche Literaturzeitung...*, Berlin, 78, 1957, col. 24; concerning the facts in targums, cf., e.g., the rendering of Genesis i. 2, 'the spirit of god' by 'a spirit before Yahveh'.

56 Schott, op. cit., p. 6.

57 Mag. Pap. Harris, v, 1; text and translation: H. Lange, *Der Magische Pap. Harris* (*MDVS*, 14, 2, 1927), p. 39; further details in Grapow, *Ausdrücke*, p. 26 (see above, pp. 88 and 99).

58 Gardiner, *JEA*, 24, 1938, pp. 157 ff.; even those who ascribe to the 'house of life' a general character (e.g., that of a university) do not call in question its task of producing sacred scriptures: A. Volten (ed.), *Demotische Traumdeutung* (*Anal. Aeg.*, III, 1942), pp. 36 ff., and finally Vergote, op. cit., pp. 74 ff.

59 *BD* 161, 11 f.

60 Ibid., 161, 10 f.

61 Pap. Louvre 3284, 1, 6.

62 Admonitions VI, 6; A. H. Gardiner, *The Admonitions of an Egyptian Sage*, Leipzig, 1909, p. 47.

63 I Kh., IV, 6 ff.; text and translation: F. Ll. Griffith, *Stories of the High Priests of Memphis*, Oxford, 1900, pp. 108 ff.

64 K. Preisendanz, *Papyri Graecae Magicae*, Leipzig–Berlin, 1928–31, I, 110, 184; II, 21, 79, 99, 105, 120, 131, 184, 185; we should like to mention in particular that the concept of ἀπόκρυφος, 'secret', has here a positive meaning, by contrast with the negative meaning which contrasts it with 'canonical'.

65 Cf. K. Sethe, *Die Totenliteratur der alten Ägypter. Die Geschichte einer Sitte* (*SPAW*, 1931, 18); furthermore Kees, *HO* I 2, pp. 30 ff., and Grapow, ibid., pp. 47 ff.

66 It may be assumed that the 'glorifications' (*sȝḥw*) which were read

out at the funerals of private persons during the Old Kingdom formed part of the spells that have been recorded and handed down: Sethe, op. cit., §18.

67 Sethe, op. cit., §33.

68 *BD* 110.

69 *BD* 144–7, 149 f.

70 Concerning the earlier title, 'Writing of the Secret Chamber (*sš n ʿt imn.t*)', which serves to indicate the location of the record, cf. S. Schott, *NAWG*, 1958, 4, pp. 315 ff.

71 The textual evidence of the Amduat has been studied by E. Hornung in *Das Amduat (Ägyptologische Abhandlungen*, 7, Wiesbaden, 1963); the bibliography of all the textual editions may be found in the works mentioned in n. 65. There have recently appeared translations of the Pyramid Texts and of the Book of the Dead which may be mentioned here: S. A. B. Mercer, *The Pyramid Texts in Translation and Commentary*, New York, 1952 (with several discussions of the material), and Th. G. Allen (ed.), *The Egyptian Book of the Dead. Documents in the Oriental Institute Museum at the University of Chicago*, Chicago, 1960. Moreover, we may once again point to the free compilations in Twenty-first-Dynasty papyri: A. Piankoff and N. Rambova, *Mythological Papyri* (Bollingen Series, New York, 40, 3, 1957).

72 We have dealt with this problem in *ZÄS*, 82, 1957, pp. 67 f.

73 In none of the earlier pyramids were such records to be found; cf. also Sethe, op. cit. §§3, 37.

74 Ibid., §37; see also p. 209.

75 There is a correspondence between the findings of the architectural historian H. Ricke (*Bemerkungen zur ägyptischen Baukunst des Alten Reiches*, II) and the Egyptologist S. Schott (*Bemerkungen zum ägyptischen Pyramidenkult (Beiträge zur ägyptischen Bauforschung und Altertumskunde*, 5, 1950)).

76 This is shown by the detailed, lucid and perceptive observations of Bonnet, *JNES*, 12, 1953, pp. 257 ff.

77 Here the observation made by Grapow (*ZÄS*, 72, 1936, pp. 37 f.) gains force, to the effect that these guides to the beyond contain no reference to their having originated from the royal domain, although we are primarily familiar with those from the royal tombs. The nether world as an abode for the dead was democratic, not royal.

78 *Pyr.*, ut. 273–4.

79 *Pyr.*, 412b.

80 *Pyr.*, 414b–c.

81 E.g., *Pyr.*, uts. 230, 293, 295 f., 297, 385, 388 f., or *BD* 31–3.

82 *Pyr.*, 240.

83 *BD* 17, 1; *Urk.*, v, 6.

84 By equating someone with Shu, the son of Atum, it is possible to emphasize the son's existence prior to the creation: *CT*, ii, 33e–34f (spell 80); cf. below, p. 257.

85 On the nature of such 'formulae of identification', and the way in which they differ from the 'formulae of presentation' with which the gods introduce themselves, cf. R. C. Bultmann, *Das Evangelium des Johannes*, Göttingen, 1937 [Eng. trans. by G. R. Beasley-Murray et al., Oxford, 1971], p. 176, with reference to John vi. 35. Unfortunately we cannot consider here the question whether passages such as *BD* 17, 1 ff., were in the first instance 'formulae of presentation', i.e. originated from spoken passages in mythological literature. It is a known fact that the literature of the dead drew its material from the most varied sources and reinterpreted it in accordance with its new purpose: Leipoldt and Morenz, pp. 126–8.

86 One should not forget the belief in the 'power' of the deceased, which becomes evident in the ancient texts of the dead, when they are simply referred to as the 'Mighty Ones (*shmw*)' or are thought of as a protection against the gods or the dead, which are mentioned in one and the same breath (see above, pp. 18, 27). With the so-called 'Letters to the Dead' (A. H. Gardiner and K. Sethe, *Egyptian Letters to the Dead*, 1928; Gardiner, *JEA*, 16, 1930, pp. 19 ff.; A. Piankoff and J. J. Clère, *JEA*, 20, 1934, pp. 157 ff.), this belief has far-reaching and significant effects throughout history. However, we are of the opinion that the idea of the dead needing help increasingly gained the upper hand in the course of time and thus became the essential motif behind the provision of supplies.

87 Instruction for Merikare, Pap. Erm. 1116A, ll. 136 f.; [*ANET*, p. 417].

CHAPTER 11

1 G. Fecht, *ZDMG*, 106, 1956, esp. pp. 51 f.

2 On this see H. W. Helck, *Anthropos*, 49, 1954, pp. 964 ff., and Fecht, op. cit., pp. 47, 51 f.

3 Material concerning Neith and Libya in Bonnet, *RÄRG*, p. 517; on derivation from the hunter culture: S. Morenz, *Orientalia*, 23, 1954, p. 86.

4 K. Sethe in L. Borchardt, *Das Grabdenkmal des Königs Sahu-Re*, ii (text), Leipzig, 1913, p. 74.

5 The same is true of other deities in the western regions such as Igai (*Igȝy*), the 'lord of the oasis', whose origin is dubious but who appears to be completely Egyptianized in his function: H. G. Fischer, *JNES*, 16, 1957, esp. pp. 230 ff.

6 On Ash and Seth cf. Kees, *Götterglaube*, p. 23. On Ash continuing to live on during the Late period: *Edfou*, i, 557, and probably also the

mummy-case from the Greco-Roman period in the Brighton
Museum: A. W. Shorter, *JEA*, 11, 1925, p. 78 (on this see Bonnet,
RÄRG, pp. 55, 577). The hypothesis offered by H. Stock (*Die Welt
des Orients*, I, 1948, pp. 142 f.) is based in part on an error in reading: Kees, *Götterglaube*, 2nd ed., p. 482 (addendum to p. 24, n. 1).

7 *Pyr.*, 803c; similarly 1017a.

8 Kees, *Götterglaube*, p. 45.

9 *Pyr.*, 1476; on this see O. Firchow, *Grundzüge der Stilistik in den
alten Pyramidentexten (Deutsche Akademie der Wissenschaften zu
Berlin. Institut für Orientforschung. Veröffentlichung* no. 21, Berlin,
1953), p. 148.

10 Hatshepsut: H. E. Naville, *The Temple of Deir el-Bahari*, VI, 1908,
Pl. 152; cf. *Urk.*, IV, 315 f.; Thutmosis III: F. A. F. Mariette,
Karnak. Étude topographique et archéologique, Leipzig, 1875, Pl. 23.

11 Stele at Abydos from the period of Sesostris III (Manchester 3306);
latest translation: J. A. Wilson, *ANET*, p. 230.

12 This is the cautious assessment by J. A. Wilson, *The Burden of
Egypt*, Chicago, 1951, pp. 134 ff.

13 P. Montet, *Kêmi*, I, Paris, 1928, pp. 90 ff. and *passim*.

14 These are the texts of ostracism edited by K. Sethe and G. Posener
(see above, p. 27) which may be assigned to the close of the Middle
Kingdom; on all the points raised above cf. A. Alt, *Die Herkunft
der Hyksos in neuer Sicht* (*BSAW*, 101, 6, 1954), pp. 26 ff. (now in
Kleine Schriften zur Geschichte des Volkes Israel, III, Munich, 1959,
pp. 89 ff.).

15 *CT*, I, 262b (spell 61); first attempt at an interpretation: Sethe,
ZÄS, 45, 1908–9, p. 8. For reminding me of this passage I am
indebted to R. Stadelmann (Heidelberg), who also most generously
allowed me to read his thesis 'Syrisch-Palästinensische Gottheiten
in Ägypten' [now published in W. Heck (ed.), *Probleme der Ägyptologie*, 5, Leyden, 1967], to which reference must be made in regard
to many points of our present theme.

16 In his *Isis-Aretalogien* D. Müller comes to the conclusion that
'Hathor, Lady of Byblos' was the only deity to be connected with
navigation.

17 I would not even wish to exclude the possibility that Hathor was of
Syrian origin, although this cannot be substantiated here, even in
outline. The sherds of vessels found at Byblos bearing royal names
of the Old Kingdom are regarded by Stadelmann neither as votive
offerings for the local deities nor as proof of Pharaonic building
activity, but simply as commodities exported to pay for the import
of timber. This would invalidate the arguments by Bonnet, *RÄRG*,
281 (left), based upon W. F. Albright, *ZÄS*, 62, 1927, pp. 62 f.

18 Ranke, *Personennamen*, I, 189 (no. 17), or 235 (no. 6); Ranke inter-

prets the use of names of gods as names of persons by the plausible argument that they are abbreviated forms (ibid., II, 234).

19 *CT*, v, 319i (spell 450).

20 É. Drioton, *Bibliotheca Orientalis*, 12, 1955, pp. 61 ff.; B. v. d. Walle, *La nouvelle Clio*, VII–IX, 1955–7, p. 282.

21 Communication from Stadelmann, who refers to *CT*, 319a and 294c, as well as to the content of the entire spell 450.

22 This is the case with the sanctuaries of Beth-Shan: A. Rowe, *The Topography and History of Beth-shan* (Pennsylvania Univ. Museum. Publications of the Palestine Section, 1, Philadelphia, 1930), pp. 10 ff. Nevertheless monuments may be found there, too, in which the pharaoh is depicted associating with *Egyptian* gods: e.g., the stele of Ramses II making an offering to Amon-Re and in return being given victory and power: text and translation now in J. Černý, *Eretz-Israel*, 5, 1958, pp. 75 ff.

23 Pap. Harris, I, 9, 1 ff., or G. Loud, *The Megiddo Ivories* (Univ. of Chicago. Publications of the Oriental Institute, 52, 1939), Pl. 63, nos. 379–82; on the entire question cf. A. Alt, 'Ägyptische Tempel in Palästina und die Landnahme der Philister', *ZDPV*, 67, Leipzig, 1944, pp. 1 ff. (now in *Kleine Schriften zur Geschichte des Volkes Israel*, Munich, 1959, I, pp. 216 ff., esp. pp. 218–21).

24 This is the case on the so-called Job stone of Ramses II at Karnaim (Bashan): Erman, *ZDPV*, 15, 1892, pp. 205 ff. and *ZÄS*, 31, 1893, pp. 100 ff.; finally, Alt, op. cit., p. 217, with further material.

25 T. Säve-Söderbergh, 'Ägypten und Nubien' (diss.), Lund, 1941, pp. 200 ff.

26 *Urk.*, IV, 815 ff.; cf. Säve-Söderbergh, op. cit., p. 201.

27 *Urk.*, IV, 199 f.

28 Alt, op. cit., p. 219.

29 Pap. Sallier, I, 1, 2–3; translation: Erman, *Egyptians*, p. 166; the monolatry claimed may be a tendentious exaggeration by later generations.

30 After information from R. Stadelmann.

31 See above, p. 223; see also Kees, *ZÄS*, 57, 1922, p. 97 (inter alia, Coffin Text from the Middle Kingdom).

32 Seth as 'lord of the thunderstorm' appears already in *Pyr.*, 261a; on the entire question cf. Bonnet, *RÄRG*, pp. 704 f.

33 Further details in Stadelmann, op. cit. (see n. 15), who has also established the reading *Hrwi-ʿnt* (instead of the untenable old version Anat-el). Cf. also H. Stock, *Studien zur Geschichte und Archäologie der 13. bis 17. Dynastie Ägyptens unter besonderer Berücksichtigung der Skarabäen dieser Zwischenzeit* (*ÄgFo*, 12, 1942), p. 64.

34 In this the most interesting problem for historians and students of

religion is the question whether Ramses II in his residence on the Delta accepted anything from the cultural tradition of the Hyksos (role of Seth and Anath or Astarte): on this see Alt, *FS. Fr. Zucker*, Berlin, 1954, p. 8 (now in *Kleine Schriften zur Geschichte des Volkes Israel*, III, Munich, 1959, p. 182).

35 Here too we must await the completion of Stadelmann's work (see n. 15). In the meantime, see Erman, *Religion*, pp. 148 ff., and the article by Bonnet, *RÄRG*, which provide information on the key words mentioned (Hurun is only mentioned there s.v. Tanis; cf. on this point G. Posener, *JNES*, 4, 1945, pp. 240–2; K. C. Seele, ibid., pp. 234 ff., 243 f., as well as S. Sauneron, *RdE*, 7, 1950, pp. 121 ff.). On Resheph, so far the best studied figure, see H. de Meulenaere, *De cultus van Resjef in Egypte (Handelingen van het Eenentwintigste Vlaams Filologencongres*, 1955), pp. 129–31, and W. K. Simpson, *Orientalia*, 29, 1960, pp. 63 ff.

36 Numerous other Near Eastern deities appear in Egyptian magical texts, although their worship cannot be substantiated: e.g., Ningal in Pap. Leyden I, 343 (Ramesside): cf. Gardiner, *ZÄS*, 43, 1906, p. 97; on the whole complex, cf. now A. Massart, *The Leiden Magical Papyrus I 343 and I 345 (OMRO*, suppl. 34, 1954). On *Smn* = Samona, which appears in it, cf. J. Nougayrol, *Archiv Orientální*, 17, 1949 (*FS. B. Hrozný*), pp. 213 ff. In a rather appealing fashion Stadelmann assumes that an onomasticon of the Near Eastern gods must have come to the hand of the author of the Egyptian magical text.

37 Again see Stadelmann for details. J. Černý, however, warns against exaggerating the important role which Syrian cults played at Deir el-Medina; he also points out that all our evidence comes from the Nineteenth Dynasty, and that at this time a foreign influx is quite unlikely. The number of foreign names at Deir el-Medina is likewise not rated very high by Černý (private communication to the author). For clarification we shall have to await specialized research.

38 Evidence for Amenophis II and Ramses II: G. Posener, *JNES*, 4, 1945, p. 240. On the other hand even the king's family was affected, as is shown by the personal name of *Bnt-ʿnt*, 'daughter of Anath', given to a daughter of Ramses II: H. Gauthier, *Le Livre des rois d'Égypte*, III (*MIFAO*, 19, 1914), pp. 102 ff.

39 H. Brugsch, *Thesaurus inscriptionum aegyptiacarum*, Leipzig, 1891, VI, p. 1434.

40 Inscription of Amenophis II at Karnak: Simpson, op. cit., p. 64.

41 Crossing of the river Orontes by Amenophis II: *Urk.*, IV, 1302; cf. Simpson, op. cit., p. 65. Later Ramses II carries out his heroic deeds 'like Baal', i.e. 'like Seth', who largely absorbed Baal: Pap. Sallier III, 3, 8 and numerous testimonies in H. Gressmann,

Abhandlungen zur semitischen Religionskunde und Sprachwissenschaft (*FS. Baudissin*), ed. W. Frankenberg and F. Küchler, suppl. fasc. to *Zeitschrift für die alttestamentliche Wissenschaft*, 33, Giessen, 1918, pp. 200 ff.; see also above, p. 77.

42 Illustrated ostracon Berlin 21826: E. Brunner-Traut, *Die altägyptischen Scherbenbilder. Bildostraka der deutschen Museen und Sammlungen*, Wiesbaden, 1956, pp. 29–31 and Pl. 8, no. 16; incidentally the cult of Astarte remained alive, at least in Lower Egypt, until Greek times and then her dominating function, as the equation with Aphrodite shows, was that of a goddess of fertility: U. Wilcken (ed.), *Urkunden der Ptolemäerzeit*, I, Berlin, 1927, pp. 37 f.

43 J. Černý has proved that in one case blood brotherhood existed between Syrians (ʿ3mw) and an Egyptian: the Egyptian concerned originated from Deir el-Medina and met Syrians somewhere in the Delta. True, the conclusion of this union was one of the matters for which the young Egyptian was reprimanded by his father: *JNES*, 14, 1955, pp. 161–3 (Ostracon Chicago 12034, period of Ramses III).

44 On this question, too, see the work by R. Stadelmann (n. 15), who notes the contrary fact that in adopting foreign deities the aspect of the god dying and being resurrected was disregarded.

45 H. Ranke, in S. R. K. Glanville (ed.), *Studies presented to F. Ll. Griffith*, London, 1932, pp. 412 ff.

46 Ranke, op. cit., pp. 412 f.; the text upon which it is based, an Akkadian letter from Tushratta inscribed on a clay tablet (J. A. Knudtzon, *Deir El-Amarna-Tafeln*, I, Leipzig, 1915, pp. 178 ff. (no. 23)) is dated by an Egyptian inscription in ink to the king's thirty-sixth year.

47 Also within Egypt proper healing deities do not acquire importance until the New Kingdom, and this apparently increases after the Late period. From earlier times, so far as we are aware, there is evidence only of divine healers who are active within the realm of the gods alone, i.e. not upon a religious plane but upon a mythical one (doctor for the eye of Horus, Lower Egypt): evidence in Grapow, *Grundriss*, III, pp. 137 ff., and Otto, *ZÄS*, 78, 1943, pp. 37 f.; see above, p. 281, n. 36. Later also kings were included among the gods of healing: É. Drioton, *ASAE*, 39, 1939, pp. 57 ff. (Ramses II).

48 I. E. S. Edwards, *JNES*, 14, 1955, pp. 49–51; see above, p. 143.

49 Against this one must set the numerous Egyptian amulets, scarabs, etc., which are to be found everywhere in Syria, especially during the 2nd millennium B.C.: A. Alt, in M. Ebert, *Reallexikon der Vorgeschichte*, I, Berlin, 1924, p. 76. We cannot consider here whether or to what extent the vigorous religious life of the Near Eastern

peoples was affected by the adoption of Egyptian pictorial motifs such as the winged sun (on many occasions: cf. O. Eissfeldt, *Forschungen und Fortschritte*, 18, Leipzig, 1942, pp. 145–7), the sign for mountain or the wavy line indicating water (on a stele featuring the Ugaritic Baal: Cl. F. A. Schaeffer, *Ugaritica*, II, Paris, 1949, pp. 128 f.), and later that of the god upon the flower (S. Morenz and J. Schubert, *Der Gott auf der Blume. Eine ägyptische Kosmologie und ihre weltweite Bildwirkung* (*Artibus Asiae*, suppl. 12, Ascona, 1954), pp. 78 ff.).

50 T. Säve-Söderbergh, 'Ägypten und Nubien' (diss.), Lund, 1941, pp. 201 f.

51 Recorded in Porter and Moss, VII, 1951, p. 207; among the centres in which Amon was worshipped in the Napata kingdom were Gematen (Kawa) and Pnubs (Argo).

52 *Urk.*, III, 110; see above, p. 63.

53 *Urk.*, III, 81 ff. (Aspelta); in his thesis on the Egyptian oracle (see above, p. 103) H. M. Schenke comes to the conclusion that the choice of the king by recourse to an oracle did not become an established custom until the time of the later Ethiopian rulers.

54 This, incidentally, is a reversion to the Egyptian Old Kingdom – i.e., a sign of classicism – which makes itself felt, for example, in Kawa, where representations and inscriptions turn out to be imitations of the mortuary temples of Sahure, Neuserre and Pepi II.

55 *Urk.*, III, 135 f.

56 Th. G. Allen, *Occurrences of Pyramid Texts with Cross Indexes of these and Other Egyptian Mortuary Texts* (*Studies in Ancient Oriental Civilization*, 27, Chicago, 1950), pp. 14 f. (on Nuri 8; Aspelta). For this and many other valuable suggestions I am indebted to K.-H. Priese (Berlin), to whose thesis we may look forward. [Cf. K.-H. Priese, 'Das meroitische Sprachmaterial in den ägyptischen Inschriften des Reiches von Kush', Berlin, 1965.]

57 *ZÄS*, 70, 1934, pp. 42 f.; it also occurs in the tomb of Aspelta's wife.

58 Porter and Moss, VII, pp. 236 f.

59 Ibid., p. 235.

60 Bonnet, *RÄRG*, 592–4. Even Justinian at first had to tolerate for some years the Isis service at Philae because the Blemmyes were legally entitled to this: W. Schubart, *Justinian und Theodora*, Munich, 1943, p. 67.

61 F. Hintze, *Studien zur meroitischen Chronologie und zu den Opfertafeln aus den Pyramiden von Meroe* (*ADAW*, 2, 1959), pp. 11 f.

62 In the meantime cf. F. Hintze, *Kush*, Khartum, 1959, 7, p. 180 and Pl. 49a.

63 H. Junker, *Die Onurislegende* (*DWAW*, 59, 1–2, 1917).

64 Rock-drawing at Gebel Qeili: Hintze, op. cit., Fig. 2 at p. 190;

nimbus of rays upon an Egyptian monument of the Imperial period: E. Loukianoff, *ASAE*, 36, 1936, pp. 187 ff.

65 On the composition of the population see, e.g., W. Peremans, *Vreemdelingen en Egyptenaaren in Vroeg-Ptolemaeisch Egypte*, Louvain, 1937; on bilingualism we have provided evidence (from the early Saite period: see Herodotus II, 154) in *HO*, I 2, p. 196; some of the effects which Egyptian–Greek cohabitation had upon literature are also discussed in ibid., pp. 202 ff.

66 E.g., by B. Schweitzer, *Gnomon*, 4, 1928, p. 192 (with bibliography).

67 On the history of this period cf. F. K. Kienitz, *Die politische Geschichte Ägyptens vom 7. bis zum 4. Jahrhundert vor der Zeitwende*, Berlin, 1953; on Egypt's cultural links with Athens in particular, see F. Zucker, *FS. Schubart*, 1950, pp. 146 ff.

68 Morenz, *FS. Fr. Zucker*, Berlin, 1954, pp. 277 ff.

69 Morenz, *FS. Schubart*, pp. 64 ff.; to my former arguments I would now add among other points that in this case it was not a doctrine of creation on the Egyptian side either, but a doctrine of evolution which could easily be adapted to Greek ways of thought: see above, pp. 170, 178. If the author quotes frequently at this point from his own earlier works, this is not because he believes them to be better than others but because those matters of which one has attempted a detailed study are clearer to the author.

70 U. Wilcken, *Zur Entstehung des hellenistischen Königskultes* (*SPAW*, 1938), pp. 298 ff.; F. Taeger, *Charisma. Studien zur Geschichte des antiken Herrscherkultes*, I, Stuttgart, 1957, esp. pp. 288 ff., 416 ff.; on the Egyptian component in 'deification' (ἀποθέωσις, ἐκθέωσις), cf. Morenz, *ZÄS*, 84, 1959, pp. 132 ff.

71 Initial 'O' misunderstood as a Greek article; this hypothesis was advanced especially by Sethe, 'Janus I', *FS. C. F. Lehmann-Haupt*, ed. K. Regling and H. Reich, Vienna–Leipzig, 1921, pp. 207 ff.

72 Tacitus, *Histories*, IV, 83 f.; Plutarch, *On Isis and Osiris*, 28.

73 G. Lippold, 'Sarapis und Bryaxis', *FS. P. Arndt*, Munich, 1925, pp. 115 ff.

74 Cf., e.g., E. Kornemann, *Aus der Geburtsstunde eines Gottes* (*Mitteilungen der Schlesischen Gesellschaft für Volkskunde*, Breslau, 27, 1962), pp. 1 ff.

75 On the entire complex we may refer the reader to U. Wilcken (ed.), *Urkunden der Ptolemäerzeit*, I, Berlin, 1927, pp. 25 ff., and the summary in Bonnet, *RÄRG*, p. 649.

76 Whether Minucius Felix (*Octavius*, 21) observed these facts may be doubted, but he is correct in saying that the service performed for Sarapis was 'formerly an Egyptian but now a Roman cult'. For modern opinions: F. W. v. Bissing, 'Ägyptische Kultbilder der Ptolemaier- und Römerzeit', *AO*, 34, 1–2, 1936, pp. 36 f., or Taeger,

op. cit., pp. 417 f. For this reason Sarapis came to be regarded by his (non-Egyptian) worshippers as an all-embracing god – as healer and helper in distress in all manner of situations: O. Weinreich, *Antike Heilungswunder* (*Religionsgeschichtliche Versuche und Vorarbeiten*, 1, 1909, pp. 118 ff.) and *Neue Urkunden zur Sarapis-Religion*, 1919, pp. 15 ff. Ample evidence is to be found in the Dream Book of Artemidorus: 148, 26; 272, 30; 273, 7; on this see S. Laukamm, *Angelos. Archiv für neutestament. Zeitgeschichte*, 3, 1930, pp. 59 f.

77 E.g., Cicero, *On Divination*, I, 23, 47; Aelian, *Varia historia*, II, 31; Kelsos (in Origen, *Against Celsus*), I, 2. This may naturally also take a negative form, i.e. instead of praise for piety, reproach for superstition. This reproach was levelled by Tacitus against Egypt in general (*Histories*, I, 11, *superstitio*) and previously by Diodorus, especially with regard to the late Egyptian worship of every specimen of certain animal species (*Hist. Bibl.*, I, 83, δεισιδαιμονία). In both cases the Latin or Greek concept has a negative meaning.

78 We are thinking of the situation as it affected the donor; the recipient's attitude does not concern us here.

79 As in a case reported by U. Wilcken, *Urkunden der Ptolemäerzeit*, I, Berlin–Leipzig, 1922, p. 84.

80 Morenz, *Wissenschaftliche Zeitschrift der Universität Leipzig*, 3, 1953–4 (*FS. A. Alt*), pp. 79 ff., esp. p. 82; in the meantime ample evidence has been found from Greek and Roman times with which I was not then familiar.

81 O. Weinreich, *Aegyptus*, 11, 1931, p. 16.

82 Frequently at Philae: several Figs. in H. Junker, *Der grosse Pylon des Tempels der Isis in Philä*, Vienna, 1958.

83 Schäfer, 'Janus I', *FS. C. F. Lehmann-Haupt*, ed. K. Regling and H. Reich, Vienna–Leipzig, 1921, pp. 194 ff.; cf. also H. Ranke, *JAOS*, 65, 1945, pp. 238 ff. (on Hathor).

84 The countless possibilities that ensued for pictorial representation by equating Isis with numerous Hellenistic goddesses are brought out by G. Vandebeek, *De interpretatio Graeca van de Isisfiguur* (*Studia Hellenistica*, 4, 1946).

85 Even the form of name Isityche occurred: e.g., *C.I.L.* 14, 2867.

86 Morenz and Müller, *Schicksal*, pp. 35 f.

87 Ibid., pp. 30 f.

88 Very convincing evidence is produced by D. Müller, *Isis-Aretalogien*. The facts we have presented above throw doubt on the thesis advanced by R. Harder that this is a translation of an Egyptian original: *Karpokrates von Chalkis und die memphitische Isispropaganda* (*APAW*, 1943, 14), esp. pp. 18 ff.

89 Mainly coins: J. Leipoldt, 'Die Religionen in der Umwelt des

348 EGYPTIAN RELIGION

Urchristentums', *Bilderatlas zur Religionsgeschichte*, 9–11, Leipzig, 1926, Figs. 32–5.

90 See above, p. 235: Hathor obtains this function by her equation with the 'Lady of Byblos'.

91 Several references in Erman, *Religion*, esp. p. 438; ample material is provided by the book-length article by W. Drexler in W. H. Roscher, *Ausführliches Lexikon der griechischen und römischen Mythologie*, II, Leipzig, 1890–7, cols. 373 ff. On the area of Upper Pannonia cf. now V. Wessetzky, *Acta Archaeologica Academiae Scientiarum Hungaricae*, II, 1959, pp. 265 ff.

92 On the connection between translation and mission, cf. Leipoldt and Morenz, pp. 66 ff. Incidentally, a 'translation' (in the Alexandrine style) is also found in Egyptian scrolls, which K. Schefold recognized as prototypes of Roman landscape painting and at the same time as a medium of the Isis mission: *Athenische Mitteilungen*, 71, 1956, esp. pp. 216 ff.

93 Pap. Oxyrhynchus 1381; cf. J. Leipoldt, *FS. Schubart*, pp. 56 ff.; see above, p. 336, n. 22.

94 S. Morenz, *Die Zauberflöte*, Cologne, 1952, pp. 71 ff., esp. pp. 85 f.

95 Apuleius, *Metamorphoses*, XI, 24; [*Metamorphoses or Golden Ass of Apuleius of Madaura*, trans. H. E. Butler, II, Oxford, 1910].

96 Ibid., XI, 27 ff. On the question of the spread of the Isis mysteries to children, cf. V. v. Gonzenbach, *Untersuchungen zu den Knabenweihen im Isiskult der römischen Kaiserzeit*, Bonn, 1957.

97 Let us bear in mind inter alia that the mystic votaries were cared for by a mystagogue: Apuleius, op. cit., XI, 23; on this see Morenz, op. cit., pp. 47 f. The effect on the individual, and also the Greek influence, become evident in the cult associations formed by Egyptians, on the model of Greek associations (θίασος etc.), under the patronage of Egyptian deities; their rules have often survived (in Egyptian Demotic): cf. W. Erichsen, *Die Satzungen einer ägyptischen Kultgenossenschaft aus der Ptolemäerzeit nach einem demotischen Papyrus in Prag* (Kongelige Danske Videnskabernes Selskab, *Hist.-Fil. Skrifter*, 4, 1, 1959).

98 Pap. Prisse 608 f.; see above, p. 224 and n. 49.

99 Deuteronomy iv. 2 and xiii. 1; Revelation xxii. 18 f.; further details in Leipoldt and Morenz, pp. 57 f.

100 II Samuel vii; I Kings iii. 4 ff.; on this see S. Herrmann, *Wissenschaftliche Zeitschrift der Universität Leipzig*, 3, 1953–4 (*FS. A. Alt*), pp. 61 ff.

101 Morenz, *ZÄS*, 79, 1954, pp. 73 f. (on the 'making of the name').

102 Isaiah ix. 6; on this see A. Alt, *FS. A. Bertholet*, ed. W. Baumgartner et al., Tübingen, 1950, esp. p. 42.

103 Proverbs xxii. 17–xxiii. 11; the thesis suggesting Hebrew or

possibly Aramaic origin was advanced on linguistic evidence by
É. Drioton, *Mélanges bibliques rédigés en l'honneur de A. Robert*,
Paris, 1957, pp. 254 ff.; his arguments seemed persuasive, but I
have not seen the contrary view recently expressed by R. J. Williams
(Toronto); [*The Alleged Semitic Original of the Wisdom of Amene-
mope*, *JEA* 47, 1961, pp. 100–6.

104 I Kings v. 13; on this see Alt, *ThLZ*, 76, 1951, cols. 139 ff.

105 Further details in P. Humbert, *Recherches sur les sources égyptiennes
de la littérature sapientale d'Israël*, 1929, pp. 110 ff., and Morenz,
HO, I 2, p. 199.

106 The Egyptian angle of this has been analysed by J. Vergote,
Joseph en Égypte (*Orientalia et Biblica Lovaniensia*, 3, 1959).

107 Further details in Morenz, *HO*, I 2, 197 ff. and *Religion in Geschichte und Gegenwart*, 3rd ed., I, 1956, cols. 118–20; there reference
is also made to the possibility that the process may be reversed,
i.e. that the Old Testament may have exerted an influence on
Egyptian religious literature.

108 Septuagint, Deuteronomy ix. 26.

109 Morenz, *Religion in Geschichte und Gegenwart*, I, col. 120; on that
occasion, too, I could provide only a few references and for this
reason should like to recommend this worthwhile theme to someone else.

110 Luke xvi. 19 ff.; the basis for this is the description of the beyond
in the so-called Setna tale (see above, p. 210): Gressmann (–Möller),
Vom reichen Mann und armen Lazarus (*APAW*, 1918, 7).

111 James iii. 4 f.; Herrmann, *ZÄS*, 79, 1954, pp. 106 ff.

112 Romans xii. 20, after Proverbs xxv. 22; Morenz, *ThLZ*, 78,
1953, cols. 187 ff.

113 Romans ix. 21, via Sir. (Greek) 33, 13, and Sap. 15, 7, from Amenemope, XXIV, 13–17 (see above, p. 67); Morenz, *ZÄS*, 84, 1959,
pp. 79 f.

114 I Corinthians viii. 4–6 and I Timothy ii. 5; it survived on an extensive scale in Christian inscriptions, particularly on Egyptian soil;
O. Weinreich, *Neue Urkunden zur Sarapis-Religion*, Tübingen,
1919, pp. 24 ff.; Pap. Leyden I, 350, IV, 17; [A. H. Gardiner,
'Hymns to Amon', *ZÄS*, 42, 1905, p. 34].

115 Revelation ii. 11 and *passim*; on the appropriate spells in the
Egyptian mortuary texts see above, p. 207. In the Greek realm
Lucian (Menippus to Tantalus) contests the existence of a second
realm of the dead and thus of a second death: *Dialogues of
the Dead*, 17, 2.

116 Revelation ii. 10 and James i. 20; II Timothy iv. 8; I Peter v. 4;
comparative Egyptian material is provided by Ph. Derchain, *CdE*,
30, 1955, pp. 225 ff.

350   EGYPTIAN RELIGION

117 A little more detail in Morenz, *Religion in Geschichte und Gegenwart*, 3rd ed., I, 1956, cols. 120 f. We have to forego completely a representation of possible ancient Egyptian survivals in the Christian (Coptic) literature of Egypt, which is mainly concerned with concepts of the beyond. Here I should like to warn the reader against the exaggerations of which I myself was guilty in my thesis 'Die Geschichte von Joseph dem Zimmermann', Leipzig, 1942 (pub. Berlin, 1951). This admission does not imply that one cannot reckon with such survivals, but one should not seek them out. On methodology cf. now J. Zandee, *Death as an Enemy*, Leyden, 1960, pp. 303 ff.

118 A late Greek derivation from *bἰk*, 'falcon', for which there is other evidence elsewhere.

119 Possibly a separate form of Hathor, who apparently was the object of a cult at Acoris (Tihna), of course only in ancient times: Bonnet, *RÄRG*, p. 13; a different view is taken by W. Spiegelberg (see n. 120).

120 W. Spiegelberg, *ARW*, 21, 1922, pp. 225–7.

121 I Corinthians xii. 4–6; II Corinthians xiii. 13; Matthew xxviii. 19.

122 The equations arrived at there may be studied in B. Meissner, *Babylonien und Assyrien*, II, 1925, pp. 47 ff.

123 Genesis xviii. 22.

124 *Quaest. in Genesim* IV, 2; on this see G. Kretschmar, *Studien zur frühchristlichen Trinitätstheologie* (*Beiträge zur historischen Theologie*, 21, Tübingen, 1956), p. 86.

125 Hippolytus, *Refutations* VII, 28, 7 and 11; cf. now also M. Werner, *Die Entstehung des christlichen Dogmas*, Stuttgart, 1959, p. 152. (This work is designed to acquaint the educated layman with a subject that has now gone out of fashion.)

126 Epiphanius, *Medicinal chest*, 62, 2. According to this opponent of heresy, this is an objectionable modalism which Roman Sabellians obtained from the Egyptian Gospel (after a reference by P. Nagel).

127 *CT*, II, 3d–e or 33e–34f; on this point, cf. the discussion on the sentence ἦν ποτὲ ὅτε οὐκ ἦν in the history of Christian dogma.

128 For this reason a link between these two entities is called in question by A. de Buck, *Plaats en Beteknis van Sjoe in de egyptische Theologie* (*Mededeelingen der Koninklijke Nederlandsche Akademie van Wetenschappen*, new series, 10, 9, 1947), p. 33; he was the first to bring to notice this and similar passages.

129 It could now be treated with greater accuracy than before on the basis of the Leipzig thesis (still unpublished) by R. Unger, 'Die Mutter mit dem Kinde in Ägypten' (1957; for references to the figure of the Virgin Mary, pp. 111 ff.).

130 The question of seclusion was raised again by Demotic papyri of

the Middle Ptolemaic period from the temple of Suchos (Sobek) at Tebtunis (Faiyum); Morenz, *ThLZ*, 74, 1949, cols. 423 ff., after Sir Herbert Thompson, *JEA*, 26, 1940, pp. 68 ff. Later Bonnet (*ZÄS*, 80, 1955, pp. 1 ff.) called in question Thompson's and our interpretation of the texts in the sense of seclusion. This important problem must be left in abeyance, but we may add that the Christian Egyptian (Coptic) word for monastery (*ḫĕnĕĕtĕ*, with variants) is derived from the old Egyptian term *ḥwt-nṯr*, 'temple' (according to references by P. Nagel and G. Fecht).

Bibliography

The following works are referred to by abbreviated titles:

ANET J. B. Pritchard (ed.), *Ancient Near Eastern Texts relating to the Old Testament*, 2nd ed., Princeton, 1955.

AOT H. Gressmann (ed.), *Altorientalische Texte zum Alten Testament*, 2nd ed., Berlin–Leipzig, 1926.

Bonnet, *RÄRG* H. Bonnet, *Reallexikon der ägyptischen Religionsgeschichte*, Berlin, 1952.

CT A. de Buck and A. H. Gardiner (eds.), *The Egyptian Coffin Texts* (*OIP*, 34–), Chicago, 1935–.

Davies, *Amarna* N. de G. Davies, *The Rock Tombs of El Amarna*, 6 vols., London, 1903–8.

Dendérah A. Mariette, *Dendérah. Description générale du grand temple de cette ville*, Paris, 1870–.

Dümichen, *Geogr. Inschr.* J. Dümichen, *Geographische Inschriften altägyptischer Denkmäler*, Leipzig, 1865–.

Edfou De Rochemonteix and E. Chassinat, *Le Temple d'Edfou*, Cairo, 1892–.

Erman, *Egyptians* A. Erman, *The Ancient Egyptians: a Sourcebook of their Writings*. Translated by A. M. Blackman. New York, 1966. (Translation of *Die Literatur der Ägypter*, Leipzig, 1923, first translated as *The Literature of the Ancient Egyptians*, London, 1927.)

Erman, *Religion* A. Erman, *Die Religion der Ägypter*, Berlin–Leipzig, 1934.

Fecht, *Habgierige* G. Fecht, *Der Habgierige und die Maat in der Lehre des Ptahhotep* (*ADAIK*, 1, 1958).

FS. Grapow O. Firchow (ed.), *Ägyptologische Studien Hermann Grapow zum 70. Geburtstag gewidmet*, Berlin, 1955.

FS. Schubart S. Morenz (ed.), *Aus Antike und Orient. Festschrift W. Schubart*, Leipzig, 1950.

Grapow, *Ausdrücke* H. Grapow, *Die bildlichen Ausdrücke des Ägyptischen*, Leipzig, 1924.

Grapow, *Grundriss* H. Grapow, *Grundriss der Medizin der alten Ägypter*, Berlin, 1954–.

Herrmann, *Untersuchungen* S. Herrmann, *Untersuchungen zur Überlieferungsgestalt mittelägyptischer Literaturwerke*, Berlin, 1957.

HO, 1 2 B. Spuler (ed.), *Handbuch der Orientalistik*, vol. 1: *Ägyptologie*; vol. 11: *Literatur*, Leyden, 1952.

Hopfner, *Fontes* Th. Hopfner, *Fontes historiae religionis Aegyptiacae*, Bonn, 1922–5.

Hopfner, *Plutarch* Th. Hopfner, *Plutarch über Isis und Osiris* (Monographien des Archiv Orientální, IX), Prague, 1940–1.

Junker, *Gîza* H. Junker (ed.), *Gîza*, 12 vols., Vienna, 1929–55.

Junker, *Götterdekret* H. Junker, *Das Götterdekret über das Abaton* (*DWAW*, 56), Vienna, 1913.

Junker, *Götterlehre* H. Junker *Die Götterlehre von Memphis* (*Schabaka-Inschrift*) (*APAW*, 1939, 23), Berlin, 1940.

Junker, *Stundenwachen* H. Junker, *Die Stundenwachen in den Osirismysterien nach den Inschriften von Dendera, Edfu und Philae* (*DWAW*, 54), Vienna, 1910.

Kees, *Ägypten* H. Kees, *Handbuch der Altertumskunde. Kulturgeschichte des Alten Orients*, III, 1: *Ägypten*, Munich, 1933.

Kees, *Götterglaube* H. Kees, *Der Götterglaube im alten Ägypten* (*MVAeG*, 45), Leipzig, 1941, 2nd ed., Berlin, 1956.

Kees, *Lesebuch* H. Kees, *Ägypten*, in: *Religionsgeschichtliches Lesebuch*, ed. A. Bertholet, fasc. 10, Tübingen, 1928.

Kees, *Priestertum* H. Kees, *Das Priestertum im ägyptischen Staat vom Neuen Reich bis zur Spätzeit* (*Probleme der Ägyptologie*, 1), Leyden–Cologne, 1953.

Kees, *Totenglauben* H. Kees, *Totenglauben und Jenseitsvorstellungen der alten Ägypter*, Leipzig, 1926, 2nd ed., Berlin, 1956.

LD R. Lepsius, *Denkmäler aus Ägypten und Äthiopien*, Berlin, 1849–.

Lefebvre, *Petosiris* G. Lefebvre, *Le Tombeau de Petosiris*, Cairo, 1923–4.

Leipoldt and Morenz J. Leipoldt and S. Morenz, *Heilige Schriften. Betrachtungen zur Religionsgeschichte der antiken Mittelmeerwelt*, Leipzig, 1953.

Lüddeckens, *Totenklagen* E. Lüddeckens, *Untersuchungen über religiösen Gehalt, Sprache und Form der ägyptischen Totenklagen* (*MDAIK*, 11), Berlin, 1943.

Morenz and Müller S. Morenz and D. Müller, *Untersuchungen zur Rolle des Schicksals in der ägyptischen Religion* (*ASAW*, 52, 1), Berlin, 1960.

Müller, *Isis-Aretalogien* D. Müller, *Ägypten und die griechischen Isis-Aretalogien* (*ASAW*, 53, 1), Berlin, 1961.

Otto, *Biogr. Inschr.* E. Otto, *Die biographischen Inschriften der ägyptischen Spätzeit* (*Probleme der Ägyptologie*, 2), Leyden, 1954.

Pap. Erm. W. Golénischeff, *Les Papyrus hiératiques no. 1115, 1116A, et 1116B de l'Ermitage Impérial à St. Pétersbourg*, St Petersburg, 1913.

Porter and Moss B. Porter and R. Moss, *Topographical Bibliography of Ancient Egyptian Hieroglyphic Texts, Reliefs and Paintings*, Oxford, 1927–.

Pyr. *Die altägyptischen Pyramidentexte, neu herausgegeben und erläutert von K. Sethe*, Leipzig, 1908–.

RAC   Th. Klauser (ed.), *Reallexikon für Antike und Christentum*, Stuttgart, 1950–.

Ranke, *Personennamen*   H. Ranke, *Die ägyptischen Personennamen*, 2 vols., Glückstadt, 1935–52.

Roeder, *Urk.*   G. Roeder, *Urkunden zur Religion des alten Ägypten*, Jena, 1923.

Sander-Hansen, *Tod*   C. E. Sander-Hansen, *Der Begriff des Todes bei den Ägyptern* (*MDVS, Historisk-Filologiske Meddelelser*, 29, 2), Copenhagen, 1942.

Sethe, *Amun*   K. Sethe, *Amun und die acht Urgötter von Hermopolis* (*APAW*, 1929, 4), Berlin, 1929.

Sethe, *Dram. Texte*   K. Sethe, *Dramatische Texte zu altägyptischen Mysterienspielen* (*Unters.*, 10), Leipzig, 1928.

Sethe, *Kommentar*   K. Sethe, *Übersetzung und Kommentar zu den altägyptischen Pyramidentexten*, Glückstadt–Hamburg, n.d.

Sethe, *Urgeschichte*   K. Sethe, *Urgeschichte und älteste Religion der Ägypter* (*Abhandlungen für die Kunde des Morgenlandes*, 18, 4), Leipzig, 1930.

Urk.   *Urkunden des ägyptischen Altertums*, Leipzig (since 1955, Berlin).

Volten, *Pol. Schriften*   A. Volten, *Zwei altägyptische politische Schriften* (*Anal. Aeg.*, IV), Copenhagen, 1945.

Volten, *Studien...Anii*   A. Volten, *Studien zum Weisheitsbuch des Anii* (*MDVS*, 23, 3), Copenhagen, 1937.

Wb.   A. Erman and H. Grapow, *Wörterbuch der ägyptischen Sprache*, Leipzig, 1926–.

Wolf, *Kunst*   W. Wolf, *Die Kunst Ägyptens. Gestalt und Geschichte*, Stuttgart, 1957.

Žába, *Ptahhotep*   Z. Žába, *Les Maximes de Ptahhotep*, Prague, 1956.

Zandee, *Hymnen*   J. Zandee, *De hymnen aan Amon van Papyrus Leyden I 350* (*Oudheidkundige mededelingen. Nieuwe reeks*, 28). Leyden, 1948.

BD   Book of the Dead
FS.   Festschrift

The following abbreviations are used for series and periodicals:

ADAIK   *Abhandlungen des Deutschen Archäologischen Instituts Kairo*, Glückstadt–Hamburg–New York.
ÄgFo   *Ägyptologische Forschungen*, Glückstadt–Hamburg–New York.
AMAW   Akademie der Wissenschaften und der Literatur (Mainz). *Abhandlungen*, Wiesbaden.
Anal. Aeg.   *Analecta Aegyptiaca*, Copenhagen.
Anal. Or.   *Analecta Orientalia*, Rome.
AO   *Der alte Orient*, Leipzig.

APAW Abhandlungen der (Kgl.) Preussischen Akademie der Wissenschaften zu Leipzig, Leipzig (from 1948, Berlin).
ARW Archiv für Religionswissenschaft, Leipzig–Berlin.
ASAE Annales du Service des Antiquités de l'Égypte, Cairo.
ASAW Abhandlungen der Sächsischen Akademie der Wissenschaften zu Leipzig, Leipzig (from 1948, Berlin).
Bibl. Aeg. Bibliotheca Aegyptiaca, Brussels.
Bibl. d'Ét. Bibliothèque d'Étude, Cairo.
BIFAO Bulletin de l'Institut français d'Archéologie orientale du Caire, Cairo.
BMMA Bulletin of the Metropolitan Museum of Art, New York.
BSAW Berichte über die Verhandlungen der Sächsischen Akademie der Wissenschaften zu Leipzig, Leipzig (from 1948, Berlin).
CASAE Cahier No. ... Supplément aux Annales du Service des Antiquités de l'Égypte, Cairo.
CdE Chronique d'Égypte, Brussels.
DWAW Denkschriften der (kaiserlichen) Akademie der Wissenschaften in Wien, Vienna.
FIFAO Fouilles de l'Institut français d'Archéologie orientale du Caire, Cairo.
JAOS Journal of the American Oriental Society, Baltimore.
JEA The Journal of Egyptian Archaeology, London.
JNES Journal of Near Eastern Studies, Chicago.
LÄSt Leipziger Ägyptologische Studien, Glückstadt–Hamburg–New York.
MDAIK Mitteilungen des Deutschen Archäologischen Instituts, Abteilung Kairo, Augsburg (later Berlin; from 1956, Wiesbaden).
MDVS Meddelelser fra Kgl. Danske Videnskabernes Selskab, Copenhagen.
MIFAO Mémoires...de l'Institut français d'Archéologie orientale du Caire, Cairo.
MIO Mitteilungen des Instituts für Orientforschung [of the Deutsche Akademie der Wissenschaften], Berlin.
MVAeG Mitteilungen der Vorderasiatisch-Ägyptischen Gesellschaft, Leipzig.
NAWG Nachrichten der Akademie der Wissenschaften in Göttingen, Göttingen.
OIP Oriental Institute Publications, Chicago.
OLZ Orientalische Literaturzeitung, Leipzig (from 1953, Berlin–Leipzig).
OMRO Oudheidkundige Mededelingen uit het Rijksmuseum van Oudheden te Leiden, Leyden.
PMMA Publications of the Metropolitan Museum of Art: Egyptian Expedition, New York.

RdE   Revue d'Égyptologie, Cairo (from 1950, Paris).

Rec. de trav.   Recueil de travaux relatifs à la philologie et à l'archéologie égyptiennes et assyriennes, Paris.

SBAW   Sitzungsberichte der Bayerischen Akademie der Wissenschaften, Munich.

SHAW   Sitzungsberichte der Heidelberger Akademie der Wissenschaften, Heidelberg.

SPAW   Sitzungsberichte der (Kgl.) Preussischen Akademie der Wissenschaften, Berlin.

ThLZ   Theologische Literaturzeitung, Leipzig (from 1947, Berlin–Leipzig).

Unters.   Untersuchungen zur Geschichte und Altertumskunde Ägyptens, Leipzig (from 1952, Berlin–Leipzig).

WZKM   Wiener Zeitschrift für die Kunde des Morgenlandes, Vienna.

ZÄS   Zeitschrift für ägyptische Sprache und Altertumskunde, Leipzig (from 1954, Berlin–Leipzig).

ZDMG   Zeitschrift der Deutschen Morgenländischen Gesellschaft, Leipzig (from 1950, Wiesbaden).

ZDPV   Zeitschrift des Deutschen Palästina-Vereins, Leipzig (1946–8, Wuppertal; from 1953, Wiesbaden).

SUPPLEMENTARY BIBLIOGRAPHY

Arnold, D., *Wandrelief und Raumfunktion in ägyptischen Tempeln des neuen Reiches*, Berlin, 1962.

Černý, J., *Ancient Egyptian Religion*, London, 1952.

David, A. R., *Religious Ritual at Abydos (c. 1300 B.C.)*. (Forthcoming publication – Aris and Phillips Ltd., Warminster, Dec. 1972.)

Griffiths, G., *The Origins of Osiris*, Berlin, 1966.

Posener, G., *De la divinité du Pharaon*, Paris, 1960.

Reymond, E., *The Mythical Origin of the Egyptian Temple*, Manchester, 1969.

Sauneron, S., *Les prêtres de l'ancienne Égypte*, Paris, 1957.

Winter, E., *Untersuchungen zu den ägyptischen Tempelreliefs der griechisch-römischen Zeit*, Graz, 1968.

Žabkar, Louis V., *A Study of the Ba Concept in Ancient Egyptian Texts*, Univ. of Chicago Press, 1968.

Indexes

A. SUBJECT INDEX

1. English

INDEXES 369

skr ꜥnḫ 49
stwt 315 (n. 17)
stny 291 (n. 43)
sḏb 132
šꜣ 70, 71, 137
šꜣyt 71, 72
šꜣw 70, 71, 72
šmꜣw 303 (n. 60)
štꜣ 100
šd-nṯr 307 (n. 126)
kꜣ 43
kmꜣ 161
Kmt 46
gmì 174
grw (mꜣꜥ) 118
grg 44, 114
tꜣ 46, 50
tꜣwy 46
tꜣ wꜥty 50
tꜣ-mrì 46
tꜣ n Kmt 50
tꜣ ḏsr 100
tr 76, 79
tmḥw 48
dwꜣt 207
Dwn-ꜥnwy 24
dḥꜣ 128
ḏt 170
ḏꜣsw 77
ḏw 105
Ḏḥwty 23
ḏsr 88

3. Coptic

me 309
nūte 19
rᵉmᵉnkēme 49
ša 89
šai 89

4. Greek

ἀγέννητος 25
ἄδυτον 100
ἄνθρωπος 49
ἀποθέωσις 346 (n. 70)

ἀπόκρυφος 338 (n. 64)
ἀρσενόθηλυς 26
ἄφθαρτος 25
γῆ 45
γνῶσις 336 (n. 22)
γραφή 222
δεισιδαιμονία 347 (n. 77)
εἰκὼν ἄψυχος 156
εἰκὼν ζῶσα 153
εἱμαρμένη 72
εἷς θεός 255
ἐκθέωσις 346 (n. 70)
ἔμψυχος 156
ἐπίπνοια 336 (n. 22)
ἐπιφανέστατος τόπος 87
ἦθος 110
θεός 19
θίασος 348 (n. 97)
καιρός 76, 77, 79, 80, 252
καλὸς κἀγαθός 49
κόσμος 45
κύριος 253
οἰκουμένη 45
ὁμοούσιος 257
ὀμφαλὸς τῆς γῆς 42, 44, 56
πανήγυρις δημοτελής 89
πίρωμις 49
προφήτης 301 (n. 32), 306 (n. 105)
σωτήρ 248
τέμενος 99
τρίμορφος 255
ὑπόμνησις 319 (n. 81)
ὡροσκόπος 8

5. Latin

colere 88
creatio ex nihilo 181
cursus honorum 76
evocatio 239
fatum 72
gloria 97, 102, 211
maiestas 287 (n. 95)
mos 110
religio 4
sanctus 305 (n. 89)
templum 305 (n. 89)

6. Hebrew

'ēl 19
'ēn-lēb 311 (n. 52)
iāšār 113

reā' 23
qādōš 305 (n. 89)
ṭabbūr-hā-āreṣ 42

B. PASSAGES

I. EGYPTIAN TEXTS

3. Literary texts, Papyri and Ostraca

4. Mortuary and Temple Inscriptions

Cairo 90434: 315 (n. 20)
Erman, *Denksteine*
  1086 ff.: 306 (nn. 107, 110)
  1089: 293 (n. 8)
  1090: 293 (n. 8)
  1094: 293 (n. 8), 313 (n. 98)
  1098: 293 (n. 8), 311 (n. 53), 312
  (n. 61)
  1101 f.: 284 (n. 61), 293 (n. 8)
  1103: 293 (n. 8)
Famine stele: 221, 285 (n. 77)
Famine stele, 5: 336 (n. 24)
Florence 7603: 315 (n. 20)
Leyden D 32: 315 (n. 20)
Leyden V 12: 324 (n. 74)
Leyden V 55: 298 (n. 103)
Leyden V 108: 315 (n. 21)
Louvre A 90: 295 (n. 48)
Louvre C 30 (hymn to Osiris): 304
  (n. 69)
Louvre C 38: 315 (n. 20)
Louvre C 46: 315 (n. 20)
Louvre C 76: 315 (n. 20)
Louvre C 213: 290 (n. 35)
Manchester 3306: 341 (n. 11)
Shabaka inscription, introduction:
  217
  2: 319 (n. 76)
  8, 10a–12a: 321 (n. 19)
  8, 10c–12c: 321 (n. 19)
  50a–51a: 284 (n. 53), 324 (n. 68)
  55: 321 (n. 29)
  56: 322 (n. 31)
  57: 322 (n. 30), 294 (n. 14), 310
  (n. 27)
  59: 283 (n. 40), 319 (n. 76)
Small plaques of annals of Udimu:
  322 (n. 38)
Turin 28: 315 (n. 20)
Turin 98: 315 (n. 20)
Turin 156: 311 (n. 59)
Turin 278: 315 (n. 20)

6. Major publications

Brugsch, *Reise nach der Grossen
  Oase...*
  13: 289 (n. 14)
  15, 13 f.: 316 (n. 38), 324 (n. 71)

  27, 40: 318 (n. 54)
Brugsch, *Thesaurus*
  918 ff.: 327 (n. 26)
  923: 295 (n. 34)
  1434: 343 (n. 39)
  625A: 327 (n. 8)
  651D: 321 (n. 11)
Dümichen, *Baugeschichte*
  12: 326 (n. 104)
Dümichen, *Geogr. Inschr.*
  II, 97: 306 (n. 99)
  III, 74: 299 (n. 119)
Dümichen, *Kal. Inschr.*
  49: 302 (n. 39)
Dümichen, *Tempelinschr.*
  II, 24: 318 (n. 60)
  III, 207d: 299 (n. 125)
  IV, 58a: 283 (n. 42), 297
  (n. 90)
  IV, 60–1: 286 (n. 94)
Lüddeckens, *Totenklagen*
  112: 327 (n. 20)
  165: 293 (n. 9)
Morgan, *Catal. Mon.*
  I, 55: 288 (n. 6)
Piehl, *Inschr. Hierogl.*
  I, 37: 311 (n. 57)
  II, 112: 298 (n. 116)
Pierret, *Rec. d'Inscr.*
  I, 21 ff.: 328 (n. 43)
  II, 21: 328 (n. 47)
Temples immergés
  I, 166: 288 (n. 116)
Wreszinski, *Vienna*
  87: 308 (n. 133)
  160: 295 (n. 46)

7. Journals etc.

Analecta Biblica
  12, 1959, 156: 292 (n. 51)
ASAE
  16, 1916, 2: 296 (n. 53)
  17, 1917, 122: 326 (n. 103)
  49, 1949, 337 ff.: 279 (n. 17)
FIFAO
  4, 1927, 38 f.: 322 (n. 42)
JEA
  4, 1917, Pl. 29: 279 (n. 17)

II. OLD TESTAMENT

III. NEW TESTAMENT

IV. APOCRYPHA

V. TALMUD

VI. GREEK AND LATIN AUTHORS

VII. GREEK AND LATIN INSCRIPTIONS AND PAPYRI